You Duped Me, O Lord

You Duped Me, O Lord

HUGH DUFFY

Foreword by Martin Sheen

RESOURCE *Publications* · Eugene, Oregon

YOU DUPED ME, O LORD

Copyright © 2025 Hugh Duffy. All rights reserved. Except for brief quotations in critical publications or reviews, no part of this book may be reproduced in any manner without prior written permission from the publisher. Write: Permissions, Wipf and Stock Publishers, 199 W. 8th Ave., Suite 3, Eugene, OR 97401.

Resource Publications
An Imprint of Wipf and Stock Publishers
199 W. 8th Ave., Suite 3
Eugene, OR 97401

www.wipfandstock.com

PAPERBACK ISBN: 979-8-3852-3994-8
HARDCOVER ISBN: 979-8-3852-3995-5
EBOOK ISBN: 979-8-3852-3996-2

VERSION NUMBER 050825

Scripture texts in this work are taken from the *New American Bible, revised edition* © 2010, 1991, 1986, 1970 Confraternity of Christian Doctrine, Washington, D.C. and are used by permission of the copyright owner. All Rights Reserved. No part of the New American Bible may be reproduced in any form without permission in writing from the copyright owner.

You duped me, O Lord, and I let myself
    be duped;
you were too strong for me, and you
triumphed.
All the day I am an object of laughter;
everyone mocks me.
I say to myself, I will not mention him,
I will speak in his name no more.
But then it becomes like fire burning in my heart,
Imprisoned in my bones;
I grow weary holding it in,
I cannot endure it.

    —Jeremiah 20:7, 9.

"When the Church does not come out of herself to evangelize, she becomes self-referential and then becomes sick."

    —Pope Francis, *Life: My Story Through History*

Contents

Foreword by Martin Sheen | ix

Part 1

Chapter 1 | 3
Chapter 2 | 9
Chapter 3 | 17
Chapter 4 | 24
Chapter 5 | 32
Chapter 6 | 39
Chapter 7 | 44
Chapter 8 | 50
Chapter 9 | 58
Chapter 10 | 67
Chapter 11 | 78
Chapter 12 | 85

Part 2

Chapter 13 | 93
Chapter 14 | 105
Chapter 15 | 113
Chapter 16 | 120
Chapter 17 | 124
Chapter 18 | 131
Chapter 19 | 135
Chapter 20 | 148
Chapter 21 | 158
Chapter 22 | 171
Chapter 23 | 175
Chapter 24 | 182
Chapter 25 | 189
Chapter 26 | 193
Chapter 27 | 198
Chapter 28 | 202
Chapter 29 | 205
Chapter 30 | 212
Chapter 31 | 217
Chapter 32 | 221
Chapter 33 | 228
Chapter 34 | 235
Chapter 35 | 241
Chapter 36 | 246
Chapter 37 | 254
Chapter 38 | 262
Chapter 39 | 271
Chapter 40 | 281

Part 3

Chapter 41 | 289
Chapter 42 | 295
Chapter 43 | 312
Chapter 44 | 321
Chapter 45 | 326

Foreword

IN THE WORLD OF human experience, few things are intertwined with as much complexity and contradiction as faith and institution. When I was approached to write this foreword to Father Hugh Duffy's memoir, *You Duped Me, O Lord*, I felt both honored and deeply moved. Though many know me primarily through my six decades in Hollywood, my own spiritual journey has run parallel to my cinematic one—sometimes harmoniously, sometimes in tension, but always with renewed understanding.

The title of Father Duffy's memoir, drawn from the prophet Jeremiah, captures perfectly the paradoxical nature of vocation—a call which both fulfills and challenges, comforts and confounds. This is no sentimental journey like Hollywood's *Going My Way*. Instead, this captivating story, beautifully written, paints a true picture of the inner workings of the church from the inside out. In telling this story, Father Duffy doesn't back away from revealing the real struggle involved in manifesting fidelity to the ministry of the gospel within a compromised institution. From the pastoral landscapes of County Donegal to the political minefields of American diocesan politics, this is not merely a chronicle of one man's journey; it is a profound meditation on what it means to pursue gospel values within structures that often work against those very ideals.

In Part One of this memoir, Father Duffy paints a vivid picture of his Irish upbringing, his early call to priesthood, and the idealism that propelled him through seminary and university training. The simplicity of his childhood in Donegal formed the spiritual bedrock upon which his vocation would be built. His portrait of life in rural Ireland—playing Gaelic football in the streets, gathering around fires for stories, and witnessing the cycles of nature up close—reveals how deeply his spirituality is rooted in community and family. His ordination in 1966 coincided with the winds of change blowing through the church following the Second Vatican Council. This timing is significant since he entered the priesthood during a period of institutional renewal, a time of *aggiornamento* or "updating," which influenced his understanding of what the church should be.

Part Two takes a dramatic turn as Father Duffy accepts an invitation to America. Here, the captivating narrative becomes a riveting account of ideals meeting reality. His work with immigrants, youth, and the marginalized in Florida repeatedly put him at odds with a "corporation sole," a diocesan structure more concerned with property, power, and image than with gospel values. What strikes me most powerfully about this memoir is its unflinching honesty. Father Duffy names the abuses of power he experienced—false accusations, the manipulation of personnel files detailed in chapter 35, and attempts to seize parish property—all while maintaining a remarkable absence of rancor or bitterness. Throughout ordeals that would embitter many, he consistently returns to the fundamental question: What does the gospel require of us? In this way, his memoir stands alongside the writings of Dorothy Day ("I loved the church for Christ made visible. Not for itself, because it was so often a scandal to me. Romano Guardini said the church is the Cross on which Christ was crucified; one could not separate Christ from His Cross, and one must live in a state of permanent dissatisfaction with the church."[1])—testimonies that do not flinch from institutional critique, yet remain rooted in profound love for the church's true mission.

The third part of Father Duffy's memoir is characterized by a deep sense of hope. Even in retirement, he faced more false accusations and a fake canonical trial that might have destroyed a lesser man's faith. Yet through these trials, his faith held firm while distilling a genuine need for church reform. Throughout my own life, I've been privileged to know figures like Daniel and Philip Berrigan and Dorothy Day—individuals who taught me that authentic faith sometimes requires standing against institutional abuse. Like the legacy of Pope Francis, whose vision resonates throughout this memoir, Father Duffy understands that true reform isn't primarily about church structures or policy changes, though these matter. Rather, it begins with a return to the radical simplicity of the gospel itself. In a time when institutional religion faces crises on multiple fronts, Father Duffy's voice offers neither facile criticism nor blind loyalty, but something far more valuable—a witness to perseverance, however imperfectly, to embody Christ's love in the world.

This is a very timely book. It needed to be written and it needs to be read—not to shame the church, but to help reform it by calling it back to its foundational mission. Through Father Duffy's eyes, we glimpse what

---

1. Dorothy Day, *The Long Loneliness: The Autobiography of Dorothy Day* (Garden City, NY: Image, 1952), 145.

Foreword

Vatican II called "the joys and hopes, the griefs and anxieties"[2] of modern Catholic life. His journey reveals both the institutional failings that have damaged so many lives and the enduring power of authentic faith to transcend those failures. I commend this remarkable memoir to believers and skeptics alike. In this unflinching, hope-filled story, we discover that true faith and spirituality always point beyond institution to a living experience of the gospel itself. As Saint Mother Teresa of Calcutta assured us, "God doesn't ask that we succeed in everything, but that we are faithful."[3]

—Martin Sheen

---

2. Pope Paul VI, "Gaudium et Spes" (Dec. 7, 1965, https://www.vatican.va/archive/hist_councils/ii_vatican_council/documents/vat-ii_const_19651207_gaudium-et-spes_en.html).

3. Mother Teresa, *The Joy in Loving: A Guide to Daily Living* (New York: Viking, 1997), 334.

Part 1

Chapter 1

THE SALTY BREEZE OF Cape May, New Jersey, carried the scent of nostalgia as I stood before my gathered family and friends on June 10, 2017. Golden sunlight glinted off the water, matching the golden jubilee we had come to celebrate—fifty years since I had taken my vows as a priest. As I gazed at the familiar faces, some etched with the lines of half a century's passage, I felt the weight of time and experience settle on my shoulders.

This wasn't just my celebration. My cousin Nancy and her husband Bernie were marking their diamond anniversary—sixty years of marriage. Our milestones had converged, much like the paths that had led us all to this moment. As laughter and congratulations filled the air, I found myself retreating inward, taking stock of the journey that had brought me here.

There's no such thing as a perfect church. A church is made up of humans, and humans are not perfect. My calling to preach the gospel was an unexpected journey of challenges and struggles, whose most formidable adversary was, surprisingly, the Church itself.

The conflict was inevitable, born from the clash between two systems: the church's flawed institutional system and the uncompromising gospel, which rejects accommodation with the kingdom of the world. As I reflected on my path, I realized that the unexpected changes in the church over the years were deeply intertwined with my own journey, challenging and reshaping my understanding of the vocation I had so earnestly embraced.

In my youth, I was taught that the world outside the confines of the church was compromised by sin. The church, in contrast, was portrayed as a safe haven, a perfect society free from the temptations and corruptions of the world it was meant to save. The Gospel of John, chapter 15, tells us we must not belong to the world, that we can be in it but not of it.[1] This teaching shaped my early understanding of my role as a priest.

---

1. There are different references in Scripture about not belonging to the world, such as John 15:19, John 17:14, 16.

But standing here, at the culmination of fifty-plus years of service, I had arrived at a deep-felt realization that diverged sharply from those early perceptions. The realms of wrongdoing and corruption, which we were always cautioned to be on guard against,[2] lurked not just beyond the church's walls but within them. It was a sobering acknowledgment, especially for someone who had dedicated a lifetime to its service.

No discerning individual could claim that the church is a perfect society. It is, after all, a social structure deeply embedded in the world. This structure, whose mission is to preach the gospel, administer the sacraments, and purify the world with the leaven of the gospel, is nevertheless subject to the same limitations and deviations as any other institution.[3] Plagued by vices of careerism and greed, the church has suffered from the short-sightedness and ambitions of individuals who, regrettably, have prioritized self-interest over the gospel's teachings.

I remember vividly the day this truth hit home. It was a crisp autumn day in 1977, and I was sitting in a meeting of clergy in Orlando, Florida. As the impressive resources for community outreach were being discussed, I watched in dismay as political maneuvering and financial self-interest took precedence over the needs of the faithful. The gospel's call to serve the least among us was drowned out by institutional self-interest. In that moment, the veil of perfection I had long attributed to the church slipped away.

This realization, though painful, was crucial to understanding the true nature of the church and its place in the world. It reshaped my perception, compelling me to look at the institution I have served with a more critical, yet hopeful, eye.

The Second Vatican Council (1962–1965) brought about a paradigm shift in our understanding of church. It taught us that the church is primarily the kingdom of Christ, not the institution. The church's own teaching recognizes the limitations of the institution in trying to embody Christ and acknowledges the perpetual need for reform.[4] These teachings stem from the recognition that the church is not impervious to misdirection and corruption.

---

2. Peter 4:3 explains that being part of the world is to surrender oneself to selfish behavior such as debaucheries, evil desires, and orgies.

3. Pope Leo XIII, in his 1885 encyclical, *Immortale Dei*, expounds on the notion of the church as a perfect society. After the Second Vatican Council, the doctrine of a "perfect society" was replaced by the Biblical "People of God."

4. The Second Vatican Council's *Dogmatic Constitution on the Church* adopted the notion of the church as "always in need of being purified."

Moreover, I've come to appreciate anew that the world is God's gift to us.[5] God's creation is full of marvelous wonders. Through human research and ingenuity in every field of learning, such as scientific and technological discoveries, God's creation reveals new blessings that can contribute to the betterment of humankind. Though the church must be in the world but not of it, it cannot reject the world created by God, but must act as a leaven to renew it through the good news of the gospel.

A critical question arises, however: How does the church reform itself? In recent times, the church has faced the need for reform in response to various critical failings—sexual abuse, financial misconduct, violations of human rights involving indigenous communities, injustices against women, and other transgressions within Catholic institutions globally.

It is striking to note that these reforms have been initiated not from within the church itself but rather propelled by external forces—public opinion, media scrutiny, and legal interventions. This external impetus for change underscores a critical failure within the church itself to create an environment in which reform is not merely reactive to external pressures, but a proactive, integral part of its ethos.

The core message of the gospel appeals directly to the individual, summoning him or her to emulate and prioritize Christ's kingdom. This is the church in its essence: the kingdom of Christ within us. The Dogmatic Constitution on the church by the Second Vatican Council makes this abundantly clear. However, a profound challenge arises when those at the helm of the church, akin to the figures in the Parable of the Wicked Tenants in the Vineyard (Matthew 21:33–43), elevate their personal greed, interests, and agendas over the Lord's kingdom. Such actions lead to corruption of the church from within. In these sad situations, the church becomes its own adversary, its own worst enemy, failing to live up to its own teaching.

The kingdom of Christ, on the other hand, demands commitment to the message of the gospel coupled with a resolute resistance to abuses, notably those committed by the church itself. The actions of Jesus towards the religious authorities of the Temple in his day serve as a powerful affirmation of this principle. He fearlessly unveiled the duplicity of those who outwardly displayed sanctity but behaved contrary to it, denouncing them as Whited Sepulchers.[6] This historical example highlights the essential obligation for

---

5. The Second Vatican Council's *Pastoral Constitution on the Church in the Modern World* embraces the positive realities and developments of the world in which we live. The Council's Dogmatic Constitution on the Church views the church primarily as the Kingdom of Christ.

6. Matthew 23:27.

each member of the church to live by the gospel's teachings, despite facing challenges from within the institution itself.

My story, unfolding over a lifetime within this flawed institution, is about the struggle to prioritize the gospel within the very church that preaches it. The Priesthood is a vocation that calls for devoting one's life to serve God and one's fellow human beings, to love God and to love one's neighbor as oneself. Throughout the fifty-plus years of my calling, I have faced challenges and struggles in following this vocation while trying to avoid the subtle pitfalls and intrigues of the very institution to which I belonged.

Along the way, I've been blessed to have had the ardent support and help of many exemplary and courageous people. Their support was not just a helping hand, but a beacon of hope in my moments of greatest need. These valiant men and women are also an integral part of this story, which began in my youth, when I first experienced the stirrings of a vocation to the priesthood.

This story, however, could only be told by telling the truth as honestly as possible. In the interest of anonymity, however, I avoid mentioning by name any of my erstwhile opponents, and have used fictitious names throughout when dealing with those who were actively working against my best interests. I bear them no resentment or ill will for I realize they were acting according to their own lights, just as I was acting according to mine. It seems to me that real growth takes place in the midst of life's conflicts and trials, and that these are part of the Lord's plan to bring about his kingdom.

These conflicts and trials are not confined to the Catholic Church alone. They resonate with anyone entangled in any institution where human liberty, respect for truth, and freedom of conscience are compromised. When I was involved in the ecumenical Kairos ministry to prisoners in Florida, I used to meet with pastors of different church denominations in my rectory. We found we had much in common. We shared similar problems, similar concerns, and similar challenges. Only the manifestations were different, illustrating that the struggles we confront within our individual spheres are, in essence, common human experiences in different guises.

The problems and obstacles we encounter throughout our lives, unanticipated though they be, are the very crucibles that serve to purify us, not shatter us. Like Dante's descent into Hell in the *Divine Comedy*, everyone must go through his or her own hell to reach paradise.

The title of this memoir, *You Duped Me, O Lord*, is taken from the prophet Jeremiah.[7] It encapsulates an important truth: There's no such

---

7. Jeremiah 20:7, 9.

thing as a charmed life. Life invariably delivers a succession of trials and tribulations that challenge our faith and resilience. Despite twists of fate and disappointments, you can still draw on a strenuous hope, like the Prophet, to keep going.

You may shout, you may argue with God out of frustration, and that is par for the course. But you cannot let whatever happens turn you into someone you're not. You are a child of God and, though you may feel duped, you cannot let go of the power of hope, which will get you through the darkest depressions. You must pass through the fire, like gold in the furnace, to emerge renewed and revitalized like Lazarus from the dead.

This story unfolds in three parts. Beginning with my earliest experiences in Ireland, Part 1 traces the formative influences in my life. This initial phase, brimming with growth and learning, serves as a prologue to Part 2, laying the essential groundwork for challenges to come.

The second phase of my story and my ministry, within the corporate structure of the American Catholic Church, was the most challenging. It goes to the heart of the struggle between commitment to the gospel and the church's intricate corporate structure. I was never prepared for this conflict, nor is anyone, to my knowledge, ever prepared for it. It is not something you are taught in the seminary.

The obstacles encountered in America came to a head when I became pastor of a country parish in South Florida. It was there that unexpected conflicts and institutional abuses conspired to prevent me from carrying out my vocation as priest and pastor. Ending these institutional abuses led me all the way to the Vatican and back.

Part 3 deals with my life after retiring from the rigors of parish administration, serving as an epilogue to Part 2. An idyllic time, this involved traveling throughout America as an Outreach Speaker, helping the needy without the pressures of church politics. As blissful a period as it was, it, too, was brought to an unexpected end by the meddling and dysfunction endemic to the very institution to which I had devoted my life.

The life I've lived was not the life I would have chosen for myself, but it was the life to which the Lord called me: If anyone will come after me, he must deny himself, take up his cross and follow Me. It is during the most severe trials and tribulations that the mind clears, guiding you towards your true purpose. The inner strength to remain true to your heart's core, despite hardships and trials, is a burning impulse. It is what the Prophet, despite feelings of being duped, described as a fire burning in the heart. It is the flame of hope that persists undimmed, defying all odds.

Honesty, it can be argued, forms the most vital component of an individual's legacy. Similarly, the church, which positions itself as a luminary of truth in a world often shrouded in shadows and falsehoods, must embody honesty in its mission. Only through honest commitment to the gospel can the church truly disseminate the Good News and live by its life-saving teachings.

The leaven of the gospel in a world riddled with imperfections is only possible when the church itself embarks on a path of transparency and self-reformation. Without an honest acknowledgment of its own failings and wrongdoings, without a sincere process of self-reformation, the church cannot be a beacon of hope and truth in our world.

As the sun began to set on that jubilant day in Cape May, casting long shadows across the gathering, I found myself filled with a sense of purpose renewed. This memoir of my personal journey within the church's flawed institution is a story of hope—written not to malign the church, but to renew it. For in the end, it is through acknowledging our imperfections that we open ourselves to true transformation, both as individuals and as institutions. And in that acknowledgment lies the seed of redemption, the very essence of the gospel we are called to serve.

Chapter 2

THE YEARS OF CHILDHOOD shape us profoundly. For me, those formative years took place in Donegal, Ireland, where I was born and raised. The lessons learned during my simple upbringing there are as much a part of me as the air I breathe. Though I've long since left Donegal, it remains an integral part of who I am.

Donegal, isolated yet majestic, stands apart as Ireland's northwestern outpost. Rugged and remote, it is the wildest and most scenic of Ireland's thirty-two counties. As James Joyce wrote in *Ulysses*, Donegal is the *coup d'oeil* of Irish counties.[1] Though Donegal lies within Ulster and is separated from the rest of the Republic by an artificial border, it firmly belongs to the Republic of Ireland.

The landscape of Donegal is ever-changing, its natural beauty often revealed in a stunning display of sun and moving clouds. Deep valleys, regal mountains, tranquil lakes, and wooded hillsides are constantly transformed by these shifts of light and shade. Donegal's rugged coastline, stretching over three hundred miles, is dotted with old, ruined castles and quaint cottages that seem to sprout naturally from the earth. The Slieve League cliffs, the highest sea cliffs in Europe, are particularly awe-inspiring at sunset, when the last rays of light cast their glow on the massive, cathedral-like precipices.

Glenveagh National Park, Ireland's second-largest, unfolds along the tranquil shores of Lough Veagh in Donegal. This verdant haven is a dream for walkers. Glenveagh Castle, with its gardens ablaze in a riot of colors, overlooks the placid waters of the lake.

Beyond the park, Donegal's reputation is further burnished by its golden beaches, home to the tallest dunes in Europe. A solitary walk along these sandy expanses, wrapped in a warm sweater to fend off the brisk Atlantic winds, is a soul-stirring experience.

---

1. James Joyce, *Ulysses*, New York: Random House: First Vintage Books Edition, June 1986, Episode 16, p. 513.

To truly experience Donegal's coastal charm, one can take a scenic train journey that meanders along majestic mountains, tracing the picturesque shoreline of Lough Finn. This juxtaposition of rugged landscapes and serene lakes encapsulates the uniqueness of Donegal, a place that leaves an indelible mark on all who visit.

Nestled within this breathtaking landscape lies Letterkenny, the town of my birth and the setting for my formative years. It was here that I learned the lessons that would shape my life.

Built on a hill, Letterkenny's name is derived from a combination of the Gaelic, *Leiter* (meaning hillside) and O'Cannon, a princely clan that ruled as local chieftains long ago. The original part of town, known as Oldtown, features the main street that winds its serpentine way up the hill and down the other side all the way to Lough Swilly. It was in number 14, lower Main Street, where I was born on April 6, 1941.

Letterkenny's neo-Gothic cathedral, with its tall spire and hilltop perch, dominates the town's skyline and is visible from all approaches. My grand-uncle, Peter Duffy, told me about attending the smaller church with the red tin roof before the cathedral was built in 1901. Peter and cousin James were conscripted into the British army during World War I. James, a pacificist, won a Victoria Cross for valor, serving in the Ambulance Corps where he risked his life to save soldiers trapped in No Man's Land. When I asked him about it, all he ever said was: "I only did my duty."

Back in the 1940s and early 1950s, Letterkenny was still a country town, with farms and farmhouses dotting the landscape around the main street. The annual Oldtown Fair was an impressive event, bringing life to the market square, where farmers displayed livestock, and hawkers sold everything from umbrellas to homemade jams.

Music filled the air with Irish Céilí dancing led by Leo Brennan, Enya's father and founder of the renowned band, Clannad. As children, we would open the top window of our farmhouse to listen to the Irish music and beautiful melodies emanating from the Literary Institute nearby.

The refined melodies of Clannad and Enya still evoke a deep nostalgia, reminding me of a time when community, culture, and music were intertwined, creating memories that continue to lift my spirit to this day.

Simple pleasures defined our days growing up in the 1940s. Having been spared the horrors of the Second World War since Ireland was a neutral country, Letterkenny was a safe haven. Summers meant football on lower Main Street, and winters brought sledding from the Cathedral to the Oldtown. The whole town would join in, either participating in the fun or playfully bombarding us with snowballs as our sleds sped by. These were times when the entire community came together to celebrate the changing seasons.

Religious and spiritual life revolved around the home, and was inspired by the Christian example of my parents—not preachy but lived. My mother often pointed to the picture of Jesus above our kitchen table, reminding us that his gaze followed us wherever we stood. As illustration of this she would say in the lazy lull of evening: "See how Jesus is always watching over us. Wherever you stand in the kitchen, he is looking right at you." We would run to one end of the table and shout: "He's looking at me!" Then we'd run to the other end of the table and observe the same marvel. Enjoying our reaction, she would add, softly: "Jesus is watching over you all the time, and if you follow him, you'll never go wrong."

Nothing I received in my seminary formation came close to the simple, Christian upbringing of my childhood where kindness to one another was a way of life. These early experiences of overcoming adversity through helping each other laid the foundation for my future calling.

In those days, few cars or trucks crowded the streets. Horse and cart were still the primary means of transporting goods. My family had a farm off of lower Main Street. Life on the farm was both challenging and joyful. My father also had a turf business that kept many of the home fires burning. Fridays meant unloading truckloads of turf for storage in the shed—a task so central we had to get a half-day off of school to complete it. Passersby were very polite and never uttered a word of complaint for having to step onto the Main Street to avoid the mountain of black turf blocking the footpath. It was all in a day's work, and the townsfolk understood this.

One Friday, I was bringing the cows home when I found the laneway blocked by a big mound of turf. The trucker had unloaded the turf, unwittingly, in front of the lane. The cows were in a hurry to be milked. They made a dash for the nearest opening they saw: the entrance to Joe and Mary Gallagher's home. Mary ran into the kitchen, waving her hands hysterically when she saw the cows entering the corridor of her house. Joe, a quick-witted man, rushed to the scene and opened the back door to the yard outside.

"Bring the cows through," he shouted to me. "You can bring them up the fields."

"Thanks, Joe," I said, gasping with relief. "Sorry for the bother," I groaned, as I followed the cows through the house and up the fields.

"Don't mention it," Joe replied tactfully.

Such kindness was a hallmark of life back then.

The most fun-loving time of year was the harvest, when we'd gather up the hay for the winter fodder. The sweet, earthy scent of fresh-cut hay filled the air, mingling with the sounds of laughter and the rhythmic swish of rakes. The prickle of straw against the skin and the warmth of the summer sun on our backs as we worked are sensations I can still recall vividly. We'd rake the low-cut hay into tidy rows for nature's windy breath to dry. Then we'd form it into little hand-cocks for further drying before it was piled into big mounds of hay, called tramp-cocks. That's when the adults would throw the wee ones, squealing with laughter, on top to trample it down. We had more fun doing this than children today on a trampoline. Cart loads would be hauled off through the town with yelling youngsters on top and then piled high to the rafters in the barn.

In the open fields, my mother and sisters would bring us food and drinks of hot tea and sandwiches that we'd eat around the tramp-cocks of fresh-scented hay.

Not a minute was wasted during harvest-time, for the hay had to be saved while the good weather lasted and, in Donegal, the weather could change at the toss of a penny. Harvest-time was always a time of new life, common sacrifice, and togetherness.

Years later, while vacationing with one of my brothers and his family in the Dominican Republic, far away from Donegal, we began to reminisce about those simple days of childhood.

"Do you remember when Dad used to bed down the animals in the barn at night, and we took turns holding the old lantern while he worked?" asked my brother.

"Sure, I remember those evenings," I replied, amused by the recollection.

"Well," he continued, fondly, "I thought there had to be a better way to make a living than that."

We both laughed.

"And now, what do you think?" I pried, curiously.

"Now I ask myself," he replied, "if I'll ever be that good."

There were two primary or elementary schools in town, one for girls and one for boys. The boys' school was run by the Presentation Brothers, the girls' school by the Loreto Sisters. Primary school was tough on youngsters in those days. Corporal punishment was the norm, and rarely questioned. There was too much of it, and it was hard to escape. You could be picked out of a bunch of lads at will and made an example of to teach the others a lesson. One day, Johnny Callaghan and I were chosen to be beaten as a warning to the rest of the class. What I recall of this horrible experience were the blows of the rod battering my drooping hands as I fought back tears of agony. I told my parents about it, and they ignored it. I expected more from my father, knowing that my grandfather had removed my father and his siblings from the Brothers' School and sent them to Bart Hall, a

Part 1—Chapter 2

Protestant school, to avoid corporal punishment. But he decided the best course of action was to let sleeping dogs lie.

I went to Johnny Callaghan's home and told his parents, but had no success there, either. They also ignored it, taking the same approach as my parents. Not so Mrs. Scoles, whose son had been badly beaten in school by one of the brothers. I'll never forget the day she came bursting and screaming into the classroom like a raving banshee, wielding a sally stick and whipping the brother responsible for her son's trouncing. She forced him out of the classroom, leaving the pupils to their own devices.

After that incident, there was a noticeable change in the brother's behavior towards the pupils.

The greatest fear in primary school was the punishment that awaited you if you turned in your lessons and didn't get them right. I'll never forget the first time I learned to read in school—one of the most frightening experiences of my life. We were given a little text, with color pictures, about the weather:

> A red star at night
> Is the farmer's delight,
> Old Sean says.
> A red star in the morning
> Is not so good; it often means rain.
> Old Sean is a good judge of the weather.

We had to take this home, and learn to read it. But how? The teacher went through it individually with each pupil the next day, testing us. When my turn was approaching, I was still unable to read it. I was petrified and felt stuck in a dark tunnel with no way out. The boy sitting next to me in the classroom could read the text and showed me where the sounds and the words matched. I got him to repeat it over and over until I memorized it, word for word. By the time the teacher came to me and began moving the ruler under the words, I was able to recite what my friend had taught me. The teacher was satisfied, and moved along to the next pupil. I breathed a deep sigh of relief. I had escaped the lash.

"How did you learn to read this?" I asked my friend when the teacher was out of earshot.

"My father taught me," was his answer.

He had help. That, I learned, was the key to overcoming obstacles in life.

Psychological abuse can be just as taxing as physical abuse. One day, a math-teaching brother insulted me in front of the class for being stupid. I was mortified, especially when he extended the insult to include my brothers before me. His insults stung to the core of my being. His piercing words, however, had the salutary effect of motivating me to prove him wrong. Thus, I devoted every ounce of energy I could muster after that to doing very well in math, which I did. There were no more insults. The old affronts, soon forgotten, were replaced by words of praise. I learned an important lesson from this early experience: what might appear to be a cruel experience can be a blessing in disguise.

Although school was a mixed bag, friendships flourished. My buddies and I gradually figured out a way to beat the painful system of instruction. About five of us would gather after school to do our lessons together. We had our secret hideout, an old graveyard across the road from the school. Huge slabs of flat stone that covered the graves served as our class table. The brighter students would do the math lessons first. If our answers matched, we'd share them with the others and explain how we arrived at them. Then we'd tackle the essay writing in English and Gaelic and help one another with story composition and spelling. The same method was used for all subjects. When we were finished with our lessons we would enjoy the rest of the afternoon, playing at the old railway station or in our family farmyard.

The teachers were pleased with our progress every morning when we arrived at school. This was how we overcame the fear of punishment—by working together and helping one another. In appreciation, the teachers gave us a special long seat at the back of the class, where we could idle away our time without fear of punishment, playing checkers.

The day everyone looked forward to during primary school was Wednesday when we were given a half day off. We'd stampede with excitement through the school gates when classes ended to catch the latest fourpenny movie at the La Scala Cinema. The La Scala was our community center, where we all gathered to watch Roy Rodgers or Gene Autrey or Laurel and Hardy or Bud Abbott and Lou Costello. Sometimes we wouldn't watch the movie at all, but would play hide-and-seek in the cinema while the movie attendant would try to track us down with his flashlight and force us back into our seats.

Another great community event came in the summer, when we took the Sunday bus ride to the golden beach of Rathmullan. It cost just sixpence for the round trip, and sometimes it took three buses or more to transport the town's boisterous youngsters to the beach and back. Rathmullan's Beach and the village's traditional New Year's Day swim in freezing water features prominently in Brand King's 2020 novel, *An Irish Winter*.

The Christmas pantomime in the Devlin Hall was the crown jewel of our town's festivities. Mr. McGuire, a reserved yet brilliant man, would take a classic folk tale like Jack and the Beanstalk and transform it into a sidesplitting comedy, weaving in anecdotes and gossip about local people and events. The actors were all townsfolk, their roles sparking whispers and speculation long before the curtain rose. On opening night, the air was electric as the hall filled to bursting, the audience ready for an evening of riotous laughter and community camaraderie. Every performance played to a full house, leaving the town buzzing with shared delight for weeks afterward.

Most townies trace their deepest relationships and bonds back to their early years in primary school. This can be seen as plain as day during the Triannual Letterkenny Reunion, when townies, like freshly hatched turtles drawn to the ocean, scurry back home from all over the world to reconnect with their childhood friends. We gather to share old memories, to enjoy the stories from our childhood, and laugh and tease one another all over again.

One particular story comes to mind from those early years.

I was walking home with my older brother. Coming towards us was a tall, dignified man with a full head of snow-white hair, shaped like an afro.

"Go on, say hello to that nice man," said my brother, brusquely, nudging me forward. I was about eight years old at the time and did as my big brother told me.

"What'll I say?" I implored.

"Say hello, Mr. Snowball," my brother replied.

Naïve to this prank at my tender age, I blurted out as instructed.

My older brother took off at a fast run, leaving me to face the consequences. The man pivoted and followed me, marching down the laneway to our house. I halted at the gable wall and apologized, explaining that my older brother put me up to it. The good man accepted my explanation, and I breathed a sigh of relief. But my sister, Bernadette, passing by at the same time caught sight of the odd exchange.

At dinner, she asked what I had been talking about to that man with the big head of white hair. My parents too, demanded an explanation. Mortified but honest, I told them that Pat got me to say: "Hello, Mr. Snowball."

My siblings roared laughing while Pat sank out of sight. Mother didn't know what to say, and my father, suppressing his urge to chuckle, feigned dismay with a shake of his head.

This was the kind of fun that defined our town, a tapestry of shared moments and spirited togetherness. From the mischievous pranks that left us in stitches to the anticipation of the Christmas pantomime, life in Letterkenny was a celebration of connection. The warmth of our community, the simple pleasures of childhood, and the enduring bonds of family helped us to deal with life's adversities and shaped not only our days but the way we would become. These memories, rich with laughter and love, remain a testament to the spirit of a town that nurtured us in faith, friendship, and unyielding resilience.

Chapter 3

As I entered my teens in the mid-1950s, my innocent vision of the world cracked like spring ice when I discovered for the first time how treacherous the world could be. The revelation came, as they most often do, on an otherwise ordinary day.

We had just finished our midday dinner—taken at noon, as was the Irish way—when my eldest brother John caught sight of our youngest, Joseph, scrambling over the wall of an old, ruined building in our yard.

"What's that ween doing climbing over the wall?" John remarked, his voice tinged with concern.

"Ah, I know well what he's at," my mother answered, her face etched with worry. "He's after the box I took off him yesterday. Tossed it o'er yonder wall, I did."

"And what was in that box?" I chimed in, curiosity getting the better of me.

My mother's frown deepened as she answered: "Nought but bullets it looked like, all packed in tight. I was minded to throw them into the fire, but something in me said no. Over the wall they went, instead."

Her words carried a weight of unease, as she sensed the danger and, instinctively, chose the best way of dealing with it. It was a moment that has stayed with me all my life, a vivid reminder of God's providential care in our seemingly tranquil corner of Donegal.

At the mention of bullets, I rushed outside, climbed the wall, and snatched the box from the hands of my embarrassed, youngest brother, who was left standing there speechless and empty-handed. Sitting around the kitchen table, we inspected the contents of the box which read: Highly Explosive Gelignite. This box contained dynamite's slightly more stable but highly dangerous cousin, gelignite. It was packed neatly into capsules that looked like bullets, as my mother described them.

Poor Joseph found himself at the center of a flurry of questions at the kitchen table, each of us eager to unravel the mystery.

"Where'd you stumble upon them explosives?" we pressed, with keen interest.

"Behind Nelly's Pub," he replied, his voice faint.

"What's that you're saying? Behind Nelly's, is it? Found them just lying on the ground, did ye?" we continued, our inquiries growing more earnest by the moment.

"No, no," Joseph clarified. "They were buried inside a wee hill of stones."

"A wee hill of stones, is that so? And tell us now, was there anyone with ye when you made this find?"

Our voices were overlapping, each laced with a mix of astonishment and concern.

The simplicity of Joseph's responses belied the gravity of the discovery, a hint of danger lurking beneath the surface of our otherwise simple life.

Joseph, twitching with remorse, reluctantly named his accomplices: the neighborhood Stephenson boys. That did it for me.

I took the box of explosives with me to the Stephenson home and showed them to Pearse, the father of the other three boys involved.

With a voice that could carry over the fields, Pearse hollered for his wife, Mary, to join us at the front door.

"Mary, come quick, will ye!" He bellowed, his voice echoing in the hallway.

As soon as Mary caught a glimpse of what I had in my hands, her eyes widened and she exclaimed: "Saints preserve us! There's a whole lot of them things tucked under the boys' pillows in their bedroom."

Her words, filled with a mix of alarm and disbelief, rang through the air.

We gathered the explosives from the Stephenson house with trembling hands, carrying our deadly cargo to the Board of Works inspector. His face drained of color at the sight: "Two boxes of gelignite," he exclaimed, "when I need a special certification for just one!"

This was no innocent find. At the time, the Irish Republican Army (IRA) was active, blowing up military installations along the Northern Irish border, just sixteen miles from our doorstep.

The police got on the case immediately, staking out Nelly's pub for several weeks to track down the perpetrators. I don't know how successful they were in finding those who hid the explosives that could have blown our home to smithereens. Some credited our safety to guardian angels, watching over little boys. But it was my mother's quiet wisdom and presence of mind that had spared us, guiding her hand away from the fire.

Part 1—Chapter 3

In the later 1950s, you could feel the stirrings of change in the town. I well remember one dreary, drizzly day, bringing the cows home for milking from the isles along Port Road. Our farmland was called the isles because it had been reclaimed from the nearby Swilly River that ran into the sea.

When I got the cows to the top of the road where the long street descended, they wouldn't advance down the hill. They were spooked by something; I didn't know what until I saw them being drawn to Rodin's Pub like a magnet to metal. The pub had recently been renovated with a polished marble front where had once been a simple whitewashed wall. The cows saw their moving shadows in the glassy surface of the marble and were attracted to it. Then, terrified by their warped and fitful reflections, the cows bolted down the Port Road from whence they came, lowing and groaning at the top of their lungs. Several times I tried to maneuver them past the pub, but I failed miserably. A man on a bike saw the commotion and sped down the street to tell my family about my predicament.

Soon, my father and brothers appeared on the run at the top of the hill, bearing ropes. We had to tie the ropes around each cow's neck and pull them, one at a time, past the pub with its glossy marble exterior.

That was the last time our cows came home for milking along Main Street. From then on, they were herded along the railway line and up the fields to the farmhouse on lower Main Street.

The town was changing.

Letterkenny, known as a border town, was only sixteen miles from the Ulster border. It had a blend of cultures, Protestants and Catholics living in harmony. We got along very well, unlike our counterparts across the border, who were constantly at each other's throats.

Across the street from where we lived were the Johnstons, who were Presbyterian. They were our neighbors and close friends, and we lived and played in each other's houses. We never let our religious differences interfere with our relationships. We had too much in common. My aunt was married to Mrs. Johnston's brother. Thus, our first cousins were also first cousins of the Johnstons.

There were many great characters in town, but Bob Johnston took the cake. He elected to be a Free Presbyterian minister and had read the entire Bible from Genesis to Revelation. He described himself as a Minister to anyone who cared to know about his religious status. Though he didn't have a church, nor did he attend one as far as I could tell, he did have a congregation. He would bring his sturdy companion, the Bible, along with him to the local pub, Fox's, and expound on it to the delight of the mostly Catholic clientele. These curious customers knew very little about the Bible, and were thrilled to learn about it in such a comfortable setting from such a genial teacher.

One night, the pub was raided by the local police for not respecting closing hours. Everyone had to leave Fox's pub, except for Bob Johnston, who continued his Bible study, alone and nonchalantly, while enjoying his pint of Guinness. The officers of the law let him be.

Bob was also a jack-of-all-trades—a practical Renaissance man: carpenter, plumber, electrician, plasterer, preacher, painter and inventor. His many services were required all over town. When my family replaced the open fire with a new kitchen range, it was Bob Johnston who installed it. He opened a fish-and-chip shop and even invented his very own potato-peeling machine, which we were taught to operate. We were his best customers—non-paying, of course—for we helped out in the shop and ate away the profits. As one could imagine, the fish-and-chips shop was not a profitable enterprise, and had to close its doors, much to the disappointment of the youngsters in lower Main Street.

My parents had several little enterprises going to augment their income, apart from the farm and my father's turf business. My mother opened the house to Scottish boarders in the summer; quite an undertaking with nine children of her own—five boys and four girls. But she was very inventive, and had an engaging, hospitable nature. One of the buildings on the farm was cleaned up, painted, and turned into a separate room for the boys. We slept there while the Scottish boarders took our room.

The Scotchies, as they were called, were like celebrities in those days, especially the girls. The lasses were highly coveted by the local lads at the dances in the Devlin Hall. Dances were also held in a marquee for youngsters at the primary school. I was often prevailed upon to introduce the young, flashy, Scottish girls staying with us to my friends eagerly looking for a dance. The Scotchies boarded with us every summer, and one of them, Sadie Kelly from Glasgow, loved it so much, she got a job in Letterkenny and moved in with us permanently until she got married.

Sadie bought herself a new bicycle to ride to work each day at Oatfield's sweet factory. One Sunday, my boyhood friend, Norman Harkin, and I decided to take a bicycle trip to Drumkeen which, to our limited perspective, seemed a whole world away. My Uncle Josie had a shop there, and we looked forward to a warm welcome and refreshments after our long ride.

We had one problem: We didn't have bicycles. We figured we could borrow Sadie's bike unbeknownst to her, and between us we could rent another from McGlynn's bicycle shop at the bottom of the town for two shillings. Norman's father had a bicycle shop at the top of the town, but Norman didn't want to ask his father for the loan of a bike. We preferred

Part 1—Chapter 3

to do business with McGlynn at the bottom of town. We raised the money by selling used beer bottles to various pubs in town for two pennies a piece until we reached the magic number of twenty-four pennies or two shillings. We were in business.

We took off on our bicycles, and when we got to the flat and open road at the top of the long hill going to Drumkeen, we raced each other for sheer joy. Our adventure ended abruptly when our bikes entangled, sending us tumbling into the gully. Bruised but undeterred, we quietly returned the damaged bikes, mine to the barn and Norman's to McGlynn's shop window at dusk. The aftermath—Mr. McGlynn's mild reprimand and Sadie's unexpected understanding—taught Norman and I valuable lessons about honesty and forgiveness.

In addition to the Scottish boarders, another source of family income came from the pigs we raised on the farm, and sold to the bacon factory. They cost nothing to keep, for we fed them the leftovers from the family table, as well as leftovers from local restaurants in town.

My mother, being from the hill country of Lanalea, west of Letterkenny, raised chickens, which provided fresh eggs for breakfast and other meals. The excess was sold to grocery shops in town. Our kitchen was always transformed into a wellspring of joy whenever the baby chickens were hatched, miraculously it seemed, beside the warmth of the kitchen fireplace. We would play with them around the floor, marveling at their simple beauty.

We didn't have much money growing up, but that didn't bother us. We had as much joy as was possible with the little amount we had; we ate well from the produce of the land and made the best of our circumstances by working together as a family.

My mother was the disciplinarian in the family, but only up to a point. When we got older and were harder to handle, she would appeal to my father to keep us in check, especially if we came home late.

At dinner one day, she said: "You'll have to do something about them three boys, Mick. They're supposed to be home at nine each night, but don't set foot 'til eleven."

She was talking about her three rambunctious teenagers: Michael, Pat, and myself.

My father backed my mother up: "Do ye hear what your mother said? I want ye fellas inside this house at nine every night. D'ye follow?"

The next time my mother brought the same matter up at dinner, my father said nothing. There was only silence. We got home at eleven as usual the following night, but passing the window, we saw the light was on and my father sitting by the fireplace, smoking his pipe and reading the paper. He had never done this before, and we knew he meant business.

When we entered the house and bolted the door, he sprang from his chair and charged at us, pounding us with what appeared to be some kind of strap. We roared and screamed and ran into the pantry, closing the door behind us. When we heard the footsteps moving away, we looked at each other and started laughing. The strap was made of rubber and felt like a harmless pounding on the shoulders. Suddenly the door burst open and we were treated to another rubber thrashing as we fled up the stairs. We ran to our room, threw ourselves down on our beds and howled laughing.

But we were never late again after that. We didn't want to incur my father's anger. We loved him just the way he was.

My parents could not have been more different. My mother was a country girl; outgoing, hospitable, well-traveled (she had been to America in her youth), and part of a large family. My father, though from a large family as well, was a quieter type and a townie to the core. He loved to have fun and had a jolly nature. My mother's folks from the country would visit our home on Saturday evenings after a day's shopping in town. It was always an exciting end to the week. My father would sit back, quietly enjoying the revelry, laughter and goings-on of our hilarious and boisterous country relatives who loved to spend a good time together. There was lots of good humor in our home, and we were adept at creating our own fun.

I remember the day one of our country relatives got into trouble in Nellie's pub, and was afraid to go back there for his belongings. He came to our house for help the following day, and I was deputized to go to Nellie's for his belongings. I did just that, but I had to listen to a mouthful of criticism from Nellie before she handed over my relative's things.

Later that evening, as my parents and I were discussing this incident, my brother, Pat, came home from a movie at the La Scala cinema. He heard the tail end of our conversation and thought he would have to share his bed with this unruly relative—a common practice in those days. My parents and I played along and Pat got more and more agitated at the thought of sharing his bed. My brother John had left for America, and Pat now had a whole bed to himself. I still had to share a bed with my brother Michael, who had gone to a dance that night and wouldn't be home until late.

My father caught my attention and nodded toward the stairs that led to the bedroom. I quietly prepared Pat's bed with pillows under the blankets to look like someone was sleeping there. The head posed a problem, so I placed one of my father's old caps on top where the head would be. When the job was done, I descended the stairs to the kitchen. Then my parents and I coaxed Pat, who reluctantly went up the stairs to the bedroom. When he saw the man in his bed with a cap on, he couldn't resist laughing at the state of this unwelcome intruder, who hadn't the decency to remove his cap in bed.

"Shush," my father muttered, "you'll wake up Johnny."

My father, leaning over the bed, spoke gently to the fake Johnny.

"Move over, Johnny, and make room for Pat," he said.

He managed to throw his voice like a ventriloquist, imitating Johnny's grudging response. It was so effective that my brother completely fell for it. My mother and I were holding each other up from laughing. When we finally composed ourselves and pulled the blankets away, Pat saw it was all a practical joke. He took it in good stride, and I felt vindicated for the Mr. Snowball affair he got me embroiled in several years earlier.

I lived all through elementary and high school in the little farmhouse on lower Main Street. But as the town grew, progress encroached. The county council targeted our property, hoping to turn it into a link road and parking lot connecting Main Street to the new road where the old railway line once was. At a council meeting, the matter was discussed, but no one, not even the bailiff, would approach my parents about moving.

"I'd rather be fired than ask Mick Duffy and his family to move," declared the bailiff.

The county manager, a neutral man from another part of Ireland, volunteered to go in person to talk to my parents about moving. Coming down the laneway, he was met by my mother, carrying potatoes into the house for dinner. She welcomed him inside in her usual, hospitable way, and offered him a cup of tea and a slice of freshly baked apple pie. She put on the kettle and when the tea was ready, she drew from the hot oven a simmering apple pie with a thin, crisp crust and served it to her guest.

She later recounted how nice the man was, and how he told her, after he finished his apple pie, that he had come to ask my parents to move. This, of course, came as a shock to her, but the man himself had a change of heart, she related. He understood why no one on the council, including the bailiff, would take on the task of asking my parents to relocate. He was not prepared to do so either, after the hospitable way he had been treated.

"You can stay here as long as you wish," he said, appreciatively.

In time, my parents decided to move, giving up farming voluntarily, and settling into a new home in Oldtown. The old homestead is now a link road, a parking lot, and a busy intersection for shops and businesses on lower Main Street.

As I reflect on this stage of my upbringing, I see how the lessons of resilience, compassion, laughter, and collaboration have guided me throughout my life. These formative years, with their alternating joys and sorrows, instilled in me the values that would guide me throughout my life.

Chapter 4

My upbringing in Letterkenny, essential though it was in my early development, was complemented by my experiences of country life in my mother's old homeplace of Lanalea, in the sprawling hill-country of Cark, County Donegal.

Every child needs a safe place where he or she can relax, be at ease, and escape the pressures of the world. For me, Lanalea sticks out in my mind as the happiest and most relaxing place to have lived. This was the Xanadu of my youth, where I spent the summer months out of school. It was my second home.

There was no need for watches or clocks or phones or any other artificial means of timekeeping in Lanalea. Here time seemed to stand still, marked only by the eternal timekeepers—the sun, the moon and the stars. There were no shops in Lanalea, no trucks or busses, no schools or TV. There was nothing but the landscape: the hills, the dales, the valleys, the livestock, the gurgling fish-filled brooks, and the vast firmament above. Intertwined with nature were the decent and endearing folk who lived there in harmony with their surroundings.

In this timeless place, hospitality reigned supreme. Every house boasted a half-door, a silent invitation for passersby to look in and for those inside to gaze out. It was a symbol of welcome, only locked at night when the day's work was done.

In the mornings, the first light of day would come peering through the little windows of my uncle's whitewashed, thatched cottage, and the cry of the rooster sounded nature's alarm to get up. I can still see my grandmother sitting by the roaring fireplace, and my Uncle Johnny, quietly reading the paper while gentle Mary was baking a fresh scone of bread. The rich aroma of this fresh bread filled the house, and Mary would warmly say: "Hughie, go to the henhouse and fetch two warm, fresh eggs and bring them here for your breakfast." I'd saunter off, sleepy-eyed, to the henhouse. No breakfast ever tasted as good or wholesome as this breakfast of hot porridge, fresh-laid eggs from the henhouse, homemade scone from the fireplace, natural butter made in the family churn, and a freshly brewed bowl of tea.

In Lanalea we made our own fun. We fished in the little burn or rocky stream below the house, we swam during warm weather in Lough Dale, captured between the rolling hills. We roamed the landscape as free as the grouse or sheep on the heathery mountains. We also worked for our keep, saving the hay, cutting or stacking the turf, and dipping the sheep.

In this timeless setting, every day was an adventure, filled with simple pleasures and valuable lessons. One such day, etched vividly in my memory, began when my sisters, Bernadette and Hannah, invited me to visit Mary Brown on the other side of Cark Hill.

It struck me as an exciting offer and I readily agreed. Skipping lightly from one stepping stone to another over the burn at the end of the cottage, we reached the foot of the mountain and started our climb to the other side of Cark Hill. As we ascended to the top of the mountain, Mary's little cottage rose up from the valley like a stage set. First the curling, bluish smoke from the chimney melting into the gray sky; then the neatly thatched roof; and finally, the white-washed walls and the half door of the cottage beckoning us inside. When we arrived at the half door, Mary screamed with joy.

"Come in, come in," she cried, ecstatically. She welcomed us with the rapture of receiving the three wise personages from the East. Turning around, she rushed to the fireplace, and came back with a little twig in her hand.

"I was sweeping the floor this morning and found this twig with three stems," she said. "I kept it on the hob, for I knew three visitors would be visiting me today."

Mary made us feel as welcome as the flowers of May. The day passed in a flash with so much fun, so much joy, so much freedom in simply being. There was no distinction between peer groups back then. We were merely children, including Mary, who had the spirit of a child. Days like this came and went like shooting stars in the night. The sparkle still remains.

In the mornings, after breakfast, it was customary to bring a few bags of fodder to feed the sheep way up the mountain. The first time I did this with an older brother, I couldn't understand why there was only one sheep track for so many. My brother Michael explained that sheep walked in line, led by the ram, to protect themselves from the cold. The sheep that ran these hills of Donegal were native sheep, wiry and weather hardened. We walked on with no sheep in sight, when suddenly, at the sound of our voices, the sheep burst forth from behind rocks and clusters of purple heather to be fed. In a frenzy of excitement, we fed these high-strung creatures, who leaped and snatched the fodder out of our hands.

One early morning, I brought the cows home from the dewy mountain to be milked. They were all feeding on the fresh, morning grass, except for one lying on the ground, showing no interest in getting up. I poked this cow gently with a stick and she jumped up suddenly, giving birth as she did so to a baby calf, smothered in placenta. The mother cleaned the placenta from her newborn lying on the ground, and nudged the calf back and forth until it stood up wobbling on its spindly legs. I watched with awe this miracle of birth take place before my eyes. In no time and to my astonishment, the little calf followed the mother down the hill and into the barn.

I ran into the house yelling, excitedly: "We have a baby calf, and it's with the mother in the barn. It walked down the mountain, all on its own."

My grandmother, my Uncle Johnny and Mary only smiled in amusement at my childlike excitement. For them, this was just a natural occurrence.

In the evenings in Lanalea, we crowded into one another's homes, young and old, to listen to stories around the open fireplace. It was here in the timeless atmosphere of Lanalea that I had my first, live introduction to the *seanchaí* or storyteller with the gift of spinning marvelous tales. The style of speech, delivery and content of this old lore had a way of capturing the youthful imagination in a way no classroom lesson possibly could. These local practitioners of the art were the keepers of a large corpus of tales passed down from one generation to the next without the need to be written down. They kept us spellbound through many an evening of what was called: raking.

I learned the meaning of raking when Mary asked me to go raking with her one evening. I thought she was talking about raking hay, a job for the daytime. But when Mary realized my lack of understanding, she laughed and explained that raking meant visiting. The expression comes from raking the ashes and coals in the fireplace to keep people warm while visiting. There was also singing and dancing during raking in these little homes. My aunt Maggie's favorite party piece was The Bonnie Wee Window.[1] She sang about the bonnie wee window with its cracked panes of glass and uneven twists and turns of the panels, yet it was the bonniest wee window you ever saw.

My uncle and mother wove tales of their childhood in the rustic environs of Lanalea. It was not an easy life for them, and had its share of hardships, but it seemed magical to me. They created their own escape from the burdens of life by dancing the evenings away at the crossroads when the

---

1. "The Bonnie Wee Window," is a traditional Scottish song that was popular in Donegal.

weather was warm, and in the hay barn when the weather was cold. For them, this was true freedom.

As a child, I loved to eavesdrop on the adult talk of my mother and my uncle, especially when it came to religion. When my mother would visit Lanalea, my Uncle Johnny liked to tease her about it.

"The law of the land is the best thing to hold people in check," he'd say. "Without it, people would run amok."

"True," my mother would agree. "But you need something more than that."

"Like what?" my uncle would return.

"God," my mother would say firmly. "Just look at the decent lives led by those who follow Him," she'd add with conviction.

"And where might these fine folks be when you're in a pinch?" Uncle Johnny would challenge. "Most times, they're nowhere to be seen. They're all for show, to impress others."

My Uncle Johnny liked to criticize false religiosity.

My mother usually got tongue-tied when arguing with my uncle, not knowing how to respond.

I was always intrigued by my uncle's way of looking at things. Whenever I listened to a replay of this frequent conversation, I felt instinctively that my uncle was overlooking something important: human conscience. Conscience, a voice within, compelling one to do right, was a greater force for good than the law of the land. The rules of men wouldn't stop me from doing wrong—it was the prospect of facing myself in the mirror of conscience. This, more than rules, deterred me from wrongs I could get away with. People will do ill if they don't get caught, but conscience prevents wrongdoing even when no one is watching.

Despite his skepticism, my uncle was a man of conscience who harbored a deep respect for the rights of others. He and I never argued about religion, nor did he pressure me to adopt his views. We were close friends.

One night I confided in him my hopes of becoming a priest. He put down his pipe and spoke bluntly: "If that's what you want to do with your life, just remember one thing: Christ is the boss."

I never forgot those words. My uncle scorned false piety and derided hollow sermons and superficial faith. He knew how easy it was to offer lip-service rather than real service in following Christ.

He had one priest friend, Father Maurice Browne, an Irish writer who visited Lanalea every year to shoot grouse.[2] When I was ordained, Father

---

2. Maurice Browne (whose pen name was Joseph Brady) was known for three novels, *The Big Sycamore* (1958), its sequel, *In Monavalla* (1963) and the semi-autobiographic novel, *From a Presbytery Window* (1971).

Browne wrote to me, inviting me to give a retreat in his parish. He confided that he visited Lanalea not just to shoot grouse, but to spend quality time with my uncle.

I was always invited to stay in Lanalea during my summer vacations from boarding school, and in case I felt uppity, my uncle would say: "You're welcome to Lanalea only if you take things the way they are. If you can't do that, don't come."

I had no problem with that. In Lanalea, I became part of its lifestyle and surroundings, which were different from what I was used to in town and at boarding school. I was happy to live the way my relatives and friends lived in this unbiased, out-of-the-way place.

One Saturday my distant cousin, Peter, living a stone's throw away from my uncle's cottage, had to go to town to buy groceries for the family. He asked me to come with him.

"That's too much for a townie," Aunt Maggie objected.

"Not at all," replied Neely. "It'll be good for him."

It was a misty day and dark clouds were forming on the mountains. Peter and I got dressed in heavy jumpers, gloves, raincoats and wellingtons for the journey to the town and back. We set off, free as birds, cycling the rocky and bumpy road from Lanalea to New Mills, a few miles out of town, laughing all the way. The paved road from New Mills to Letterkenny made the last leg of the journey easy going.

Once in town, we purchased the groceries as instructed. I didn't visit my own folks, though they lived nearby. It felt strange yet cozy—a country boy adrift in his hometown. And I liked it that way.

We tied our boxes of groceries to the carriers of our bikes and set off for the return journey. The weather then changed, and the dark clouds discharged torrential sheets of rain. At New Mills, we pushed our bikes up the steep and rocky, rain-drenched hill until we reached level ground. We hadn't the strength to utter a word on the way up. At the top of the hill, we paused a while, like two weary athletes, to get our second wind. We hung tight to our bicycles for support, letting the tiredness drain from our bodies. Then, after resting a while, we continued the journey on the flat ground to Lanalea. The rain never let up and continued to drench us as we bicycled the rest of the way. We were dripping wet when we entered the cottage. Maggie and Neeley came rushing over, grabbing the raincoats off our backs, the wellingtons off our feet, and rinsing and drying the socks and gloves we wore. They set the wet things on the iron rack over the fireplace before sitting us down to dry on the big hobs next to the roaring fire. Neeley piled fresh turf onto the open flames to keep us warm. The loud crackling, the flashing flames, and the dancing shadows curling up the dark chimney transported me into a delirium of pure delight. I was as close to heaven as I could possibly be at that moment in the Donegal of my youth.

The patriarch of my mother's family, my grandfather, John Kelly, emigrated to the U.S. in the late nineteenth century, and worked in the Klondike before settling down again in Lanalea. He was only eighteen when he left his native land to work in Alaska. I was always intrigued by how he managed to travel so far afield into a strange land in search of work.

As an aside, many years later, I found myself serving as a chaplain on a cruise ship. During a stop at Skagway, Alaska, I encountered an acting troupe. They performed an interactive play, offering glimpses into the lives of Klondike pioneers from days long past. You had to pick a name to be in the play, and I chose John Kelly, my grandfather's name. It was then that I got a feeling for what it was like for my grandfather to survive the Klondike experience: the run-in with unscrupulous and dangerous conmen who stole the pioneers blind, the inflated cost of shovels, buckets and pick axes, and the terrible journey by foot through snow and slush to Carson City before landing work in the Klondike.

My tour guide and I visited the Red Rooster, a popular gathering spot for Gold-Rush miners. I could easily picture my grandfather among the regulars. After a thrilling but exhausting day of kayaking through Alaska's rapids, we bellied up to the bar and I ordered drinks to cap off our adventure.

Out of nowhere, a lady in a dazzling red dress made a grand entrance on the balcony. She descended toward the bar, her every step punctuated by uproarious music and cheers from the crowd. It seemed she was headed our way.

"Do you know her?" my guide inquired.

"Absolutely not," I replied.

Before I could say another word, she approached me, grinning from ear to ear.

"Methinks you're as bored as a parson in a whorehouse," she said.

I was speechless. Around me, the Red Rooster erupted in laughter. Glasses were raised high in jest. It turned out they were all cruise members, and I had just fallen for their elaborate prank; hook, line, and sinker.

My grandfather did not settle in the Yukon where he was mining for gold. As the eldest son, he had to return to Lanalea after his father's death to take possession of the family farm. Ireland was a crown colony of the British Empire, and my grandfather was a British citizen. According to British law, the farm would have reverted to government ownership if he didn't come back to claim it.

Thank God my grandfather made it possible for the likes of me to experience the hospitality of Lanalea.

I remember once my uncle and I went raking at dusk to the McMenamin home on the other side of Cark Hill. The shortest and best way to the other side of the mountain was through it. We could have bicycled along the narrow, country road around the hill, but that would have meant a much longer journey, and a lot of climbing up winding hills. A car, on the other hand, would have cut the journey down to nothing. But it was a blessing to walk over the mountain. A car did away with space and robbed you of the joy of planting your feet solidly in nature and seeing vividly what lay before you. We're used to moving so fast today that it's difficult to enjoy what lies before us.

When we got to the house, there was no one home, and that was unusual.

"Let's try the windey," my uncle said. "Git a holt of the sill," he added, raising the window up and pushing me through.

Once inside, I unlocked the door. My uncle entered. He lit the kerosene lamp and we both settled in until the family came home. I heard a car approaching. The McMenamins of Cark had a car, the only one around. I nudged my uncle, nodding off by the fire.

"What's going on?" he asked.

"The McMenamins are here," I replied, "but they're afraid to get out of the car. The lights keep flashing."

"Run out and let them know we're here," my uncle instructed.

I rushed out to make myself known, and the family recognized me immediately. There were shouts of laughter as we all settled into an extended evening of raking by the open fireplace.

We returned home again the way we came, through the wide and open mountain, guided by the light of the amber moon. Now and then we'd disturb a little speckled grouse and it would take off, gliding on the reins of the wind, until, once safely distant, it would nestle in a cluster of purple heather. The wild heather of the mountain, illuminated by the moon's mesmerizing sheen, bore the semblance of a carpet, mixed with purple and gold. When we got to the foot of the mountain, we tip-toed our way across the gurgling brook, going straight by crooked steps, one stone at a time, to the lush meadow fronting the cottage in Lanalea. All about us the rich fragrance of fuchsia and hawthorn bushes filled our senses.

In Lanalea, you lived in communion with nature, or you didn't live at all.

During my parents' golden anniversary, many years later, I returned to Lanalea with my Philadelphia cousins. We came to see the ancestral home where their faither and grandfather were born. The transformation was stark and poignant. Life had drained from the place, leaving behind a shell of memories. Even the well, once a vital source of life, had run dry. Its stones stood silent, the tiny underground veins that once fed it now clogged and lifeless from disuse.

We had to park our car about a mile away, the little rocky road to the house now hidden beneath a tangle of rushes and weeds. As we walked, each step stirred memories of the vibrant life that once filled this place. The contrast between the Lanalea of my youth and the abandoned landscape before us was a powerful reminder of the passage of time and the inevitability of change.

Lanalea, for me, has always been more than a physical place. It was like an eternal state of being, where nature, family, and faith intertwined to shape the essence of who I became. My summers there were a symphony of connections—to the land, to our neighbors, and to a way of life that valued simplicity and togetherness. Those moments, steeped in the beauty of creation and the richness of community, continue to inspire and ground me, a reminder that the spirit lives on, unbroken by time or distance.

Chapter 5

It was during my fourteenth and last year in elementary school that a vocation to the priesthood began to take root. Father Oliver McGettigan was introduced to the class one day to talk to us about a vocation. We were all ears as he described a vocation to the priesthood as a calling to dedicate one's life to the service of God and our fellow man, like the early apostles, missionaries and some priests we knew.

At the end of talk, he said: "If anyone feels he has a call to the priesthood, please give your name and address to the teacher."

Several youngsters volunteered their names and addresses. I was not one of them. I had a deep respect for the priesthood, but felt it was out of my reach. When the priest received the names and addresses of the pupils from the teacher, he did something unexpected. He said he'd ask another pupil who didn't volunteer his information if he had ever considered the priesthood.

I got an uneasy feeling he was going to ask me. Well, that's exactly what he did. Pointing directly at me, he inquired: "Have *you* ever thought about a vocation to the priesthood?"

Reluctantly, I nodded my head, but I didn't offer my name and address.

Later that afternoon, as my pals and I were playing in the barn of our farmhouse, one of my friends said: "That priest who came to our class today is in your house talking to your parents."

This came as quite a shock, as I hadn't expressed any interest in the priesthood to my parents, and I hadn't revealed any of my personal details to the priest. He must have got the information from my teacher, Master Ferry.

When I entered the house, I saw Father Oliver seated in the kitchen, deep in conversation with my parents. I heard my parents say to him: "We never heard him say anything to us about the priesthood."

Obviously, my parents were surprised to hear that I was interested.

At the same time, my parents made it clear to Father Oliver that they would support me if that was what I wanted to do.

It's strange the way the Lord works. He uses others to show you the way, just as Andrew guided his brother, Simon (later to have his name changed to Peter), to follow Christ.[1]

If Father Oliver had not entered the classroom that day and put the question to me, I doubt I'd be a priest today.

The hardest part of my decision was how it might affect my relationships with my closest friends. I didn't want to lose them by choosing such a different path in life. I was heartened when they all encouraged me and gave me their full support. We have remained close friends to this day and have stayed in touch all through the years.

Father Oliver was a priest of the Carmelite Order, and he prevailed upon my parents to send me to the Carmelite College in Castlemartyr, County Cork, Ireland, for my secondary education. All through my years of secondary schooling, he visited my home when I was on vacation to nurture the vocation he had awakened in me.

I began my preparation for the priesthood in earnest in the fall of 1959, after I graduated from high school. Pope John XXIII, or Good Pope John, as he was affectionately called, was the reigning Pontiff. This was a time of great optimism and expectations in the church, as the jovial Pope John, born to a family of sharecroppers in Lombardy, Italy, broke with traditional church protocol. He decided to walk through St. Peter's Basilica rather than be carried aloft on the ceremonial throne. He won the hearts of the world with his Christ-like gesture of visiting the inmates at Rome's Regina Coeli prison.

My first year of preparation was called a novitiate or spiritual year, and it took place at the Carmelite friary in the town of Loughrea, County Galway. Loughrea ("gray lake," in Gaelic) is located in the peaceful countryside of Galway, and it takes its name from the gray lake on the edge of town.

The day I left home for Loughrea is clearly etched in my memory. Bob Johnston came strolling into our kitchen, his hands casually clasped behind his back. He took his place, his back against the kitchen range he had installed some years before.

"That was a fierce gale we had last night," he remarked to my father, seated at the kitchen table.

"Aye, that it was, Bob," my father responded, his smile tinged with a hint of shared understanding.

---

1. John 1:41 relates how Andrew brought the news to Simon Peter: "We have found the Messiah."

"Some houses lost their slates," continued Bob.

"You don't say!" replied my father, shaking his head.

As this jovial conversation continued, my mother ushered my younger brother, Joseph, out of the house, pressing two cans of milk into his hands for delivery to our neighbors. Reluctant to leave, Joseph lingered, and I knew mother's coaxing stemmed from a desire to spare him the pain of watching me depart in the taxi waiting outside. After Joseph left the house, I steeled myself and headed for the taxi parked outside our door.

Just then, Bob came over to me, shook my hand firmly and said, "Good Luck young fella," wishing me very best.

With a big wink and a smile to my father, his parting words were, "Stay away from the women and the drink."

Bob did not have a bone of religious bigotry in his body. In Letterkenny, Protestants and Catholics lived and worked alongside one another, went to the movies together, played sports together, and supported one another. This spontaneous, ecumenical camaraderie prevailed in my hometown, long before the ecumenical movement was launched by the church's Second Vatican Council.

As the taxi carrying me and my mother passed Joseph on Main Street, I twisted in my seat for one last look. There, frozen in the middle of the street, stood Joseph. Our eyes met through the rear window, and in that moment, time seemed to slow. The milk cans, once gripped tightly in his small hands, now slipped free. They hit the pavement with a hollow clang, white liquid pooling around his feet. Joseph's face crumpled, his wail cutting through the air and piercing my heart as pedestrians rushed to help him. At that moment, I understood what Kahil Gibran meant by love knowing nothing of its own depth until the hour of separation.

As I was borne away that morning, I knew my life would never be the same again. One chapter had closed, and a new uncertain one was beginning.

The taxi brought us to Sligo and from there I said goodbye to my mother, and took a bus to Loughrea. Joining me on this last leg of the journey was another young man in a black clerical suit. Frederick Wilberforce was from England and we met for the first time on the Loughrea bus. We were the only two people clerically dressed, so we became acquainted immediately because of our common purpose and destination.

As the bus rumbled along, Frederick and I exchanged tentative smiles.

So, I ventured, my Irish brogue a stark contrast to his crisp English accent, "What brings you to the Carmelites?"

Frederick's eyes lit up. "It's a family tradition of sorts," he said. "My ancestor, William Wilberforce, dedicated his life to abolishing the slave trade. I suppose I'm following in his footsteps, in a way—answering a call to serve."

I nodded, impressed. "And here I am," I remarked, "just a farm boy from Letterkenny."

Frederick laughed warmly. "We're not so different, you and I," he replied. "We're both answering the same call, aren't we?"

Despite our different backgrounds, I felt a kinship with Frederick. We were two young men on the same journey, finding comfort in each other's company as we stepped into the unknown.

Upon our arrival, the novice master greeted us kindly. I met my colleagues from the Carmelite College in Castlemartyr, who had arrived before us. Ushering us to the refectory, the novice master offered refreshments. My gaze fell upon a skull encased in a wooden box atop a table. It was a jarring sight, evocative of the Knights Templar or Yale's notorious Skull-and-Bones society.

When I inquired about it, the novice master replied, "It's a reminder of death." Odd, since no such *memento mori* graced the Carmelite refectory back at the college.

Afterwards, he led us one by one to our quarters.

I entered a dark corridor, the air heavy with silence. The novice master stopped, his silhouette barely visible in the gloom. He nodded towards a sign, its gilt letters gleaming faintly: Grand Silence. The floorboards creaked beneath our feet as we moved forward, each step seeming to echo in the stillness. The darkness pressed in around us, making every rustle of fabric, every breath, sound thunderous in comparison to the enforced quiet.

Part of our initiation was to be robed in the Carmelite habit. The day of robing arrived. As each piece of the Carmelite habit was placed upon me—the coarse woolen tunic, the flowing scapular, the enveloping cloak—I felt like a caterpillar entering its chrysalis. The weight of the fabric seemed to press away my old life, my old self. When the hood was finally drawn over my newly tonsured head, I hardly recognized the figure I saw in the mirror. I was in a cocoon of sorts, suspended between my old life and whatever new form I would take. The symbolism was unmistakable. This was more than a change of clothes. It was the beginning of a new life, the shedding of the old in hopes of emerging as something new. I emerged... changed, yet somehow still the same. But the real work of initiation lay ahead.

During Lent, we were encouraged to do extraordinary mortifications.[2] My fellow novices volunteered to do at least one, such as foregoing

---

2. Extraordinary mortifications were also called "works of supererogation" because they went beyond what God requires.

meals, while going around the refectory tables, plate in hand, from person to person, begging for food. Presumably, this was to instill within us a sense of humility. Thus, I found myself under pressure to conform, for I didn't volunteer to do any of the extraordinary mortifications. I didn't see any point in them. There was enough pain in life, I thought, without adding to it by some kind of extraordinary mortification.

One day during Lent the novice master came into my room.

"I see you didn't volunteer to do any of the extraordinary mortifications," he said, grievously.

"That's right," I replied. "I don't see any point in them."

"Everybody else has done one, so I'd like you to do one also," he continued, as he patiently explained what he wanted me to do.

Though I viewed imposed extraordinary mortifications as unnecessary, I played along for the sake of communal accord. Better to endure a little inconvenience than become a discordant note in the collective song.

As I knelt in the refectory, plate in hand, I couldn't help but question the purpose of this mortification.

"This is for your spiritual growth," the novice master had insisted earlier.

But was it really? Or was it just an exercise in imposed humility?

So, there I knelt in the heart of the rectory, a spectacle of imposed mortification. With great ceremony, a small table was placed before me, soon to be graced with food scraps, if any of the brethren deigned to donate. Suppressed chuckles echoed around me while I grinned at the sheer folly of it all. There I was, performing this strange ritual under the pretense of piety and sacrifice. Fortunately, it was the first and last time I was persuaded to perform an act of extraordinary mortification.

Father Cormac, the kindly superior at the college in Castlemartyr, came to visit our class in the novitiate at the closing of the year. He asked us: "What do you think of the Order?"

There was an awkward silence, but I couldn't hold it in any longer.

"What Order?" I asked. "This is not the same Order we knew in the College in Castlemartyr."

Everybody began to snigger. Soon, the snigger erupted into a sudden burst of laughter, beginning with Father Cormac.

The priests we knew at the Carmelite college were personable and engaging, and were not bound, as far as we knew, by the rules we were now asked to abide by in the novitiate.

The purpose of these rules, among other things, was to isolate one from the "world." Thus, we were forbidden to talk to lay people, for example, including those good people who worked in the kitchen and on the grounds. We also were told to practice mortification of the eyes, for it was in the rules that you should keep your eyes cast down, only looking the length of your coffin. I was unable to take these rules seriously.

When the novice master asked me to practice mortification of the eyes, I told him, "It's not the way I was reared."

"What do you mean?" he asked, genuinely.

"I've been taught to look people in the eye when you talk to them," I replied, all the while making eye contact with him.

He had nothing to say to that, and he let it drop.

Each of the novices had a small garden to care for. I knew little about growing flowers and plants, but Paddy Casey, the gardener, knew a lot. So, I asked him what I should do. He gave me good advice and offered me a bunch of tulips to plant. Word got back to the novice master, who came into my room.

"You could get Paddy Casey sacked," he said, steaming with anger.

"Paddy Casey had nothing to do with this," I replied. "He was only helping me by doing the Christian thing when I asked him what I should plant in the garden."

"You know you shouldn't be talking to seculars," continued the novice master. "That's against the rules."

But how could that be right? I pondered. Wasn't Christ himself known for speaking with all manner of people—tax collectors, prostitutes, the sick and the poor?

"Seculars" was the term used for lay people, but I didn't see the point in this rule since it was against the example of Christ, in my view. Thus, I had to listen to a lecture about prudence, and my lack of it. When the spiel was over, I remarked quietly, "Paddy Casey has a soul too."

The novice master got red in the face and didn't know what to say. He left the room in silence.

I closed my eyes, reflecting: *If I'm wrong, Lord, show me. But if treating all of your children with kindness is a sin, then I fear I'm not meant for the priesthood.*

I realized that my journey to the priesthood would be filled with trying moments—times when I'd have to choose between what I believed to be true Christian charity and blind obedience. It was a path I was only beginning to navigate and I knew it wouldn't be easy.

I was not dispatched from the novitiate for these infractions. Shortly thereafter the novice master came into my room again. I was expecting another dressing down, but I was mistaken. He began to compliment me on my progress, not on keeping to the rules, but on my spiritual growth and demeanor. His sense of empathy and encouragement were like rays of sunshine after a dark and cloudy day. After he left the room, I felt like Sidney Poitier in the classic movie, *Lilies of the Field*, when he jumped for joy upon hearing the mother superior, a walking rule, utter the human compliment: "Thank You."

Rules are okay in the life of a Christian if they bring you closer to Christ and your fellow man, but if they don't do that what's the point? It only means they have outlived their usefulness. The downside to these rules, I found, was that some of my friends who took them to heart ended up with nervous breakdowns and had to leave the order to regain their sanity. One of my friends joined up a little later than the rest of us. When he first arrived, we were introduced to him and enjoyed his conversation and good spirit. He had a wonderful sense of humor. After he was there for only a short time, a morose, funereal change came over him. A fellow novice remarked to me: "Have you noticed how he's changed?"

"Of course, I have," I replied, assuredly: "He's lost his lively sense of humor because of the weight of these rules."

Over half a century later, I received a call from Mick McQuaid, my old, novitiate friend, his humor revived after countless seasons. Now he tended the botanical gardens in Dublin, Ireland. We picked up as though no time had passed, reminiscing through laughter at the follies and foibles of human nature in general and our seminary formation in particular. The decades between us melted away. He thanked me for lighting his spirit during darker days. Though an ocean and endless tomorrows separated us, we were young again, but wise enough to laugh at the absurdities we were forced to endure. The phone call finally ended, yet a warm glow lingered, kindled by the timeless gift of friendship.

Apart from the imposition of senseless rules, I enjoyed the novitiate or spiritual year. It was, primarily, a year of spiritual reflection, meditation, and preparation. There was plenty of quality time to read and meditate. To me, this was a gift as precious as gold. Living in community also energized me to get along with others and support them, in spite of differences.

I also was able to brush up on my Latin during this time. I knew it would come in handy when I went to the major seminary in Dublin, where all our textbooks were in Latin. I studied conversational Latin in my room every day during my spiritual year.

At the major seminary, I was proficient enough in conversational Latin, the common language of the church, to be able to communicate quite fluently with the foreign seminarians from Spain and Italy.

Chapter 6

THE 1960S WAS A time of exhilarating promise, especially within the seminary halls of Dublin. When Pope John XXIII announced the need for an ecumenical council to a gathering of cardinals on January 25, 1959, he launched a spiritual renaissance in the church. He viewed this council as necessary for the renewal of the church and as a means for all Christians to join in the search for unity. This was extraordinary news, discussed in colleges and seminaries, in the secular media, in cafes, barrooms and institutions across the globe. As I delved into my studies, the impending council felt like a divine wind, a new Pentecost sweeping through the church.

Yet this new Pentecost met with resistance from the *Curia*, the Vatican's nerve center and ecclesiastical bureaucracy. Entrenched in a view of the church through the austere lens of judicial absolutes and external perfection, they questioned the need for change. Their stance was not surprising: We too had been immersed in Cardinal Bellarmine's centuries-old concept of the church as an immutable, Perfect Society.[1] Why change what was already perfect? was the mindset of the time. Though some clung to the old certainties, the Second Vatican Council dawned with the promise of *aggiornamento*, bringing the light of the gospel to the modern world.

Pope John saw the need for a more pastoral church that would focus not only on doctrinal statements or pronouncements, but on the following of Christ, on living by the gospel, reaching out to the marginalized, to the poor, to people of other faiths, and to all people of good will.

I'll never forget the day we heard about Pope John's visit to Regina Coeli Prison. As one of our professors read the news to us, a hush fell over the classroom. The image of the Pope, standing among the prisoners, saying: "You could not come to me, so I came to you," struck me like a thunderbolt. Here was the church I had always dreamed of—not a distant, judgmental institution, but a living embodiment of Christ's love, reaching out to the

---

1. Cardinal Bellarmine's definition of church as a perfect society was the prevailing definition found in theological textbooks in the early 1960s.

forgotten and the marginalized. In that moment, I felt my own calling deepen and take on new meaning.

Pope John gave witness to this pastoral ideal and approach through his own actions. Example, they say, is the best sermon and speaks louder than words. His example spoke volumes.

He was the first pope since 1870 to make pastoral visits in his own Diocese of Rome. He visited children suffering from polio at the Bambino Gesù, Children's Hospital in Rome. The very next day, he visited the Hospital of the Holy Spirit, the oldest hospital in Europe, also located in Rome. He also visited a reformatory for juvenile delinquents and abandoned the informal *We* when referring to himself, so he could talk to the youth on their own level.

He opened dialogue with the communist countries of eastern Europe, so that eastern Christians could find refuge from persecution. He also initiated dialogue with the Russian Orthodox Church to heal the sad divisions in the church going back to the eleventh century. In his 1963 encyclical, *Peace on Earth*, Pope John sought to prevent nuclear war and tried to improve relations between the United States and the Soviet Union. He condemned antisemitism in the Catholic Church and in 1960 he eliminated the description of Jews as *perfidious* in the church's Good Friday liturgy.

In the refectory of the Major Seminary in Dublin, a book about the council by German theologian, Hans Küng, was read during meals, and discussed by the students during walks in the seminary grounds afterwards.[2]

One crisp autumn evening, we were huddled in the common room, our well-worn copy of Hans Küng's book opened on a table before us. The air crackled with excitement as we debated the possibilities of change in Küng's remarkable work on church reform.

"Can you imagine," whispered Jerry, his eyes wide with wonder, "a church that truly speaks to the modern world?"

I nodded, feeling a surge of hope. "It's like we're on the cusp of a new Pentecost," I replied, my voice trembling slightly with emotion.

As we talked, I felt as if the very walls of the seminary were expanding, making room for a broader, more inclusive vision of our faith.

We were all ardently involved in this extraordinary conversation to renew the church and to make it more relevant in a changing world. I remember when a vote was taken in the seminary about the discipline of celibacy as a requirement for the priesthood. Everyone, with only one

---

2. The title of Hans Küng's book was *The Council, Reform, and Reunion*. Küng was arguably the most important Catholic theologian of the twentieth century. He wrote over fifty books on theology, and founded an Ecumenical Center devoted to fostering unity among world religions.

exception, voted in favor of having married priests in addition to celibate priests in the church.

The preparatory stage of the Council (1959–1962) exhibited the widest preparation of any council in the history of the Catholic Church. It consisted of ten commissions to oversee the collection of information, and produced twelve volumes of suggestions, comments and input from bishops, the Vatican *Curia*, seminaries, theologians, and higher institutes of learning throughout the world.

Outside lecturers were brought into our seminary to explain the major issues of the council. The Second Vatican Council, the largest in church history, called 2,400 bishops, a large number of theologians, auditors, and observers from other denominations to attend its four sessions or periods from 1962–1965. George Williams, Professor of Divinity at Harvard University, with whom I later became a close friend, was an observer at the Council.

Over a three-year period and four sessions, the council promulgated sixteen documents.[3] The most important and fundamental of these are the four constitutions: *On Revelation, On the Church, On Sacred Liturgy*, and *The Church in the Modern World*.

Next in importance are nine Decrees on various subjects: *Ecumenism, The Media, Oriental Churches, On Bishops, Religious Life, Training of Priests, Lay Apostolate, Missionary Activity*, and *Ministry and Life of Priests*.

The final three documents are called Declarations and deal with *Christian Education, Non-Christian Religions*, and *Religious Liberty*.

The large body of work that emerged from the Council was primarily pastoral. It changed the way the church viewed itself and how it should meet the needs of the gospel in a changing world. Unlike previous councils, this council promulgated no dogmas, canons or anathemas.

The present-day synodal process by Pope Francis[4] is a continuation of the reforms of the Second Vatican Council, and has as its goal the broadening of the church's decision-making process by involving lay members. The church's teaching and mission has, regrettably, been hampered by dysfunction in the church's institution, exemplified by resistance to change, sex abuse, financial wrongdoing, and abuses of authority.

During my seminary training, the ability to communicate in Latin became an enormous asset. It was even more important than the subject

---

3. *The Documents of Vatican II*, New York: The American Press, 1966.

4. The Synod on Synodality was a three-year process of listening and dialogue in the universal church. It began with a solemn opening in Rome on October 9 and 10, 2021 with each individual diocese and church celebrating the Synod on the following week of October 17. The synodal process concluded in 2024.

matter itself. I had had the advantage of preparing myself by brushing up on my Latin during the novitiate or spiritual year. Thus, I found it easier to do well in exams. The Examiners, normally three priests during our oral exams, would read the questions in Latin from a textbook. If you could answer them somewhat eloquently in Latin, they would not attempt to engage you in any discussion. They preferred to advance to the next stock question.

As I finished my oral exam, gasping from relief, the elderly Monsignor O'Malley leaned back in his chair, a twinkle in his eye.

"Well, young man," he said, his voice gruff but kind, "that was quite a performance."

"Thank you, Monsignor," I replied, uncertain whether to be relieved or worried.

He chuckled, sharing a glance with the other examiners. "Oh yes, well done indeed," he continued. "We'll be wondering after you leave us what exactly you were talking about."

The room erupted in laughter, and I felt myself relax, joining in their mirth. It was a reminder that even in the serious business of our priestly examinations, there was room for humor and humanity.

There were some bright spots in our seminary training. A weekly class on public speaking by Ray McAnally was like a blast of sunshine that lit up the entire seminary. Everyone looked forward to this class. Ray was an accomplished actor in the famous Abbey Theatre in Dublin, and he played major roles in movies like *The Mission* and *My Left Foot*. He knew how to communicate. He would have us in stitches with laughter when one of the seminarians might be delivering a sermon to the class. Ray would mimic the reaction of some poor soul in the pews in church attempting to understand what was being said. Theological words such as "incarnational," "transcendence," "hypostatic," and "eschatological" evoked Ray's funniest facial gestures. He made us think about what we were saying, and taught us how to communicate theological truths in simple language, and in a way ordinary people, including ourselves, could understand.

Another radiant chapter in our seminary journey was the final pastoral year in Dublin, working with media experts at the national broadcasting station, RTE. Ray McAnally's preparatory lessons proved invaluable. They were a compass that guided us through the diverse worlds of communication, from the airways of radio and the dynamism of television to the pulpit.

As the Council progressed, I felt as if I was undergoing my own personal transformation alongside the church. Each new document, each step towards renewal, resonated within me like a bell being rung. I remember sitting alone in the chapel one night, overwhelmed by a mix of excitement and trepidation. The seminary I had entered was changing before my eyes.

Was I changing too? As I grappled with these thoughts, I felt a profound sense of peace wash over me as the rigid boundaries of the institutional church were dissolving, revealing a vast, beautiful landscape of possibility.

And so, my spiritual landscape expanded beyond the confines of rules, regulations and religious observances to a vivid, living relationship with the Lord. That epiphany has continued to illuminate my way, long after the Council ended. Its animating spirit has endured and moves me still.

Chapter 7

ON THE EVE OF my ordination, a profound peace enveloped me like a warm summer slumber. As I drifted to sleep in the seminary dormitory, no restlessness stirred my soul. The next day, December 16, 1966, the Archbishop of Dublin would lay hands on my head, conferring ordination upon me.[1] My life was securely in God's hands, I felt, and no effort of mine could augment Christ's accomplished work. In the morning, I would make my vows to try to walk the path set before me. But that path's destination dwelt not in my power. Like Abraham, I would set out for a promised land which I knew not. All I could do was try to be faithful, one step at a time, to the way of Christ. That night, God's grace gifted me with untroubled sleep.

My family and relatives attended my ordination in Dublin, followed by a reception in Jury's Hotel, before driving to my hometown of Letterkenny to celebrate my first Mass the following day.

As our car approached Letterkenny, the wind howled and rain lashed against the windows. Despite the tempest, the streets were alive with color and sound. Bright buntings flapped wildly in the gale, their cheerful hues a stark contrast to the gray sky. At the town border, a group of familiar faces huddled under umbrellas, their warm smiles cutting through the chill. The local band, their instruments gleaming with raindrops, struck up a lively tune. As we processed through the town, the music battled with the storm, a joyful defiance of the elements. The air was thick with the scent of wet earth and the metallic tang of rain. It was a sensory whirlwind, impossible to forget.

I celebrated my first Mass in the cathedral in Letterkenny. Every pew was packed, with people standing in the aisles and at the back. As I made my way from the sacristy to the altar, the rustle of clothing and muffled sounds filled my ears. My hands trembled slightly as I began the Mass, but when I

---

1. John Charles McQuaid, C.S.Sp. (July 28, 1895–April 7, 1973), served as the Catholic Primate of Ireland and Archbishop of Dublin from December 1940 to January 1972.

spoke the familiar words, a sense of calm washed over me. After the final *Amen*, I turned to give my first blessing. A hush fell over the congregation, and I saw tears glistening in many eyes. In that moment, I felt the full weight of my new role, a conduit between these people and God. I prayed I was up to the task.

I could not complete the individual blessings at the altar rail because of the crowds and also because I had to attend a reception in town. The local priest asked me: "Could you come back again to celebrate benediction at 6 p.m. and continue blessing the people?" I said I would, and he informed the congregation in turn. When I returned at 6 p.m., it was to another full church of people.

In the days following my ordination, I found myself in a strange new world. The familiar streets of Letterkenny seemed unchanged, yet everything felt different. People I'd known all my life now addressed me as "Father," their eyes filled with a reverence that made me feel uncomfortable. Neighbors who once asked me to join their card games now sought my blessing or spiritual advice. I was the same person I'd always been, yet in their eyes, I had been transformed. As I walked down the street, I felt the weight of their expectations settle on my shoulders. I wondered if I could live up to the kind of person they now saw me as. The priesthood, I realized, was not just a vocation, but a profound shift in identity. I was no longer just myself, but a symbol of something greater. It was exhilarating and terrifying all at once.

A few days into my ordination, my mother said, "A family in the Oldtown wants you to visit their son. Gangrene has taken one leg, and the other one is infected."

I approached the young man's bed, my heart heavy in my chest. As I administered the sacrament of the sick, my mind raced. *What am I doing here? I'm barely ordained, and already I'm face-to-face with such suffering.* His anguished moans filled the room, each one piercing my soul. I sat beside him, feeling utterly helpless. All my years of theological study seemed useless in the face of this raw human pain. God, I prayed silently, give me the strength to be what he needs right now. It was a brutal initiation into the realities of priesthood, far removed from the lofty ideals I'd held just days before.

The young man's eyes, glazed with pain, met mine. "Father," he whispered, his voice hoarse, "why would God let this happen to me?"

I leaned closer, clasping his hand gently: "I wish I had an answer for you," I said softly.

He turned his face away, a tear sliding down his cheek. "Death would be better than this," he muttered.

I squeezed his hand, searching for words. "I can't pretend to understand your pain," I finally said, "but I'm here with you. You're not alone in this."

He looked back at me, a flicker of something—gratitude, perhaps—in his eyes. We sat in silence then, the weight of his suffering hanging between us.

No facile answers came to mind, only the ache of sorrow. I could not untangle the why of his suffering, but I could endure it with him.

In my time as a priest, I would come to know many of these painful moments, facing much heartbreak with no solutions except a sympathetic presence.

Soon after this bedside visit, another urgent summons came from a family member: "Would you visit your cousin in hospital, she's had two miscarriages already, and this baby she's carrying will not settle in her womb?"

Entering the hospital room, I found my distant cousin lost in prayer, frantically reciting the rosary. Amidst a tableau of holy cards on her bedside table, she treasured one in particular. It was a prayer to St. Gerald Majella, patron saint of expectant mothers, a saint I learned of for the first time.

I sat beside her, thinking of Martha from the gospel, consumed by worry as Christ counseled calm. My cousin had every reason to be upset, given her past history of failed pregnancies.

"Let go and let God," I gently urged as I anointed her, adding, "don't be anxious; put your troubles in God's hands."

Switching on the radio to a channel of calming melodies, I said: "Lie back and relax, and listen to this soft music. You have nothing to fear, nothing to be anxious about. God is in charge."

Her face softened into a beautiful, serene smile as her head melted into the soft cheeks of her pillow. She was at peace. I left the room.

Just as I was leaving through the corridor, one of my old primary school classmates came up to me. He was an employee in the hospital.

"How do you feel being ordained when many priests, such as Charles Davis,[2] are now leaving the priesthood?" he asked, provocatively.

I was not expecting this.

Charles Davis had just made headlines as a renowned English theologian who had left the priesthood. At the time of his departure, he famously remarked, presciently: "The church is losing its soul to save its face."

"I cannot speak for Charles Davis," I replied, "because everyone is different. He is a fine theologian and I love his writings."

---

2. Charles Alfred Davis (February 12, 1923–January 28, 1999), an English theologian and priest, was Professor of Theology at St. Edmund's College, Ware, and later Professor of Religious Studies at the University of Alberta.

Part 1—Chapter 7

My friend didn't push me any further and left it at that.

The following morning, when I came into the kitchen for breakfast, something felt amiss. Nobody was talking. That was strange in our family kitchen, always an oasis of chatter and laughter.

My brother, home from America, sat at the kitchen table, his tea untouched. He had always been a kind of jokester, questioning humorously everything from religion to politics.

"What's eating you?" I inquired, a look of bewilderment crossing my face.

"Mother says you've performed your first miracle," he remarked with a hapless smirk.

"What kind of talk is this?" I asked my mother, who was standing by the fireplace, blushing nervously.

"The nurses in the hospital got the shock of their lives after you anointed the mother," she explained. "The baby settled in her womb and a healthy baby boy was born."

My mind had not been on my visit to the hospital when I came down the stairs for breakfast, but I was glad to hear of the happy outcome for the mother who had given birth to a healthy baby boy. Her faith had come through.

Many years later, during a reunion in my town of Letterkenny, a tall, handsome young man came up to me.

"We're related," he said. "I wanna buy you a drink."

He then explained how his mother and my mother were cousins from the same part of Donegal. As I was listening to his story, I realized who his mother was—the very same woman who had given birth to a baby boy in Letterkenny hospital in December 1966. And now he was standing right before me, all grown up.

You were born in December 1966, I remarked, calmly.

His jaw dropped. "How did you know that," he inquired.

The words came easy to me. "You were born during the time I was ordained," I replied. "It was big news back then."

The Lord works in strange ways. It was just like yesterday when I offered the sacrament of the sick to his mother in the hospital.

We had a great time talking about our family ties and the days spent in Lanalea. But I didn't have the heart to tell him about anointing his mother the day he was born.

My brother's in-laws from County Cork attended my ordination, and were put up in a guest house across the street from where we lived. Mrs. Huston, a kindly neighbor, provided accommodation free of charge.

She recounted a story to my friends and myself about her lovely daughter, Ann, who entered a convent the same time I entered the seminary. Ann was a sweet girl, and we had grown up together. Mrs. Huston recounted how she had journeyed to see Ann in Dublin and didn't recognize her own daughter. Ann was so subdued and inhibited in the convent, she had lost the naturalness that nature and nurture had blessed her with. It reminded me of my friend from the novitiate years, who called me fifty years later in Florida. Mrs. Huston held her daughter in her arms, clothed in a nun's habit, and cried out mournfully: "Where are you Ann, my darling? Come out wherever you are."

Mrs. Houston didn't leave Dublin until she got her daughter out of the convent. She was a strong woman whose love for her daughter was not to be trifled with.

I could sympathize with Mrs. Huston and her daughter Ann's plight, because I too experienced, first-hand, how oppressive rules tend to repress one's personality.

A most joyful moment occurred during the time of my ordination, when a telegram arrived from America. We were all jovially seated around the kitchen table in Letterkenny. The telegram was for my brother, whose wife was pregnant with their first child.

Pat fumbled, mangling and tearing the telegram into pieces trying to open it. He was that nervous. We were all laughing, for we knew the news had to be good. The torn telegram had to be reassembled and patiently read to Pat, who learned he was now a father. A baby girl, Erin, had just been born. What joy filled the house that day! There was both a new birth and an ordination in the family in December 1966.

Before returning to the seminary, I visited my neighbor and old friend, Bob Johnson. I found him in his kitchen armchair, visibly moved as I entered. He asked for my blessing. As I finished my blessing, I looked at Bob's weathered face, transformed. Tears welled in his eyes, spilling over onto his cheeks. When I asked for his blessing in return, something shifted in the air between us. Bob closed his eyes, his calloused hands reaching out to grasp mine. Then, in a voice thick with emotion, he began to pray. The words flowed from him, raw and sincere, yet filled with a sincerity that took my breath away. In that very moment, the denominational lines that had always been there in the background seemed to blur and fade away completely. We were simply two souls, united in our faith and our shared story. As Bob's prayer washed over me, I felt a profound sense of coming full circle—the boy he had watched grow up was now a priest, yet still receiving his blessing, gratefully.

Part 1—Chapter 7

With Bob's eloquent blessing, it was back to the seminary again to await my next assignment.

Chapter 8

When I got back to the seminary, an assignment was waiting for me. The superior of the seminary did not want me to go to Rome for higher studies. He preferred the University. A Scripture scholar himself with an impressive academic background, he had experience of studies both in Rome and at University College, Dublin (UCD).

He went further: "Those Roman degrees are not worth the paper they're written on."

I was surprised to hear him say this. His remark, I imagined, surely could not apply to Pontifical Roman universities such as the Gregorian and the Angelicum. Perhaps he was referring to other institutions in Rome run by different religious orders. His stated opinion, however, was confirmed by the priests who taught me and had studied in Rome's theological institutions. They told me about the restrictions imposed upon them by their training, depriving them of the ability to learn and communicate in their own language.

And so, in the fall of 1967, as a student-priest, I embarked on an English and French honors degree at University College Dublin with minors in philosophy and Latin.[1]

Those early semesters at the university were a true test. The bustling lecture halls of University College Dublin were in stark contrast to the austere seminary walls I'd left behind. The air hummed with intellectual energy, the corridors echoing with rapid-fire debates. My mind, accustomed to the quiet recitation of rote learning, reeled under the onslaught of critical thinking and scholarly discourse.

---

1. UCD is a public research university in Dublin, Ireland and is a member institution of the National University of Ireland. It first opened as the Catholic University of Ireland with St. John Henry Newman as its rector in 1854. Five Nobel Laureates are among UCD's alumni. Four Irish prime ministers, three Irish presidents, along with a president of India, graduated from UCD.

No longer just textbook knowledge, the courses consisted of vast reading lists, lectures brimming with insight, and regular term papers that demanded original thought. My grades struggled to keep up under this onslaught of critical analysis and scholarly discipline.

At first, I floundered in this new environment, overwhelmed by the sheer breadth of knowledge required. But gradually persistence paid off. Immersed in the university's diversity and standards of scholarship, my mind stretched beyond prescribed texts that had to be committed to memory, to embrace new vistas of knowledge. With each completed essay, my confidence grew and so did my grades.

At the end of a very competitive year called First Arts, I was able to drop my minors in Philosophy and Latin and concentrate on English and French language and literature.

When I received the news of my Group 4 classification in English Literature, a rare achievement, I felt a surge of accomplishment tinged with uncertainty. The path of a creative writer beckoned, promising freedom of expression I'd never known. Yet, as I stood at this crossroads, the rational part of me—the part shaped by years of disciplined study—whispered of practicality. Honors in English and French offered stability, a clear trajectory. As I made my choice, I couldn't help but wonder if I was closing a door on a part of myself that I'd only just discovered.

Pursuing an honors degree in French in addition to English allowed me the opportunity to travel abroad. I was intrigued by the possibility of studying French in the land of France itself, a country that produced so many gifted literary writers.

Every summer, my journeys through France to delve deeply into the language and culture unfurled countless opportunities that would have eluded me had I remained ensconced within the seminary.

These annual voyages were nothing short of transformative. As I meandered through bustling cities and serene countryside, engaging in university courses whenever feasible, France gradually unveiled herself to me. Layer by vivid layer, her rich tapestry of history, art, innovative ideas, and enlightening conversations was revealed.

I stayed one summer in Tours, France, and had the privilege of offering Mass and preaching in the magnificent Cathedral, a towering Gothic edifice. Yet what struck me most was the scarcity of parishioners. While an Irish church overflowed, here only a smattering could be found in the cavernous nave. Most Sundays, the stillness was broken only by the voices of occasional tourists echoing off the stone walls. The glorious Cathedral of Tours felt more like a museum than a place of worship.

France was famous for its Catholic scholars and intellectuals, whose writings were well known worldwide in academic circles. But France itself, the eldest daughter of the church, had lost the masses of the people.

And so, I was surprised to find a large crowd blocking the entrance to the Cathedral one Sunday morning. Cameras clicked and lights blared in the midst of all the excitement. I asked someone in the crowd, what was going on? A film, came the reply.

Making my way to vest for Mass, I saw another priest in the sacristy taking off his vestments.

"Did you already say Mass?" I asked innocently.

"No," he said, "I'm only an actor."

It dawned on me then that this magnificent Cathedral was being used as a stage-set for a movie. Regrettably, it only evoked a slice of history for most people. It had become more like the temple Jesus found bustling with commerce than a place of prayer.

The next year in Paris, I watched the film with friends. It was a comedy. The opening scene focused on the imposing building of the Cathedral and, as the camera panned inside the building, the same actor, whose name I don't recall, appeared playing the role of a priest. He was playing a kind of Walter Mitty character who fancied himself in different roles.

One day, as I stood in the eerily quiet Cathedral, I asked the rector, my voice slightly shaking, "Why are the churches here so empty?"

The rector's face tightened, lines of worry etching deeper around his eyes. He was silent for a moment, then turned to me with a gaze that spoke volumes.

"My friend," he said in French, his voice heavy with emotion, "the church in France is in full crisis."

"But how can this be?" I pressed, gesturing to the magnificent architecture around us. "With such beauty, such history."

He shook his head sadly. "Beauty and history are not enough," he continued. "We've lost touch with the people, with their needs and struggles. "This," he said, sweeping his arm to encompass the empty pews, "is the result."

In hindsight, the cinematic vignette in the Cathedral that day exposed a real quandary. This storied bastion of faith was relegated to the realm of the aesthetic or historic monument. While revered as a cultural icon, the Cathedral was no longer the place of a vibrant spirituality. It was a mere curiosity. My actor acquaintance was merely playing a role, mimicking the rituals of the church without meaning or substance.

As I stood in the shadow of the towering Cathedral, a thought struck me with the force of revelation. These soaring spires, these intricate stone carvings—they were not the true embodiment of faith. My mind flashed to the faces I'd seen on the streets of Tours: the weary shopkeeper, the boisterous students, the elderly woman feeding pigeons in the square. It was in their lives, in their joys and struggles, that the real work of the gospel took place. It is not to be found in these towers of stone, but in the lives of people who live by the gospel, brought down to earth and made new in human hearts.

How had the church lost sight of this fundamental truth? I asked myself. *And more importantly, how could we reclaim it?*

The rector's generosity afforded me a special opportunity to lead a parish pilgrimage to Lourdes. I jumped at the offer. Having just obtained my advanced, language certificate from the French language Institute, I eagerly boarded the train to the famed Marian shrine nestled in the foothills of the Pyrenees, straddling the border of France and Spain.

Accompanying me was a group of excited French pilgrims. Their eager chatter and laughter filled the train. A pilgrimage, as Chaucer so aptly described in his famous *Canterbury Tales*, brings together people from all walks of life. And indeed, like Chaucer's quixotic band, we made for exciting company. Pilgrims of all ages and backgrounds mingled in our train, each a trove of different stories and experiences. We were all bonded by a shared spiritual quest.

The long, leisurely journey south, through Poitiers and Bordeaux, did not feel at all tedious, as I was captivated by the changing scenery of this charming region of France. Traversing verdant landscapes, we made our way to our destination at the French-Spanish border.

The hotel lobby in Lourdes buzzed with a cacophony of languages and the scrape of luggage across tiled floors. Exhausted from our journey, we stumbled through the doors, only to collide with a group of animated Irish pilgrims. The familiar accents cut through the French chatter, a familiar melody in this foreign symphony.

As we untangled ourselves and our belongings, apologies gave way to laughter. Soon, we were swapping stories of our travels, my Irish countryfolk regaling us with tales of delayed flights and lost suitcases, while my French pilgrims shared anecdotes from our long train journey. Language barriers melted away in the warmth of shared experience and purpose. Before long, it felt as if we'd known each other for years, united by our common quest for spiritual renewal in this sacred place.

Though divided by tongue and custom, good humor united everyone and we soon bonded. Though we were there to enrich the spirit, we also reveled in camaraderie. Our time was filled with laughter and deep reverence as we explored the sacred site and celebrated Mass. Bathed in candlelight, the sacred grotto fostered deep devotion. Barriers separating people dissolved in a spirit of unity.

The university culture I had embraced encouraged travel abroad, any kind of travel, including my pilgrimage to Lourdes. I remember when I entered Paris for the first time. The cacophony of voices, the aroma of fresh baguettes, and the sight of the Eiffel Tower overwhelmed my senses. The stark difference from the hushed corridors and the unchanging routines of the seminary hit me like a Mack truck. Here, life pulsed with energy and possibility. For a moment, I felt a pang of regret for the years spent in seclusion, followed by a rush of excitement for the adventures that lay ahead. The world was opening up before me, and I was finally ready to explore it.

The world of the university offered a broader culture which exposed me to the influence of creative writers and scholars in different branches of literature. I loved the intimate tutorial system at UCD which divided students into small groups, each with an assigned professor or lecturer to provide practical guidance and supervision.

Wednesday afternoons, our small group of six would gather in Dr. Seamus Dean's cluttered office. The smell of old books permeated the air as we huddled around his ancient oak desk. Dr. Dean, with his piercing eyes, would lean forward, gesturing emphatically as he dissected Yeats's poem, "Sailing to Byzantium." The walls seemed to disappear as we lost ourselves in heated debates about symbolism and meter. It was in these intimate sessions that I truly learned to think, to question, to see beyond the surface of words.

In my childhood, I had experience of group study during primary school, when my buddies and I voluntarily gathered together after school to do our classroom work together, but the university tutorial brought this to another level. These tutorials allowed the students to benefit from the knowledge of qualified supervisors and scholars and to receive valuable input from the various students themselves. It was a very effective, collegial way of learning. Hearing our peers' perspectives, our collective understanding was enriched.

In addition to our scheduled times in class, the tutorial group I belonged to would also meet regularly in students' apartments, or in one of the local pubs in Dublin. The literary culture we were privileged to absorb in the university was not bookish or impersonal. It involved, of course, broad reading, which was highly stressed, but it also involved applied knowledge in the best sense, because this knowledge was imparted to us through quality lectures from living Irish poets, novelists, short story writers and dramatists. The impact of this kind of education was life changing.

Part 1—Chapter 8

The great advantage of the study of the classics of literature, old and new, was that it enabled me to appreciate spiritual truths and struggles in a new way, as part of life itself.

The works of Shakespeare are full of spiritual insights, embodied in the experiences of living humanity. When the King in *Hamlet* knelt down to pray, he couldn't, because his prayers lacked heart and the vital connection to forgiveness: "My words," he groaned, "fly up toward heaven, but my thoughts stay down on earth."

The Brothers Karamazov by Dostoevsky impressed me by the way Christian experience and conflicts were described through ordinary experiences. Boris Pasternak's *Doctor Zhivago* gave me an appreciation of liturgy as a dynamic activity within the context of the changing seasons of nature, rather than the observance of *rubrics*, which I had been trained to follow. All of Charles Dickens's works are imbued with a Christian ethos, especially the celebrated *A Christmas Carol,* which did more to rehabilitate Christmas than anything else in the industrialized world.

I found the writings of James Joyce to be imbued with a knowledge of Scripture and Catholic theology. In one powerful sentence in Episode One of *Ulysses*, Joyce encapsulates the four great Trinitarian heresies.

James Baldwin's *Go Tell It on The Mountain* was full of biblical symbolism. Tolstoy's *The Kingdom of God is Within You,* exposed the tendency of institutional religion to stifle the kingdom within rather than liberate it.

It is commonly imagined that spirituality should be confined to the church's doctrines, to the catechism, to Biblical commentaries, or to specific religious writings. What's often missed by this approach to spiritual growth is the human dimension or personal experience. Mankind's great literatures, the writings of Dostoyevsky, Tolstoy, and contemporary writers such as Pasternak and Solzhenitsyn, address faith and spiritual truths through the lens of human experience, engaging the heart as well as the head.

As I pored over Joyce's *Ulysses* late one night, a memory surfaced. I recalled sitting in the seminary classroom, dutifully memorizing theological arguments, my mind feeling like a well-organized filing cabinet. Now, as I navigated the stream of consciousness flowing through Joyce's Dublin, I realized how much I'd changed. My mind was no longer a static repository of facts, but an organic entity, capable of making connections I'd never dreamed possible. The rigid boundaries of my seminary education were dissolving, replaced by a fluid, dynamic understanding of spirituality and human experience. I closed the book, marveling at how far I'd come, and how much further I had yet to go.

My seminary education, which focused solely on the scholastic method of inquiry, left me bereft of literary enrichment. The embers of a literary education were stoked during my childhood in Donegal, where I was exposed to the Irish tradition of storytelling at an early age. But it was at the university that this early need was reignited and found its mature expression.

I recall vividly the day Dr. Morris Harmon, poet and scholar, lectured on George Herbert's lyric poem, "Love," a profound poetic meditation on the agape love of Christ in the Eucharist. It was an epiphany for me.

My theological training taught me to view the Eucharist rather abstractly, as the separation of substance and accident, in which the substance of bread and wine are transubstantiated into the body and blood of Christ. This perspective, while valuable, remained somewhat detached from experience. Herbert's poem spoke to the humanity of Christ and opened up a new dimension of understanding for me, transforming the Eucharist from a doctrinal concept to a tangible experience of Christ's love.

Through this poetic journey, the Eucharist was revealed, not just as dogma, but as an intimate encounter with the love of Christ, forever altering my spiritual perspective.

As Dr. Harmon's final words hung in the air, a hush fell over the lecture hall. I sat motionless, my mind reeling from the profound beauty of Herbert's poem. Suddenly, I felt a tap on my shoulder. Turning, I met the wide-eyed gaze of Sarah, a fellow student.

"Did you . . . did you appreciate the Eucharist like that before?" she whispered, her voice trembling slightly.

I opened my mouth to respond, but found I had no words. How could I explain that in those few minutes, my understanding of a sacrament I'd performed countless times had been transformed into an amazing love story. I simply shook my head, feeling the inadequacy of words.

Sarah nodded with understanding in her gaze. "Me neither," she murmured. "It's . . . it's beautiful, isn't it?"

The most practical advantage I derived from my literary education was a better understanding of the Bible. The Bible is a marvelous work of literature with unparalleled power to touch every mood and movement of human experience. I learned to appreciate it, not only as the revealed word of God, but as a work of moving literature in the words of men. No wonder it has influenced the arts and literature of western writers more than any other book. The works of a writer, like John Steinbeck, are a case in point. Even though Steinbeck was not a believer, his writings are steeped in knowledge of the Bible. One of his works takes its title, *East of Eden*, from it.

Opening the Bible was like stepping into a vast literary museum. Each page revealed a new exhibit: here, the epic frescoes of myth and legend; there, the delicate watercolors of lyrical poetry. In one corner, the stark photographs of historical accounts; in another, the impressionistic swirls of popular stories. Drama unfolded on a grand stage, while collections of poetry whispered from intimate galleries. Every turn offered a new perspective, a new way of seeing the world and our place in it.

While passages can be turgid and controversial, the Bible maintains a high level of style, both in its prose and poetry. The literature of the Bible embraces the whole symphony of nature and human life, speaking of sunrise and sunset, of birth and death, of war and peace. It offers promise and fulfilment binding all nature together: The mountains, the streams, the vineyards, the olive groves, the desert places, the sheep and the cattle, the wild ass, the lion in the wilderness, the tender grass, the rocks, the sea and the ships upon the sea, the fishes beneath the waters, the stars, the firmament of the sky, the rain, and the whispering wind. This earthly symphony of nature and people, both the good and the bad, going about the business of life, is united and tied together by the presence of the eternal spirit, touching it all with glory.

After I got my degree, I was given my next assignment: to teach English and French at the Carmelite College, Castlemartyr, County Cork. This is where I had spent five years of my secondary-level education from 1955 through 1959.

Now in 1970, I was going back to my old alma mater to teach.

Chapter 9

I LOVED TEACHING.

The moment I stepped into the classroom at Carmelite College I knew I was home. For five exhilarating years, my classroom echoed with the sounds of poetry recitations and literary discussions. Each day brought new discoveries, both for my students and myself, as we navigated the rich worlds of English and French literature together.

I had one great advantage: The students were curious to learn. With an attitude like that, there were no disciplinary problems to speak of in the classroom.

Every secondary schoolteacher in Ireland is required to have a Higher Diploma in Education (H. Dip) from the national university in order to be salaried by the government.[1]

Education was free to every pupil in the country, including those attending boarding schools such as the Carmelite College. Thus, in my first year, I studied for the H. Dip at University College Cork. The courses involved a series of academic classes on the history, philosophy and methods of education, and also required submitting a written thesis on the subject.

The most practical part of the H. Dip was classroom supervision by professors and lecturers from the University. They would come to the school and observe the method of instruction in the classroom.

The students, I discovered, were just as anxious as myself that I should do well whenever the supervisors from the university arrived to observe. As the door closed behind the departing supervisor, a flood of students would surge towards me, their faces a mix of anxiety and hope.

"Father," Timmy blurted out, his eyes wide, "how did we do?"

"Yeah," chimed in Michael, running a hand through his disheveled hair, "do you think we impressed them?"

---

1. In Ireland, a higher diploma in education is a post-graduate qualification and is necessary to teach at a second-level institution.

Part 1—Chapter 9

I couldn't help but smile at their earnestness: "You were all brilliant," I assured them, feeling a surge of pride. "Absolutely brilliant."

The students felt they too were being graded and wished to put their best foot forward. The whole experience was, in fact, a cooperative activity of teacher and students working together.

With such an engaging and engaged group of pupils, one could take risks and be creative when preparing classes in anticipation of the supervisors' arrival from the university.

The night before a class, I'd often find myself surrounded by a sea of paper, the soft scratch of my pen against notebook pages punctuating the late-night silence. The air sang with possibility as I crafted lessons that would challenge and inspire. Come morning, the classroom would buzz with nervous energy, the students' excitement palpable in their whispered conversations and the rapid tapping of pencils against desks.

John Dewey was the rave in educational circles back then.[2] He had outlined a new approach to education based on the active involvement of pupils in the learning process. Dewey's challenging vision, however, did not address the practical problems of a teacher with limited time and resources, and a classroom setting that could include unruly students or at least some students difficult to teach.

Since the students and I lived on the same campus, we had the advantage of more resources and time at our disposal to prepare classes in line with Dewey's vision. Thus, the classes we prepared were more creative than typical classes. For example, when it came to giving a class on the short story, by such authors as Frank O'Connor, Brendan Behan and Liam O'Flaherty, I found it helpful to turn them into one-act plays, with the students playing the different parts. We could take full advantage of the school's facilities to offer these interactive classes, or one-act plays, on the big stage in the hall.

The supervisors enjoyed these classes thoroughly and looked forward to visiting the school.

As for classes in poetry, the same interactive method was applied. "The Kingfisher," by William Henry Davies, for example, aroused the special interests of the supervisors when one of the priests, Father Herman, a nature lover, showed a rare film he had taken of a kingfisher behaving exactly the way the poem described. I included Father Herman's creative film in my class to illustrate the accuracy of Davies's poetic depictions of the kingfisher in flight.

---

2. John Dewey (October 20, 1859–June 1, 1952), an American philosopher, psychologist, and educational reformer, profoundly influenced educational methods in Western society through works such as *Democracy and Education* (1916).

Motivation is, perhaps, the most valuable trait in students. As a teacher, my main task was finding ways to motivate them.

As I watched my students huddle over their essays, brows furrowed in concentration, I pondered the nature of motivation. What spark ignites a young mind's curiosity? How could I fan those embers into a real love of knowledge? Each day presented a new puzzle, challenging me to find innovative ways to inspire and engage. It wasn't just about imparting knowledge anymore; it was about kindling a lifelong love for learning.

One highly effective motivation tool was the essay competitions for secondary-school youngsters available across Ireland. The Department of Education and other institutions sponsored these competitions at the national and regional levels. For talented students, these contests gave them a chance to have their work evaluated beyond the walls of their own school.

The regional competitions were held in each of Ireland's four provinces: Ulster, Munster, Leinster and Connaught.

Students who participated produced some surprising results. One student took first prize nationally and was honored for his achievement by the Minister of Education at a grand ceremony in Dublin. More locally, a lad from Donegal won the top spot in the Munster regional competition, earning himself a handsome cash prize of one hundred pounds.

After the ceremony, I quipped in jest: "And what's the grand plan for your newfound fortune?"

His response took me by surprise.

"I'd like to treat my classmates to something special. That's what I really want," he said earnestly.

True to his word, that's exactly what he did. Our entire class clambered into the old truck, our customary conveyance in those times. Off we went to the renowned coastal gem of Youghal in County Cork. The day was spent in high spirits, commemorating our friend's accomplishment. For the students, it was also an invaluable lesson: Education was not just a worthy pursuit, but one that could yield rich rewards.

When it came time for the written exams for the Higher Diploma in Education, some unexpected trouble arose. Apart from a written thesis and supervised classes, the actual exams were held at the university. You had to register there beforehand by submitting forms and a fee. My heart sank as I approached the registration office, only to find the door firmly shut, a hastily scribbled *Closed* sign mocking my punctuality. Panic rose in my throat as I realized the implications. Without registration, I couldn't take the exam. Without the exam, I would forfeit receiving a degree with honors. I pressed my forehead against the cool glass window of the door, my mind racing to find a solution to this unexpected obstacle.

Part 1—Chapter 9

As I stood perplexed outside the locked door, another student shared a simple solution: "Just put your ten-pound note in an envelope with the forms and drop it in the mailbox."

Taking his advice, I deposited my registration packet and payment in the outside box and left, confident the office would receive it.

But when it came to sitting for the exam on the specified day, I was refused admission and was told I would have to take the exam in the fall. The reason given: The university had not received my registration form or fee payment.

I immediately suspected that the young man who advised me to drop the envelope in the mailbox had stolen it.

There was an unfortunate disadvantage to sitting for the exams in the fall. Such students couldn't qualify for an honors grade, and I was well on the way to receiving a first-class honors grade, based on my strong thesis and practical classroom examinations.

Professor V. A. McClelland of the education department advocated for me, pleading with the president of the university to allow me to take the exam, without prejudice, as planned. He argued that what had happened had been out of my control.

The university president refused to bend the rule. This particular university college in Cork was the only one in the national university system with such a strange policy. The rationale, it was explained to me, was that those taking the exams in the fall would have more time to prepare.

"But wouldn't a longer delay also allow them more time to forget what they had studied?" I asked myself.

We appealed to the Minister of Education in Dublin, no less, to bring the university's practice in line with the other university colleges. After much legal wrangling, I was finally permitted to sit for the exams, without prejudice, as originally scheduled. In the end, I earned a first-class honors degree.

There was one more hurdle to overcome before I could become a salaried teacher. I had to take an oral exam in Gaelic since it was the official language of Ireland. When I sat for this oral exam, I found it difficult to follow the examiner, who spoke Munster Gaelic. I spoke Gaelic in the dialect we used in my native Donegal. As a result, this exam didn't go well. I was packed off to study Munster Gaelic for a month in County Kerry.

This detour turned out to be a rare blessing. Living with a Kerry family, I experienced the warm hospitality of the locals on a daily basis. After a month immersed in their dialect and armed with newfound linguistic confidence, I returned to Dublin to retake the oral exam. This time, I passed with no issues.

With the Higher Diploma in Education finally in hand, I took my place as a fully certified, salaried teacher. As tradition dictated, my earnings were dutifully contributed to the Carmelite Order.

I next began studies for an MA in literature at the University in Cork while still teaching high school. I chose the writings of Samuel Taylor Coleridge as my research subject. Coleridge appealed to me because he was a poet, a philosopher and a theologian, thus bringing together three major forms of knowledge that interested me.

At the promptings of Professor McClelland at the department of education, which seemed a more appropriate department for the subject of my research, I transitioned my academic focus from the English department to this department. There, I wrote my master's thesis on Coleridge.[3]

Coleridge's mind was a vast, sprawling library, each internal shelf lined with volumes of diverse knowledge. His notebooks were like intricate maps, guiding readers through the winding corridors and hidden chambers of human consciousness. To study Coleridge was to embark on an intellectual treasure hunt, each discovery leading to new, unexplored territories of thought.

My research led me to a thrilling revelation about the anatomy of creativity which Coleridge broke down into three pivotal stages:

1. Comprehensive mastery of all aspects of the subject matter, encompassing broad reading, study, and a thorough understanding of its many facets.

2. Allowing that knowledge to percolate into "the deep well of the unconscious" to create links and form a web of intricate connections.

3. The conscious act of creation itself, bringing to light the ideas and insights nurtured in the unconscious realm, through writing or other creative activity.

For Coleridge, creativity was the union of the conscious and the unconscious. I dare say creative minds in any field, whether it be in science, literature, philosophy, or music, exhibit this three-fold process of creative endeavor. The interplay of broad learning, unconscious processing, and finally conscious creation seems universal to human creativity.

A special bonus to studying Coleridge was a visit during the summer to the Houghton Library in Cambridge, Massachusetts, to examine the author's notebooks.

---

3. Duffy, Hugh. "The Origin and Development of Creative Knowledge in the Writings of Samuel Taylor Coleridge." Master's thesis, University College Cork (1975).

Part 1—Chapter 9

During the Easter break, I was able to work on my thesis at Trinity College, Dublin. My friend, Senator Trevor West was professor of mathematics there, and he offered me the use of his rooms in the old Rubrics Building, free of charge. It was an ideal situation, including the privilege of having meals with Trinity faculty members in the community refectory, called the commons.

A strange illness overcame me at this time. I had developed an awkward pain in my back, and Trevor directed me to a doctor he knew in Dublin. The doctor was leaving on vacation for his family cottage overlooking the Atlantic Ocean in my native Donegal, and couldn't see me in Dublin. I told him I would also be visiting my parents in Letterkenny during the Easter break. When he heard this, he said that we could kill two birds with one stone, and meet at his cottage where he could take care of the problem.

This sounded like a good solution.

"I could drive to your place on the afternoon of April 6, my birthday," I said. "If that suits you."

The doctor agreed, and on April 6, I drove to his cottage.

"The problem with your back," he said after a brief examination, "is a touch of arthritis. Nothing to worry about. Get plenty of rest and stay warm."

To commemorate my birthday, he uncorked a bottle of Bushmills whiskey. As we reveled, his parents departed for Belfast in another car. My body felt drained, not having eaten much all day. As dusk settled, I sensed I should be on my way.

Slipping into my car and turning on the heater, I found myself enveloped in a surreal haze, a dreamlike state.

In this foggy condition, I navigated the rocky road that hugged the untamed Atlantic Ocean. Suddenly, my car crashed into a boulder. Colliding with this rock was providential, as it prevented a fatal plunge over the cliff.

I rolled down the window, inviting the cool, crisp air to rouse me from my stupor. It was now dark, and I didn't know what to do. Just then, a kindly male face appeared at the window and a benevolent voice instructed: "The fender is shattered, but you still can drive. Put the car in reverse and go down the hill in second gear."

He filled me with peace. I did as he said, arriving at the bottom of the hill onto the paved road that brought me safely home to Letterkenny.

I had a fitful night's sleep and every time I woke up, I thanked God for the gift of life. Without the intervention of that kindly stranger, whoever or whatever it was, I knew I wouldn't be alive.

When I returned to Trinity College, I asked Trevor how his doctor friend was doing.

"You haven't heard what happened?" asked Trevor.

"What are you talking about?" I inquired nervously.

"He was driving home from his cottage in Donegal in his sports car," he replied, "and ran the car over the cliff into the Atlantic Ocean. He died."

As Trevor's words sank in, a cold dread washed over me, leaving me light-headed and nauseous. The image of the doctor's car plunging over the cliff flashed before my eyes, quickly replaced by a vision of my own vehicle meeting the same fate. My legs weakened, and I had to sit down to steady myself. In that moment, the full weight of my narrow escape crashed down upon me. The mysterious stranger on that rocky Donegal Road hadn't just given directions—he'd reached across the veil between life and death to pull me back from the brink.

During a Christmas break from teaching, I spent a month at Gladstone's Library at Hawarden, in Wales.[4] Professor McClelland, my university supervisor, recommended that I go there to pursue further research for my thesis.

My specific purpose was to study another collection of Coleridge's notebooks. Of the seventy-two that have survived, twenty-four are preserved in the Gladstone Library. These notebooks are evidence of Coleridge's broad reading in various subjects. They contain his reflections on his various lines of inquiry, along with his musings, dreams, lecture notes, puns and prayers. You could trace in his notebooks, the origin of the ideas, words, and phrases that later appeared in his poetry and other writings.

Coleridge was a man who put into practice his prescription for broad reading, allowing what he read to sink into the deep well of his unconscious. For example, "Kubla Khan" was influenced by Coleridge's reading of the travel writings of Samuel Purchas, especially about China. When he used the expression "myriad-minded" to describe Shakespeare, he borrowed it from a Greek monk who used it to describe the mind of Christ. Later, W. B. Yates improved and simplified the expression by referring to Shakespeare as "many-minded." Perhaps Yeats, who was influenced by Coleridge, drew inspiration from Coleridge's description of Shakespeare.

Hawarden was not all about study and research, however. We had a fun time there, and I made friends with many interesting people. After dinner, the warden would take all of us to the nearest pub for a nightcap before going to bed. The warden told me he was a close friend of Hans Küng, the well-known German Catholic theologian. He had many a good story to tell about the great theologian's academic prowess, and down-to-earth way of

---

4. Gladstone's residential library is the only Prime Ministerial Library in Britain. Live-in writers and scholars from around the globe gather at this center to pursue research on various subjects.

speaking. They got to know each other when Professor Küng stayed with him and his family in Australia.

On weekends, we would visit nearby cities, such as Chester, on the border of Wales, to watch the famous Christmas mystery plays being performed in the open square by groups of students.[5]

Christmas Eve at Hawarden dawned crisp and clear, the promise of a frosty yuletide hanging in the air. As the scent of roasting turkey and plum pudding wafted from the kitchen, our motley crew of scholars decided to earn our feast. Bundled in woolen scarves and mittens, we set out into the Welsh countryside, a far cry from the bucolic image portrayed in Llewellyn's novel, *How Green was My Valley*. The stark beauty of the winter landscape unfolded before us—bare trees etched against the pale sky; their branches laden with a delicate frosting of snow. Our breath plumed in the frigid air as we trudged along, the crunch of frozen grass beneath our boots the only sound in the hushed, expectant stillness of Christmas Eve.

We traversed the rugged North Wales terrain. By afternoon, we retraced our steps back to where we were staying, our bodies hunched over from fatigue. We resembled a caravan of weary Bedouin shepherds stumbling upon a desert haven, as we shuffled into a Hawarden pub. Laughter filled the air as we discussed our day's misadventures.

One memorable obstacle we faced was an obstinate Welsh shepherd driving his sheep along the open road, forcing us to scale a steep hillside to get around the blockade. We complied, laughing, for in Wales, sheep had the right-of-way. We were merely intruders.

The impulse that drove our group to embark on that grueling hike deep into the Welsh countryside, not knowing anything of the land's contours, was a blessing to all of us, a way to break the ice and bond as a surrogate family in a foreign place. Miraculously, it worked.

We emerged from the experience as more than mere acquaintances. Through shared struggle, we became a tight-knit community of kindred spirits, exchanging warm smiles, engaging in lively conversations, and acknowledging each other's presence whether we crossed paths in the library corridors or during meals.

The Christmas dinner the following day was brilliant. We were able to have an excellent time, celebrating into the wee hours of the morning.

As I boarded the ferry back to Ireland, my briefcase heavy with notes and my mind brimming with new ideas, I felt a profound shift within

---

5. Medieval mystery plays were devoted to the representation of Bible stories in churches as tableaux with accompanying antiphonal songs. These plays evolved into presentations shown in courtyards and town squares for the enjoyment of the populace. Popular themes included the Nativity during the Christmas cycle.

myself. The young priest who had left for Hawarden was not the same man returning to the Carmelite College. My experiences had broadened my perspective, deepened my understanding, and rekindled my passion for learning. When I finally sat for my master's degree exams, I approached them not with trepidation, but with a quiet confidence born of rigorous study and newfound maturity. The First-Class Honors I earned were more than just an academic achievement—they were a testament to my growth as a teacher, and a person.

My five years of teaching in Cork were happy ones. These bountiful years involved teaching in the classroom, taking university exams, learning Munster Gaelic in Kerry, traveling by boat over the Irish sea for research at Hawarden in Wales, and flying to Boston for further research studies at Cambridge.

As I reflect on those five years at Carmelite College, I realize they were more than just a period of academic growth. They were a crucible in which my vocation was tested and refined. The challenges I faced in the classroom, the intellectual stimulation of my studies, and the camaraderie I found among fellow scholars all played their part.

But it was my growing involvement with the needy across Ireland that truly shaped my path forward. In the faces of those I served—the handicapped, the homeless, the forgotten—I saw the true meaning of my calling. These experiences, more than any academic studies, would come to define my journey as a priest and as a human being. Little did I know then how profoundly these experiences would alter the course of my life.

Chapter 10

My path towards helping the needy was sparked by a family crisis. My youngest sister, Kathleen, was born with a disability. Seeking the kind of help she could not receive at home, my parents enrolled her in a residential center for the handicapped, run by the La Sagesse Sisters in Sligo. Under their care, Kathleen thrived. She developed vocational skills and could vacation at home every Christmas, Easter, and Summertime. It was an ideal arrangement.

In 1970, however, the Center abruptly closed due to financial hardship when government assistance was cut off. Unable to provide a sheltered workshop and accommodation for the handicapped, the sisters sent the children home. Kathleen and others like her returned to families ill-equipped to provide the care they needed, especially during the vulnerable years of adolescence. This placed a heavy burden on the parents.

While studying at the university, I volunteered with a group known as Building Companions. Founded in Belgium in the aftermath of World War II, this selfless community dedicated their time and skills to constructing homes and essential facilities for those less fortunate. Inspired by their example, I envisioned a similar initiative for Sligo, focusing on the needs of the disabled.

To translate this vision into reality, I founded Christian Community Action (CCA) based on the selfless agape love depicted in the Sermon on the Mount and specifically outlined in the Gospel of Matthew, chapter 25. This parable from Scripture beautifully encapsulates the requirements for belonging to Jesus's kingdom: feeding the hungry, clothing the naked, quenching the thirst of the thirsty, welcoming the stranger, and providing shelter for the homeless. To me, this was the very essence of being a Christian, practicing Christ's agape love in the Sermon on the Mount (chapters 5–7), also clearly stated in the following Scripture passages:

"Do unto others what you wish them to do unto you" (Matthew 7:12). "Love your neighbor as yourself" (Mark 12:30–31). "Love one another as I have loved you" (John 13:34).

To build a sheltered workshop and housing for the handicapped in Sligo, we needed volunteers, especially those with construction skills. As fortune would have it, Verolme Dockyard in Cobh, County Cork,[1] employed large crews of skilled workers: carpenters, plumbers, painters, electricians, metal workers, and welders who were ideally suited for the job. The Dockyard was close to where I taught school. These skilled artisans were a perfect match for the deserving endeavor I envisioned. Recognizing this incredible synergy, I saw the dockyard as the ideal venue to seek out dedicated volunteers for our project.

The Verolme Dockyard throbbed with activity as I approached the management office. The air was thick with the rhythmic clanging of tools against steel. My heart raced as I prepared to make my pitch, knowing that the success of our project hinged on the generosity of these hardworking men.

I asked management for permission to seek volunteers from among the workers for the project in Sligo during the weekends when they were off work.

Permission was generously granted. I spoke to a large group of workers on the floor of the dockyard about the project, and what it would entail. A hush fell over the large gathering as I outlined our project's aims and urgent needs. The workers listened in silence, exchanging subtle, sidelong glances among themselves, gauging each other's reactions as they communally weighed the meaning of this call to service.

"You would be staying with local families in Sligo," I said. "They are also volunteers and would provide you with room and board during the course of the project."

Finally, I put the question to them: "Would you be willing to work on this project by giving up your weekends of leisure to help the needy?"

To my great surprise and delight, all hands went up. These men accepted the challenge to help the needy as the proper thing to do. It was just what the Lord ordered: "Do unto others what you wish them to do unto you."

Helping one another in need was something these men took to heart. When they later appeared on an Irish television program, the interviewer leaned forward, microphone in hand.

---

1. The Verolme Cork Dockyard, owned by a Dutch firm, employed over 1,200 workers at its peak and closed in 1984, although ship repair continued to be carried out on the site.

"What drives you to give up your weekends for this work?" she asked, her tone a mix of curiosity and admiration.

The dockworker paused, wiping his brow with a calloused hand.

"It's simple, really," he said, his voice warm. "Today it's them needing my help. Tomorrow, it could be me needing someone's help. We're all in this together, aren't we?"

Riding a wave of collective enthusiasm, we marshalled an army of volunteers. Skilled artisans from Cork eagerly jumped into their vehicles, forming a spirited caravan to Sligo. Generously sacrificing their weekends, they breathed new life into our plans for a new shelter and accessible housing for the disabled.

Since I didn't own a car, I always relied on hitching rides between Cork and Sligo, coordinating the work as best I could. But destiny had a surprise up its sleeve. My father's land in the Isles was designated an industrial zone and, in an act of generosity, he gifted me a much-needed car with the proceeds from the sale of some of the land.

Now with wheels under my feet, I became part of the enthusiastic procession of vehicles coursing between Cork and Sligo each weekend. A grassroots effort was born.

There was a great spirit of selflessness in these excursions every weekend. Everybody seemed buoyed by the same sense of freedom and service. In Sligo itself, local businesses and building suppliers showed the same spirit and donated everything we needed free of charge. Materials such as essential lumber, sand to make concrete, construction blocks, and paint for the shelter when it was completed were all donated. Business owners told me they were privileged to be asked to contribute to such a worthy project.

Word of our cause spread, and flocks of volunteers joined us from across Ireland and overseas. My own senior students joined our ranks during their summer vacations. Young men and women came from as far away as America to help.

Together we lodged on-site in quaint chalets, forming a family bond by our shared experience. The chalets creaked and groaned in the night wind, their wooden walls barely containing the laughter and chatter within. As we huddled around the flickering warmth of a fireplace, sharing stories and dreams, the bonds between us grew stronger than the structures we were building.

Our downtime saw us boarding a bus furnished by the center, heading to the beach for respite after work. Some of our members playfully started calling each other brother and sister.

When one of my pupils who lived nearby in Sligo took a summer job, our circle felt incomplete. After a few days, the magnetic pull of camaraderie drew him back. He missed the warmth that enveloped our new-found family. His return validated the adage that love is its own reward.

Each weekend brought fresh excitement, brimming with anticipation as the crews arrived from Cork, eager to unite with the younger men and women volunteers. Their playful interaction infused the project with good natured fun and unity.

Our path was not without its pitfalls. Halfway through construction, the center's chaplain, whose residence served as my temporary home, revealed disturbing news.

"Board members," he said, "were paying themselves for the work you were doing."

The implications were dire. If word spread of personal profit from donated work, it could only damage our reputation and sink the entire project.

As the chaplain's words sank in, a tight knot formed in my stomach. I could almost hear the delicate framework of trust we'd built beginning to crack. How could I face the volunteers who'd sacrificed their weekends, their sweat, their skills? The weight of responsibility pressed down on me, threatening to crush the very spirit of generosity that had brought us this far.

Without hesitation, I immediately convened my committee. I was advised by some to let the matter drop since this bad news, if it got out, would disillusion our volunteers, and do more harm than good. But I couldn't cover it up. It would be wrong. The weight of conscience bore heavily upon me. I owed it to the volunteers, to myself and my faith to pursue the path of integrity. Thus, we dispatched a strongly worded letter to the superior of the La Sagesse Sisters, stating: "We would withdraw from the project if board members continued compensating themselves for our voluntary work."

In the aftermath, I gathered our volunteers on the trampled floor of Cork's Dockyard. As I laid bare the unsettling truth, a palpable silence descended upon the group. Their stunned expressions slowly gave way to relief and gratitude, however, when I explained what happened.

One by one, they approached me, sharing whispers of rumors that had been circulating in local pubs. Some confessed to heated altercations with residents, their loyalty to our cause leading them to deny the very accusations I now confirmed. Yet, in the face of this difficult truth, they found solace in my stand to uphold the project's integrity. At that moment, amidst the dust-tinged air of the dockyard, I witnessed the power of honesty to fortify bonds and restore faith in our shared purpose.

This episode taught me an important lesson: Worthy ends cannot justify unworthy means. Integrity in the execution of any project mattered a great deal.

Part 1—Chapter 10

The project was completed. The handicapped youngsters were then able to return to their community home, afforded the kind of facilities they badly needed.

Some of the volunteers who kept pouring in for this project came from Northern Ireland, an area torn apart by sectarian conflict. Victor Bewley, a Dublin businessman, philanthropist and good friend, came up with the idea of bringing Catholic and Protestant youngsters together from the turmoil-ridden streets of Belfast to work on a common project. Victor was a Quaker, and he knew that getting these youngsters to work together to help others would bring out the best in them. He was right, and it was heartwarming to see these youngsters working in harmony for a change. Their common, benevolent purpose left no room for hate. What they had in common was much greater than the sectarian divisiveness that had been tearing them apart in the British Province of Northern Ireland.

*　*　*

After the Sligo Project, I received all kinds of invitations from different organizations and people in Ireland to help them with their needs. Each plea for help, piled one upon another, threatened to overwhelm me. I'd lie awake at night, the faces of hopeful community leaders swimming before my eyes, their voices echoing in my ears. How could I choose one worthy cause over another when each represented an opportunity to do good?

I was contacted by a dedicated nun, Sister Patricia in Freshford, Country Kilkenny. Her dream to convert the old school at the center of town into a community home for seniors seemed like a worthy project in which to engage.

Sister Patricia's weathered hands told the story of her dedication. Each wrinkle on her face was a testament to the countless miles she'd traveled, the meals she'd prepared, the wounds she'd bandaged. Her eyes, though tired, sparkled with an unwavering determination to improve the lives of the elderly she'd come to see as family.

She felt she should bring them all together into a group home where they could live together in the center of town. She also felt that the homes the seniors vacated could be repurposed into homes for young couples in need of housing. Sister Patricia was a practical visionary.

This was the kind of worthy project we couldn't turn down. The townspeople of Freshford rose to the occasion, becoming very active in this project. They not only opened their homes to the volunteer workers from outside the community, they actively worked on the project itself.

This project, like the one in Sligo, was also completed successfully. Nineteen homes were built for the senior citizens, in addition to kitchen facilities, dining room, living room, laundry room and medical service area.

As impressive as the work was, it was not all smooth sailing either. Doing what the gospel demanded was never easy. It always involved struggle, and oftentimes persecution.

The old school building in Freshford belonged to the parish, and the pastor was not willing to let it go. He wanted to sell the building and make money for the parish, even though it was being put to good use to help the most vulnerable members of his community. As a Cathedral Canon, he wielded considerable influence within the diocese. Thus, he objected to the project at a meeting of the Cathedral chapter, insisting that our Sunday work contravened the sanctity of the Lord's Day. This allegation shook up Bishop Birch, the Diocesan Ordinary, causing him to waver in his support of the project.

When Sister Patricia shared news of the Ordinary's wavering support, panic set in. I had to halt the next wave of volunteers, just as over fifty Dockyard tradesmen readied for the journey to Freshford, County Kilkenny. The disappointment of the volunteers was sorely felt as they wondered what was going on.

I drove to Kilkenny to meet with Bishop Birch at his residence. Sister Patricia let him know I was driving from Cork to meet him. The road to Kilkenny stretched before me, each mile amplifying my anxiety. What if the bishop remained unmoved? The fate of the project, the hopes of the volunteers, the dreams of the elderly—all hung in the balance. As I pulled up to the bishop's residence, the imposing structure loomed over me.

The bishop was in a bad state of ill health when we met and had to drag himself out of bed, sniffling and coughing.

"I'm very sorry I cannot support this project," he said vigorously, between coughs.

I felt bad for him, realizing the pressure he was under.

"I'm sorry too," I responded, "and I'd like to know the reason for this sudden turnaround."

His answer did not really surprise me. I already knew. The canon's objections to breaking the Sabbath, and the fact that the job was being done in plain sight of parishioners going to Mass, were the main reasons for withdrawing support.

"The volunteers are working on Sundays while people are going to Mass. This unfortunately is a scandalous situation," he elaborated.

"I don't see the scandal when people are helping one another, even on a Sunday," I returned. "After all, Saint Jerome, way back in the sixth century made a convincing case for nuns working on the Sabbath to help those in need."

The bishop sniggered.

"I totally agree with what you say," he replied, "and have no objection to your argument, but my back is up against the wall. There is nothing I can do about it. If the church can allow people to work on Sundays so publicly, then everybody else will use that as an excuse to break the Sabbath."

I realized the bishop was in a bind. He wanted to uphold Sunday as the Lord's Day in his Diocese at a time when secularism was making deep inroads into Irish society. This problem did not arise during our previous project in Sligo because it was hidden from public view. But in Freshford the project was a work in progress right across from the church.

"So, your problem is that we're working on Sundays. Is that it?" I asked the bishop.

"That's it in a nutshell," he said.

"I'll see what we can do about this," I told him. "I'll have to speak with my committee when I get back to Cork."

Bishop Birch softened after this. We spoke warmly about our common interests in teaching. He became more relaxed and the coughing and sniffling stopped. He told me his happiest years were when he taught English to secondary-level pupils in Kilkenny. I could identify with this, since I had similar experiences as a teacher of English literature at the Carmelite College in Cork.

We parted on very good terms. He was a good man, I could see, and had a reputation for promoting the gospel message of helping the needy. He had no problem with the project itself, and would have liked it to succeed for the benefit of the senior citizens in his diocese. He was under pressure, however, to oppose working on Sundays because it constituted a scandal. This I understood.

I returned to my base in Cork and met with the members of my committee, explaining why the bishop felt he had to put the project on hold. But I emphasized that it still could be salvaged if we could manage to avoid working on Sundays.

Someone asked the obvious question: "Would it be worth traveling all the way from Cork to Kilkenny to put in only a day's work, on Saturday?"

Like a bright light piercing a somber sky, the Dockyard's management emerged as our saving grace. In a providential decision, they donated employees' labor on Fridays toward the project. Thus, all volunteers could now travel to Freshford on Thursday evenings after work instead of Friday evenings.

This new arrangement reignited our momentum. The crews could devote full days on Fridays and Saturdays before returning home on Sundays. In actuality, no time was lost; we still achieved two full workdays each weekend.

With the Sunday work issue resolved, our project was like a river that had found its way around a stubborn boulder. It flowed with renewed vigor, carving out progress day by day, reshaping the landscape of Freshford and the lives of its elderly residents.

The Freshford project to build nineteen homes and facilities for senior citizens was on again. Needed now was increased cooperation from the good volunteers of Freshford to have everything ready and in place, so the skilled workers from Cork could hit the ground running when they started work on Friday mornings. Sister Patricia organized everything that needed to be done locally at Freshford, while I organized the outside help from Cork and elsewhere. This cooperation between local and outside volunteers was as harmonious and efficient as it could possibly have been. Not a minute was wasted.

Kilkenny is a hurling county, with Ireland's all-time record of national hurling championships. I was staying with Pa and Teresa Dillon and their family in Freshford while working on the project. Pa was a Kilkenny hurler and local legend. Often members of the Kilkenny hurling team and their wives would visit his home for an evening of fun. I got to know them all. These men were local heroes as well as national sports personalities. They offered to lend a hand to the project. Some of them were skilled workers like Fran Larkin, a plasterer by trade. When they turned up as a group to work on the project, the news media in Ireland got wind of it and covered the event. Radio, television and the press interviewed workers and published photos of the Kilkenny hurlers taking part in an activity different from winning national hurling championships.

After the coverage of the Kilkenny hurlers, news of our project spread throughout Ireland like wildfire in a forest. Wesley Burrows, script writer for the popular national television show, *The Riordans*, heard of the project and contacted me about incorporating our activities into the show. Thus, *The Riordans* blended fiction with reality as it invited Kilkenny hurlers to appear on the show and talk about the experiences of CCA volunteers working on the Kilkenny project.

Our efforts, as I already mentioned, attracted the notice of the well-liked television program, *Tangents*, known for exploring social issues. Our grassroots work appeared to be a natural fit for this show.

Soon a documentary crew visited the Verolme Dockyard in Cork, interviewing craftspeople, one by one, as they meticulously assembled cabinets destined for Freshford. Later, the TV crew traveled to the site of the project, speaking with volunteers and capturing on film the moment these cabinets were assembled into the apartments for the elderly.

These candid camera exchanges afforded a compelling look into the rich community effort the project embodied.

While work on the Freshford project was in progress, we had the misfortune of an accident. I was on the premises and saw what happened. One of our volunteer workers, a plasterer, fell. I immediately rushed him to the local doctor and had him treated. He insisted it was nothing and kept assuring me on the drive back to Cork, in my car, that he was okay. With time, however, he developed pains and had some difficulty walking.

Later, Sister Patricia called me: "The plasterer who fell is suing the diocese for damages," she related, frantically.

"That's the first I've heard of that," I replied. "I'll have to look into it and get back with you. Things like this happen, but are no reason for panic, Sister."

Then I got with my attorney and committee. My attorney advised us that the man had a right to sue for damages. The committee agreed. Further, they asked me to visit the man and his wife to see how we could help them in the meantime since the plasterer was one of our volunteers. We decided to give the man a check for one thousand pounds from our CCA account to help him in the meantime.

When I visited the man and his wife, they were cautious with me in the beginning. But they were overjoyed when I offered them financial assistance to tide them over in their time of need.

"This is the kind of help we never expected but are so happy to get," said the wife.

"The last thing we need are bad feelings," I replied, happily. "We're just privileged to help one of our own volunteers in need just as we help others."

As I handed over the check, I saw the tension in the man's shoulders ease, the worry lines on his wife's face soften.

"We're a family here, and family takes care of its own," I said, my voice full of emotion.

The gratitude in their eyes, the trembling of their hands as they accepted the help was a powerful reminder of why we did this work in the first place.

We enjoyed a good chat, a cup of tea and freshly baked scones together. We parted as good friends.

The matter was finally settled, amicably, out of court.

I learned another important lesson from this experience. Always respect the dignity of those who work for you.

You Duped Me, O Lord

* * *

My mother called me while I was working on the Kilkenny project.

"Your uncle, Dan Duffy, has come back after forty-two years in America," she told me. "You have to come home and spend some time with Dan, his son, Michael, and his wife, Peg. They want to meet you."

"I'm bogged down with this project in Kilkenny," I explained to my mother. "We've had some setbacks, and I don't want to abandon the project in the middle of its completion."

That wasn't good enough for her.

"The project can wait," she said, earnestly. "It had to wait before you started it, so it can wait another while."

I couldn't argue with my mother's insistence or her logic.

I drove to Letterkenny and had a wonderful two weeks with my Uncle Dan, his wife Peg and Michael. We drove all over Donegal in two cars, visiting our relatives and those of Peg in the lovely townland of Fanad, at the farthest tip of Donegal.

Upon my return to Freshford, the sight that greeted me was almost surreal. Our once bustling project had come to a standstill. The site was now lifeless, save for one stalwart local fellow soldering on in solitude. Mustering my courage and gathering every shred of resolve, I did what I could to breathe new life into the stalled project. Our grassroots machine churned back to life. Soon, caravans of volunteer work crews rolled back into town, their enthusiasm invigorating local support. We were back.

After the project was completed, I heard some interesting news. In a final ironic twist, the canon who had vehemently opposed the project became one of the first residents of the senior housing complex in Freshford.

CCA was a voluntary operation entirely. As an ecumenical organization, we pulled together people of all faiths and good will, united by the common goal of service to one another. Despite no one receiving monetary compensation, each project was executed with a level of professionalism that could rival any paid venture. Our volunteer pool was a wide array of diverse skill sets: architects, engineers, tradesmen and laborers, all lending expertise pro bono. Most of these experts came from local communities.

As I reflect on our journey, I'm struck by the delicate balance we managed to strike. Our army of volunteers, armed with nothing but goodwill and donated skills, accomplished what many thought impossible. We didn't just build homes and facilities; we constructed bridges between communities, between faiths, between the haves and the have-nots. In a world often divided by profit and self-interest, we showed that the currency of compassion could build just as effectively—if not more so—than corporate interests. Our relationship with unions stood as a testament to this truth: when the goal is the greater good, traditional barriers fall away. We had created more than buildings; we had nurtured a model of community action that honored both the spirit of service and the dignity of labor.

Chapter 11

WHAT WE ACCOMPLISHED IN Sligo and Kilkenny became better known throughout the country, especially after CCA was popularized in the national media and on television.

One day, I was called out of the classroom to answer an urgent call. As I lifted the receiver, I had no inkling what the voice on the other end would be asking of me.

"Father Duffy. This is the aide-de-camp to President Erskine Childers," his crisp voice intoned.[1]

As a man of the people, the President of Ireland had a keen interest in any work that was devoted to helping needy causes. He had been Minister for Health in the Irish government when the Center for the Handicapped in Sligo was closed due to a funding shortage. The aide-de-camp told me that he was intrigued that we could achieve through voluntary help what the government could not.

As I listened to him, I could almost picture President Childers—a man known for his progressive views and commitment to social justice—leaning forward in his chair, eyes alight with curiosity. Here was a leader who had grappled with bureaucracy and budget constraints, now marveling at how a group of volunteers could succeed where his own efforts had fallen short.

This was good news. CCA had a modest budget, but we needed seed money to get projects we undertook off the ground.

As I hung up the phone, a mix of excitement and trepidation washed over me. The President's interest was a validation of our work, yes, but it also raised the stakes. How would we balance the increased attention with our grassroots ethos? Could we maintain the spirit of volunteerism that was our lifeblood while navigating the corridors of power? I took a deep breath, realizing that CCA stood at a crossroads.

---

1. Erskine Hamilton Childers (December 11, 1905–November 17, 1974), an Irish politician and statesman, served as the fourth president of Ireland from June 1973 until November 1974. He remains the only Irish president to have died in office.

When I spoke to President Childers, I let him know how much I appreciated his offer of help, and asked if he could sponsor a fund-raising event we were planning for CCA in my hometown of Letterkenny. He agreed.

A popular Irish folk singing group from Letterkenny, the Pattersons,[2] offered to perform, gratis, during the benefit. The main hotel in town offered its facilities free of charge. The president, who enthusiastically accepted my invitation, visited Donegal in January 1974. This would be his first official visit to my county as President of Ireland.

I was kept busy beforehand sending out invitations for this event. The Catholic Bishop of Raphoe, whose jurisdiction covered Donegal, was the first to receive one. The Anglican Bishop of Derry was invited, as well as ministers of Anglican and Presbyterian churches in town. The list also included government officials of the Irish parliament whose constituencies were in Donegal. The benefit requested a goodwill donation of three pounds. We had a full house.

This event offered a simple wine and cheese reception before the main program. The president was the main attraction, and he delivered an impassioned address about CCA. Following up on this, I gave a slide show with commentary that described the different projects we had undertaken. Given the ecumenical nature of our work, the Anglican and Presbyterian ministers spoke eloquently about the need for people of different faiths and denominations to overcome their differences, and work together in the service of the community.

In the second part of the program, the Pattersons singing group, gave a lively performance. As the group took the stage, the room hushed. The first haunting notes filled the air, sending shivers down my spine. The rich harmonies wove through the crowd, feet tapping in rhythm, faces softening with nostalgia.

Townspeople in attendance were very impressed by the accomplishments of CCA in such a short time. One thing, however, upset them. The Catholic bishop of the Diocese of Raphoe, who resided in Letterkenny, did not attend the event. Members of the town council quizzed me about this, which I found rather embarrassing. I was glad to invite the bishop to the event but if he couldn't come it didn't bother me, for the work of CCA would continue, regardless. Still, I was upset that the bishop's absence had become a sticking point.

One town council member asked me, his tone accusatory: "Did you invite the bishop?"

2. The Pattersons were an Irish folk band from County Donegal in Ireland during the 1960s and 1970s. The group released five LPs and achieved international recognition in the 1970s.

I felt heat rising in my cheeks.

"Of course I invited the bishop," I shot back, my voice sharper than I intended. Taking a breath to calm myself, I added: "He was the first person on our list. I even followed up with a phone call when I was in Letterkenny to make sure he received it, since I had not heard back from him."

Another curious member of the council wanted to know what the bishop said.

"He told me," I replied, "that he might send a representative from St. Eunan's College, Father Lafferty, and that's what he did."

As much as I tried to explain away the bishop's absence with understanding, I couldn't calm the troubled waters. The event in Letterkenny brought Catholics and Protestants together, but not the bishop, even though what we were doing was in line with the church's ecumenical outreach. Why the bishop would ignore such an auspicious occasion, attended by the President of Ireland, continued to bother many people. It didn't bother me, but I could not make it go away.

The whole matter reached a new level of controversy when the public relations officer (PRO) for CCA decided to write to Cardinal William Conway, the Archbishop of Armagh and Primate of All Ireland.

At John's home in Cork, I found him hunched over his typewriter, brow furrowed in concentration.

"What are you working on?" I asked, peering over his shoulder.

My stomach dropped as I read the salutation: "Your Eminence, Cardinal William Conway."

The clacking of keys felt like a ticking time bomb, each letter bringing us closer to a confrontation I'd hoped to avoid.

I tried to persuade John not to write this letter because I felt nothing worthwhile would come of it, and I didn't want to make matters worse. The last thing I wanted was to muddy tranquil waters by having a conflict with the bishop, who might feel his authority was challenged. I have always respected authority, even when I didn't agree with decisions emanating from the office. John, however, insisted on writing the cardinal since he had attended the event himself and heard the reactions of the Catholic community to the bishop's absence. So, on February 16, 1974, he wrote the cardinal and sent copies of his letter to the bishop and me.

The cardinal responded to John's letter positively on February 25.

The bishop, on the other hand, disregarded John's letter, stating in a note to him on February 27: "As I have not the advantage of a PRO, I consider it preferable to take the contents of your communication up with the Founder Director of CCA. I am writing Father Duffy."

Part 1—Chapter 11

The bishop's long letter of February 27 to me arrived. The envelope sat on my desk like a coiled serpent, the bishop's seal hinting at danger within. With nervous fingers, I opened the envelope and unfolded the letter. Each word seemed to leap from the page, sharp as dagger points: "ill-conceived, disregard for authority, grave disappointment." As I read, I could feel the weight of church hierarchy bearing down on me, threatening to crush our fledgling organization beneath its unyielding traditions.

Our affair was ill-conceived, in his view, because we hadn't received his "written permission," as Ordinary of the diocese. The tone of this letter was strictly juridical; a stark reminder of the long-standing tension between the gospel and the institutional church. The bishop prioritized his juridic authority over the gospel mandate to help the needy. He failed to realize, it seemed, that his decisions should align with the gospel, not the reverse. It seemed to me that he got it backwards.

The cardinal, on the other hand, saw things differently from the bishop, and adopted a pastoral approach. He raised the issue at a general meeting of the Irish bishops in Maynooth, County Kildare. Following this, an announcement, published in the *Irish Press*, commended our efforts and conveyed "the openness of the bishops to attend and support such work." Where the bishop saw an affront to his power, the cardinal saw an opportunity to nurture the gospel mandate of helping the least among us.

Father James McDyer,[3] who achieved extraordinary results for the people of his parish in Donegal by getting them to work collectively for the good of the community, also wrote a letter to the *Irish Press* supporting our work. He was familiar with CCA because we had sent volunteers to help out with one of his projects, building housing for young married couples in his parish.

It is a fact of life that anyone who does some good is likely to get into some sort of trouble. As our work expanded, I began to realize that doing good was like walking through a minefield. Each step forward, each life improved, was a victory—but all around us, the ground was peppered with the explosive devices of tradition, prejudice, and bureaucracy. We treaded carefully, but knew that sooner or later, one of these hidden dangers would detonate beneath our feet.

John Lewis, the American civil rights leader, called this "good trouble." It's the kind of trouble that is not intended, but comes with the territory.

---

3. Father James McDyer (September 14, 1910–November 25, 1987) achieved national fame as a campaigner for the rights for disadvantaged and rural areas of Ireland. He developed in his own parish in Donegal a model housing community, hotel and guest houses, attracting numerous tourists from around the world.

Take, for example, the minister of Letterkenny's Presbyterian church, who spoke so eloquently at the reception. I had noticed his flock abstaining from the wine and cheese reception, standing apart. I respected their convictions. Still, the event's inclusion of wine drew the ire of the elders of his church, and they ousted the good minister from his post. The minister and the few members of his flock in attendance never touched a drop of wine, yet he was punished regardless, forcing him to find work teaching in England. I was saddened by this and thought of Christ's first miracle, changing water into wine at Cana's wedding feast.

After the event, I was vacationing in Letterkenny with my family. I walked into the Hibernian Bank, finding the people inside in a jovial mood as we greeted one another.

In the bank, a man had his back to me at the counter, but he suddenly disappeared. I wanted to say hello to him, for I was sure it was the kindly Brother Elmer, who I knew from my school days. I asked the bank manager, a friend, why Brother Elmer had left so suddenly.

The bank manager smiled.

"That wasn't Brother Elmer," he said. "That was the bishop. When he saw you, he asked me to let him out by the back door."

We both looked at each other and laughed.

The President of Ireland, a Protestant, once shared with me tales of the subtle opposition he faced from some clergy during his travels. As he recounted particular incidents, I chose not to tell him about the bishop's reaction to his Letterkenny visit. People often respond negatively based on their entrenched beliefs and prejudices. Better to let sleeping dogs lie, I felt.

Later that year, during classes at the Carmelite College in Country Cork, I was called out of the classroom to take an urgent phone call. It was the aide-de-camp again, calling on behalf of the President of Ireland.

"The president is attending a meeting of Rotarians in Cork City and he'd like to stop by to visit you at the college," he said.

Naturally delighted to have a visit from the president, I told the aide-de-camp I very much looked forward to it. This was also a great honor for the school, so I let the superior of the college know right away that the president of Ireland would be visiting.

Excitement spread throughout the school. Students were given the day off in honor of the president's visit and everything was done to make him feel welcome.

The president was in great form himself. He strode into the college, his energy infectious, his handshake firm and warm.

"Just got a clean bill of health," he told me, his eyes twinkling with the vigor of a man half his age. We laughed together, reveling in the moment, blissfully unaware of the cruel surprise fate had in store for him.

During the fall break, when I was in Boston attending a benefit for CCA, I heard the news that President Childers of Ireland had died of a massive heart attack—at an international meeting of doctors in Dublin. How swiftly joy can turn to woe in our lives!

* * *

After the Freshford project, the next job we undertook was closer to home. This project was in Midleton, only a few miles from the college where I taught. A priest in Midleton had built up an impressive athletic service for young people by involving them in a wide range of sports activities, amassing a remarkable number of all-Ireland medals for their efforts.

His vision was to build a community center and an indoor track for youngsters, so they could practice all year round, come rain, come hail.

When he approached me about this project, I brought it before the committee. Once the project was approved, we worked on it during the summer of 1974. As usual, the Catholic and Protestant communities of Midleton came together to see this project through. Among our dedicated volunteers was my friend, Senator Trevor West, whose family lived in the area. He had no knowledge as a bricklayer, plasterer, carpenter or electrician. But he used his influence to promote the organization's work. This kind of self-effacing sacrifice was common during all CCA projects. Distinctions of class and denominations were put aside for the common good.

The cast of *The Riordans* television show also came to Midleton to support the project. This was a big day for the community. They attracted thousands of people far and wide to the site to catch a glimpse of the actors in the flesh and to mingle with them.

The last project we undertook involved restoring the Carmelite college in Castlemartyr to its original Georgian luster. Desmond Guinness, president and founder of the Irish Georgian society, offered to help with this project. He selected the color scheme for all the different rooms and parts of the building that needed renovation and was there to give advice when needed. This color scheme, applied by CCA volunteers, accentuated previously obscured architectural features of the building.

The new look of the building, which was actually a return to the original look, took most people by surprise. When the students returned from their summer vacation they were in shock. So were some of the priests and college staff.

An emergency meeting was called by the superior of the college shortly after the project was completed.

"We would like you to restore the building to the way it was," said Father Francis in a worried tone of voice.

"I wouldn't feel good asking the volunteer workers to undo what they did after all the work they put into it," I replied. "They were only following the directions of Desmond Guinness, a world authority on Georgian architecture and design."

Father Francis replied in good faith: "Regrettably, I'm getting bad vibes over this and something needs to be done about it."

The only response I could think of was to ask for more time so that people might get used to the changes.

"I know the changes are rather striking, but could you give it a few more weeks?" I implored. "If the bad vibes are still there, I'll ask the volunteers to put things back the way they were."

"Okay," said Father Francis, in a conciliatory tone. "We'll give it a few more weeks."

In the span of two weeks, the critics had changed their opinions. The once-wary priests admired the renovations and the students embraced the original aesthetics, newly revealed. Familiarity had worked its magic, and no one spoke anymore of rolling back the changes. Everyone had moved on.

Such is our deep-seated resistance to change. Yet often, time is the salve that soothes transition's pain.

Standing before the Castlemartyr resort today, its Georgian splendor restored and celebrated, I'm struck by how it mirrors the journey of CCA itself. What began as a controversial endeavor and met with resistance and skepticism, had blossomed into something beautiful and enduring. Our work faced initial opposition, but through persistence and faith, we created something that continues to serve and inspire. The transformation of this Georgian building to a prized destination echoes the broader impact of CCA—proving that with vision, hard work, and a willingness to challenge the status quo, we can indeed create lasting change in our communities and in people's lives.

The Georgian Mansion's renovations have endured, unaltered, to the present day. It was eventually sold, and is now a renowned resort hotel.

In 2022, it was selected as the premier five-star resort hotel in Ireland.[4]

4. Charlotte Ryan. "Irish Hotel Awards 2022: Cork Resort Named Best 5-Star Hotel." *RTE* last modified October 25, 2022. https://www.rte.ie/lifestyle/travel/2022/1025/1331285-irish-hotel-awards-2022-cork-resort-named-best-5-star-

Chapter 12

IN THE FALL OF 1974, at the invitation of Monsignor John J. (Jack) Egan, director of the Center for Pastoral and Social Ministry at Notre Dame, Indiana, I came to participate in a seminar on social ministry.[1]

The chill autumn air of Indiana filled my lungs as I stepped onto the hallowed grounds of Notre Dame. Golden leaves crunched as I walked beneath the golden dome, a fitting prelude to the exciting seminar that awaited me. Little did I know that this gathering would be the catalyst for a seismic shift in my life's trajectory.

This seminar attracted leaders of organizations throughout the U.S. and elsewhere to discuss the gospel's social ministry in all its dimensions. Here I met people like Monsignor Higgins, well known for his courageous efforts supporting Cesar Chavez and helping to pass just laws for migrant farmworkers in California.

There was no platform like this in Ireland to bring together people of like mind, people with a common interest in the gospel's outreach to the needy, and to allow them to listen and learn from one another.

During the course of this seminar, Monsignor Jack and I became well acquainted and I was able to discuss with him topics of importance to both of us.

"What got you into your work with CCA, Hugh?" he asked me, curiously.

"I got into this work quite by accident to build homes and a sheltered workshop in Sligo for the handicapped," I told him. "I also felt it was the Christian thing to do. From there, it just took off."

"Is that what you want to do in the future?" Jack asked me, surprisingly.

---

hotel/.

1. The seminar by the Catholic Committee on Urban Ministry was presented at the University of Notre Dame, Indiana, 1974.

Having thought seriously about this question, I answered: "I've been a teacher of English and French at the Carmelite College in County Cork, I replied, but I don't want to do that for the rest of my life."

"You don't like teaching?" he asked.

"Oh no," I replied. "I love teaching. It's just not what I think a priest should be doing with his life. There are many good lay teachers who can do as good a job."

Jack smiled, giving this some thought.

"I see," he said. "You'd like to change what you're doing?"

"That's it, more or less," I agreed. "I don't want to continue teaching, as much as I love it, but I do want to continue what I've been doing to help people, especially the needy, in a practical way. I feel this is the essence of being a Christian."

Jack could not agree more. His eyes lit up, a spark of recognition flashing across his kindly face. He leaned forward, elbows on his knees, as if physically drawn into our shared vision.

"You're preaching to the choir, my friend," he said, his voice warm with enthusiasm.

In that moment, I saw not just a fellow priest, but a kindred spirit who understood my desire to put faith into action.

"It's not possible to continue this work if I remain in the Carmelite Order in Ireland," I said. "It was different, however, when it came to the Carmelites in France who were socially engaged," I explained.

Jack was intrigued. His brow furrowed as he leaned back in his chair.

"But haven't you been doing this work with the Carmelites in Ireland?" he asked, his tone a mix of curiosity and concern.

I sighed, running a hand through my hair. "I have," I admitted. I paused, searching for the right words. "It's like trying to fit a square peg in a round hole. The Order moves in a different direction."

"And you?" Jack prompted gently.

I met his gaze, feeling a surge of determination.

"I can't go backwards, Jack, not now that I've seen what's possible. I got a letter from my provincial notifying me that I would be receiving a new assignment in the Philippines."

And you have a problem with that, naturally? he concluded.

"Indeed. I don't want to spend the rest of my life, after what I've been doing, living what's called the regular life within four walls."

This got Jack's attention, and I could see he understood the dilemma I was in.

We spoke about the regular life in a monastic setting, contrasting it with the fluid life of Christ which was episodic rather than regular; that is, open to meeting the needs of the gospel in the changing circumstances of life itself.

Jack said he would help me in any way he could and that he would begin by putting me in touch with some bishops he knew in the U.S.

Thus, Jack enabled me not only to reassess my vocation, but to discover my vocation within a vocation. As his words sank in, I felt a strange mix of exhilaration and terror. It was as if a veil had been lifted, revealing a path I'd always known existed but had never dared to tread. My vocation, I realized, wasn't just about wearing a collar or living within monastery walls. It was about answering the deeper call of the gospel, one that echoed from the streets and the struggles of everyday people. This revelation both thrilled and unsettled me. I felt like a bird standing on the edge of a cliff, knowing it must jump off to truly fly.

After the seminar at Notre Dame, before returning to Ireland, I attended two benefits in the U.S. for CCA: one in Chicago and another in Boston. The one in Chicago was organized by Irish immigrants living in the south side of the city, and the benefit in Boston was organized by Irish immigrants living there.

I was invited to appear on Robert Cromie's TV show in Chicago.[2] On the show I was introduced to Irish author Ulick O'Connor.[3] We struck up a friendship and Ulick offered to host a benefit in Cork, Ireland, to support the work of CCA. He followed up on his offer later by bringing his celebrity team of rugby players to Midleton, County Cork, to play a soccer game against a team assembled by myself. The game was a major success, much like the earlier visit of *The Riordans* cast members to the Midleton project, especially when it became known that some of the cast members of that TV show, such as Benji, were to play on our team.

I was about to fly back to Ireland from Boston's Logan International Airport when I heard of the death of President Childers on November 17, 1974. His widow, Rita Childers, would later write to me about the sad passing of her husband.

Arriving back at the Carmelite College, the familiar scent of polished wood enveloped me. Sunlight streamed through the narrow window of my room, illuminating two crisp white envelopes on my desk. My heart quickened as I recognized the official seals, knowing that within those paper

---

2. Robert Cromie (February 28, 1909–May 22, 1999) was a writer for the *Chicago Tribune* and the creator of the television shows *Book Beat* and *From the Editor's Desk* as well as the radio show *Authors' Forum*.

3. Ulick O'Connor (October 12, 1928–October 7, 2019) was an Irish writer, historian, playwright, critic, and noted sportsman especially in boxing, rugby and cricket. He was also a master debater.

folds lay the keys to my future. One of the letters was from Bishop Charles Buswell of the Diocese of Pueblo, Colorado, inviting me to join his diocese. The other was a similar request from Bishop Thomas Grady of the Diocese of Orlando, Florida.

My past journey in Ireland, arduous though it had been, was familiar territory, its challenges known. The road that beckoned ahead was uncertain. I stood at my window of the Georgian mansion, gazing out on the lake and rolling fields that graced my vision every day.

My fingers traced the smooth paper of the letters from America, their contents pulling me towards a horizon I couldn't yet see. My throat tightened as I imagined leaving Ireland behind—the familiar faces, the lively sense of humor, and the rhythms of life I'd grown accustomed to.

Yet beneath the fear, a current of excitement thrummed through me. What new challenges awaited across the Atlantic? What lives would I encounter, what changes would I have to deal with in a land of seemingly limitless possibilities?

My first choice was the Diocese of Pueblo. I wrote to Bishop Buswell that I would be staying in Philadelphia in July of 1975 with a friend in Maple Shade, New Jersey, and that I would be happy to fly from there to Pueblo to visit him. Bishop Buswell offered to spare me the inconvenience, writing that he would be in New England for a bishops' conference and would gladly come to see me in Philadelphia. This was indeed a gentlemanly offer.

But fate, in its unpredictable nature, intervened. Before we could meet in Philadelphia, Bishop Buswell was urgently summoned back to Pueblo. Thus, I now stood at a crossroads in my life: Pueblo on one side, Orlando on the other. I had to choose between them.

I flew to Orlando to meet with the bishop. While there I attended a clergy convention and spoke with several priests from Ireland who worked in the diocese. In fact, over 60 percent of the clergy in the Diocese of Orlando at that time were Irish-born. The reason: Florida was an Irish mission, and most of the priests working there were recruited from Irish seminaries. I felt quite at home among so many Irish compatriots.

And so, I found myself choosing the warmth of Florida over the cold and rugged beauty of Colorado.

Upon my return to the Carmelite College in Cork, the provincial's letter lay on my desk. I hesitantly opened the envelope and read its contents. I was being offered, as I expected, a new assignment in the Philippines, half a world away from everything I'd been working towards. I paced my room, the weight of impending confrontation heavy on my shoulders. How could I explain that my heart was pulling me in a completely different direction? The pen felt leaden in my hand as I sat down to craft my response, informing my provincial of a new opportunity to work in the Diocese of Orlando, Florida.

His reply expressed regret at the prospect of parting ways. He sought a meeting, and we soon found ourselves talking things over at St. Teresa's Church, Clarendon Street, Dublin.

Initiating the conversation, he remarked, "I've been following the remarkable work you've undertaken across the country."

His words caught me off guard.

"I was worried you'd object that my work was not aligned with the Carmelite Rules," I replied.

With a gentle smile, he countered: "What stands out about your efforts is the discretion with which you've carried them out. No criticism, no objections have reached my ears."

This revelation was unexpected. Memories of my inadvertent clash with the bishop of my native Donegal diocese resurfaced, leading me to ask: "Did any criticisms ever find their way to you?"

His reassuring response was: "Not a single one."

Our conversation was very cordial. The provincial offered to help me any way he could, just like Monsignor Jack Egan. For this, I was grateful. We kept in touch as friends throughout the process of being transferred from the Carmelite Order to the Diocese of Orlando. Whenever I came home on vacation to Ireland each year, we would meet in Dublin to enjoy a good time over a meal. The transitional process, known as incardination, was rather painless.

Before departing the Emerald Isle for the sunny shores of Florida, I met with the CCA committee in Cork to hand over the reins of running the organization's programmatic affairs. The committee's sentiments were bittersweet. While the members deeply lamented my departure, likening it to becoming orphans, they understood my reasons and wholeheartedly offered full support.

But without the founder, they felt they would be unable to sustain active involvement in social programs throughout the country. Recognizing the difficulty of continuing the legacy of CCA, the committee decided on another course of action. They would provide from our financial resources seed money to deserving causes like we did in the past, sustaining our mission for as long as financial resources allowed.

My good friend, Paddy Duggan, who had selflessly contributed to several programs, graciously took the helm of the restructured CCA.

On my last night in Letterkenny, I stood atop the hill overlooking the town I'd called home. The lights below blurred as tears filled my eyes, each one a bittersweet mixture of gratitude for what had been, and a new hope for what was to come. My heart felt like it might burst, torn between the comfort of the known and the allure of the possible. As the cool Irish mist settled around me, I savored this moment of in-between, knowing that come tomorrow, I would step into a new world, leaving a piece of myself behind even as I carried forward all I had learned.

I had no inkling of the vast contrasts I'd encounter in America compared to my experiences in Ireland. There was no way I could have imagined then how starkly different and contradictory my new experiences in America would be.

And so, like a sailboat cast off from familiar shores, I drifted toward unknown horizons, led only by the winds of Providence.

As I boarded the plane to Orlando, I felt like a tree being uprooted from its native soil. My roots, nurtured in Irish earth, ached as they were torn free. Yet I also felt the exhilaration of a seed carried on the wind, not knowing where it would land but trusting in the fertile ground of God's plan. America lay before me, a vast and unknown region, where I would exercise my ministry.

As the plane lifted off Irish soil, I pressed my palm against the cool window, as if I could hold onto my homeland for just a moment longer. Below me, the patchwork fields of green gave way to the vast blue of the Atlantic. I closed my eyes, feeling the vibration of the engines resonating through my body. In that moment, suspended between two continents, I realized that this journey was more than a physical relocation. It was a leap of faith, a commitment to carrying the spirit of my work in Ireland into new, uncharted territory. The familiar shores of home receded, but the compass of my convictions pointed steadily forward.

Whatever challenges lay ahead, I was ready to face them, armed with the lessons of my past and the hope for a future where faith and action could make a difference.

Part 2

Chapter 13

THE FLORIDA HEAT CAME cascading over me like a tsunami as I stepped off the plane in November 1975, a stark contrast to the chilly Irish autumn I'd left behind. Two Irish priests, their familiar accents a comfort in an alien land, greeted me with warm smiles and firm handshakes. As we drove through the palm-lined streets to St. Charles Parish, my temporary home, I couldn't shake the feeling that I had stepped into a different world entirely.

The following day I met with the bishop.

"The assignment we have for you was put on hold because another post needed to be filed urgently," he said, with a slight snigger.

I just smiled and nodded.

"Have you had any experience with marriage counseling?" the bishop inquired.

I hadn't, of course. I had plenty of experience dealing with married couples, including my own married siblings. Feeling this qualified me well enough, I nodded affirmatively, pleasing the bishop.

As I soon learned, however, marriage counseling was readily available through Catholic Charities counselors in the Orlando Diocese. There was no need for me to offer counseling in an area where I had little or no expertise. Thus, I was able to guide couples towards these counselors. This saved me from the subtle pitfalls and self-inflicted troubles often experienced by well-intentioned but ill-equipped priests who offered marriage counseling without proper training.

The bishop then shifted the conversation to Marriage Encounter, a movement I knew nothing about. Apparently, it was a big deal in the Orlando Diocese, aimed at making good marriages better, I was informed. I listened respectfully despite my lack of familiarity.

Curiously, he never mentioned anything about the parish where I was being assigned: what it was like or even the pastor's name. I found this odd since he had assured me, in writing, that he would match me with a parish suited to my skills, and where I'd be comfortable. Instead, his focus remained fixated on Marriage Counseling and Marriage Encounter.

As the bishop extolled the virtues of these ministries, a nagging doubt began to gnaw at me. Here I was, a man who had sworn off marriage, being asked to guide couples through their most intimate struggles. What insights could I, with my vow of celibacy, possibly offer to a husband and wife navigating the complex waters of matrimony? It felt like being asked to captain a ship I'd only ever seen from shore. Yet, wasn't empathy at the heart of our calling? Perhaps, I mused, it was precisely our distance from the issue that allowed us to see it clearly. Still, the question lingered, a pebble in my spiritual shoe.

When the bishop and I had finished discussing these aspects of pastoral ministry, he said: "You can meet with the chancellor next door and he will fill you in on anything else you need to know."

The chancellor's office door swung open, revealing Father Nathaniel Ring (not his real name) who seemed to have stepped out of a Hollywood movie. His impressive frame, draped in clerical black, was crowned by a mane of wavy hair, artfully quaffed and seemingly defying gravity. As he fixed me with a steady gaze, I caught a glimpse of the rugged western Ireland that had shaped him—in the set of his jaw and the cocky gleam in his eye. Here was a man who had traded the west of Ireland for the appealing corridors of ecclesiastical power, yet hadn't quite left the old country behind.

He extended a firm handshake. With a practiced motion, he gestured towards a chair, inviting me to sit. Meanwhile, he assumed a pose that seemed almost studied in its precision. He perched himself on the edge of a grand mahogany desk, one foot slightly elevated, the other planted firmly on the floor, as if anchoring himself in his domain.

I had only seen this seating position before in American movies.

He explained the reason for the delay in my assignment: "What we are dealing with here is the domino theory. Are you familiar with the domino theory?" [1]

I was familiar with the domino theory as it related to Cold War geopolitics. I never imagined it could apply to diocesan assignments.

In my attempt to look impressed, I must have released an involuntary smile, because the Chancellor's face got very red and he bounded from his desk to a standing position.

"You are being assigned to Resurrection Parish in Lakeland, Florida," he said, in an officious-sounding tone.

---

1. The Domino Theory posits that a political event in one country will cause similar events in neighboring countries, like a falling domino causing an entire row of upended dominoes to fall.

I was glad at last to know where I was going, even if I didn't know where Lakeland was. I thanked him for his help.

As it happened, there was a seminar for priests taking place in Orlando the following day, which I attended with the rest of the clergy. It was offered by the well-known moral theologian and scholar, Father Bernard Häring,[2] who played an important role as an expert at the Second Vatican Council (the Latin term for expert is *peritus*).

During the course of the seminar, an announcement suddenly came over the intercom: "Would Father Duffy please report to Resurrection Parish in Lakeland to celebrate evening Mass and attend a meeting of the parish council."

Upon hearing this, all the priests in attendance at the seminar laughed out loud.

I made my way to the office. A priest, Father Pat Sheehy, was standing there.

"I heard the announcement on the intercom," he said. "I'm from St. Joseph's, the neighboring parish in Lakeland, and I'd be glad to drive you to Resurrection Parish."

"Oh, thanks a lot. I had no idea where the parish was or how to get there, and I don't even have a car," I replied, gratefully.

After picking up my belongings at Orlando's St. Charles Parish, Pat drove me to Lakeland. It took a little over an hour.

During the journey Pat asked me: "Were you told anything about the situation at Resurrection?"

"Not a thing," I replied.

It now dawned on me that the bishop's comforting letter was nothing more than a carefully crafted piece of rhetoric designed to please. In stark reality, I was on my own in a new country, an unfamiliar diocese, and an unknown parish.

Pat shed light on what awaited me. He spoke candidly of the pastor's struggles with alcohol, which severely hindered his ability to fulfill his priestly duties. I was grateful for this forewarning; it braced me for the challenges that lay ahead.

At the rectory, the doorbell was answered by a French-Canadian priest, in residence. He kindly showed me to my room, gave me a key to the rectory, and directed me to the church where I celebrated the evening Mass. There I was introduced to Kay, the sacristan. She had meticulously

---

2. Bernard Häring (November 10, 1912–July 3, 1998) was a German moral theologian who attended the Second Vatican Council as an expert.

arranged everything for the Mass, which was a real help since I was new to everything.

After Mass, the meeting of the parish council took place in the parish hall. The absence of a prearranged agenda lent an air of informality to the occasion. Taking the lead, I introduced myself and encouraged each member to do the same.

"What's on your minds?" I asked.

The responses were immediate and overwhelming. A cascade of queries and concerns flowed from the council members.

"What are you going to do for the parish youth?" was the first question, followed by another's observation: "We have no youth activities."

A third voice chimed in: "And what of religious education? We have nearly two hundred youngsters, yet no structured program for their spiritual guidance."

I absorbed their concerns, noting the palpable sense of urgency that filled the hall.

"I've just set foot in this parish, and have had no prior knowledge of this," I admitted. "But rest assured, addressing the needs of the community will be my priority once I've found my footing."

I thanked all the council members for their frankness and openness. The meeting ended on an optimistic note, and we parted in good spirits.

Returning to the rectory, I watched television in the living room. The pastor suddenly emerged from his room to join me, drink in hand. He was a big, affable Irishman from County Clare.

He welcomed me to the parish with the words: "Would you have a drink?"

"Not really," I replied, unwilling to contribute to his problem.

"Ah, come on," he insisted. "You have to have a drink."

He poured me a vodka and tonic and refreshed his own drink. I knew it was going to be a long night.

Casting his eye on the big television set in the living room, he said: "You need a television in your room."

"Oh no," I insisted. "I prefer quiet when I go to bed."

"But *everybody* has a television set in their room," he asserted.

"Not me," I stressed again. "I prefer to read."

We talked amiably for hours, comparing our memories of Ireland where we grew up. Finally, we retired to bed for the night.

The next morning, the cook made me a delicious breakfast.

The aroma of sizzling bacon and freshly brewed coffee wafted through the rectory, drawing me to the kitchen like a siren's call. There, I found the cook, Mama Ruby, her ample frame swaying to a silent rhythm as she

Part 2—Chapter 13

flipped pancakes with the skill of a seasoned short-order cook. The kitchen was warm and steamy, filled with the comforting sounds of butter hissing on the griddle and eggs cracking against the side of a mixing bowl. As she placed a plate piled high with golden pancakes, crispy bacon, and scrambled eggs before me, the rich, homey scents enveloped me with all the warmth of legendary Southern charm.

"Your mama's back in Ireland, but while you're here, I'm your mama," she insisted, giving me a big hug.

This jovial, affectionate Black woman did all she could to make me feel at home. The name she had bestowed upon herself, Mama Ruby, was more than apt; it was richly deserved, a testament to her generous heart and nurturing soul.

I walked outside after breakfast on my first morning to explore the grounds and property. What I saw was eye-opening. In addition to the beautiful rectory and the church, the grounds of the parish had a large tennis court, a big corral for horses, and a brand-new parish center. This was like no parish I had ever seen. It was like a country club.

At lunch, the pastor kindly offered to drive me to nearby Bartow to buy a new car. We set off together after lunch. I bought a new car with a down-payment from the sale of the car my father bought for me in Ireland. My new car was a Vega.

A lady named Loretta was tasked with running the religious education program. But with no educational background or experience of her own, she badly needed help. She asked me to design and implement the program. First though, I wanted to meet the parish families.

Loretta provided a list of addresses and helped print calling cards for my visits.

As I stood outside a door on my first stop, hand poised to knock, the silence struck me. No children's laughter spilled from open windows, no distant radio hummed, no kettle whistled a welcome. The manicured lawn and pristine exterior spoke of order. The house seemed to hold its breath. I slid my calling card under the door. As I moved from one silent home to the next, leaving my cards like breadcrumbs, a longing for the busy kitchens and chatty neighbors of Ireland overcame me. Here, in this land of plenty, I felt a new kind of poverty—a lack of connection, of community.

Soon, calls came pouring in from parishioners, inviting me to their homes at a mutually acceptable time. It was actually a lot of fun meeting the parishioners in their own homes, and they were always welcoming. I had dinner or lunch with the families and played card games afterwards as we got to know one another.

One day as I was making my rounds, I drove up to a stately home. The house loomed before me, a monument to American prosperity perched atop a manicured hill. The Stars and Stripes snapped in the breeze, a silent sentry guarding the home. My finger hovered over the doorbell, hesitation gripping me. What if this visit went like the others: nobody home. The chimes echoed inside, each second of waiting stretching into eternity. Finally, the door creaked open, revealing a woman whose guarded expression did little to quell my nerves. I offered her my most disarming smile.

"Good afternoon," I began. "I'm Father Duffy, making a pastoral visit."

"I know who you are from the church," she acknowledged.

I didn't know what to say but, to make conversation, I asked if her husband was home.

"Yes, he is," came the reply.

"Could I talk to him also?" I asked.

"Let me see," replied the lady, and she went off to converse with her husband.

At this point I felt I was an unwelcome intruder, but I resisted the urge to run away.

The lady returned and said: "My husband will see you."

I was led into a living room where the husband was relaxing, watching baseball and sipping a highball. Feeling instantly at ease in this casual atmosphere, I began to relax also.

"I didn't want to meet you, Father, or become friends," he said. "You're only passing through like the others before you. After the last priest left, I told my wife I'd never put myself through this again."

I appreciated his frankness. His remark about me passing through was spot on. He highlighted a real problem with the church's domino policy of assigning priests to parishes for brief periods, especially associate priests. They didn't stay long enough to truly know the parishioners or be known themselves. This institutional policy frustrated priests and parishioners alike. Parishioners need time to get to know a priest and build a pastoral relationship.

"I'm only trying to meet the parishioners," I returned. "I hope you understand."

"What you're doing is commendable, Father, I know," he replied. "What I'm telling you is that you're not going to be long here, either. Give it a year and a bit, at the most, and you'll be gone just like the others. I just don't want to go through the same disappointment all over again."

I heard the same refrain from other parishioners I visited. Some explained that they grew up with their priests in their home parishes, but now they see priests coming and going like dust in the wind. What I heard from these parishioners was borne out only 15 months later. I was switched from Resurrection parish to make room for another priest who was unhappy with his assignment in Orlando.

At the parish council meeting I attended on my first night in Lakeland, two urgent matters were raised: 1) the need for a youth group and 2) the need for a religious education program. These were the two areas where I needed to focus my efforts.

I knew nothing of American sports: baseball, basketball, American football, but I knew something about soccer, having played it back in Ireland. With just a ball to kick around, it was an inexpensive, easy youth activity for both boys and girls. There were no soccer programs in Lakeland then, so I announced from the pulpit that I'd be starting one. I invited any interested boys and girls to show up at the parish center the following Saturday.

Twenty-nine boys and one girl came that first day. A few adults, originally from various foreign countries also arrived with soccer balls, offering to coach: Nat from Argentina, Flavio from Columbia, Arlene from England and Tom from Scotland. Arlene became the first coach of an all-girls team. These soccer enthusiasts formed the nucleus of the fledgling program, along with volunteer coaches, mostly fathers of participating youngsters.

The first thing we did was lay out a soccer field on the parish grounds, with goal posts at both ends.

More and more youngsters turned up every Saturday. The youth soccer program spread like Florida wildflowers in spring, taking root in the fertile soil of community need. It spread across Lakeland, reaching into schools, parks, and the very fabric of family life. Once barren, the church's field now bloomed with the colorful jerseys of young players, their laughter and shouts breathing new life into the parish.

Soon, I was getting phone calls from parents outside the parish asking if you had to be Catholic to join. An aide to Governor Lawton Chiles called on behalf of the governor's grandchild.

"Do you admit youngsters who are not Catholic into your program?" he asked.

"Of course," I replied. "We welcome everyone."

Thus, the governor's grandchild joined the soccer program. Soccer, like any sport, had nothing whatsoever to do with religious affiliation.

The Lakeland school system served many parish youngsters, so as word of the new sport spread, I was invited to various schools to promote it. The American coaches, feeling threatened, were initially unhappy with this unfamiliar, competitive program. I made it a priority to alleviate their fears by talking with them and gaining their cooperation first.

The soccer program grew so rapidly all over Lakeland that we expanded it into the Greater Lakeland Soccer League. The dedicated coaches, parents, and youngsters assured the success and continuance of the program.

Back in Ireland, the need for insurance was never a problem. We didn't have it. But in a litigious country like the U.S., every child had to be insured.

One day, the owner of the largest sports emporium in Lakeland stopped by to see me.

"I understand you were turned down by my store in Lakeland when you asked if we had any soccer uniforms," he stated.

"That's correct," I replied. "We were rather disappointed you couldn't help us."

"I apologize for that mistake," he returned, "and I would like to make it up to you."

"What changed your mind?" I inquired curiously, "and how would you like to make it up to us?"

"We lost 250 of our basketball youngsters overnight to your program, and I want to get in on it," he said.

"What would you like to do?" I asked.

"I'm prepared to charge fifty percent less than any and all outlets that have been providing you with soccer uniforms," he explained. "I'm prepared to do this to be admitted to the program."

"I'd be happy to invite you to the next meeting of the coaches in the parish hall," I replied. "There you can make your pitch to them."

He agreed. When he offered the generous deal of fifty percent less on all uniforms, the coaches enthusiastically accepted the offer.

A major professional game was slated for Tampa's stadium, pitting the local rowdies against the renowned New York Cosmos. I was asked to bring our youth teams for free, provided they'd parade around the field in uniform before kickoff. The youngsters were thrilled at the prospect of this once-in-a-lifetime experience. Quickly, we organized a convoy, a mixture of cars and a bus to shepherd our uniformed players to the big event

As the young athletes from Lakeland, twenty-five teams strong, marched around what is now Tampa's Raymond James Stadium, a wave of applause cascaded from the stands. It was a heartwarming sight, witnessing our young players basking in the limelight, their faces aglow with joy. It also gladdened our coaches' and parents' hearts to witness our Lakeland youth teams receiving the acclaim of the crowd.

The owners of the Rowdies came up to me on the pitch, elated by what they saw.

"We've been told you are responsible for arranging this extraordinary group of young soccer players," they remarked.

"That's an exaggeration," I replied. "It's a team effort by many people: volunteers, coaches, and parents. I just happen to be one among many."

"How long do you think it will take for soccer to become a national sport in America?" one of the owners asked.

"These youngsters would have to grow up first and bring their kids to the professional games before that could happen," I proffered.

"We've been told soccer will be a national sport in five years. Do you not agree?"

"I don't think it will happen that quickly," I returned. "The game will have to grow from the bottom up before it becomes a national sport, it seems to me."

The owners of the Rowdies had an awakening that day. They were a little bit too ambitious about the prospects of soccer becoming a national sport so rapidly.

The youth program for youngsters in the parish drew a lot of families back to church who had been inactive, and prepared the way for the second goal discussed at the parish council meeting; namely, a religious education program. With more youngsters now active in the parish, we were able to fashion a very effective religious education program.

Volunteer teachers came forward, full of goodwill. With my educational background, good text books and much needed training were offered to the teachers. Youth enrollment began to increase every week. It was heartwarming to receive letters from grateful parents, describing the positive effects of the program on their children. The growth was nothing less than astounding, as it seemed to come from an unusual source: soccer. As the soccer program grew, so did the parish religious education program.

Many formerly married Catholics, feeling alienated from the church, began to return. Their children were in the soccer program and, after I got to know the parents, they told me they thought they had been excommunicated. Once I explained that they were still bona fide members of the church, they were so relieved that they rejoined the church and registered their children in the religious education program. Thus, the program that began with less than 200 youngsters, soon grew to over a thousand. We had to organize several sessions every weekend at the education center for the religious instruction of so many youngsters.

The Lord works in strange ways. Soccer became a tool of evangelization in bringing families back to church. Some clergy members were critical of my involvement in the soccer program, believing it alien to the real vocation of a priest to bring people to God. Little did they appreciate the real world. Human nature is a mixture of body and soul; you cannot have one without the other. The sense of connectedness we all felt by being part of the soccer program only strengthened our spiritual bonding. This bonding has never left us.

The parish had several organized adult groups for different kinds of ministry: Charismatic Ministry, Alcoholics Anonymous, Marriage Encounter, Cursillo. Formally Married and Divorced Catholics, Transactional Analysis (to improve communication between couples) and Choral Ministry.

One adult group I found particularly fascinating was called Enjoy Doing It Yourself Group (EDIYG). I asked a member of this group what it was all about.

"Well, there's a ministry for everything else," she explained, "so we thought a group of laid-back, fun-loving people with no imposed agenda would be a welcome addition."

I was drawn to this group.

It met every Wednesday morning and became my favorite. I always enjoyed the company of these personable people who spread joy, shared refreshments, and laughed a lot, without imposing anything on you.

Things took a sad turn for me when my Aunt Marie, in Philadelphia, developed cancer. This was a great sorrow to all my family. The pastor was very supportive, encouraging me to pay a visit to my aunt and relatives during this trying time. I left the parish for a week, but when I returned it seemed all hell had broken loose.

In my absence, the pastor's drinking got worse and, lacking support, he began to fall apart. Things were out of control and news reached the diocesan chancery.

The bishop called me when I got back from Philadelphia.

"How are things at the parish?" he inquired. He was obliquely referring to the pastor's drinking problem.

"The same as when I got here," I replied.

"What do you mean?" he asked.

"Well, I was told nothing about the situation prior to my arrival at Resurrection parish, and things have been the same ever since," I explained.

It was actually Father Sheedy from a neighboring parish who filled me in on the pastor's situation when he drove me to Lakeland for the first time. Neither the bishop nor the chancellor mentioned a thing about what to expect.

Surprisingly, the bishop asked me: "What do you think I should do?"

This was a hopeful sign.

"I think you should help the pastor who is going through a tough time," I replied.

The bishop thought for a moment.

Part 2—Chapter 13

"I'll drive down and should be there in an hour or so," he said.

I was glad to hear this, but I cautioned him: "The pastor may not be here when you arrive because he has a habit of taking off suddenly."

That was the end of our conversation—indeed, it was the first real conversation I ever had with the bishop about the parish.

As promised, the bishop arrived about an hour later. And as I'd warned, the pastor was not in when the bishop inquired about him with the parish secretary.

He let it go at that and then turned to me, asking me to walk outside with him.

Donning a pair of dark glasses, he asked me: "When did the pastor fall off the wagon?"

"I didn't know he was ever on it," I replied.

He then began to ask more questions, but I said: "I feel uneasy talking about a fellow priest behind his back."

I then suggested the bishop should talk to him personally and try to help him.

Eventually, the pastor did get help. Kaye, the sacristan, and I drove him to Orlando, where he was to catch a flight to Michigan, and from there to a center for alcoholics. Before the flight, we entered a restaurant and the pastor immediately ordered a double Manhattan. A strange feeling suddenly came over me. I stepped outside the restaurant to case the surroundings. I spotted the bishop and the chancellor at the ticket counter, obviously making inquiries. I rushed back into the restaurant.

"The bishop and chancellor are here," Bill, I said.

He swallowed the drink with a single gulp, arose, straightened himself to a standing position and walked outside with Kaye and myself.

The bishop and the chancellor saw us and came over to bid the pastor farewell and wish him the best.

On the drive back to Lakeland, Kaye could not stop laughing. Her recollection of the pastor gulping down a double Manhattan before saying farewell to the bishop at the airport amused her immensely.

* * *

A new pastor was appointed to Resurrection Parish.

In 1976, America's bicentennial filled the air with patriotic fervor, with jubilant celebrations taking place across the nation. Amidst this historic zeal, I read James Michener's novel, *Centennial*, to appreciate the significance of the 200th anniversary. Celebrations included my own planned vacation back to Ireland in July of that year.

Later, in February of 1977, I received a new assignment at St. James in Orlando. The diocesan policy mandated assigning new priests to two different parishes within three years.

As I packed my meager belongings, each item stirred a memory: the stack of thank-you notes from parents, their gratitude a bittersweet ache; the spare key to the parish rectory where we'd built so much more than just a youth program. My heart felt as heavy as the boxes I carried, laden with the weight of unfinished plans and severed connections. Lakeland had become more than just an assignment—it had become home. And now, once again, I was being uprooted, leaving behind another garden I'd only just begun to tend. The thought of saying goodbye to the families, the children whose growth I'd witnessed, the community we'd forged, left an emptiness in my chest that no amount of priestly stoicism could fill.

Fortunately, I ensured continuity in the soccer program, meeting with all the coaches to elect the very capable Tom Joyce to succeed me as league president. I knew that under his stewardship it would continue to thrive.

As I stood at the threshold of St. James in Orlando, poised to step into yet another new beginning, the words of that candid parishioner in Lakeland resonated within me: *You're only passing through.* This was the consequence of the ecclesiastical version of the domino theory.

With a deep breath, I crossed the threshold, ready to serve where I was planted.

Chapter 14

ST. JAMES STOOD LIKE a stone sentinel amidst the bustling streets of downtown Orlando. Entering the church, the cacophony of traffic faded, replaced by whispers of prayers and the soft flicker of votive candles.

There, amidst the divine and the day-to-day, I was a fresh-faced priest, swapped for one who preferred a more bucolic and tranquil setting over the clamor of city life.

Scarcely a month had passed in my urban ministry when flames engulfed the Cathedral of St. Charles Borromeo. The devastation meant that a new cathedral had to be designated, and St. James was chosen. And so, the parish was thrust into the limelight as the Diocese of Orlando's new Cathedral Church.

The Dedication of the Cathedral of St. James in 1977 was a grand event. Dignitaries such as the Papal Nuncio were there, and the air crackled with the recitation of the Papal decree by a Vatican representative, designating St. James as the Diocesan Cathedral.

The guest list consisted of wealthy Diocesan members; those who had donated over $1,000 to the bishop's annual appeal. Conspicuously absent were the very souls who called St. James their spiritual home. This was a far cry from Jesus's parable of the banquet welcoming everyone without distinction. Instead, the list of attendees consisted of the diocese's biggest benefactors, quite the antithesis of the Gospel's open table. Not surprisingly, the barred parishioners of St. James voiced their dismay. The rector tried to make the best of a bad situation by requesting that the diocesan chancery forward to him any left-over invitations to be made available on a first-come, first-served basis to local parishioners. However, it was too little too late. The local parishioners weren't interested. To mollify the locals' hurt feelings, the bishop decided, post-dedication, to greet the parishioners after weekend Masses at St. James.

Alas, the Saturday Vigil Mass became less a service and more a tribunal as parishioners offered the bishop some choice sermons of their own on their way out of church. Unaccustomed to such forthright feedback, the bishop beat a hasty retreat and didn't show up for any of the Masses the following Sunday, as promised.

Whenever the bishop celebrated Mass at the Cathedral after that, it was not unusual for the Cathedral secretary to call me on behalf of the bishop, requesting that I offer the sermon at his Mass.

The Cathedral parish hosted a seminar on lay ministry when I was there, drawing the dutiful laypeople working at various offices of the diocesan chancellery. I was eager and excited to learn from these seasoned, diocesan administrators. Each ministry was introduced by an official from the chancery and was followed up by a practical demonstration from a leader of some ministry or other in the cathedral parish. A problem arose when the parish representatives were conspicuously absent, afraid to show up as the ministries they headed only existed on paper. Impressive on parchment, these ministries held little substance beyond it.

Thus, the rector asked me to account for each of these absent ministries.

"I don't know anything about this or that ministry," I protested to the rector. "So how do you expect me to talk about them?"

"Oh, just go to the podium and say something about them. You can do it, you have a way with words," he returned.

Compelled by a blend of duty and desire to oblige, I ascended the dais to speak about different parish ministries I wasn't sure actually existed. My impromptu remarks struck a chord, appealing to the collective, ecclesiastical imagination, and were taken as gospel by the diocesan administrators. I was surprised by this unexpected reaction.

As the diocesan administrators nodded approvingly at my improvised descriptions, a wave of unease washed over me. How could they be so impressed by mere words or illusions? The ease with which my words were taken as truth unsettled me, forcing me to confront the fine line between faith and fabrication. I left the podium with a disturbing awareness of the power of words and their danger, especially when spoken from a position of authority.

There were, however, several effective ministries at St. James: ministries to the sick in three different hospitals, a prison ministry, a ministry to shut-ins, and a most effective food pantry to help the poor of Orlando. It was the hands and hearts of lay volunteers that brought these ministries to life, offering comfort and sustenance with unwavering regularity.

The ministry to the homebound held a special place in my heart. Perhaps it was the isolation I felt in this new city as well as my experience with visits to the empty homes in Lakeland.

Part 2—Chapter 14

One Sunday, I stood before the congregation. "I need a guide," I announced, my voice wavering slightly. "Someone to help me get around Orlando's streets and neighborhoods."

As the words left my lips, I realized I was asking for more than directions—I was seeking a connection in this unfamiliar city.

One morning, a kind gentleman arrived at the cathedral.

"I'd love to be your guide, Father, to navigate the neighborhoods of our shut-ins," he said, most helpfully.

"That's very generous of you," I acknowledged, gratefully.

Every week, my new-found friend and I made the rounds. A life-long Orlando native, he possessed an intimate knowledge of every side street and dead end in the city, guiding us efficiently to each destination.

We became fast friends, not just with one another, but to all those confined to their homes in Orlando. The sincere gratitude of the shut-ins made it all worthwhile.

When our day's chores were completed, we would stop off at the IHOP, a pancake restaurant, where laughter and stories were shared over steaming coffee and syrup-sprinkled pancakes. The warmth of community experienced during these travels nourished our spirits.

When the day came that my steadfast companion would be absent, bound for a well-deserved vacation with his wife, he assured continuity by lining up another volunteer to fill in for him.

"Wherever did you find this volunteer?" I asked.

"Oh, he's a lifelong friend who was quite critical of me for offering my services free," my friend explained.

"Why would he want to do this now if he disapproved of you doing it?" I inquired.

"Well, we grew up together in Orlando, so I know him well," he said. "He's a bit of a loudmouth, but it's mostly bluster."

"After hearing me describe our uplifting visits," he continued, "my friend had a change of heart and offered to substitute if needed."

The substitute proved his merit, his humor as dry as autumn leaves.

"So, you just got off the boat from the auld sod, eh?" he jested, as we set off on our journey.

"Plane, actually," I returned, evenly.

"Didn't think they had planes in Ireland," he quipped.

"Oh yes," I shot back, "quite reliable ones, too. Irish Airlines—Aer Lingus, has never had a crash." When he couldn't counter with another wise crack, he changed the subject. Despite his arid wit, he was a fine guide and we got along well.

I've found that people often voice doubts about selfless service to seek clarification, not criticize. Such was the case with my provisional chauffeur. His jest veiled a kind heart and an affinity for charitable endeavors. When my original guide returned from vacation, the familiar rhythm resumed.

Within the vibrant world of St. James, the charismatic movement was very active. This ministry was a strange by-product of the ecumenical movement, ushered in by the Second Vatican Council to foster understanding between denominations. My own ecumenical endeavors in Ireland had been pragmatic, uniting Catholics and Protestants to work on common projects to help the needy. It intrigued me how adherents of the charismatic movement attributed spiritual gifts to themselves without evidence, it seemed. Some Catholic mystics, like St. John of the Cross, cautioned against this very thing, saying it could cause spiritual pride by leading people to make claims that were not actually true.

The group's leader claimed he had performed every Gospel miracle, save for walking on water.

Each Sunday evening a special charismatic Mass was celebrated in church. I asked the rector to excuse me from having to celebrate this Mass. I just didn't feel I had a role to play in this ministry, even though I was very impressed by the Christian example of some of the members.

One Sunday evening, as twilight crept into the rectory's living quarters, I was approached by a member of the charismatic group.

"There's no priest around," he announced. "Would you celebrate the Mass?"

I could not refuse.

What ensued was a liturgy ablaze with fervor, evocative of the so-called holy rollers. The pews creaked and groaned as bodies swayed in rhythmic fervor. Indeed, the loud and freewheeling celebration resembled an old-fashioned tent revival. As we processed into church, I was directed to sit in a pew, not in the sanctuary, while the charismatics led the liturgy with much clapping and alleluias. I read the gospel, then a member gave an impassioned sermon. Placing his shoe on top of some object or other, he addressed it like he was speaking to a live person, letting his feelings and emotions run like a gushing torrent.

A voice shouted: "Amen! You tell it, brother."

Breaking into the gift of tongues, called glossolalia, some charismatics responded to the speaker, reminding me of the sounds Bedouin women made at weddings or other important occasions. Others joined in with loud applause and more alleluias. Soon the church vibrated to a cacophony of discordant sounds as the congregants began to speak in tongues, clap hands, and utter alleluias. I was baffled by it all.

Part 2—Chapter 14

I continued with the Mass and Communion. As I uttered the final blessing, a familiar figure materialized at the pulpit. My heart skipped a beat—it was the rector, his unexpected presence as jarring as a clash of cymbals in a quiet church. Our eyes met for a fleeting moment; his expression unreadable. As he turned to address the congregation, praising their "inspirational service of praise," a cold tendril of suspicion crept up my spine. Had this been a test?

I retired to the living room when it was over. The rector joined me there a little later. He took a seat beside me and asked: "What did you think of the charismatic Mass?"

"It's not the way I like to worship," I replied.

"That was a very poor service tonight," he replied.

"Then why did you describe it as an inspirational service of praise?" I asked.

"Oh, well, we have to say things like that," was his answer.

"No, you don't," I returned. "The Holy Spirit has nothing to do with deception."

I was never again asked to celebrate a charismatic Mass at the Cathedral of Saint James. I've met some wonderful people who belong to the charismatic movement, and I wouldn't want to denigrate their Christian commitment. One of my closest friends. in fact, is an evangelical Christian and we share more in common than what divides us.

In Orlando as in Lakeland, soccer took a prominent role in my ministry. One day I got a call from Tampa, where a meeting of the Florida Youth Soccer Association was being held. I was asked to attend.

"Why do you want me there?" I asked.

"You're the commissioner of the Central Florida Youth Soccer Association," he informed me.

"That's the first I've heard of that. Who appointed me commissioner?"

"It's automatic," came the reply. "You've registered the highest number of youngsters in South Florida, and we need you to cast your vote."

We spoke about the issues involved and I asked the caller to cast my vote, since I couldn't be present at the meeting.

Soon after my surprise appointment as commissioner of the Central Florida Youth Soccer Association, I was approached by Joe Davis, a parishioner who worked for a TV station. He wanted to start a soccer club in Orlando.

"What's your interest in soccer?" I asked him.

"I want to offer something for my nephews," he said, "and I can't think of a better way to get them involved than by participating in a sport like this. With you as commissioner, it should be easy to put together a club here, too."

Thus, inspired by Joe Davis's vision, we started a new club, the Downtown Orlando Soccer Club (DOSC), later to be renamed Orlando United. As in Lakeland, all players, boys and girls alike, could register in the U.S. Youth Soccer Association. We invited schools in Orlando and surrounding areas to participate in the league. Established clubs in Winter Park, Altamonte Springs and Apopka signed on as member associations. Our league expanded quickly, soon comprising about a dozen clubs, with teams differentiated by age and united by a common purpose. DOSC was one of those clubs.

My job as commissioner was to look out for the welfare of young players, not coach them. I mediated disputes between different clubs, players and families. Our collective efforts bore fruit when one of our own, a young standout named Mark McKane, made us all proud by earning a spot on the U.S. Olympic Soccer team.

A memorable chapter unfolded when youth teams from Mexico converged upon Orlando, staying with local families. One game was televised on a local channel, exposing our league to the wider community. Soon after, during a prison visit, the inmates excitedly told me they saw the match and my subsequent interview as commissioner. This opened up a whole new conversation about our shared interests, unlike our prior, somber interactions. It helped diffuse the intense sadness I felt when I heard the harsh, cruel sound of clanging iron doors shutting behind me.

Soccer became a universal language in this concrete purgatory, its rules and rhythms a bridge spanning the chasm between myself and the incarcerated. As we discussed the game, the iron bars seemed to fade, if only for a moment, turning the visiting room into a warm and friendly place where these men could discuss their passion for the sport.

Even the guard noticed my changed demeanor.

One day he remarked: "You're looking more relaxed now."

"What makes you say that?" I asked.

"When you first came, you were white as a sheet. Now you're at ease," he noted, perceptively.

Association with a normal human activity like sport humanized all of us.

The simple joy of heart-to-heart conversation brought me closer to them and them to me, diffusing the oppressive weight of that dismal place.

Indelibly etched in my memory is the day I kept vigil by a dying man's bedside. I was summoned to perform the last rites at a hospital. As the words were spoken and the sacrament bestowed, the dying man's last words to me were: "That's a wonderful thing you're doing, helping the youth of Orlando."

His words pierced through the somber veil of impending death, catching me off guard. In that sterile hospital room, with the rhythmic beep of monitors marking his final moments, I had expected his mind would dwell upon the last things, or on his family, or on the pain he was suffering. No. Instead, his fading voice carried a spark of life, of concern for others that transcended his own suffering. In that moment, I saw not a dying man, but a soul radiating with the purest form of love—one that reached beyond the self even at life's twilight.

He quietly passed away in my presence.

* * *

In August 1977, I went on my annual vacation to Ireland, dividing my time between my family and the Yeats Summer School in Sligo. My cousin, Niall, let me borrow his car for the event in Sligo.

Returning from the seminar in Sligo, a dangerous bend in the road sent my valise flying off the passenger seat. As I grabbed for it, the car went soaring over the mountain precipice. I said a quick prayer as I braced for impact, imagining my imminent demise. I needed a miracle, my own Lazarus moment cheating death.

Yet providentially, the car landed in the welcoming, outstretched arms of two sturdy trees, their leafy embrace holding the car just six feet above the ground. I sat stunned, suspended in mid-air and surrounded by foliage, yet unharmed.

Climbing down to the ground, I began scaling the hill to rejoin the living. Atop the hill, a crowd of locals, as if witnessing an apparition, had gathered with their trucks and tractors. Drawing near, I called out: "Can you help carry the car up to the road?"

Without a word, these big-hearted men descended the hill, positioning themselves under a car-lift of branches. With their robust frames forming a human cradle, they hoisted the vehicle aloft from its leafy berth and carried it up to the road. A tow truck then arrived from the town of Ballybofey to haul the car away for repairs. I rode along with the driver, still marveling at my deliverance.

I spoke with the wife of the garage owner, tending the gas pumps, about my predicament. She couldn't concentrate on what I was saying. Heartbroken, she was listening to the music of her idol, Elvis Presley, who had just passed away that same day. My near-death experience in Donegal happened the day Elvis died.[1]

Caught again in the swift current of ecclesiastical tides, my time at St. James Cathedral proved as ephemeral as my time in Lakeland. I enjoyed my work at St. James, especially my interaction with the parishioners, the camaraderie of my fellow staff workers, and the satisfaction derived from the various ministries I took part in. No parish is perfect, but St. James did a lot of good in downtown Orlando.

I was switched suddenly to St. Mary Magdalene in Altamonte Springs to replace another priest who took my place at St. James Cathedral.

Here I was, a man dedicated to stability and community, constantly uprooted by the institution. The domino theory, once a geopolitical concept, had become a disturbing reality in the ecclesiastical world.

---

1. Elvis Presley was pronounced dead at Baptist Hospital on Union Avenue in Memphis, Tennessee at 3:30 p.m. August 16, 1977.

Chapter 15

THE PASTOR OF ST. Mary Magdalen had written to me while I was in Ireland, inviting me to work at his Altamonte Springs parish north of Orlando. In my reply, I mentioned having a good friend, also with the same name (let's call him Matt Conway), from Cork who turned out to be his first cousin, and who volunteered on some of our CCA projects. I wondered if they might be related.

I received no response.

This pastor was gifted with impressive oratorical skills and excelled at fundraising, especially for the bishop's annual appeal, thus currying favor. His controversial methods of extracting money from the laity didn't faze him, as long as it produced results. Nor did it faze the bishop, either.

His lack of academic credentials, however, deeply bothered him. He had no degrees and hadn't attended high school in Ireland, either; just a substitute school for "late vocations," a term to describe older seminarians. From there he entered an Irish missionary seminary, which prepared him for the Florida missions.

As I observed Father Matt navigate his duties with a natural charisma that no degree could confer, I couldn't help but wonder about the wounds that drove him to fabricate his past. Behind his confident facade, he was a man haunted by imagined inadequacies, his true talents overshadowed by the specter of a formal education he never had.

Insecure about his educational deficit, he tried to compensate by inventing degrees he didn't possess. To impress Americans, he gave himself a B.A. from Mount Mellory and an M.A. from Carlow Seminary (both in Ireland), when neither of these institutions awarded degrees. He also gave himself degrees from various institutions of learning in the U.S.

Walking the tightrope of this new kind of parish politics felt like a daily test of my patience and principles. I was as careful as was possible not to step on the borrowed plumes my pastor wore with such pride.

It was smooth sailing for a while until something totally unexpected occurred.

A call came through to the rectory from a woman in Jericho, New York. She said she was calling on behalf of Matt Conway, but the parish secretary misinterpreted what she said and thought the call was for the pastor of the same name. He took the phone call.

As I sat at the desk in my office, I could hear the muted drone of the pastor's voice from the adjacent room. His usually composed tone wavered, rising in agitation, only to dip as if weighed down by an unseen burden. Every word uttered reverberated with mounting tension, thickening the atmosphere with a sense of unease. It was the kind of voice you couldn't ignore, even if you wanted to.

"Father Duffy. This call is for you," he roared.

I took the call wondering who it could be, since I had just arrived at the parish and few if any of my friends knew I had been assigned there.

The woman at the other end of the phone was the mother of a young lady who was engaged to my old friend, first cousin of the pastor. The woman knew nothing about this, and she simply wanted to surprise her future son-in-law by putting him in touch with me, an old friend. She quickly passed the phone over to her son-in-law to be.

Within earshot of the pastor, I said: "Great to talk to you, Matt. What brings you to America?"

Matt was all excited to be in touch again.

"I'm getting married in Jericho, New York," Matt laughingly told me. "I want you to do the wedding. Remember, we discussed this back in Ireland."

I never expected this, and I knew things were about to get complicated.

"You're getting married, Matt. That's great news," I replied. "Guess what? I'm assigned as associate pastor to your cousin, Father Matt Conway. I'm sure you'd love to invite him to do your wedding."

My old friend caught on right away.

"Of course, I'd love to invite my cousin Father Matt to do the wedding. And isn't it lucky," he added, "that I could get in touch with both of you at the same place and at the same time!"

"It sure is. It's providential," I said, hoping it would be.

After this conversation, the two Conway cousins spoke on the phone. Father Matt, who by this time had calmed down, told his cousin in Jericho that he'd be delighted to officiate at the marriage ceremony.

But that's not what happened. Instead, I was asked by the pastor to officiate at the wedding, which I did. But from then on, our relationship was never the same.

Part 2—Chapter 15

It is a dangerous thing to rattle the skeletons in another man's closet, even inadvertently.

I was rescued from this assignment when I got a call from the chancellor.

"There's an opening for the position of school pastor at a Catholic high school in Fort Pierce, Florida. I think it would be a good fit for you," he intoned.

"What makes you say that?" I prodded.

"You're working on a PhD. You'll have the summer off for research," he said.

The offer sounded good. I did not look favorably at the prospect of being involved in an American Catholic High School, a totally different proposition from my experience in Ireland. The position seemed to have its advantages, however, and I decided to take it.

* * *

My work at the Catholic school was mainly pastoral, and that pleased me. I offered Masses for the student body every Monday, held retreats every month or so, and was available to listen to students and help them with their problems. The students loved to stop by at my little office to relax and discuss their many concerns.

We had Mass for the student body in the parish church nearby. There was a good mix of students who were not Catholic attending the school. I was very happy that these students chose to attend Mass rather than abstain when they were perfectly free to do so.

Interacting with the students at the school proved invaluable. They openly critiqued my sermons, which was refreshing.

One day after Mass, a girl approached me in the sacristy to comment.

Her eyes met mine, a mix of respect and challenge in her gaze.

"Father," she began, her voice steady. "Your sermons are interesting, but . . . " She paused, seeming to gather courage. "They come across more like college lectures than spiritual guidance," she continued. "I come from a Protestant background where the Bible lends authority. I want you to know where I'm coming from so you can better relate to the likes of me. Do you see what I mean?"

Stung and intrigued at the same time by her remarks, I replied: "I certainly do, and I appreciate your feedback."

After this blessed encounter, I decided to change my approach to preaching. I now started my sermons with Scripture, and then developed its implications and relevance to real life.

The young girl later returned to speak to me in the sacristy.

"Your sermons are so much better," she said. "The message is much more powerful now when you tie it into Scripture."

I thanked her for the compliment but wasn't ready to let her off the hook.

"Wouldn't you like to participate more actively in the liturgy, given your interest?" I asked.

She reacted enthusiastically: "What do you have in mind?"

"You could prepare the prayers of the faithful at Mass," I explained, "and get other willing students to submit intentions to be included."

"Oh, that's a wonderful idea," she exclaimed.

Each Monday morning when we had Mass, the young woman would arrive at school early, her desk overflowing with slips of paper. Students of all kinds—athletes, the studious, the popular and the nondescript—would stop by her desk, slipping their handwritten prayers into her hands. There was a quiet reverence in the way they approached her, as if they were entrusting her with their deepest hopes and fears. She worked diligently, her pen moving silently across the page notes, assembling their words into a collective prayer that echoed the desires of the entire student body.

Attendance surged. The dean had to nix the optional study session, since students now preferred attending Mass. Through this participation, the liturgy was transformed into something more engaging and uplifting.

Beyond weekly Masses, our retreats made a profound impact by actively engaging students, who signed up in droves.

The retreats took place under the towering pines of a camp that smelled of damp earth. As the sun filtered through the trees, casting long shadows on the forest floor, the students gathered around a campfire, their faces illuminated by the flickering flames. One by one, they stood to speak, their words hesitant at first, but soon finding a rhythm that blended with the crackling of the fire and the distant call of owls. The stillness of the night was only broken by the occasional laugh, the rustle of leaves underfoot, and the profound silence that often followed a heartfelt revelation.

These weekend retreats forged lasting friendships. Students could laugh together, have fun together, and cry together while sharing poignant stories. The intimacy of the retreat setting allowed the students to expose and share their vulnerabilities, forging indelible bonds.

One day the mother of a student came to see me.

"What's my son Keith doing on these retreats?" she inquired.

Part 2—Chapter 15

"Oh, Keith is my right-hand man," I responded. "He works with me on the retreats and helps me with nearly everything. He's a fine young man. You should be very proud of him."

"As his mother, I'm very proud of him anyway. But what's this about Communion services? I've never heard of such a thing in my church," she declared.

"It's usual to have a Communion service when we don't offer a Mass," I told her.

"Not at Saint Paul's Lutheran," she replied.

"Are you telling me that Keith is a Lutheran?" I asked, dumbfounded.

"Yes, he is," was the mother's reply.

"Keith never mentioned that to me," I replied. "He just plunged into the retreats with the enthusiasm of a child in a playground, becoming part of everything we were doing. He has been an inspiration to all of us."

Keith later told me he wanted to take a gap year before college to help the underprivileged, and that's what he did. Several other students felt compelled toward service to others before entering the privileged domain of higher education.

In Ireland and England, national Departments of Education standardized curricula countrywide, so school boards didn't exist as in America. I was surprised when the board asked me to offer a class to boost grades for students struggling to meet requirements.

"Why not provide tutoring to raise grades in these subjects?" I asked at a board meeting.

My pleas went unheeded. I was maneuvered into teaching an ethics class to inflate the grades of students unable to meet standards in regular subjects. This would be unthinkable in the Irish and English educational systems.

In the first summer months, I was happy to spend my time in Boston doing PhD research in the marvelous libraries at Harvard University. While I was there, I received a phone call from the chancellor.

The chancellor's words hit me with the force of a tornado, knocking the air from my lungs.

"The Board of Education at the high school wants to replace you," he informed me.

"Replace me?" I echoed, my mind reeling. The room seemed to tilt as the implications sank in. Everything I'd built, every connection I'd forged with the students, was suddenly balanced on a knife's edge.

"But why?" I managed to ask, my voice sounding distant to my own ears. As the chancellor began to explain, I felt the ground shifting beneath my feet.

"It's about money," he said, emphatically. "The diocese wants the school's large endowment to be transferred into the diocesan bank, and the board is blaming you for squealing on them, and wants you out."

"I knew nothing whatsoever about this endowment," I replied to the chancellor.

"I know that," he said. "But the board wants to make you a sacrificial lamb, a sort of a trade-off," he replied.

He advised me to meet with the bishop, which is what I did when I returned to Florida.

When I met with the bishop, his first words to me were: "You did nothing wrong."

I knew that, but I could see that my removal was a done deal, as the chancellor made clear.

I was a bit miffed. I knew I had done nothing wrong, so why was I being asked to move?

The bishop continued: "In these circumstances it would be best to take another assignment."

I stared at him, a chill creeping up my spine.

"Are you not concerned about the truth?" I asked, my voice firm.

His response, when it came, was like a hammer shattering any illusions I might have had: "Not as long as your truth doesn't come out," he chuckled, his eyes crinkling with amusement at what he clearly saw as naivety on my part.

In that moment, I realized there was a chasm between what I had always believed about the church and the reality that stood before me. The church should have been a bulwark of truth and integrity, yet here I was, confronted with the cold reality that sometimes the truth wasn't welcome.

Now that I was being asked to leave the high school, I asked the bishop if, in lieu of an assignment in a parish, I might be allowed to finish my PhD research at Harvard University in Boston.

He was surprised to learn that I was a PhD candidate, and he acceded to my request. Soon, I was on my way to Boston. It was a good trade-off.

However, I felt like a modern-day Billy Budd, sacrificed on the altar of the institution. I had entered the school's halls as a willing pilgrim, seeking to guide young minds. Instead, I found myself navigating a labyrinth of institutional politics, each turn revealing not spiritual enlightenment, but the all-too-human foibles of power and pride. It was an odyssey, yes, but one where the gospel message was often hidden beneath layers of intrigue and personal vendettas.

As I left the meeting with the bishop, each step felt like a decision. The corridors of power had revealed themselves as a maze where truth

Part 2—Chapter 15

could easily be lost. Yet, paradoxically, this disillusioning journey had only crystallized the essence of my vocation. I realized that the true work of the gospel often happens not in the sanctioned spaces of the church, but in the margins, in the quiet moments of genuine connection with those seeking meaning and solace. I would navigate these turbulent waters, but my compass would always point towards the truth of my calling.

For in the end, it was not the institution, but the message of the gospel that really mattered: the love, compassion, and justice I had sworn to uphold. And that message, I knew, could weather any storm of politics or power.

Chapter 16

Stepping off the plane into the crisp Boston air, the weight of recent upheavals seemed to lift from my shoulders. The Hume family's welcoming embrace awaited me. Their cozy home, with its smell of freshly cooked meals and the familiar cadence of Irish accents, became my temporary haven before I found permanent lodgings.

It wasn't long before the pastor of Annunciation parish in Melrose, a graduate from Harvard himself, requested my assistance. Close to the university, the parish rectory served as my permanent place of residence while in Boston.

After settling into the rectory, I next drove to the university to register as a PhD research student. The process was quite simple. Once I showed my academic credentials and my PhD acceptance from the University of Hull, I was given access to the university's very impressive library system. There was no fee involved. I had my own stall at the Widener Library to pursue research, and I could avail myself of the services of the Houghton Library for rare books.

Weekends were devoted to pastoral duties, while weekdays immersed me in the rich world of research. This balance brought a deep sense of fulfillment—both spiritually and intellectually.

Mr. Charles Montalbano oversaw the sixty doctoral students, including myself. He introduced me to Professor George Williams, holder of Harvard's Hollis Chair of Divinity. A man of slight frame but formidable intellect, he occupied his position with an authority that was as gentle as it was commanding. His voice, calm and steady, drew you in, and his sharp wit often left me both enlightened and humbled.

George and I would meet weekly at his private study, Study K. He took a keen interest in my research on faith and reason, since parts of this topic overlapped with his own work on Pope John Paul II. He published the book *The Mind of John Paul II* while I was there.

Part 2—Chapter 16

As an observer at the Second Vatican Council (1962-1965), George Williams had become friends with bishop Karol Wojtyla, the future Pope.

As Professor Williams recounted his friendship with the future Pope John Paul II, his eyes sparkled with a mixture of reverence and fond reminiscence. His hands gestured animatedly as he painted a vivid picture of the young Bishop Wojtyla— brilliant, intense, yet surprisingly humble. Through George's stories, I began to see not just the iconic religious leader, but the man behind the papal robes, a fellow seeker of truth whose journey had intersected with my mentor in such a profound way.

Leaning forward in my chair, I couldn't resist asking: "Professor, how did you and Bishop Wojtyla become friends?"

George's eyes twinkled with memory.

"Ah," he chuckled, "it was quite serendipitous. He was familiar with my writings on Polish history."

"And that sparked a connection?" I prompted.

"Indeed," George nodded.

"You met often?" I asked.

"Every week," he replied. "I always had a lot of questions for him."

"And did the future Pope ask you any questions?" I pressed.

George paused, pondering.

"An interesting question, and I never really thought about it until now. Actually, I don't think he ever asked me a single question," he answered.

"Those had to be interesting conversations," I replied, and we both laughed.

I learned much from George Williams, both as a mentor and friend. He gave me a copy of the Pope's doctoral dissertation (written in Latin) entitled, *The Concept of Faith in the Writings of St. John of the Cross*. This document was important to me since I was studying the relationship between faith and reason in Catholic theology.

The notion of faith put forward by the Pope in his doctoral dissertation adhered to the scholastic mindset of faith as an assent of the will to the doctrines of the church. In his much later work after the Second Vatican Council, which he described as a *Vade Mecum* (pocket handbook), he adopted a pastoral approach to faith, as the response of the individual to the living word of God in Scripture. Evidently the Pope's understanding of faith had evolved since he wrote his doctoral dissertation prior to the Second Vatican Council.

Faith is akin to a sixth sense. It is a gift and it transcends the doctrines of any one creed. It is much broader than a belief system and relates to man's mysterious connection to an invisible God. It touches lives in so many ways: through the glory of creation, the light of conscience, and most palpably for the faithful, through the resonant word of God in Scripture. The Bible provides the written narrative of faith, the teachings and the lived experiences of the people of God in both Testaments, Old and New.

By studying or reflecting upon this narrative, we arrive at a better understanding of faith. St. Anselm's portrayal of theology as faith seeking understanding echoes true, for it is in the contemplation of these holy Scriptures that our grasp of faith is both deepened and brought to light. While doctrine has its place as guidance for Christians, true faith penetrates deeper to a personal encounter with Christ.

My period of study in Boston was a creative one. Not only did I enjoy the association of academics like George Williams at Harvard and Bernard Lonergan at Boston College. I also was able to participate in the Irish-American experience of Boston with my many friends who lived in the area.

As I mentioned previously, after completing research work at Harvard, I submitted my PhD at the University of Hull in England, under the tutelage of Professor V. A. McClelland. We had met at least once a year during vacation, sometimes in Hull itself, sometimes in Cambridge, England, and even in Tortola in the British Virgin Islands, where the University of Hull maintained a branch location.

When I first presented the outline of my doctoral dissertation to Professor McClelland, he asked: "Where did you get the idea to write on this amazing topic?"

I reminded him that the seed of my inquiry was planted by none other than himself when he asked me to explore the relationship between faith and liberal education. Though the genesis of my work slipped his mind, he was gratified by the result.

A truly liberal education is a concept often misunderstood. It is not the same as liberalism, with a false liberty of thought, but an education in the liberal arts and the liberal sciences devoted to the pursuit of truth for its own sake. Within the realm of Catholic theology, I charted the course of theology's relationship to liberal education up until the Second Vatican Council. My dissertation was later published in 2004, entitled, *Queen of the Sciences*. To my astonishment, the book caught the eye of the renowned Catholic theologian, Professor Hans Küng, who wrote to me describing it as a "precious book." He was reading it at his summer retreat in Switzerland when he wrote to me. We maintained a correspondence that lasted until his passing in 2021.

Harvard Square, a perpetual hive of activity, attracted all sorts of attention. Not a day passed that wasn't energized by the vibrant hum of life. Emerging from lunch one afternoon, I stumbled upon a protest directed against the oppression of the American worker.

Part 2—Chapter 16

The square buzzed with energy as the protest gathered steam. The voices of demonstrators clashed with the steady thrum of everyday life. I stood on the periphery, drawn in by the passion of these protesters, and their promises of much larger, nation-wide protests on May Day itself in support of the American worker.

But just as quickly, the mood shifted. The roar of armored cars, the heavy thud of boots on pavement, and the swift, silent efficiency of the police filled the square, leaving behind a silence that echoed louder than the protesters themselves.

I approached a rotund policeman, monitoring the scene, hands locked on his belt.

"What was that all about?" I asked.

"You won't be hearing from them again," was his reply.

The promised May Day protest never materialized.

While in residence in the Melrose parish, the Cardinal of Boston visited to confer confirmation. His diminutive stature belied the grandeur of his office. As he proceeded down the aisle, he was flanked by two even shorter altar boys, the sight evoking a ripple of chuckles from the pews.

At the reception in the rectory, the Cardinal displayed a good sense of humor. With a twinkle in his eye, he plucked a choice *hors d'oeuvre* from the tray, remarking: "This is what my mother served daily."

I laughed.

"That's what my Irish pastor used to say," he added.

He then invited me to join the Archdiocese of Boston. But having endured the turmoil of Florida, I wasn't keen on switching dioceses again. I respectfully declined the offer.

After Boston, my next assignment was to Our Lady of Lourdes parish in Daytona Beach, Florida.

Chapter 17

THE FIRST THING I noticed as I stepped onto the grounds of Our Lady of Lourdes Parish in Daytona was the vibrant pulse of the Beach. The salty tang of the sea hung in the air, mingling with the distant roar of engines and the hum of motorcycles. The church, standing aloof, was in stark contrast to the restless energy of the beach just steps away. As I breathed in the intoxicating mix of sun, sea, and speed, I realized this place was a unique intersection of the sacred and the secular, where the reverent hush of Mass would often compete with the exuberant cries of beachgoers.

One Sunday after celebrating Mass, I was greeting members of the congregation as they were exiting church.

A gentleman with an engaging smile shook my hand.

"Have you ever been to the races?" he asked.

I admitted I hadn't.

"Would you like to see the Daytona 500? I'd be glad to take you," he offered.

The altar servers, usually quick to disappear, were oddly lingering, listening to our exchange. I suspected the man had to be important to cast such a spell on them.

"What's your name?" I inquired.

"Bobby Allison," he replied.

Of course! The famous, race-car driver. And he was inviting me to the big NASCAR event at the Daytona 500 Speedway. What an opportunity!

When Bobby pulled up in his car, it was hard to reconcile the unassuming man I met in church with the legendary name known across American racetracks. His hand, hardened and strong from years of gripping the wheel at breakneck speeds, moved with surprising gentility as he opened the door for me. In the pit area, surrounded by the organized chaos of mechanics, engines, and flashing lights, I watched Bobby transform. The easy-going demeanor he had at church was replaced with a laser-like focus, his eyes scanning every detail of the track. But even in this high-stakes

Part 2—Chapter 17

environment, he never lost that graciousness, introducing me to his family and crew as if we were all part of the same team. It was in these moments, between the roaring engines and the adrenaline, that I saw the man behind the driver—the complex, humble, and deeply grounded friend I would get to know.

I watched the race from a privileged position in the pit area, with Bobby's wife, family and crew team.

The deafening zoom of cars roaring past in thunderous clusters was unlike anything I'd experienced. Every minute or so, a loud, concentrated zoom erupted as cars in tight formation sped by. This repetitive zoom-sound created a mesmerizing effect. The crowds loved the adrenalin rush of lightning-fast vehicles and daring maneuvers. Pit stops added frantic drama as crews scrambled to refuel and replace worn tires in seconds. Here, time was the relentless adversary, and the crew's frenzied dance was as crucial to victory as the driver's skill.

It was in this rarefied environment that my friendship with Bobby Allison took root. As our friendship grew, we were able to spend time together at his home in Hueytown, Alabama.

I once asked him: "What is the most important attribute of a racecar driver?"

"Handling," he replied.

The word "handling" covered a multitude, not just forty cars roaring round the track in bursts of thunder for two and a half miles. A lot of other things ran with them. There was the strategy of the pit crew, the car's condition leaving the garage, the skill and courage of the driver; when to hold back, when to maneuver, and when to give more speed. These factors were all part of handling and when they flowed together, it made all the difference between winning and losing.

The racer had to have the split-second ability to assimilate information, calculate risks and execute his strategy. The higher the speed, the less the reaction time. A split second for most may go unnoticed, but for a racer it is the difference between life and death, between crashing or avoiding it, between winning and losing. It seemed to me that handling served as a metaphor for life itself, with its constant twists and turns and changing conditions.

As Bobby skillfully maneuvered through the chaos of the race, a thought took root in my mind: wasn't life itself much like this? Each of us is a driver, navigating through the sharp curves and unexpected obstacles of our journey. Every decision—whether to push forward, pull back, or change course—had to be made in the blink of an eye, often with little room for error. Watching Bobby on the track, his reflexes honed by years of experience,

You Duped Me, O Lord

I couldn't help but wonder: had I faced my life's twists and turns with the same level of grace? How often had I swerved when I should have stayed the course, or hesitated when I needed to act? These reflections stayed with me long after the race, and I began to view my own path through a new lens, one shaped by the art of handling whatever life threw my way.

And so, my first Daytona 500 race, when Bobby seized the winner's crown, was particularly memorable. In the afterglow of victory, Bobby inquired if there was a cause to which he could lend his support. I suggested he might speak to our new parish youth group. He loved the idea and chose a date for his appearance.

Word of Bobby's impending visit was carried over the airways of Daytona, and through the eager whispers of the grapevine. The appointed day saw our hall packed with excited youngsters plus more outside in the parking lot, eager to see the racing legend. Not only was he the national driving champion at the time, he was also voted by his peers as most likeable.

True to form, Bobby embraced the moment with the grace of a true champion, signing autographs before entering the hall and addressing the overflow crowd with kindness. His status as racing's most likeable driver was self-evident.

Inside, eager fans were treated to dramatic race footage before Bobby spoke and took questions. The questions were as candid as the youth themselves.

In the crowded room, a young boy anxiously raised his hand.

"Mr. Allison," he asked, his voice barely audible above the murmurs of the crowd, "did you ever get into fights with other racers?"

The question hung in the air as the audience laughed. For a moment, Bobby's face clouded with a mixture of regret and reflection.

Locking eyes with the boy, as if to make sure his message would truly land, he replied: "I did, son," his voice steady but tinged with remorse. "And I wish I hadn't. Those fights, they were mistakes—moments when I lost sight of what really mattered."

He let the silence linger for a beat before continuing: "You see, racing, like life, isn't about the punches you throw, but the way you handle the race. It's about integrity, whether you're winning or losing. Those scuffles taught me that what matters most isn't where you finish, but how you carry yourself on the way there."

The boy nodded, his eyes wide, as Bobby's words seemed to settle over the entire room, a lesson that transcended the sport itself.

His graceful handling of this opener won the hearts of all. He imparted a lesson on sportsmanship that transcended the raceway. We could not have asked for a better role model to inspire our youth. The applause that rang out at the conclusion of the event was not just for a famous driver, but for the man who stood before them, an exemplary role model.

At Easter, thousands gathered for a grand celebration of faith at an outdoor Mass in the Dome, overlooking the sun-kissed beach of Daytona. I was entrusted by the pastor with leading this service, attended by thousands, young and old, along the golden, sandy beach. The cacophony of beach-clatter, sea breezes and the gulls' calls didn't disturb the deep, collective reverence of worshipers on this Easter Sunday morning.

The pastor, let's call him Larry Delaney, and I got along well. Each morning over breakfast we discussed parish needs. He appreciated that I could ease his burden, wearied as he was after the Herculean task of building a new church. The bishop considered him a wizard with finances.

When the priests' pension fund was mismanaged and depleted, the bishop asked Larry's advice on a replacement board member.

"I don't know anyone to recommend," Larry told me over breakfast. "Do you know anybody?" he asked.

"Yes," I replied. "I know a successful Wall Street investor, a man of integrity, who is now retired. We're friends."

I gave Larry his name, and added that he knew his father, a very capable and upright man living in the parish.

"But he might be too honest!" Larry cried.

"It's our pension," I reminded him. "Who do you want managing it, a dishonest or an honest man?"

"You're right," said Larry.

When it came to securing our communal future, the choice was clear: honesty was the best policy.

So, Larry recommended my friend, who soon resigned from the board. Alas, the honest man found the diocesan morass too sullied for his principles, choosing to resign rather than risk the tarnish of association.

Larry described himself as a survivor, a term he forged in the crucible of ecclesiastical politics. He harbored a dread of bishops, knowing too well how they could abuse power.

He recounted one incident from his early days in the American diocese. Having arrived fresh from Ireland, he had a fateful encounter with Archbishop James Patrick Hurley during a clergy meeting.

The archbishop was giving a summary of his agenda and asked for questions from the priests. A young priest dared to offer a suggestion. Turning to his vicar general, the archbishop instructed him to ask the priest if he meant what he said. The vicar general did as he was ordered and approached the priest: "His Grace would like to know if you meant what you said."

"Of course, I meant what I said," the young priest replied.

"That priest got a letter in the mail the following week," declared Larry, "removing him from the parish and reassigning him to the boondocks of the diocese without explanation."

The memory of this arbitrary abuse of power was etched into Larry's psyche, a cautionary tale that kept the specter of hierarchical abuse ever-present in his mind.

From Larry, I learned much about the inner workings of the church's "inequitable institution," as he described it. Some of the machinations he described made my blood boil. But I learned from him how the system worked, and was determined to avoid its sinister pitfalls as far as possible, and to be, as Christ urged, in it, but not of it.

"You must play the game," Larry insisted.

"I know where you're coming from, Larry," I replied. "I've been told the same thing by others before, but aren't you forgetting something?"

"What's that?"

"You're forgetting that if you play the game, the game will play you," I warned.

That thought never crossed his mind, yet it was prophetic. Indeed, the inequitable institution ultimately turned on him despite his loyal service. Though he fought back bravely, it played him in the end.

Our beach parish, like St. James, pulsed with the fervent groans of aggressively active charismatic members. Larry, ever the survivor, rode the crest of this wave. He uneasily promoted the charismatics to avoid their clout, even going so far as to declare "he was slain in the spirit." But they went too far eventually, insisting that the parish change the name of the church from Our Lady of Lourdes (not found in Scripture) to a biblically based name, Maranatha (1 Corinthians 16:22), which translates as Come, Lord. This Aramaic phrase, *Maran Atha*, was used by charismatics as a mantra during their prayer meetings.

Fearing the diocese might remove him from the parish if he changed its name, Larry stood his ground and rejected the name change. The schism that followed led the main group of charismatics to form their own breakaway church. They did not disappear completely, however, and every now and then some of them would make their presence felt.

Larry and I made weekly sojourns to a nearby spa. It served as an oasis, away from parish problems, until the day the steam room, where we were relaxing, became the stage for an unsolicited worship service. The leader of the breakaway group entered, calling upon brother Larry to join hands with him in praising the Lord. I made a quick getaway with some other spa members to the pool, but vulnerable Larry endured this ambush disguised as prayer, his evening of relaxation transformed into an evening of torture.

Part 2—Chapter 17

In the whirlpool another day, the same man hijacked Larry's hand. As I bolted the scene with other folk, he bellowed: "Brother, won't you offer praise with us?"

"There's a time and place for everything," I replied, abandoning the whirlpool.

These unwanted incursions during Larry's downtime grieved him greatly. We had to discontinue our weekly spa-rituals to avoid further entanglement with zealous, charismatic leaders.

After three years in Daytona Beach, my time to be appointed pastor arrived.

One day the chancellor called.

"There's a parish open in Okeechobee," he said. "Would you like to take it?"

"What's it like?" I asked.

"Well, it's a books-or-booze parish. If you like books you'll survive, but if you like booze you'll die," he quipped.

"You know I like books. What else do you have to say about the parish?" I inquired.

"It's a small country parish, around one hundred and fifty families, and it has no debt. You can hang out there for a year until you get a big parish on the coast."

His words, though cloaked in the semblance of guidance, rang with the hollow timbre of careerism, not vocation. Sadly, the restless pursuit of ecclesiastical advancement, a malaise denounced by Pope Francis as the leprosy of careerism, was undermining the gospel. It wreaks damage, fostering self-aggrandizement over service, in defiance of the call to humble stewardship. Christ's call to ministry is no glittering ascent up the rungs of power, but rather service to the least among us.

"It sounds good," I said to the chancellor. "It looks like the kind of place where I could do some good."

I had a lot of experience in Ireland building up communities that needed help, and I felt that Okeechobee would suit me well.

"You have one problem," he added.

"What's that?"

"When your name came up for a parish close to Daytona Beach, the pastor would not recommend you," he said.

"I already know that," I told him. "My pastor sees himself as a survivor and felt threatened at the thought that I might draw parishioners away from his parish. This won't be the case if I'm assigned to Okeechobee. It is far enough away and will not constitute a threat. You're the politician in the ranks," I added. "You can verify what I've said when you talk to him yourself."

"Okay," said the chancellor. "I'll give him a call right away."

Things happened very quickly after that. Larry came pounding on my door with both fists, shouting: "The chancellor is on the line, and he wants to talk to you!"

I picked up the phone.

"Congratulations," said the chancellor. "You are the new pastor of Sacred Heart in Okeechobee. You were absolutely right. You're no threat to the pastor, and he will not stand in your way. He recommends you highly."

Larry showed me the very positive letter he wrote for my files, recommending me for the position.

I was busy over the next few days, preparing to take up residence at the new rectory at Sacred Heart parish. Boxes of books, clothes and other personal items needed to be packed and readied for transport to Okeechobee. My friends, Pete and Nancy Tupas, assisted me during this hectic period, helping me organize, pack and transport all my personal effects.

One day before leaving Daytona, Larry came into the living room where I was seated and stood before me.

"You know, Hugh, we've always been the best of friends, and I'd like to maintain this friendship," he said, warmly. "If anyone should say anything to you that might harm our friendship, don't believe it."

I knew he felt guilty about steering me away from a parish within reach. Yet, I harbored no ill will. He was a survivor and, in a way, he couldn't help it.

"Don't feel guilty about the parish nearby that I might have gone to," I assured him. "I know all about it."

He froze like a snowman, speechless.

He left the room but returned later. Facing away from me and, with his right hand extended behind his back, he offered it to me, saying: "Thanks for understanding me, Hugh. You're the only one who ever did."

We shook hands warmly, letting it go. He then did everything he could to help me settle into my new Okeechobee parish.

Careerism is something I've been fortunate to reject early in my ministry. Its pervasive mark runs deep within the church's institution, and it can do ghastly things to a priest, even to undoing his vocation.

Chapter 18

THE FIRST TIME I heard of Okeechobee was at a clergy retreat in Orlando. The retreat master began: "Every diocese has a parish somewhere that is designated as its Siberia. Tell me, what is the Siberia of this diocese?"

Everybody burst out laughing and roared: "Okeechobee!"

I turned to the priest beside me and asked, "Where is Okeechobee?"

Eight years later, in September of 1984, I embarked on my first journey to Okeechobee. I was not arriving as a casual visitor, but as the new pastor of the modest church that served both the rural town and surrounding county. Accompanying me were two friends: Larry Delaney, my former pastor in Daytona, and Des Kavanaugh, our appointed driver and close mutual friend.

As we drove along Highway 70, slanting sunbeams burst through the foliage, casting shifting patterns of light and shadow. Eventually, the deep forest opened up into expansive dairy farms and ranches that sprawled for miles in all directions. Signs like McArthur Farms and Larson Dairies marked the land, with tiny worker cottages clustered near the ranch and dairy entrances.

As we neared Okeechobee, the world around us seemed to shift. Gone were the bustling coastal towns, replaced by a vast, sun-scorched plain that stretched to the horizon. The town emerged like a mirage, poised on the northern tip of the great lake, standing sentinel over its shimmering waters. From a distance, Okeechobee seemed less a town and more an outpost, suspended between the endless sky and the lake's still surface. It was a place where time seemed to slow, where the vastness of the landscape held a quiet presence, a humble oasis in this sea of grass and sky.

We couldn't help but notice a huge sign greeting us, listing all the local churches: Twenty-five Baptist churches, one Catholic, one Episcopal, one Methodist, and one Lutheran.

"We're in Baptist country," Des proclaimed.

You Duped Me, O Lord

The church was located on Southwest Sixth Street in the heart of town, but finding it proved difficult. We drove down the street, passing a large Baptist church on the right. I stopped into the office and asked the receptionist for directions to the Catholic Church. She looked at me quizzically and stated: "There's no Catholic Church here."

I returned to the car bemused, telling my companions: "Apparently, there's no Catholic Church in this town."

Larry and Des erupted in laughter.

We continued down the narrowing street.

"There's nothing down there, but pasture," Larry insisted. "Look at it. Nothing but open fields and trees."

Des paused the car, wondering what to do.

"Keep going," I urged.

We crept forward slowly, until we saw it. A cluster of buildings hidden far back from the little road, in a sprawling twelve-acre pasture. No signs of parking marked the secluded church grounds. We parked in the grassy field, having finally arrived at our destination.

Getting out of the car, we were met by a kind-looking man coming toward us.

"You must be Jimmy Winnie," I said.

I had spoken with him on the phone, and he was expecting us.

Jimmy moved through the parish grounds with an effortless grace, his every step reflecting the quiet authority of someone who had long taken responsibility for the place. His kindly face, creased with deep lines of care and experience, bore a quiet pride as he spoke of the parish, each word tinged with affection. It wasn't just facts he shared, but stories—anecdotes about the people who made up this close-knit community, stories of their joys and struggles. In Jimmy, I saw more than just a caretaker. He was a man who had filled the absence of a full-time priest with a steady hand and an open heart, tending to the flock with a humility that spoke volumes about his character.

Jimmy led us inside the modest church, which could seat about a hundred worshippers. Adjoining it was a hall serving two purposes: Monday night bingo and overflow seating via an accordion door for visiting snowbirds during the season.

We entered the hall on the left, walking to the far end, where a kitchen provided meals and refreshments during bingo nights. Next, Jimmy brought us to the priest's residence, attached to the hall. Across from it, a small corridor led to an unused parish office that stored odds and ends.

Stepping inside the rectory was like entering a dark tunnel. With the flick of a switch, Jimmy dispelled the darkness, revealing a living room held captive by brown draperies that prevented the light outside from getting in. With a heave, he pulled them back. Sunlight flooded the previously dim space. The windows opened out to a lush green pasture, alive with the vibrant sights and sounds of nature.

I asked Jimmy, "Would it be possible to have the place painted before I took up residence in about a week."

"I know two people in the parish who can do the job," Jimmy replied.

Jimmy seated himself at the table and proceeded to go through the mail. I observed him as each envelope was opened, its contents examined, and finally filed away. He then meticulously logged into the parish register the names of parishioners he had visited that day who were ill or homebound. I was impressed by his attention to detail, and ability to keep accurate parish records.

I couldn't help but marvel at the efficiency with which Jimmy handled everything.

"Jimmy," I asked, breaking the silence, "where did you learn to do all this—so meticulously?"

He paused, a distant look clouding his eyes.

"The Army," he replied quietly. "North Africa. During the war."

"The Army taught you this?" I asked, incredulous.

A faint, bittersweet smile crossed his face.

"Not in the way you'd think," he replied. "But when you're tasked with keeping track of the wounded, the dying. . . when you have to write letters to mothers and wives, telling them their loved ones won't be coming home. . ." His voice trailed off for a moment, heavy with memories.

"You learn quickly," he went on. "You learn the importance of detail and compassion, things that make all the difference."

He returned to his work, but his words lingered, offering a glimpse into the depth of his experience, a weight that he carried with quiet grace.

As I observed Jimmy meticulously filing parish records, I couldn't help but feel a profound sense of gratitude. Here was a man forged in the crucible of war, who had witnessed the worst of humanity, now offering his skills in the service of this peaceful community. The contrast was striking. The U.S. Army had trained him for conflict, but God had repurposed those very same skills for a mission of mercy. It was one of those moments that gave me pause—how often does God use the least likely of us for his work? As I watched Jimmy, I wondered: *If he could turn his past into something so lifegiving, what might I accomplish in this humble parish, if I, too, embraced the unexpected gifts of my journey?*

Stepping out of the rectory, we paused to take in the sight of the interconnected structures once more. Their state of decay was unmistakable. The roofs of both the church and the adjoining hall drooped wearily, like an old mare burdened by time. Scattered pebbles strewn across the grass crunched underfoot, evoking the haunting solitude of the Traveler in Walter de la Mare's poem "The Listener."

Plenty of work awaited here, but that's the way I liked it. It would take time to do what was necessary, not all at once, but one thing at a time. I was committed to working alongside these parishioners for as long as it took. My prior experiences in Ireland, building community centers and homes, would serve me well in this out – of – the – way place.

The most indelible impression from my initial 1984 visit to Sacred Heart was my soulful encounter with Jimmie Winnie. The buildings, weathered and wanting, were of little concern. The true cornerstone of any congregation lies not in bricks and stones, but in its people. In meeting Jimmy, I could tell that this parish was abundantly blessed where it mattered most: in the souls of those who embodied the gospel's glow. The parish of Sacred Heart may not have been rich from the point of view of wealth or its physical structure, but I could sense, after meeting Jimmy, it was rich in people who lived by the gospel. That was all that mattered.

We left the church grounds, driving to the lake's edge. The rickety bridge straddling the water groaned under our steps. The vast, distant horizon blazed red from the setting sun, bounded by still waters. The Seminole Indians named the lake, Okeechobee, meaning Big Water, an apt description of this giant, pulsating heart-shaped body of water serving all of south Florida down to the Keys. It was truly the liquid heart of Florida, tucked away in the center of the state, but for most Floridians it was as remote as the man on the moon. People failed to grasp its vital role in the ecosystem. Should this lake falter, succumbing to pollution, for instance, the whole of south Florida would face grave peril.

Surrounding the sprawling lake was a man-made dike to protect the surrounding areas from flooding.[1] It was constructed after the Great Hurricane of 1928, which pushed the waters of the lake over the banks with such ferocity that thousands of people—the actual number is unknown—lost their lives. In the many hurricanes since, this bulwark has shielded the surrounding communities from nature's fury.

Having set eyes on the great lake and the modest Sacred Heart Church for the first time, we retraced our route back to Daytona.

---

1. The dike around the waters of Lake Okeechobee in Florida is called the Herbert Hoover Dike because it was built during the Hoover Administration.

Chapter 19

OUR DIFFICULTY IN LOCATING the church when we first visited Okeechobee in September 1984 was not the kind of challenge I would wish on anyone. Consequently, one of our earliest priorities was the installation of a conspicuous signpost at the church's driveway. In a heartwarming display of community spirit, the men's club dedicated their time and expertise to erect a robust concrete marker. It was easily visible from a distance, guiding anyone towards our place of worship.

We next gained approval from the city to place a sign on the corner of Highway 441. The heat of the Florida sun shimmered over the long, cracked asphalt of the highway snaking its way through Okeechobee. As we stood at the crossroads, hammering in our sign, its metal face catching the sunlight, it felt as if we were embedding our community into the heart of Okeechobee County.

With these twin signs of welcome in place at strategic locations, the church's visibility dramatically improved. Attendance swelled as newcomers could readily find our house of worship.

A man came up to me after Mass one day.

"Me and my family were attending the Episcopal church for years because we thought it was the Catholic Church," he said. "We didn't know the difference because everything looked the same."

"How did you know where to find us?" I asked.

"The sign on Highway 441 and the big entrance sign to the church," he replied.

Exterior changes like this were important in attracting people who didn't know where the church was. Changes to the interior of the church, however, did not go as smoothly. In Okeechobee, the design of the altar area predated the Second Vatican Council. Altar rails were no longer necessary, since people could receive communion standing rather than kneeling. Moreover, statues around the altar prevented the overflow, seasonal congregation in the hall from viewing the Mass.

I consulted with the architect, Andrew Mixon, who designed the chapel, before making any changes to the interior. He was very helpful and apprised me of the different aspects of the church's structural design.

The day after meeting with Andrew I was having breakfast with Jimmy Winnie at the Boulevard Restaurant in town. Andrew and another man took a seat next to us, unaware of our presence. I was not wearing my clerical collar, which was probably why Andrew didn't recognize me.

The two men struck up a conversation.

"What'd the new priest have t'say?" began Andy's friend.

"Oh, he was askin' how the new changes might fit the structure of the hall next t'the church," Andy drawled.

Jimmy and I could hear everything and we began to snicker. It was too late to do anything about it without embarrassing Andy, so we just listened.

"What sorta changes was he on about?" the other man inquired.

"He was ponderin' if it was possible to yank out the pillar in the hall next door," said Andy. "But I said it wouldn't work, seein' as it's holdin' the roof up."

"And he took to that alright?" the man pressed.

"Yep, he did indeed," Andy agreed.

"What else did he get to saying?"

"He brung up 'bout them altar rails not bein' needed no more accordin' t'some church Council."

"What's that?" the friend asked. "An old Baptist like me ain't got no clue about such things."

"Nor did I, not till then," Andy admitted. "The council happened back in the early sixties, shakin' things up, but Okeechobee never caught up."

"And y'alls okay with these changes?" the man questioned.

"Sure," said Andy. "Makes it a heap easier, 'specially for us old timers like me, t'receive Communion standin' up."

We were finishing breakfast at this point and were getting ready to leave. Jimmy went over to shake hands with his friend, Andy.

When Andy saw me, I shook his hand, saying: "A real pleasure meeting you again."

Then I shook hands with his Baptist companion. Okeechobee was a small town and news traveled fast. I was happy that Andy relayed our conversation accurately to his friend in the restaurant.

We implemented several changes to the sanctuary, but there was push-back.

Frances, the resolute owner of the local Piggly-Wiggly franchise, bore the weight of decades of tradition in her sharp eyes. When I moved the statues, I didn't just rearrange objects; I disturbed something deep within

Frances. Her gaze, usually soft with the familiarity of routine, became a fortress guarding a history of devotion she was unwilling to relinquish. In her stiff posture, I saw more than displeasure—I saw a woman whose identity had intertwined with the unwavering traditions of her faith.

Despite the best efforts of the Women's Club to assuage her feelings during their market trips, she remained steadfast in her opposition to the changes. They asked me to talk to her. I was grateful for their solicitude.

I called Frances on the phone.

"I don't like where you stuck Mary," said Frances.

I tried to explain the reason for placing the statue of Mary at the entrance of the church, but I couldn't soothe her unsettled disposition.

A short time later, I was greeting people entering church for the Saturday evening Mass, and Frances was among them.

"How are you, Frances?" I asked.

"You're not interested in how I feel," Frances replied.

"Frances, we may differ on aspects of the liturgy, but we cannot differ when it comes to Jesus's message to love one another as he loved us," I pleaded. "Surely, we can love each other despite our differences."

Frances looked at me with a distraught face, saying nothing.

After Mass was over, she came up to me with an entirely different attitude.

"It is a custom in my family to receive a blessing from the priest before going on vacation," she said. "Can I have your blessing?"

I was thrilled to be asked, and gladly gave Frances a blessing.

Upon Frances's return from holiday, I was heartened to see her seated in the hall looking very relaxed and smiling. This marked a stark departure from her former rigid demeanor. She would never sit in the hall before, nor would she dare smile in church, especially at me. A profound change had come over her. From that point forward, we became the dearest of friends. In that spirit of newfound kinship, she divulged a secret that helped me understand her resistance to change.

"When I was a little girl, about thirteen years of age, the Blessed Mother appeared to me," she said. "She looked just like the statute in the church," she explained. "Have you not noticed that whenever I enter the church, the first thing I do is light a candle to the Blessed Mother?"

"I sure do, Frances. I couldn't help noticing that," I replied. "You are very devoted to the Blessed Mother."

Frances had forgotten her resistance to relocating the statue by this time, since she had moved beyond that. But I understood, for the first time, why she was so upset over the moving of the statue. I had moved the embodiment of her vision—the statue—from its venerable space at the altar.

That was something she found very hard to stomach. But with time, however, and a little love and understanding, she came around.

No priest is ever prepared for the reactions of parishioners like Frances. There are no courses in the seminary to prepare you for the likes of this. People have all kinds of feelings, resentments, and imaginings that we cannot possibly fathom. My good friend, Frances, was only one example.

One man thought the church in Okeechobee was exactly like the church he grew up with in Ohio. He loved the old Sacred Heart because it reminded him of his church at home, one that didn't change with the times. The changes to the church in Okeechobee upset him to no end, and he went with a few others to complain to the bishop. He was deeply disappointed when he was told he might just be too old to change.

Another lady invited me to a rodeo, the biggest annual event in Okeechobee. She told me her daughter's boyfriend was competing in it, and he wanted to donate the prize money, should he win, to the church. I went with her to the rodeo and got a big kick out of it when the young man won the prize money. We celebrated with a dinner at Okeechobee's Brahma Bull Restaurant and Lounge. Then the lady explained the real reason behind this magnanimous gesture.

"I was part of the group that went to the bishop to complain about the changes in the church," she said. "But when push came to shove, I couldn't join the others."

"What changed your mind?" I probed gently.

"What changed my mind," she explained, "was the fact that you didn't do anything wrong."

"I appreciate that," I replied.

"Of course," she added, "I'm not telling you anything you don't already know."

In fact, I knew nothing about her involvement in this little conspiracy. But I was glad she was able to get this troubling matter off her chest.

Her next words floored me.

"I discussed it with my psychiatrist," she said, "who helped me see that I was projecting anger and authority issues I had with my mother onto you."

I offered silent thanks for the psychiatrist's probing analysis which paved the way for healing and reconciliation.

As I grappled with the resistance to change, a sobering realization dawned on me. The church, in its haste to embrace Vatican II reforms, had neglected its greatest responsibility—its people. The church had pushed forward, expecting members of congregations to follow blindly, but left them grappling with expressions of faith that suddenly felt unfamiliar. How could we expect them to embrace change when we hadn't taken the time to explain, to reassure, to connect the dots between tradition and change? How could we, as shepherds, expect them to find their way when we had failed to illuminate the path? This oversight weighed on me, a reminder of the delicate balance between tradition and change.

Catholics today are still divided over the Latin Mass. Yet I discovered, when parishioners understood how the Council and its reforms actually enriched their spiritual lives, they welcomed the news with open hearts.

Beyond redesigning the sanctuary, we faced other pressing needs. We had no facilities for the religious instruction of the youth, and few youngsters darkened the church's doors. But once we launched Okeechobee's inaugural soccer club, the youngsters flocked as they had in Lakeland. Our league swiftly grew to nine teams, drawing many youngsters. Dowling Watford, a Methodist city commissioner, eagerly assisted this ecumenical effort benefitting all Okeechobee youth.

Soon our swelling ranks of youth highlighted the necessity of proper religious education facilities. Toward that end, we began a campaign to erect our first Catechetical Center, the largest construction project since the church itself in the 1960s. My worthy predecessor, Father Sloane, left the parish a reserve fund of $60,000 which served as seed money for constructing the center.

Some parishioners were not in favor of making pledges to the new project and preferred to give what they could afford to a second collection every month. One kind lady, Eileen Kalie, expressing the views of most, approached me.

"Father," Eileen began, "we want to help with the new center, really, we do."

She hesitated, eyes cast down.

"But making a pledge . . . It's like wearing a heavy chain. What if something happens, and we can't keep it? The guilt . . . it would eat us alive."

Her words revealed the silent struggle between her desire to contribute and the weight of responsibility that pledging carried.

There was no arguing with the sincerity of what she said, and I took her suggestion to heart.

"That's perfectly fine," I said. "We can take up a monthly collection, and the parishioners can give whatever they can afford. If it's God's will, we will be successful in raising another hundred thousand dollars to build the education center."

I put Eileen, who had a background in accounting, in charge of keeping records of all the monthly collections.

The next step was to seek approval for the project. We met with the Building Committee at the Diocesan Pastoral Center in North Palm Beach.

Jerry Jenkins, an engineer, and Jack Hofer, an architect, both residents of Okeechobee, offered their services free of charge, and attended the meeting with me.

Our request to build the center was met with general skepticism and condescending smiles when we arrived at the diocesan center.

"How do you expect to pay for this when you have a debt of sixty thousand dollars?" asked the chairman of the committee.

"We don't have any debt," I replied.

"This form you filled out states you are carrying a debt of sixty thousand dollars," said the chairman.

"May I see the form?" I asked.

"It reads 'Deposit' on this form, so we entered sixty thousand dollars," I pointed out. "What's the problem?" I asked.

We naturally understood Deposit to mean the amount of money we already had deposited in the bank.

"Oh, that's a typo," the embarrassed chairman hastened to say. "It should have said: 'Debt.'"

After the committee realized the mistake on the form, the condescending smiles morphed into smiles of approval. We got permission to proceed. The project was completed debt-free, with $250 left over. Eileen Kalie did a detailed job keeping the financial records. The new center was dedicated by the new bishop in 1986.

On the day of the dedication, as clergy gathered for a celebratory dinner prior to the ceremony, an unexpected knock came to the rectory door. I answered, expecting a tardy guest, but found a man requesting use of the telephone instead. Obliging him, I directed him to the phone.

I could hear him on the phone offering to sell the contents of his truck, meant for our education center, in exchange for narcotics. After he left, I told my guests what I just heard the man say on the phone. Everybody was amazed. But soon the phone rang again, and this time it was the dealer himself on the line. He was sobbing.

"Father, I'm not a good person," he cried, "but I'll not rob the church."

He vowed to return the stolen goods immediately. I thanked him for his sense of remorse. Before the dedication ceremony every item was restored to its rightful place.

Okeechobee was an out-of-the-way place, the people were decent country folk who lived there because they liked a peaceful environment where fishing was good, and the cost of living relatively low. Parishioners were down-to-earth, outgoing, and easy to get along with. Many were old Catholics with a long and faithful history of service to their church community. To me, this was an idyllic parish.

But shortly after I arrived at Sacred Heart, I experienced another shock. A lady came to see me, saying: "Okeechobee is about to see the biggest drug bust in the country."

"How do you know that?" I asked.

"My husband is an undercover FBI agent," she explained, "and as a disguise, he plays with a rock band in different joints around the county."

"Why are you telling me this," I asked, feeling very uneasy.

"I attend this church without my husband, and I wanted you to know what's going on," she replied. "I didn't want you to get the wrong impression."

I was grateful to know what was going on, but disappointed to learn that Okeechobee was not the simple, country place I thought it was. What the lady told me was true. A short time later, news stories broke about the big drug bust in Okeechobee. One newspaper article announced that Okeechobee, hitherto viewed as a tranquil country retreat, had "lost its innocence." It was a sad story and, unfortunately, one with consequences for the parish as well.

At the diocesan level, clergy were abuzz with excitement, belonging to a new diocese. A spirit of optimism and new beginnings took hold as we embarked on this journey alongside the first bishop of the Diocese of Palm Beach, fresh from the archdiocese of Boston. Okeechobee had originally fallen under Orlando's domain when I was first assigned there, but now it had transitioned into the new diocese of Palm Beach.

Eager to aid our fledgling diocese, I penned the bishop a letter offering help. Given my literary background, I offered my skills should he have need of them. Not hearing back from him, I rested easy, content he was sufficiently served.

He visited the parish shortly afterwards. He was in a buoyant mood.

In an enthusiastic tone of voice, he said, "I received your letter."

"I wrote to you in case you might need help," I said, "but if you have what you need, that's great."

"I could use your help," he replied.

I was glad that I might be of some help to the first bishop of the fledgling Diocese of Palm Beach.

He spoke to me about his special relationship with Cardinal Medeiros in Boston, to whom he stressed: "I owe everything."

I was surprised to hear him make this confession. It appeared to me that he might have attributed this honor to Christ who called us to imitate Him. But he was talking in terms of career, I realized, not the following of Christ.

The conversation then took a strange and disturbing turn.

"Are you afraid of me?" he asked.

What a question! I thought.

"Of course not," I replied. "Why would I be afraid of you? Aren't we following the same Lord?"

But that's not what he had in mind as I soon discovered.

"We need to be careful about priests," he said, "surprising me by this remark."

My guard went up. I didn't like being drawn into a conspiracy against fellow priests, especially when he said, "we." I had thought he held his priests in high regard. That was the impression he gave whenever he spoke to us in public.

"The laity are no problem because they don't know," he continued. "Priests are different. They can cause us trouble."

I had no problem with fellow priests, and spoke freely: "Aren't we all, bishops and priests, in the same business, the business of following Christ? What's wrong with that?"

He didn't answer, but gave a censorious glance, ending the conversation.

I never heard from him again after that, except to receive from him some written material that needed refining. I had no stomach for church politics. The concerns of the parish were my business.

* * *

There were hundreds, if not thousands, of Mexican farmworkers living and working in Okeechobee County. But few ever came to church, and those who did attended Masses in English. The rest just didn't come.

A young Mexican, Jesus Torres, turned up one day at the door. A crew leader who arranged transportation and work for Mexicans who picked oranges, he spoke good English. Jesus knew the lay of the land and offered to work with me to serve the Mexican community. He was the right man in the right place at the right time.

We discussed the Mexican situation at length, and decided if the Mexicans wouldn't come to church, we'd bring the church to the Mexicans.

We contacted all the camp owners around the county and sought their permission to bring Masses to the camps every Saturday evening at 8 p.m. The owners, to our surprise, were overjoyed and pitched in to help us.

As the sun dipped below the horizon, painting the sky in hues of orange and purple, our old truck rumbled into the camps. The air was dense with the scent of citrus and soil, mingling with the faint hum of distant crickets. We unloaded chairs that creaked under the weight of weary bodies, and set up a simple wooden table that would serve as our altar. The flickering flames of candles danced in the gentle evening breeze, casting shadows across faces etched with the day's labor. Above us, the stars pierced the night sky, and the low strum of a guitar blended with the gentle singing of hymns, weaving a sacred connection between God above and these humble people.

In the open fields we offered confessions, catechism classes and performed baptisms. We also informed the people that a Spanish Mass would be offered every Sunday in church at 12 noon and encouraged them to attend.

The people came to the Sunday Mass, and as they got used to coming, the congregation swelled. With the addition of a Spanish Mass on Sunday, I needed the help of another priest. Father John Morley had just retired from St. Richard's parish in Philadelphia, and he offered to assist me. We converted the old car garage that was part of the rectory into guest quarters for Father John, and built a new car port at the back of the rectory.

The Mexicans were in the habit of coming to church 15 minutes late, so we pushed the time forward to 12:15 p.m. As they arrived late again, we pushed the time again forward to 12:30 p.m. We finally set the time for the Mass in Spanish at 12:30 p.m. and not a minute later, whether they came late or not.

It was like an epiphany when the Mexican families filled not only the church, but the entire hall during the 12:30 p.m. Mass. As the Hispanic congregation grew, the need for religious instruction (catechism classes) for the children of migrants became urgent. Thanks to the public school system, the children of Mexican immigrants were taught English, and served as interpreters for their parents in stores, in the hospital, at the flea market—wherever they were needed.

Our new education center was built not a moment too soon, and was well positioned to embrace the influx of Mexican youth. Attendance in religious instruction swelled accordingly. The diocese hosted a teacher seminar, assessing fees based on enrollment. Ours being the largest enrollment in the diocese, we faced steep charges. I appealed to the director, an understanding man, noting the injustice of penalizing us by demanding fees since our own classes were tuition-free. Seeing the wisdom in this, the director created a scholarship to cover the diocesan training seminar.

Soon after, the need arose for a bus as parents worked on Sundays. Providence smiled when actor Paul Newman gifted a new bus for the migrant children in nearby Indiantown. Their pastor then passed his old bus on to us. Now with our own bus, volunteer drivers shepherded the children to and from catechism classes.

One morning after Mass, a Mexican woman approached me with her two children. She was accompanied by Refugio Luna, who had replaced

Jesus Torres as my helper when Jesus returned to Mexico. She was very nervous; even Refugio was nervous. Her two children seemed embarrassed and kept squirming, as they approached.

"I was doing the laundry in the morning and had a pile of clothes to fold before the children left for school," she said, "when I heard this sweet music enter the house from outside."

"Did you go outside to see what was going on?" I asked, gently.

"Yes, I did, and I saw this beautiful lady," she explained. "The children were with me and were frightened when they saw the lady."

I looked at the children and they turned away. They were scared. I did not ask them any questions.

"And then what happened?" I inquired.

"The lady asked me to tell the priest to do for the parents what he's doing for the children," she replied.

"Was that everything?" I probed.

"No," added the woman. "The lady vanished, and the clothes in a pile were all neatly folded when we went back to the house."

I looked at the two children, too shy to say anything. Strange encounters like this were not infrequent among Mexicans.

The message conveyed was a good one, but what to do about it was another matter.

After his return from Mexico, Jesus Torres approached me and asked: "Can we form an adult soccer league like the soccer league for the youngsters?"

I agreed.

This idea took off like a kite in a summer breeze. Groups from parts of Mexico I had never heard of formed their own teams. Thus, an Adult Soccer League was born.

Life in the parish was an endless succession of surprises. One Saturday morning brought an unexpected visitor to my door. A lanky stranger introduced himself as Colman McCarthy, a writer for the *Washington Post*. He was penning a piece on Okeechobee's immigrants and had been directed my way.

I welcomed him inside. I found him very engaging, with impressive credentials in human rights journalism. Once seated, I inquired who exactly had referred me.

"The immigrant families I've visited," he replied. "They say you're the one who helps them."

"What can I do for you?" I asked.

Part 2—Chapter 19

Colman didn't speak Spanish, so he wondered if I would drive through different immigrant neighborhoods with him and translate discussions about living conditions. I agreed to accompany him.

Colman's article caused quite a stir upon publication, and to good effect. Soon the city zoning director approached, requesting I guide him through the immigrant neighborhoods to identify improvement areas. Additionally, two representatives from the Department of Housing and Urban Development arrived at the rectory with word of over a hundred houses, newly available for needy families. The Mexican immigrants, valued for filling labor needs on dairies and ranches countywide, took advantage of this housing opportunity.

At this time, the bishop announced he'd be visiting Ireland, and would like to visit the parents of priests serving in the diocese. He wanted the addresses of all the Irish priests serving over here.

What a sensitive gesture, I thought, maybe the bishop loves his priests after all.

I sent his secretary the address of my parents and called to tell them to expect a visit from my bishop in Florida. They were delighted. But when I spoke to some of the Irish priests in the diocese about this magnanimous gesture, they were not as enthusiastic as I was. In fact, they were downright suspicious of the bishop's motives. I was eagerly looking forward to hearing about the bishop's visit with my family when I would be home on vacation later that summer.

Sitting in the kitchen of my home in Letterkenny during my vacation I asked my parents: "How did you find the bishop's visit?"

"He drank several cups of tea," my mother said, "using the same tea bag several times."

A humble prelate.

My father sat kitty-corner by the kitchen window overlooking the green pasture outside, quietly laughing to himself while drumming his fingers on the window sill. He had nothing to say.

Just then Uncle Peter, who lived next door, walked in.

"Was that American who visited your parents really a priest?" He asked, incredulously.

I gathered that the bishop had made quite an impression on Uncle Peter.

"Of course, he's a priest. He's my bishop in Florida," I retorted.

"He was the most ignorant man I ever met," said Peter bluntly.

My father, seated by the window, rollicked with laughter.

Peter was a man who didn't mince words.

I asked my uncle to elaborate.

"I was fixing the window in my upstairs bedroom when I saw this priest wandering about outside like he was lost," Peter recalled. "Leaning out the window, I said to him, 'I'll be right down, Father.' He looked like he needed help, and I opened the door."

"'I'm Hughie's bishop,' were the first words out of his mouth," said Peter.

The bishop mistakenly thought Peter was my father and was trying to impress him with the lordly announcement.

"Hughie's in school," replied Peter. "You don't look like the bishop."

Peter was talking about my nephew, Hughie, and as far as he knew, this priest bore no resemblance to the bishop who lived in Letterkenny.

"I'm Hughie's bishop in Florida," the bishop countered.

Peter, put off by this superior attitude, said: "Oh, it's Father Hugh you're talking about. I'm only the uncle, but if it's his parents you're looking for, they live next door."

With that, Peter closed the door on the Bishop of Palm Beach.

When I got back to Florida after my summer vacation and met the bishop at a deanery meeting, he could not stop talking about my Uncle Peter. Clearly, he was obsessed with Peter, never mentioning his visit with my parents. Peter had exposed something about his character, and it didn't sit well with him.

Great news for immigrant farmworkers in Okeechobee arrived with the passing of a new law allowing them to be legally documented.[1] This required proof that an immigrant worked as a farmworker ninety days out of the year. The Immigration and Naturalization Service (INS) opened an office in Okeechobee to process the immigrants' documents. I was asked to bless the INS building on opening day. This was a watershed moment for immigrants, and a time of real hope for them.

At Sacred Heart we opened an office for Immigration Assistance to help immigrants fill out their paperwork, getting past difficulties with language and documents. Our assistance was offered free of charge. We were a QDE (Qualified Designated Entity) because of the trust that existed between the church and the immigrant families. We were kept very busy with this program, which helped document thousands of families in the parish and surrounding areas.

The new immigration law offered Mexican families new hope and new opportunities in America. It would change their lives forever.

---

1. In 1986 Congress agreed to allow immigrants in the country illegally to get legal status—with a special provision focusing on farmworkers.

Part 2—Chapter 19

But for me, it presented my greatest challenge since arriving in Okeechobee.

Chapter 20

BEING NOTICED CAN BE a good thing, but it can also attract the wrong kind of attention. The parish in Okeechobee was a country parish far away from Diocesan bureaucracy. That's the way I liked it.

The column by Colman McCarthy in the *Washington Post* about our outreach to immigrants, and an article in the *National Catholic Reporter* describing the parish as *a shining buckle in America's Bible Belt*, attracted national attention at the time. The parish in Okeechobee couldn't hide any more.

One beautiful day in June, when the air was still fresh, and all about were the pungent scents of new life, a mysterious visitor stopped by the rectory. As I opened the door, sunlight streamed through the entrance, casting golden rays across the floor. Framed in the doorway stood a small figure, his presence as unexpected as a sudden Florida thunderstorm.

"I've heard of the great work you're doing to help immigrants," said the little man at the door. He had a smile that switched on and off like a lightbulb. I invited him inside. Seated comfortably on the sofa, he continued: "I'm an immigrant too and I'd like to help you."

"Where are you from?" I asked him.

"From Nicaragua," he replied.

"And how would you like to help?"

"I could help by offering Masses in Spanish for you," he beamed.

"Oh, so you're a priest," I exclaimed, pleasantly surprised.

"I'm a bishop in exile from my own country, sadly," he replied.

Bishop Pablo Antonio Vega was indeed a bishop from Nicaragua. He had been the president of the Nicaraguan Conference of Catholic Bishops, and General Secretary of the prestigious Latin American Episcopal Council, CELAM.[1] He was exiled by the Sandinista government in Nicaragua for

---

1. Based in Bogotá (Colombia), the Latin American Episcopal Council, better known as CELAM, is a council of the Roman Catholic bishops of Latin America, founded in 1955.

his support of the Contras, a right-wing pro-Somoza faction that garnered a lot of attention during the Reagan Administration in the arms-for-hostages debacle.

Daniel Ortega, leader of the Sandinistas, conferred upon Bishop Vega the title of Generalissimo of the Contras and had him air-lifted by helicopter and dropped off in Honduras. From there he made his way to Rome to meet with the Pope, and then to Miami where he was staying in the Archdiocesan Seminary, and finally to Okeechobee.

When he arrived at my door, I took the little bishop at face value, knowing nothing of his background.

As Bishop Vega spoke, his eyes flickered with a complex mix of emotions. Each word seemed carefully chosen, as if he were still addressing a council of clergy rather than a regular parish priest. His small stature belied the weight of his past roles, and I sensed that here was a man struggling to reconcile his former glory with his current exile.

He appeared to be a kindly man. My assistant, Father John Morley, was on vacation in Philadelphia. I could use the help for sure, so I offered Bishop Vega the use of Father Morley's apartment in his absence. He was grateful for the kindness shown to him.

I notified the diocese, as was the custom, about Bishop Vega's offer of help and got diocesan *faculties for him*; namely, permission for him to help me in Okeechobee.

No sooner did Bishop Vega begin to celebrate the Mass in Spanish than the Mexicans began to attend the Masses in English. This was an inexplicable turnaround, disappointing after all the effort we put into providing the Mass in Spanish for the Mexican immigrants.

I found the reaction of the Mexicans to Bishop Vega baffling. *What's going on?* I wondered. And, why would the Mexicans attend the Masses in English when they had their own Mass in Spanish, and didn't understand English very well?

The adult soccer tournament was in full swing at the time, and various teams competed every Sunday afternoon on the soccer field at the church. I always attended the games, if I could, as an enthusiastic spectator.

During the half-time period, I spoke with the group of soccer players.

"Why are you attending the English Masses when you have your own Mass in Spanish?" I asked.

The Mexicans squatting on the grassy field began to laugh among themselves.

One parishioner, Gilbert Navarro, speaking for the bunch, said: "This is the United States, and this bishop doesn't seem to understand that."

Another interjected: "We don't like this bishop's sociopolitical sermons."

Fernando Rodriguez then spoke up: "We know he had a bad experience in Nicaragua, but Nicaragua is not America. We are content here with the way things are and with the opportunities we have."

After listening to the Mexicans, I was left with no choice—I had to take over the Spanish Mass myself, asking Bishop Vega to celebrate one of the English Masses to lessen my load.

As the word got around, the Mexicans returned to their scheduled Mass in Spanish.

We had a meeting of the parish finance council in the rectory one evening, and as a courtesy, I asked the bishop if he would like to meet the members. I thought he might like to express his appreciation to the council for the kindness shown to him in Okeechobee. He said he would like to attend the meeting.

But when he didn't show up, I went to retrieve him from his room. I was in shock. He was wearing his full, Episcopal regalia: red flowing cape and matching waistband, red skullcap, and a ruby ring—which I had never seen before—perched on his ring finger. Gone was the on-and-off smile. With a solemn expression, he was waiting for me to escort him into the meeting.

The members of the finance council looked surprised when they saw him dressed in what looked to them like a Halloween outfit. They greeted him warmly, nonetheless.

Taking a seat apart from the rest of us, he demanded: "I want you to build me a house on the parish grounds for a Nicaraguan colony."

We were all stunned upon hearing this. Here was a man who was invited to attend our parish finance council meeting as a guest, and he was telling us what to do.

"Why would we do that?" asked Bill Gernat.

"I have no *confiance* [meaning confidence] in the Mexicans," he replied.

"Is he saying the Mexicans aren't as smart as the Nicaraguans?" one of the council members asked.

Everyone laughed.

The exiled bishop continued: "I've invited Nicaraguan friends from Miami to come here next weekend to see for themselves what we need to do."

Our guest had asked me, prior to this, if he could invite his Nicaraguan friends to Okeechobee for the weekend, and if I could find a place for them to stay. I spoke about this with Vinny La Mariana, President of the Finance

Council, and he graciously offered to put them up in mobile homes on his ranch. Neither Vinny nor I had any idea the bishop was planning to establish a Nicaraguan colony in the parish.

Members of the finance council simply ignored the bishop's colony request. It wasn't part of the council's agenda. He was disappointed and sat apart, all through the meeting, eyeing the proceedings disapprovingly.

The following weekend, the Nicaraguans from Miami arrived, consisting of exiled Contras, including the sister and other relatives of the dictator, Somoza. They stayed in the mobile homes on Vinny's ranch. Vinny had stocked the refrigerators with food for them.

When it came time for breakfast, however, they came knocking on Vinny's door— demanding to be served.

"We always had servants to serve our breakfast in Nicaragua," they insisted.

Vinny had had enough.

"You have everything you need," he said, sternly. "Serve yourselves."

During this time, a friend invited me to spend a few days with him and his family in the Dominican Republic. I needed a break, but the timing was not the best. I needed to watch my back now, and that posed a problem if I was going to be out of the country.

Bishop Vega agreed to take the morning English Masses in my absence. But the night before my departure, I noticed a change in his manner, talking down to me as if he were laying down the law to one of his subjects. He had never behaved like this before. I sensed something was afoot, but I didn't know what.

The following morning just prior to my departure, I went over to the office to speak to my secretary, Dorothy.

"You know what Jesus says," I explained. "Do as they say, but don't do as they do."

Dorothy understood.

"When I'm away," I continued, "treat Bishop Vega respectfully, but keep any evidence for me about his plans until I get back."

Just then, Vinny arrived at the office and filled us in on the bizarre behavior of the Nicaraguan Contras on his ranch over the weekend. We now realized this little bishop was very serious about establishing a Nicaraguan colony in Okeechobee at the expense of the parish.

We also feared that he had help from the diocesan bishop.

Our fears were soon confirmed. After I had left the church's grounds to fly to the Dominican Republic, the diocesan bishop drove into the church parking lot to confer privately with Bishop Vega in the rectory. Vinny was leaving the parish grounds when the bishop of the diocese was pulling in.

He promptly called Dorothy on his mobile phone to let her know that the diocesan bishop had just arrived.

As the wheels of my plane left the ground, I imagined that the tranquility at Sacred Heart wouldn't last long. Secrets, like shadows, were gathering under the rectory roof when I was away.

When I got back from the Dominican Republic, Dorothy met me at the airport in West Palm Beach. She gave me a file containing a letter from Bishop Vega to the members of the parish finance council, which she never sent. I read it on the drive to Okeechobee.

"Bring this letter to me in the morning when I'm having breakfast with Bishop Vega," I instructed Dorothy.

The following morning, Dorothy dutifully walked into the rectory at breakfast time and handed me the file. I opened it in the bishop's presence.

"What's this, Bishop Vega?" I asked. "You're ordering the members of the finance council to build a house and Nicaraguan center for you on parish property."

Unable to contain his uneasiness, the bishop rose from the seat to leave the dining room.

"No, stay there," I pleaded. "This is a very serious matter."

"I was only suggesting," he said, sitting down again.

"These are not suggestions. These are demands," I countered. "You're pulling rank when it doesn't apply, and you've been trying to impose these demands on the finance council without my knowledge while I was away. You are a guest here and have been treated very generously, but I'm afraid you have mistaken kindness for weakness."

Bishop Vega's face flushed, his carefully cultivated calm cracking.

"I'm not a guest," he fumed, rising from his chair. His eyes, usually warm with practiced charm, now blazed with indignation.

"I'll talk to the bishop," he declared, his voice quivering with barely contained rage.

I met his gaze steadily, keeping my voice low and even.

"Bishop Vega, let's not pretend. You've already spoken with the diocesan bishop, haven't you?"

His mouth opened, then closed, like a fish out of water. In that moment of stunned silence, I saw the mask slip, revealing the calculating man beneath the pious exterior.

I added: "Didn't my housekeeper serve both of you coffee in this dining room the day I left? Do you deny that?"

Bishop Vega had no response.

As the realization dawned that I was caught in a web of episcopal intrigue, I knew I had to watch my step. Here I was, a simple parish priest,

Part 2—Chapter 20

suddenly thrust into a game of ecclesiastical chess with two skilled players. I was shocked that men who had sworn to shepherd God's flock were now engaged in political maneuvering that would make Machiavelli proud. How could I navigate this minefield without compromising my calling and the wellbeing of the parish?

The only way out of this mess was to stop it from festering. But I was dealing with two bishops, and had to be very careful. Thus, I dealt with the matter in the best Christian manner.

"Let's handle this like Christians," Bishop Vega, I continued. "And let's part as friends. What you've done is wrong, and I'm prepared to put it behind me."

He softened when I said this, and I was glad for this attitude. I thanked him for helping me by offering Masses during the time he was here. I wished him the best in Washington, where he had planned to meet with members of a Nicaraguan organization called the National Opposition Union (UNO).

"We will do everything on our part to help you move your belongings," I said.

Bishop Vega had nothing to say in response, and he left the parish quietly. I informed the diocesan bishop by letter of his departure. At the end of the summer, Father John Morley returned to the parish to assist for the season.

I'll never fully know what the two bishops were concocting among themselves, because it was all done in the utmost secrecy. All I know is that their behavior had nothing to do with the wellbeing of the parish. It had everything to do with church politics.

The diocesan bishop didn't respond to my letter in the usual timely manner. He let time lapse until the Nuncio in Washington got involved. Only then, six weeks later, did he respond to my letter, acknowledging that I had taken appropriate action.

The man responsible for maintenance in the parish was Roy Padgett, and he happened to be from Nicaragua. He was well acquainted with Bishop Vega and his activities in Nicaragua when he lived there. Roy told me that Bishop Vega didn't return to his diocese in Nicaragua, but returned to Honduras, where Daniel Ortega, the president of Nicaragua, originally exiled him. He joined a junta and ran for the office of president there, according to Roy, receiving just two percent of the vote.

Shortly after the Nicaraguan bishop's departure, we held confirmation for the youngsters in the parish. This was always an enjoyable time for the parish, the priests and bishop of the diocese. We had dinner for the priests and bishop in the rectory.

Just as dinner ended, the doorbell rang. Standing on the threshold was Vinny La Mariana, smiling cheerfully, as usual.

"I'm busy right now with confirmation dinner Vinny," I said. "This is not a good time to talk."

"I have a meeting with the bishop," Vinny relied.

This was indeed a surprise. Vinny never told me anything about this meeting.

I told the bishop that Vinny was here to see him and showed them both to the guest room to conduct their meeting.

After a while, Vinny emerged from the meeting and asked me to join them.

"The bishop is making an accusation," Vinny said when I entered the room. "He says that altar boys were playing strip poker during a parish picnic."

"What's strip poker?" I asked. "I know what regular poker is, but I've never heard of strip poker."

"The players play for their clothes instead of money," Vinny explained.

I knew youngsters did dumb things, but what amazed me was not what the kids were alleged to have done, but that the bishop would use this cockamamie story to discredit me in the eyes of the chairman of the finance council. Thankfully, Vinny did not fall for this ruse.

"Excuse me," I said, stepping out of the room to ask Father John Morley to join us.

"Father John," I said, "the bishop is accusing altar servers of playing strip poker. You were present at the altar servers' barbecue, weren't you?"

"I was indeed there," replied Father John, "and it was a wonderful event."

"Did you see any altar servers playing strip poker?" I asked.

Father John just laughed it off. Unlike me, he knew what strip poker was. It was obviously an American thing, and he ignored this silly insinuation by the bishop. He saw it as I did: a red herring, introduced by the bishop to discredit me.

"You should visit the parish more often, bishop," said Father John, "and see for yourself what marvelous things are being done for all parishioners, young and old."

The bishop fidgeted with a toothpick, stifling snarls as he realized he'd been ensnared in his own trap.

After Father Morley left the room, Vinny revealed the true reason for the bishop's attempted ambush: Cover-up of diocesan abuses in the immigration program.

Part 2—Chapter 20

As a developer, Vinny rented a property to the INS. He had presented evidence to the bishop of exorbitant fees charged by people in the employ of the diocese to desperate immigrants.

I had never expected to be part of this meeting but, since I was brought into it, I made it clear that our services were offered free of charge to all farmworkers. Yet the diocese, under the guise of legal services, was asking for sixty dollars per head for our service. We did not go along with this because we were not engaged in the business of law. We were helping immigrants fill out their paperwork as their trusted helpers.

The bishop withdrew into himself like a child caught with his hand in the cookie jar. He would not deal with the issue brought up by Vinny. This meeting made him feel very uneasy, so much so that it was the last time he visited the parish for confirmation, calling upon a retired archbishop, Thomas J. McDonough, to perform the confirmations the following year.

I later learned from Vinny that it was Father John who had advised him to meet with the bishop about these diocesan abuses in the immigration program. The bishop, however, seemed to think I was responsible for arranging it.

The matter of corruption in the immigration program did not go away. I was utterly taken aback when the bishop later announced to the clergy of the diocese that he was bringing a class action suit against the INS in Okeechobee. His surrogates contacted volunteers working in our parish office of immigration assistance, directing them to give false evidence that we were withholding over five hundred applications for fear of reprisals from the INS. Our volunteers would not go along with this disinformation as I made it perfectly clear to them that it would be wrong.

We never withheld any applications to the INS office in Okeechobee.

I later read in the *Palm Beach Post* the false allegation about Okeechobee withholding five hundred applications for fear of reprisals. I was very disturbed by this disinformation, and went to see the head of the INS in Okeechobee.

I told the director that I was prepared to tell the truth in court, if necessary, that we were *not* withholding any applications to the INS.

"I don't want to get you into trouble with the diocese," Father, he said. "That's a ruthless organization."

As a result of this lawsuit, the INS office in Okeechobee was closed, to the detriment of Mexican farmworkers. We continued to offer our assistance at the parish's office by filling out paperwork, free of charge. At great inconvenience, these farmworkers now had to travel for appointments all the way to the INS office in Miami.

Every year, the diocese celebrated the annual meeting of the diocesan Women's Convention. In 1989 it was another big affair; the women from the different parishes looked forward to it. I was happy, as were most priests of the diocese, to join the women from our parishes in celebrating their big event. No excitement can compare to that of a bunch of women, jittery with glee, gathered together for a good time. It was a special time for me to treat our dedicated women.

This annual meeting of the Women's Convention, however, was important for another reason.

A priest of the diocese was canvassing all the priests at the convention to write letters of recommendation to the bishop on his behalf. This kind of thing was unheard of. I asked the priest what brought this about.

Father John Cranberry (not his real name) had met with the bishop about serving as pastor in a Spanish-speaking parish since he was bilingual. The bishop, as related to me by Father John, didn't particularly like him and told him he had heard "negative vibes" about him.

"From the laity?" asked Father John.

"No, from the clergy," replied the bishop.

"The only clergy I can think of are the two I worked with in the seminary," explained Father John. "We differed in our theological perspectives."

Theological differences are quite normal among the clergy, especially after the changes following the Second Vatican Council. Indeed, theological differences are part of the church's intellectual life. Religious orders, such as the Dominicans and Franciscans, differ in their theological perspectives.

Father John pressed the bishop on the matter.

"How am I to rehabilitate my reputation in the diocese?" he asked.

"You'd need letters of recommendation from the clergy of the diocese," replied the bishop, categorically.

Father John left the office of the bishop crushed, not knowing what to do.

Suddenly, he was hit by a penetrating insight, he told me. He turned around and, walking into the bishop's office, pointed his finger at him, saying: "Bishop, you'll get your letters."

Letters of recommendation from the priests of the diocese poured into the bishop's office. The bishop scarcely knew what hit him. Blindsided, he decided to hold deanery meetings in the diocese to discuss the morale problem of the clergy.

Meetings were held in the three deaneries of the diocese. At the meeting of the northern deanery to which I belonged, the priests were very frank, telling the bishop that *he* was the morale problem, not the priests.

Father John was at this meeting and spoke up, explaining to the assembled clergy what had happened.

"I don't know about the rest of you," responded the bishop, "but I'm very happy being the bishop of the Diocese of Palm Beach."

After the deanery meetings concluded, rumors circulated that the bishop was leaving the diocese willingly. The rumors were true. He was appointed bishop of another diocese.

Whenever a bishop leaves a diocese, the period during which the diocese is without a diocesan ordinary is called an *interregnum*.[2] This period, for me, was a time to breathe a long sigh of relief. I took full advantage of this opportunity to take a welcome break.

I decided to travel to Mexico to experience, first hand, what it was like for our Mexican immigrants in their own country.

---

2. An *interregnum* is a period when a diocese is without an Episcopal Ordinary, such as a bishop.

Chapter 21

In May of 1990, I found myself peering through a plane window as Mexico City stretched out beneath me, a sprawling, chaotic labyrinth. The afternoon sun bathed the endless sea of buildings with piercing rays of light, while snow-topped volcanoes stood silently in the distance, their majestic peaks brushing the sky. My heart quickened in rhythm with the city below, as I prepared to touch down into this lively world that had long called to me.

As the plane edged gently over this landscape, chills curled up my spine. With every second of the plane's advance, a vast panorama of houses kept unfolding. Some homes, mere shacks with corrugated tin roofs, crawled up the mountainsides while others kept appearing in greater numbers along the horizon.

Just when I thought there would be no end to this, the plane took an unexpected dive and the airport appeared as if out of nowhere, having been lost in an intricate camouflage of hills, houses and buildings.

I was heartily relieved when my feet touched the soil of Mexico.

The cab driver at the airport directed me to the Bureau of Exchange, where I exchanged American dollars for pesos. The peso was almost valueless, at that time 2,600 to the dollar. Trying to count this new money and calculate the rate of exchange was impossible. I had to take the cashier at her word, for there was no way to quickly verify the exchange rate of dollars into so many pesos, especially when the taxi driver was waiting patiently for me.

The taxi ride through Mexico City was full of surprises. There were little children everywhere selling periodicals, balloons and snacks. Women were busily frying, cooking and selling food on the street paths or in the doorways of their small homes. Whenever the taxi came to a stop, little hustlers rushed to the car window seeking a quick sale. They were not annoying, for even if you weren't interested in buying something, they still greeted you with a smile. These appeared to be hardworking people trying to make a living in a tough world. Wherever I traveled in Mexico, this impression was reinforced. The caricature of Mexicans as *mañana* people, unconcerned about making a living, was not borne out by any of my Mexico experiences.

I stayed at the Best Western on the Avenida Francisco Madero in the city's historic center. The first thing I did after securing my room was to go to bed and rest. I never wear a watch, nor do I carry an alarm clock with me when traveling. If I want to get up at a certain time, I simply ask the person at the desk to give me a buzz. When I awoke, I walked out into the city again. On almost every street corner there was a newsstand filled to capacity with popular picture magazines. Mexicans seemed to like to read little pocket magazines resembling comic books, except that the subject matter was more risqué.

Everywhere I went, people showed me courtesy, even when they were trying to sell me something. On the way back to the hotel a young go-getter asked me for money.

"Everybody wants money," I said in Spanish. "Do you agree with that?"

Displaying a broad smile, he nodded in agreement. Then I asked him, jokingly: "Do you have any money to spare for me?"

He gave me another big smile. I reached into my pocket and gave him some dollars for which he appreciatively exclaimed, *gracias*.

After walking as far as I could, I hailed a taxi and asked the driver to give me a tour of the city. He obliged and we drove around the highways and byways of Mexico City, but I couldn't take it all in. His fee was only a few dollars in American currency. (The value of the Mexican peso today has much improved.)

My eventual destination was the city of Dolores Hidalgo in the state of Guanajuato, where my friend, Jesus Torres, and his family lived. I was anxious to get there as soon as possible.

The trip to this historical town from Mexico City took me nearly five hours. My journey by bus, on the day after I arrived, went through most of the central region of Mexico, known as the lowlands. On the way, I reached the town of Guanajuato, after which the state is named. I got off the bus to see this beautiful town. The main streets are a network of tunnels stretching beneath the town's historical center, constructed in the sixteenth century from a riverbed.

The illuminated tunnel streets of Guanajuato revealed the magnificent stonework and engineering of the Spaniards who built this town centuries ago. The labyrinth of tunnels diverted the rivers flowing beneath the streets, protecting the homes above during the rainy season. Perched over this subterranean web, Guanajuato's seven splendid plazas provided gathering spaces where townspeople sang, played music, or simply sat and watched the world go by. As I approached the main plaza, resplendent with colorful hedges, mimosa trees and blossoms, a troupe of costumed Mariachis entertained the crowd. Students joined in song, loudly and melodiously filling the plaza air. Across from this lively scene stood the brilliantly constructed Teatro Juarez, a nineteenth century theatre that still today hosts concerts, plays and recitals.

With its large university population, Guanajuato was a town of students. That evening they paraded through the streets in costume, serenading onlookers as they passed by. I spent the night taking in the sights and sounds of this unique place before continuing my journey the next day. My final destination was the more modest town of Dolores Hildago, where my friend Jesus awaited my arrival.

Arriving in Dolores Hidalgo by bus, I settled into a room at the El Caudillo hotel situated along the town's central plaza. This modest community would serve as my home base during my time in Mexico. After unpacking, I visited the imposing Spanish colonial church that dominated the local landscape. Though late in the evening, the doors were open in welcome. It was within this sanctuary in 1810 that Father Miguel Hidalgo gathered the townspeople and rallied them to revolt against Spanish rule by ringing the church bell. He amassed a ragtag army of 50,000 and marched upon nearby Guanajuato, achieving independence for the city. Ultimately, Father Hidalgo sacrificed his life in service of his beloved Mexico, which won independence just a decade later. The church bell that rang out loudly to awake a nation resides today in Mexico City, a proud reminder of that fateful day, much as the Liberty Bell commemorates American independence in Philadelphia.

Inside the church, I found the pastor, instructing parishioners about baptism. I introduced myself during a break in his presentation and asked him if he knew Jesus Torres and where I could find him. Father Cerna did not know Jesus personally, but he directed me to where he lived when I mentioned the name of the ranch, Las Palmitas.

The next day, I took a taxi to El Rancho, Las Palmitas. As I approached Jesus's modest home, the yard filled with the warmth of family. His wife, her eyes bright with welcome, clasped my hand in a way that made me feel as if we had known each other for years. Nearby, his grandfather, his face softened by age but still radiant, watched from under the shade of a wide-brimmed hat, a quiet smile touching his lips. His grandmother and sisters, animated and full of life, greeted me like an old friend, their laughter filling the air as their children darted in and out of doorways. In their faces, I saw the same openness and strength that I had come to admire in Jesus, and I felt immediately at home.

"Welcome to the real Mexico, Padre," said Jesus in Spanish when we met.

He introduced me to all the members of his family and invited me to stay with them. I thanked him and said I was staying at El Caudillo hotel in Dolores.

"My family is saying you have the same curly hair as my favorite uncle," Jesus told me.

After hearing this, I knew I was one of the family.

I never really understood before what a Mexican meant when he said he lived on a *rancho*. A rancho to me conjured up a large, landed estate owned by a family or by one person with many hired hands working on the property such as you find in Okeechobee. In Mexico, *El rancho* signified a townland, populated by many families living near each other. These ranches had their own school, church (called *templo*) and convenience store. It wasn't unusual for the families to be related in these ranches.

As we walked through Las Palmitas Ranch, everybody Jesus introduced to me was either a relative or close friend. Each family tilled a small portion of the land and lived off the produce. When families got too large and there were more mouths to feed than food available, the young men had to emigrate to the U.S. in search of work. That is why so many of them ended up in places like Okeechobee, harvesting citrus during the picking season.

It was exhilarating to experience life as it was lived by these ordinary Mexicans on the ranch. These were an industrious people, tending to their livestock daily, tilling the soil, and selling their produce to the neighboring towns or cities. Jesus, along with his wife and children, showed me every part of the ranch, laughing and talking with everyone they met. Serving each other was not just a spiritual injunction: Love your neighbor as yourself, but a form of survival for these folks. They were not rich by the world's standards, but rich when it came to caring for each other. The equity they stored in the granaries of their souls was of the order of grace which valued acts of love and good deeds above everything else. This was a helping community, and I felt at home in it.

Jesus and family members drove me back to my hotel where I invited them to join me for dinner.

We took a leisurely walk through the park after dinner. It was a tranquil evening and the setting sun hovered gently over the park and its people, enveloping them in a purple glow. The music played, the children ran about gleefully, and the birds frolicked with them through the park. It was nature at its best, this communion of children and birds joined in play. At 9 p.m. the music stopped and the birds stopped chirping. Everything became quiet at the same time. A peaceful silence settled over everything and everybody. Nature and people became one and the same, whether brimming with energy or asleep at day's end.

I retired to my hotel. Jesus and his family drove back to Las Palmitas.

The next morning, I visited the museum in Delores dedicated to the life of Father Hidalgo. The town is now known as Dolores Hidalgo, after its famous priest-patriot. As you enter this little town, a striking sign reads: Dolores Hidalgo, the humble Bethlehem where Mexican independence was born.

The comparison with Bethlehem could hardly have been more appropriate. Everything about this town and its people breathed humility. Dolores Hidalgo seldom sees a tourist, and when tourists appear it is only because they are passing through. I was the only visitor at the museum. Everything was laid out and explained in great detail. I read several of the priest's displayed writings. Obviously, he was a man of letters as well as a man of the people.

Jesus arrived later to pick me up. We set out to visit the great monument dedicated to Christo Rey (Christ the King). We had a pact between us to converse only in Spanish because I wanted to brush up on the language. This monument, Jesus explained, is the spiritual heart of Mexico and rivals the Shrine of the Virgin of Guadalupe. I had never heard of it before. It is a wonder how the Mexican people could erect such a monument atop the highest mountain in the heart and center of Mexico. Although we could see the monument from afar early on in our journey, the drive up the hill seemed interminable as we zig-zagged back and forth without seeming to get anywhere.

"This is nothing compared to what the people have to do on foot to get up to the top of the mountain," said Jesus.

Time has a different value for Mexicans. They don't worry about it. It's a common sight to see houses not yet completed, but that doesn't mean they won't be finished. I observed men arriving in the afternoon to work on a house, do a little bit of work and then take off again. They were working, but they were taking their time. I learned to accept this mentality while in Mexico. Mexicans are a hardworking people but are not obsessed with work itself.

After many twists and turns, we arrived at the top of the mountain where Christ the King looks out over Mexico. The huge bronze statue rises far above the gaze of any mere mortal. At the feet of the statue two crowns are held by angels; a regal crown on one side and a crown of thorns on the other, representing Christ as King and Christ as suffering servant.

Part 2—Chapter 21

On the way down the mountain, Jesus began to have problems with the car.

"The brakes are not working," he exclaimed fretfully. "What will we do, Padre?"

"You're asking me?" I gulped. "Keep driving as best you can, Jesus. We're now in God's hands. He brought us up here and will bring us back down again."

By some miraculous intervention, the car continued down the hill, twisting and turning and avoiding crashes at every twist of the road. It kept gaining speed and there was no way to slow it or stop it since the brakes were useless. Jesus kept swinging his car this way and that, like a Mexican Bobby Allison. By some grace the car stayed on the road. I kept my mouth shut. Jesus was doing the best he could. I put my trust in him and in the Lord.

What's going to happen when we get to the bottom? I wondered, but I dared not say this aloud. At the bottom of the hill there was another hill facing us. This was to our advantage, as the uphill climb slowed us down, the road then leveling off and the car coming to a dead stop right in front of a little roadside garage, placed there just for us, it seemed.

"God has been watching over us, Padre," said Jesus, tossing his shock of dark hair into place with a jerk of his head. A grateful smile like a ripple in a pond rolled over his face.

"He sure has," I offered. "God most assuredly has been watching over us."

We climbed out of the vehicle in silence, weary and exhausted from nervous energy. We had nothing more to say, but there was much to ponder. Jesus went to talk to the garage owner about repairing the brakes. Buoyed with a sudden burst of joy, I squatted in a pool of shade under a palm tree. I was alive, thank God.

When we arrived back in Delores after this unforgettable pilgrimage to Christo Rey, I celebrated the evening Mass in the parish church. Jesus assisted me throughout the Mass just as he had in Okeechobee. He read the readings, led the congregation in singing, and translated my English words into Spanish. The people were extremely attentive. When I finished Mass, the congregation showed their appreciation by breaking into spontaneous applause.

In the plaza outside the church after the Mass, people came up to talk, and express thanks for coming to visit them. Little children came running in twos and threes, stopping to say, "*Buenas noches, padre.*" The Mass had brought us together and things were never the same in Dolores after that.

Families came to talk with me every evening in the lounge of El Caudillo hotel. Parents brought their children, who were always very well behaved. There was entertainment in the lounge, and a talented guitarist and singer regaled us with Mexican songs every evening. Most of the fathers of these young families had worked in different parts of the U.S., some in California, some in Arizona, others in Texas, Chicago and Florida. They had a lot to talk about.

"Why did you not settle down in the U.S?" I asked one young parent who worked in California.

He paused, cradling his young son in his arms.

"It wasn't about the money," Padre, he said, his voice soft yet resolute. "In California, I saw children talk back to their parents, acting as though family didn't matter. They were losing something, something I couldn't name but knew in my heart. Here, family is everything. I want my children to grow up knowing respect and love of family."

His voice wavered slightly, and I saw the weight of his decision reflected in the way he held his son, as if protecting him from a world that had forgotten its values.

His sentiments were echoed by many others who, despite appreciating the financial opportunities in the U.S., did not want to raise their families there. As I observed the well-mannered children of the ranches, I understood these parents' desire to raise them with a love for family. Though the lure of prosperity tugged them north, tradition and family brought them home.

* * *

Father Cerna had arranged an audience with the bishop of Celaya, but our unreliable car was unfit for the journey. A few blocks from the hotel we secured passage on a bus bound for San Miguel de Allende, the most celebrated of the "magic towns" in Mexico, as they are called. This charming city lay halfway between Dolores and Celaya along our route. In San Miguel we transferred to another bus that carried us the rest of the way to Celaya.

The early morning bus ride that began in Dolores had an excitement all its own. As we entered the bus, we were greeted with the liveliest of Mexican music, an experience that lasted the whole trip. People were animatedly chatting, and the trip had all the feeling of a joyride, Mexican style. There were many stops along the way, and even though the bus was full to capacity, there was always room for more passengers. Sometimes the ticket inspector would worm his way to the back of the bus to urge the people to stand closer together, in order to make room for more passengers.

I will never forget one particular sight along the road. A Mexican family, weighed down with baskets, buckets and trinkets, was waiting for the bus. A youngster, no older than ten, had his hands full while he anxiously directed an elderly couple onto the bus. Since the couple had difficulty moving, the youngster managed to grab hold of them and pull them along while carrying his own heavy burden. The inspector got off the bus to help the old couple and the driver left his seat to lend another helping hand. Suddenly, the bus began to slide backwards, and to stop it, a passenger ran up the aisle and slammed on the brakes. There was quite a bit of bumping and shoving as the bus finally settled down. It was then I noticed that the old couple in the group were blind. Everyone wanted to help them.

This was typical of the deep love and respect you find in Mexican families.

Finally, we arrived at the residence of the Bishop of Celaya. A man of about fifty years, he breezed into the living room where we were waiting, effusively apologizing for his tardiness. In his haste to greet me he brushed right past my companion, Jesus. After a quick greeting, I introduced Jesus to him. Then the three of us sat down and I attempted to explain the plight of his migrant parishioners in Okeechobee. To my surprise, the bishop initially responded critically, blaming them for abandoning their families.

Recognizing the need for firsthand testimony, I encouraged Jesus to share his personal experience. As a married man with a wife and three children in Dolores, he had no choice but to spend eight months of the year working in Florida to provide for them. The bishop listened intently to Jesus's story, clearly unaccustomed to hearing directly from those who sacrificed so much. His heart softened with understanding and empathy. Before we departed, the bishop gave me his card to maintain contact. I had work awaiting me back in Las Palmitas, so we promptly took our leave.

In Mexico, each ranch has its own church, called a *templo*, built by the residents themselves to serve the people. In Las Palmitas, Jesus's wife, Juanita, was busy preparing the children for First Communion. A huge crowd had gathered in this little church. I heard the children's confessions for a few hours before Mass, and during Mass itself the children crowded around the altar. The congregation, which extended into the street outside, prayed and sang aloud. When Mass was over, the crowd just stood there, not wanting to leave. Nobody was in a rush to go anywhere. When I walked outside, the crowd was still there, quietly waiting, smiling and coming forward to extend a hand of welcome.

Jesus's family prepared a fiesta after the Mass. Food and drinks were brought forth, the music began and everyone had a wonderful time. In the afternoon, a group of ranchers from another ranch came forward and asked Jesus if they could bring me to their ranch at 3 p.m. I agreed and set out on a fifteen-mile trek to a ranch called San Nicolas. The mountain roads to this ranch were the most difficult I've ever travelled, even more challenging than the little country road in Lanalea, County Donegal, where my uncle had his cottage. Whenever we came to a stream we had to get out of the car and lift it across. I wondered if the car could take all this manhandling, but we made it all right. When we arrived, a local boy climbed the church steeple and began ringing the bell. In minutes, people assembled and in no time the church was full and ready for another Mass.

One man in the group was from Austin, Texas, and he was married to a Mexican woman.

"What's it like living here?" I asked. "It's very different from Texas."

"I love it here," he replied. "The people here are the best I've ever encountered in my whole life."

The migrants who worked in Okeechobee during the season and were natives of San Nicolas had prepared another fiesta. With two fiestas in one day, I was almost worn out with celebrating. The festivities went on for hours. In pauses between merrymaking, I gave the Sacrament of the Sick to an old lady who was confined to bed, and I visited another family to bless their home. I appreciated the busy schedule of a Mexican priest. And yet, I only spent a single weekend in parish work at Dolores Hidalgo.

As I lay in bed that night, exhaustion pulled at my limbs, but my mind was still alive with the day's encounters. I marveled at the endless energy of the Mexican priests, whose days blurred into nights filled with the constant demands of their flock. In just one weekend, I had glimpsed a life driven not by schedules or rest but by an unwavering devotion to service. It was a stark contrast to the more measured, often solitary life of American priests. This whirlwind of activity left me both awed and humbled, forcing me to question whether I had ever truly understood what it meant to give of oneself entirely to God and community.

This parish, Father Cerna told me, had 120 ranches in addition to the large town of Dolores.

I asked him how many people he had in this sprawling parish.

"We have more than a hundred and fifty thousand," he answered.

"That's as many as are in some of the dioceses in the U.S.," I observed.

I marveled at how only three priests could manage to serve so many people, but they did. The priests had help from the people in the ranches who built their own little chapels, and offered catechetical services for children and families. These simple, integrated Christian communities reminded me of the Ireland of the 1950s. Poor, but rich in spirit.

When Jesus drove me back to Dolores that evening, I went to my room and retired for the night. The plaza in front of the church was full of people having fun, but I was too tired to join any more festivities.

I was asked to visit one of the local schools to give a class in English. This turned out to be a technical school, with boys and girls of high school age. They all stood at attention when we entered the classroom, and they listened carefully to every word. The teacher and I decided I would talk to them about the lives of Mexicans in America, and he would serve as translator. The eyes of the pupils went wide with wonder in hearing the sounds of English spoken in person.

After each talk, I invited the students to ask questions. They were shy and began to shuffle a bit out of embarrassment. Eventually a student was brave enough to ask a question.

"How old are you?" he asked.

"I am a young, forty-nine-year-old priest," I replied.

The teacher translated this into Spanish for the youngsters and they all laughed.

As I was about to leave the classroom another student shouted to me in Spanish, "I'll see you in Okeechobee, Padre, when I go there to pick oranges!"

"I look forward to meeting you," I replied, with a laugh. "But don't forget to introduce yourself to me when you get there. I meet a lot of people and my memory cannot handle all the names."

* * *

We left Dolores Hidalgo for Mexico City the following day at 5 a.m., to meet with Bishop Mena at 11 a.m. The early morning hadn't chased the night away, and the color of day was a hazy gray. I slept a little on the journey and this helped me regain some of the strength I had lost for lack of sleep. The bus rolled into Mexico City around 10 a.m. We took a taxi to the Hotel Jehna in city center. After checking in, we hailed another taxi at 10:30 and went to the residence of Bishop Mena.

We were received enthusiastically. The bishop was a man of about seventy years in age, and he was full of good nature and laughter.

He enjoyed our visit and did not want us to leave when we were ready to go. He was interested in our meeting with bishop Velasquez of Celaya and wished to know what he said. When we told him about his initial reaction to migrants from his own diocese in Florida, he laughed out loud. Bishops like priests, are not alike. And Bishop Mena was a different kind of bishop.

He told me how nearly all the able working men from his area migrated to California. Because of his own experience with immigration, he was intensely interested in everything we were doing and wished he could be of more help.

He also had insight.

"You're going to suffer persecution for what you're doing," he said.

"I'm well aware of that," I replied. "That's what brought me down this way, having survived persecution from my own bishop over our free immigration program in the parish. I needed a break."

"That's what I'm talking about," he said. "You cannot do that work without being persecuted."

The bishop understood my situation and well he should. He had suffered persecution within the church for his outspoken stance against social injustices. The profound irony is that you can suffer as much *from* the church as *for* it.

Bishop Mena then asked me if I would join him that evening at the Shrine of Our Lady of Guadalupe to celebrate Mass with him. I said I'd be honored. We made arrangements to meet at the shrine around 5:30 p.m., for Mass to start at 6 p.m.

At 6 p.m. Jesus and I entered the sacristy of the basilica and Bishop Mena rushed to greet us. During the Mass, I read the gospel and gave the homily. Toward the end of Communion, a woman asked me to bless her child. I did so, and suddenly a long line formed of people bringing children and the infirm to be blessed. Bishop Mena was at the president's chair trying to conclude the service, but he couldn't. As soon as I saw a break in the line, I made for my seat beside him so as not to appear out of place.

Once inside the sacristy, we were also approached by groups of people who simply wanted to shake hands. The naturalness of the Mexican people stood out. People felt free in church to move about anywhere at will, and no one was ever disruptive.

The visit to the shrine of Our Lady of Guadalupe was another highlight of my trip to Mexico. As you enter the basilica, the first thing you see is a cluster of lights, netted together like the Milky Way behind the altar. A constant steam of people flowed through three different passageways, gazing up at the miraculous image of the Lady. The two outer passageways had moving platforms, while the center one was stationary.

The image of the Lady of Guadalupe enshrined in this basilica is extraordinary in its vividness and clarity, rivaling the work of the great

Part 2—Chapter 21

masters. Yet there is somehow more to the experience of viewing it than the merely visual.

Every Mexican knows the simple tale: Juan Diego, a native fleeing Spanish oppression, was met by the vision of the Virgin on this very spot. She told him to gather roses in winter's barren chill, cloaking them in his mantle to present to the bishop. When Juan Diego unfurled his mantle before the bishop, it revealed not roses but the miraculous image we see today above the altar. This wonder saved the natives from continued tyranny, as the Spanish halted their persecution. The shrine erected here, though rebuilt through time, has remained a sanctuary of pilgrimage and refuge ever since.

Early in the morning of May 31, Jesus gave me his own personal tour of the city. Our first visit was to the Zocalo, which contains the national palace and government buildings and the remains of the Montezuma's palace in the great Aztec city of Tenochtitlan, destroyed by Spanish conquistadors in 1521. This area is also known as the Plaza of the Three Cultures; that is, Aztec, Spanish and Mexican—a mix of the first two. Montezuma's palace has been recreated by archeologists from the old ruins that were only discovered in 1978. The museum adjoining the ruins houses an excellent collection of Aztec artifacts. I was struck by the great similarity between the Aztec and the Egyptian cultures and wondered if they were somehow related.

The museum traced the primitive history of Mexico from the time of the earliest settlers until the establishment of the dominant Aztec culture in the fourteenth century. Group after group of students were taking the tour and making notes of their observations.

Chapultepec Park was our next stop. It contains the national museum of history and the famous Chapultepec castle. Many of the national museum's halls are dedicated to various aspects of Mexican history, beginning with the Conquistadors and covering the Vice-Regal era, early independence, the Second Empire and the Revolution. Dolores's famous priest, Father Hidalgo, is featured prominently as one of Mexico's heroes in the halls that deal with the Revolution. Indeed, I found the name of Hidalgo displayed throughout Mexico City: on street signs, in subways and in shops.

Our final stop was The Palace of Fine Arts, home to magnificent murals by famed Mexican artists. Within this cultural center, we were treated to a dazzling performance of classical and contemporary dancers showcasing Mexico's rich traditions. As the sun set over the capital, this was a fitting end to our day's cultural journey across this vibrant city

On my final night in Mexico, as Jesus and I shared a room in the Hotel Jehna, I was stirred from sleep by the unsettling tremors of my bed. Befuddled in those first moments between dreaming and wakefulness,

I wondered, *What's this?* After things settled down, I shifted and moved about a bit to see if my own involuntary movements had caused the bed to shake. The only movement I felt was that of my own body. I went back to sleep but the movement of the bed woke me up again. Glancing over at the other bed, I saw that Jesus was slumbering soundly, unaffected by the odd trembling. The fleeting thought of an unearthly poltergeist crossed my mind but I dismissed such fanciful notions and again, went back to sleep.

In the morning the sound of the TV woke me up.

"We had an earthquake last night," said Jesus.

"What," I exclaimed. "You mean to say what I experienced last night was an earthquake?"

"You felt the earthquake last night?" asked Jesus. "It's all over television. Look."

Just as dawn, inevitably, follows the dark, the television broadcasts that morning were saturated with coverage of the previous night's earthquake. If I had known what was taking place I would have panicked, for we were on the fourteenth floor of the Hotel Jehna. Thank God for the blessing of not knowing. Ignorance is bliss, sometimes.

My sojourns with Jesus across the varied landscapes of Mexico etched profound impressions on me. Immersing myself in the richness of its people, culture, and their enduring struggles gifted me with insights that could only unfold through such intimate, personal experiences.

While my exploration covered merely a fragment of this expansive country, the places I visited, the individuals I met and the experiences I embraced were enlightening. Each interaction ignited a flame, illuminating the profound humanity of the Mexican people. Engaging with its people and immersing myself in the vibrancy of its culture, I developed a deep-seated admiration for the resilience and enduring spirit of a people sculpted by the relentless forces of history.

Leaving Mexico, I felt rejuvenated and enriched, having shared moments of kinship with those who call it home. Yet, as my journey turned back towards Florida, a different chapter awaited: the installation of a new bishop, the second Ordinary of the Diocese of Palm Beach—a major event marking the beginning of a new era.

Chapter 22

THE INSTALLATION OF THE new bishop, the second Ordinary of the Diocese of Palm Beach, was a theatrical and triumphant affair. Normally it would have taken place in the cathedral, but this installation was different. It took place in the West Palm Beach Auditorium, capacity 4,000.

The sunbaked asphalt of Congress Avenue shimmered beneath the oppressive Florida heat as I drove through the growing traffic. Suddenly, my car jerked to a stop, the grinding of brakes echoing through the humid air. This was no ordinary day. Ahead, a procession of white stretch limousines and polished buses glided past, their windows dark and impenetrable, while policemen briskly directed the grandiose parade. This was the entourage of the new Bishop of Palm Beach as he made his grand entrance.

Even uninvited observers along the highways of West Palm Beach could not help but be impressed by this resplendent motorcade on this sweltering, humid morning of July 31, 1990. I noticed that the clouds formed themselves into wisps of mist, spread like a burial shroud over the auditorium where they had come to rest.

Prelates from all over the U.S. and the Vatican were dressed out in finery of red, crimson and gold. Hundreds of priests and deacons and over a thousand Catholic laity from every parish in the diocese were present.

After the installation, the dignitaries, priests, and a select number of laity from each parish dined at a posh golf and country club on PGA Boulevard. At every table, each guest had a marble place-setting, displaying the new bishop's coat-of-arms emblazoned in gold. The new bishop's motto, With Joyful Trust, draped over the coat-of-arms.

As the post-installation party was breaking up in the dining room, and as dignitaries were exiting past throngs of adoring fans, something unusual happened. The previous bishop, the first of the Palm Beach Diocese, was among the dignitaries present, and began pushing his way through the crowd to our table.

"He's coming over here," said Manny Garcia, unable to contain his surprise.

Vinny La Mariana, another table guest, was not as giddy as Manny about this intrusion. He focused an even, steady stare on the approaching bishop. I could not see what was happening behind my back. But suddenly, my shoulder received a snappy pull from behind.

"I wish you all the best," said the ex-bishop of our diocese, as he speedily melted into the crowd like a shadow in a dark forest.

When I got back to the parish later in the day, I retired to my room to rest a while. No sooner was I settled than I heard a banging on the door.

"There are two priests in the church, Padre," Roy announced. "And they are taking bulletins and anything they can find."

"I'm coming right out, Roy," I replied.

In the corridor, Roy explained how the two priests got him to open the church so they could pray, but once inside they started grabbing whatever materials they could lay their hands on.

"Thank you, Roy," I said. "You did well to tell me this."

I stepped into the silence of the church, my footsteps echoing faintly across the floor. The two priests turned abruptly; bulletins and other material clutched in their hands like guilty secrets they didn't want to reveal.

"Welcome to Sacred Heart. I'm Hugh Duffy," I said, my voice cutting through the silence. "I don't believe we've met."

The taller of the two cleared his throat, shifting uneasily.

"We . . . we were just admiring your beautiful church."

I smiled, noting the tension between them.

"Well, if you've come all this way, I insist you join me for a cup of coffee in the rectory. It would be rude of me to let you leave without proper hospitality."

Seated in the rectory, I learned they were both monsignors and longtime friends of the new bishop. They had worked with him when he was chancellor of the diocese of St. Petersburg on Florida's west coast. Monsignor McNulty, the talkative one, had served as vicar general to Archbishop John P. Hurley when Florida was just a single diocese. I'd heard of him. An old hand at ecclesiastical politics, he had developed quite a reputation among the clergy. It didn't bother me that he would be reporting back to his friend, the new bishop, especially if he reported the truth. I had nothing to hide.

"The bishop will be out to see you," he assured me.

"He'll be most welcome," I replied.

The two monsignors finally left. I expected I'd be getting a visit from the new bishop soon after they reported back to him. True to form, the bishop wasted no time in visiting the parish. He was very well received. He was generous with his time and met with the parishioners after all the weekend Masses. The parish sign at the entrance to the church welcomed him to Sacred Heart. The last thing he did as he was leaving the grounds was to step out of his car and take a photo of the sign. The kind words of welcome pleased him greatly.

The rhythms of parish life hummed along through the sweltering summer of 1992. On August 24, the wind picked up speed, shrieking through the streets like a living thing, and the trees bowed low under its strength. Windows rattled, roofs trembled, and the world outside became a blur of rain and fury. Hurricane Andrew, a powerful category 5, had arrived, not with a whisper but with a roar, leaving nothing untouched in its path.

Andrew forced us to open the doors of our facilities, Education Center and Parish Hall, to anyone needing shelter, especially those living in fragile mobile homes.

As darkness fell on the eve of Andrew's arrival, a frantic knock at my door revealed a woman, her eyes wide with worry.

"There's a man, a Mexican, who won't leave his home," she pleaded. "I've tried everything, but he won't listen." She was a devout Baptist, but felt I might have more luck rescuing this poor man who was, most likely, Catholic.

Her voice cracked with the weight of fear and anxiety, and I felt the need to rescue this man immediately.

I thanked her for her solicitude and gathered a bunch of Mexicans who travelled with me in Jesus Torres's truck to rescue this gentleman. He was seated stoically with a six-pack of beer at his feet in an open area of a little, vulnerable dwelling. The Mexicans with me began to laugh.

"This little man is in serious trouble and needs help," I said to my helpers. "Go and carry him in his chair and put him into the bed of the truck."

They rushed to the Mexican and took hold of him, chair and all, and put him on the truck. He didn't protest or say a word. He was in God's hands.

"Don't forget the beer," cried Jesus from behind the wheel.

This was retrieved and placed at the feet of the rescued Mexican before we drove off.

We were very busy during this hurricane. Time seemed to accelerate as Andrew approached. Every nail hammered and every sandbag placed felt like a desperate attempt to hold back the inevitable. The wind's howl grew louder with each passing hour, a constant reminder of our race against nature's wrath. As we worked, sweat-soaked and hearts pounding, I couldn't shake the nagging fear: Would our efforts be enough?

While we were doing everything we could to protect the church, I noticed a group of Mexicans giggling among themselves.

"What are you laughing about?" I asked.

Pointing through the glass door entrance to the church, the Mexicans drew my attention to a lone man in a car, buffeted by the wind in the parking lot. He had arrived for the Saturday evening Mass, hurricane or no hurricane. We gestured to him to leave, but he wouldn't budge. He was confused. Finally, Jesus got a long rope. Tying it around my waist for safety so I wouldn't fly away, he let me through the door, extending the rope and holding it fast until I reached the car.

"Please go home," I roared as the man lowered the window.

"Do you not have an evening Mass?" he inquired. "I've driven all the way from the coast to attend Mass here."

"There are no Masses anywhere," I replied.

With that, he swerved his car about, and drove away.

We survived Hurricane Andrew, shaken but standing. But other parts of South Florida did not fare so well. The city of Homestead was levelled to the ground. The U.S. Air Force had left two jets in a concrete bunker in Homestead, thinking they were safe, but Andrew pulverized the bunker and planes inside.

In the hurricane's wake, as the first tentative rays of sunlight pierced the clouds, I stood amazed at the sight before me. Where I expected to see devastation, I instead witnessed resurrection. The church grounds, once strewn with debris, now buzzed with the energy of volunteers—Americans, Filipinos, and Mexicans working alongside each other, their differences swept away by the storm's indiscriminate fury. When Florida Power & Light (FPL) announced that our power was restored, it felt like more than just the promise of electric light. It was a spark of hope, igniting our collective spirits.

As we celebrated Mass the very next day, in a church that had weathered the storm just as we had, I realized that Andrew had not only tested our physical foundations but had revealed the unshakeable spirit of the community. In its fury, the hurricane had stripped away our differences and laid bare our shared humanity.

Chapter 23

As we settled into a new diocesan administration, the second bishop, it appeared, harbored a desire to imprint his legacy upon the diocese, a tangible testament to his tenure long after his departure. This notion has always struck me as perplexing. In my simple view, the most authentic legacy of any Christian was the quiet assurance of having tried to walk in the footsteps of Christ.

I recall coming across an article in the *National Catholic Reporter* that profiled a truly extraordinary bishop. His distinction lay not in the grandeur of his projects or the visibility of his achievements, but rather in his remarkable restraint. This bishop was deeply cherished by his priests, not for the legacy he tried to craft, but for what he chose not to do. He didn't seek to etch his name into the annals of the diocese. Instead, he devoted himself to empowering his clergy, supporting them in fulfilling their vocations. His legacy was one of unassuming support and love, qualities that endeared him to those he led.

The second bishop of Palm Beach seemed determined, however, to leave his mark on the diocese. One day the priests were summoned to the diocesan pastoral center to hear the bishop's ambitious five-year plan. Following his opening statement, the priests were divided into focus groups to discuss the plan and to offer a summary of their deliberations.

I was selected by my group to offer a summary.

The reactions to the bishop's plan by those speaking before me were rather critical. When my turn came to speak, I adopted a positive approach, suggesting that the diocese develop a mission statement first to guide the deliberations.

The bishop, impressed by my approach, spoke: "Father Duffy, I'd like you to take the lead on drafting our mission statement."

His words, though complimentary, carried a weight that felt heavier than praise.

I was not happy about this assignment because the bishop had appointed a Vicar for Evangelization in charge of the five-year plan.

Later, when he approached me privately, I asked him again: "Why not let the Vicar for Evangelization draw up the mission statement?"

A sense of unease began to form in my stomach when he would not listen to my objection.

I accepted the task, reluctantly. It was a somewhat difficult process, as I had to get feedback from all the priests before finally agreeing on a mission statement acceptable to everyone. The bishop was very happy when I presented it to the council of priests, of which I was an elected member.

Nothing more was heard of the mission statement or the five-year plan until the bishop began sharing his strategy at meetings of the priests' council. Priests present asked why they could not see the plan, rather than just be told about it. I was also interested in knowing how the strategic plan developed from the mission statement I had helped to formulate.

The upshot of all this was that the bishop invited me to his office after a meeting of the priests' council.

"Here is the five-year strategic plan," he said, dropping a large manuscript into my hands. "I want you to go through it and write your comments on the margins."

"What you are asking of me should be the job of the Vicar for Evangelization," I again stressed.

"No," he continued. "I want you to do this for me and bring the manuscript with your comments to the cathedral sacristy before the Chrism Mass."

The Chrism Mass was offered for priests by the bishop on the Tuesday of Holy Week.

"Why can't you discuss this manuscript at the regular meeting of the priests' council?" I entreated.

The bishop wouldn't hear of that.

Instead, he insisted I take the manuscript home with me so that I could return it to him with my comments by this deadline. There was no way of getting out of this without incurring the bishop's displeasure, so I did what he asked. I handed it back to him with a cover letter in the sacristy before the Chrism Mass. He radiated gratitude.

As it turned out, though, he was highly displeased with my comments, because I had highlighted problems that ran counter to our mission statement.

He decided to visit me at the parish, manuscript in hand. He asked me to alter all my corrections, deletions and additions to the text right then and there in his presence.

Part 2—Chapter 23

"That's not possible, Bishop," I replied, "when we were seated together in the rectory."

"Why not?" he asked.

"I believe the document needs to be re-written, as stated in my cover letter," I said.

Still, he persisted in asking me to make the changes there and then.

I pleaded with him.

"Please do not insist I do something against my better judgement, bishop."

That ended the discussion about the manuscript and the five-year plan. It was abandoned. The process had cost the diocese $119,000 in terms of money but a lot more in terms of human frustration.

The bishop later made another parish visit.

"I'd like you to leave Okeechobee and take a different parish," he declared.

Surprised by this remark, I replied: "I'm happy where I am."

Suddenly producing a map, he showed me a parish in the diocese that had a university and, as he thought, an upscale population.

"I think you'd be well suited to this parish," he urged, pointing to the map. "You can take six months off or even a year before you take up your new assignment."

Never before had I been offered such an enticing assignment. Even so, I wasn't impressed. I felt happy and content where I was doing the Lord's work.

"I'm happy where I am, Bishop, working among the immigrants and the poor," I told him.

He appeared perturbed.

"Is there any parish in the diocese I can offer you to get you to leave Okeechobee?" he asked, finally.

"Not really," I answered.

His eagerness to see me leave Okeechobee surprised me. Most priests I knew felt the diocese was lucky to have a priest willing to take a parish regarded as the Siberia of the lot. It was not a plum assignment by any stretch of imagination. But that's what I liked about it because I could contribute more and, hopefully, make things better.

Our meeting was cordial enough, and I was hoping fervently that this would be the end of the matter.

Father John Morley had gone into a retirement home in Philadelphia. His family was worried about his health, and so was I. One day, I had found him stretched out on the floor of his room, the result of a stroke from pills he had taken to reduce his weight. He was a kind and gentle man and was sorely missed by all at Sacred Heart.

He was replaced by Father Tom Cleary. I spoke to Tom about the bishop's request.

"The bishop wants me to leave and take a plum parish in Palm Beach County," I told him.

"Did he give any reason?" asked Tom.

"No," I replied. "It looks like he wants me out of here."

"Why?"

"He's upset I didn't go along with the manuscript dealing with the five-year plan for the diocese," I said. "I could not agree with everything in the document, and I told him so, truthfully, when he came out here to discuss it."

"That makes sense," admitted Tom.

"The strange thing is he could simply have ignored my comments about the document," I remarked, "and that would have been the end of it. All I've ever wanted was to do my work as pastor in the parish."

"He doesn't like being told what to do," Tom pointed out, "and this is his way of getting back at you."

"Perhaps," I replied. "He actually tried to bribe me by offering me six months or a year off if I took the plum parish on the coast," I added.

"Many priests would jump at that offer," Tom noted with a laugh.

"Tom, I fear that this is just the beginning," I added, "and it's not just about the manuscript. Our meeting was civil, but the next time it could get nasty."

Things settled down again. At the next presbyteral council meeting, the bishop announced that the year 1992 would be The Year of Communications in the diocese. He asked all pastors to use the media to showcase the work of the church in their respective parishes.

At Sacred Heart, we produced a video—*A Parish for All Seasons*—that was widely viewed on different TV channels.

The bishop called my secretary.

"Why is the parish showing that video on TV?" he asked her.

"Because it's The Year of Communications in the Diocese," she replied.

"Why didn't I get a copy of the video?" he inquired.

"We can send you a copy, Bishop," she replied. "I'll tell Father you'd like to have one. I know he'd be delighted to send it to you."

A copy of the video was sent to the bishop with my compliments. After receiving it, he called me.

The bishop's voice crackled over the phone, tinged with suspicion: "Are you profiting from this video, Father Duffy?"

I paused for a moment, praying for patience. "No, Bishop. We're not making a cent."

"Then what's the purpose of it?" he pressed.

"We're doing our part for the Year of Communications, just as you asked," I replied.

"Are there any appeals in the video for funds?" he asked.

"Not a one," I replied. "If you've watched the video, you'll see for yourself there are no appeals for funds."

I never heard anything more from the bishop or the diocese about the video after this phone call.

* * *

During this time, a problem developed in Okeechobee that needed an immediate response from the parish. The Ku Klux Klan (KKK) planned a rally in front of city hall aimed at recruiting new members to their cause. This was bad news for Okeechobee, for it gave the impression that the KKK had the support of the town's citizens, which I knew was not the case.

The NAACP (National Association for the Advancement of Colored People), an American organization formed to advance civil rights, got in touch with me to stage a counter-rally to oppose the KKK's rally. I agreed to be part of a peaceful counter rally.

One day before the rally, I was having lunch at the Brahma Bull restaurant in Okeechobee. Sheriff Raulerson came over to my table. He heard about the counter-rally I was organizing in conjunction with the NAACP.

"There could be serious trouble if you organize a counter-protest against the KKK," he said.

"There will be no trouble, Sheriff, if you place a line of police officers between the two groups," I said. "We are only exercising our Constitutional rights to protest peacefully."

The sheriff was impressed by what I said and took my suggestion to heart.

On the day of the event, a line of police officers was placed between the KKK and our counter-rally in front of City Hall. The midday sun bore down on us as we gathered, the heat pressing heavily on our bodies. Between our peaceful rally and the KKK's, the thin line of uniformed officers stood like a human wall, their badges catching the sharp glare of sunlight. The tension mounted as the chants from both sides collided, creating a cacophony of clashing ideologies.

Roger Azcona, head of the church's family outreach center, and his helpers, organized the Parish's Martial Arts Group to walk in formation to City Hall and join with the NAACP in the counter-rally.

Opposite City Hall, the Martial Arts Group put on a demonstration of their skills in the town park. The KKK were asked to remove their white hoods, show their real faces and join in the celebration. To our surprise, they complied. These were not angry or bitter faces as expected—but smiling faces, befitting human beings. From that point forward, the atmosphere changed. The KKK, caught up in the spirit of celebration, forgot about the reason for their being there. No new members were signed up by the KKK at the City Hall in Okeechobee.

The NAACP leadership asked me to conclude the event with a prayer. As the leader turned to me with hope and anticipation, I felt the weight of the moment. This wasn't an idle prayer; it was a bridge between communities, a balm to heal old wounds, a whisper of possibility. As I stepped forward, the crowd hushed, and I could almost feel the collective heartbeat of our divided town, waiting in expectation, yearning for unity and peace.

As I delivered the prayer, calling for unity in diversity, and peace among all people, the responses from the effusive African-Americans were different from what I had been used to. Each part of the prayer was met with loud bursts of applause, Amens, Praise the Lord, and Alleluias.

What began as a disturbing KKK rally turned into a celebration that ended with a Prayer for Peace.

Good fortune smiled on us that year when a parishioner decided to leave her home to the church in her last will and testament. A donation like this meant a lot to a little country parish. I discussed this bequest with the diocesan comptroller, since Gladys, the donor, had made me the personal representative of her estate.

"How should this donation be made out?" I asked the comptroller, since I was new to this.

The diocese is what is called a corporation sole, which meant that the bishop held title to all parish properties. The comptroller explained this to me, and advised me to have the donation made to the Bishop's Appeal, which helps parishes, adding that he would tell the bishop it was meant for Sacred Heart.

"Are you sure the parish will receive the money when the property is sold?" I inquired.

"Absolutely," he affirmed. "I'll make that clear to the bishop."

One day, at a clergy meeting, a priest asked me: "When are you going on vacation to Ireland?"

Part 2—Chapter 23

Once I told him the date, I noted the instant reaction of the bishop, standing close by. The bishop's reaction, when I mentioned my vacation, had been too eager, too unsettling for me. Something didn't sit right, and I couldn't shake the feeling that when I was away, events might unfold that I would have no control over. To cover my tracks, I called the comptroller to let him know when I'd be on vacation.

When I returned to Okeechobee following my vacation in Ireland, I called the comptroller to again discuss the property.

"The bishop sold it when you were on vacation," he informed me, alarmingly.

That's what I suspected.

"Did you not let him know it was meant for the parish?" I asked him.

"I surely did," he said. "You'll have to be very careful the next time, how you word a donation of property meant for the parish."

That day I learned a hard lesson about corporation sole[1] and the workings of the institutional church. As the intricacies of corporation sole dawned upon me, a realization rolled over me. The complex, hidden machinery that drove the institutional church didn't always respect the rights of the people of God in the parishes. What the bishop had done was legal, but he didn't take into account the intentions of the donor and the needs of the local parish.

I realized more clearly that I wasn't just a pastor guiding my flock—I was also a small cog in a large, bureaucratic machine where decisions weren't always guided by the gospel, but by legal and financial concerns.

The abuse of corporation sole didn't go away. It came back to haunt me again when the parish of Sacred Heart became the beneficiary of another donation of property.

---

1. Corporation sole is a corporate office that is occupied by a single, natural person. Thus, the diocese and all its churches and lands are incorporated as part of the corporation sole. So, on paper and in civil law, the bishop is the owner and controller of everything.

Chapter 24

George McKay had joined Sacred Heart Church in the early 1990s. Though his health was failing, he came to see me one day with an offer: "I'd like to leave my house to the church," he said, "and I'd like you to be the personal representative of my estate."

I hesitated: "Do you have no family of your own, George, to whom you could leave your house?"

I was wary of inserting myself into a potential feud over his property.

No, he replied simply. "I'm single and have no children."

"That's very generous of you," George, I remarked. "The parish could certainly benefit from the donation."

"I've thought a lot about it," said George. "You're doing a lot for needy people, including immigrants. I thought you could use the house for something like that."

George then told me he was thinking of leaving his savings to a seminary, called Sacred Heart, in Hales Corner, Wisconsin. Now he was having second thoughts and felt he should leave his savings to Sacred Heart Church in Okeechobee.

"There might be a conflict of interest if you do that," I told George.

"Why?" he asked.

"I might be blamed for exerting undue influence as your personal representative," I answered. "Besides, the seminary is a good cause."

George agreed to leave the will as it was. He left his savings to the Sacred Heart Seminary in Hales Corner, Wisconsin, and he left the house to the parish of Sacred Heart in Okeechobee.

When George passed away, I had the responsibility for his estate.

Tom Conley, a highly regarded lawyer in Okeechobee, was the attorney for the estate. One copy of the will was sent to the bishop of the diocese of Palm Beach, and another to the provincial of the sacred Heart seminary in Hales Corner, Wisconsin, a beneficiary.

Part 2—Chapter 24

What started as a relatively simple and straightforward matter soon devolved into a complex one, with the diocesan attorney informing me that the bishop wanted to sell the property. My attorney answered the diocesan attorney, pointing out that the house belonged to the parish according to church law, even though the title was in the name of the bishop as corporation sole.

Failing to sell the house, however, the diocesan administration decided on another tactic: to convert the parish house into an office of Catholic Charities with an employee in residence.

Now, we were thrust into a canonical conundrum. The property belonged to the parish as a juridic personality according to canon law, but it came under the legal title of the bishop as corporation sole. What were we to do?

I met with the members of the finance council and explained the situation to them.

"The house," I said, "was occupied by an employee of Catholic Charities and his wife."

"Have them evicted," said George Fitzpatrick

"It doesn't work like that," George, I explained. "The bishop holds title to the house, and in the eyes of the law he is the owner."

"What then can we do?" someone else asked.

"It will have to be handled canonically," I said. "And that could be a lengthy process."

The members of the finance council understood nothing of the complicated intricacies of canon law or corporation sole. There was nothing more I could do but hold out in the hope that justice might prevail.

I was fearful that what I had told Father Cleary earlier might now come to pass: that things could even get nasty. It looked like troubled waters ahead, but that was the hand I was dealt. I prayed God was on our side.

As the final hours of 1994 slipped away, the sun beat down on Sacred Heart. I stepped out of the rectory for my midday walk, the Florida heat shimmering off the pavement. What I thought was a routine stroll was about to lead into a far more significant series of events.

Faye, the church secretary, was dutifully locking the office door before noon when she spotted me. Turning around, she smiled, benignly.

With her soft crown of silvery hair that always seemed to catch the sunlight just right, Faye had found solace in Sacred Heart after her husband Bernie's death. Her smile, radiant and full of warmth, was her gift to everyone, a quiet strength that had become the heart of the parish. In her, I saw the embodiment of quiet faith—a woman who had weathered storms and emerged more compassionate for it.

"Wouldn't it be a good idea, Father, to close the office for the rest of the day?" she said, pushing a bunch of keys deep into her purse.

On a hunch that there might be more to her remark than mere comment, I pressed her gently,

"Do you want me to close the office, Faye?" I asked.

"Well, Father," she continued. "We're all very busy preparing for the New Year's party in the pavilion. I just felt it might be too much pressure to keep the office open."

As Faye spoke, a sense of unease crept over me, like a shadow passing over the sun. It was a feeling I'd come to recognize over my years in the priesthood—a sort of spiritual alarm bell, warning of unseen dangers. I'd learned to trust this instinct, born from years of dealing with the often-treacherous waters of church politics. I had a feeling that, unbeknownst to herself, Faye was acting as an unwitting conduit to save me from danger. As if compelled by a benign force, I decided to close the office at noon for the rest of the day.

Faye, unaware of my feelings or the fact that she was acting as my guardian angel, beamed a big smile and replied: "Well then, the office is closed for the rest of the year."

She took off, waving her hand and shouting, gleefully, "Happy New Year!"

On small things great issues hang. Little did I know then that this simple act of closing the office at noon on the last day of the old year, 1994, would save my life.

I was in good spirits after talking with Faye outside the office. When I returned to the rectory after my walk, the savory smell of fresh food, cooking in the kitchen, filled the living room. My little dog, Rocky, lay on the floor curled up like a hedgehog while Fran, the housekeeper, could be heard scraping carrots and cutting up vegetables for the evening dinner. In the apartment next to the kitchen, Father Finn, who had replaced Father Cleary after he retired to Ireland, was doing what he loved best: quietly reading. All was calm and all was well.

I followed Father Finn's lead, relaxing into a good read: Nicholas Evans's novel, *The Loop*. In this comfortable state, I began to ponder the good fortune of the parish over the past ten years and how the Lord had led us safely through stormy waters. We had much to be grateful for as the old year was ending and a new one about to begin. The parish had grown in leaps and bounds, from a sleepy backwater into a mixed community of Americans, Hispanics, Asians, and French Canadians. Sacred Heart was the first trilingual parish in the diocese to celebrate Masses in English, French and Spanish. The growth in congregants came about through the influx of domestic migrants from different parts of the U.S. and the arrival of international migrants from Latin America, the Philippines, and French Canada. Fortunately, I was proficient in all three languages to serve the needs of this diverse community.

The parish had also attracted national attention. It was profiled in the *Washington Post*, the *National Catholic Reporter*, and in the Catholic Network (EWTN) as a new kind of inclusive parish. Nothing, it appeared, could hinder the Lord's work. Or so it seemed.

My reverie was jolted suddenly by the ringing of the doorbell. Rocky, my little Shi-tzu, barked loudly, bounding up from his crouched position, eyes focused on the door. Fran entered the living room to answer the doorbell. She stopped when she saw that I was already on my feet.

"That's okay Fran, I'll get it," I said, making my way to the door with a touch of anxiety, book in hand. Waiting at the door was our temporary receptionist, Annabelle (not her real name), who I had given a job until the end of the year. She assisted Faye in the office. Now she was returning from lunch, on her last day on the job, having had no idea that the office was closed. She spoke Spanish but her English was very poor.

"Glad to see you Annabelle," I said warmly, and explained that the office was closed. She told me she was looking forward to going to Miami to celebrate the new year with family. I was happy for her. Wishing her all the best in the new year, I asked her for the office keys since she had no further use of them. The mood suddenly changed.

"*I wanna lutta*," she snapped, abruptly.

"You want a letter?" I replied, taken aback by this request and sudden change of tone. I had been as helpful as I could to Annabelle, offering her a parttime job that was to last until the end of the year so she and her child could get on their feet. Annabelle was a single mother. She had never behaved like this before, and the radical change of attitude threw me for a loop. I smelled a rat.

"The office is closed, Annabelle," I continued. "And there is no way of typing a letter now. You'll have to come back in the New Year or we can mail one to you if you wish."

Annabelle was not cooperative and would not hand over the keys, nor did I insist she do so. I knew better than to press the matter any further, given her negative attitude. It also struck me as highly unlikely that she was doing this on her own. Somebody had put her up to it, I felt. It looked like she was being coached by people who were using her for their own nefarious purposes. I did not know yet what those purposes were, but I had my suspicions they involved the property the diocese was trying to wrest from the parish.

Providentially and out of nowhere, Fran poked her head around the corner to see what was up. The timing could not have been more perfect. Fran's sudden appearance threw Annabelle off balance. Not knowing what to say or do next and visibly shaken, she turned around and disappeared like a witch on a broomstick.

The indominable Fran, who was never afraid to speak her mind, simply shrugged her shoulders and quipped: "What's she up to?"

"I don't know," I replied. "But we'll find out soon enough."

I tried to continue reading after this but I couldn't get the incident out of my mind. Just when everything was going right and could not have been much better, the devil had thrown a monkey-wrench into the works.

The encounter at the door with the woman I had been actually helping, her refusal to hand over the keys, the strange request for a letter, the confusion when she saw Fran—all this bothered me.

Who was behind this? I wondered. This incident did not happen in a vacuum, I knew. I had a hunch it had something to do with the diocese's attempt to remove me as pastor and take over the parish property donated by George McKay.

Some prior incidents came rushing into my mind, casting a piercing light on this strange development with Annabelle.

Sometime earlier, a parishioner, Mel Gentry, had been brutally murdered, sending shockwaves through the parish and leaving a particularly painful scar on the senior citizens who also lived alone.

The question that haunted us all was, why?

Mel was murdered, I learned from the sheriff, for being willing to tell the truth. Like several others in the parish, Mel had been a victim of a financial scam. The perpetrator of the crime was already imprisoned, but his biggest fear, as the sheriff explained, was that Mel would testify truthfully at the trial. She was the kind of person who couldn't tell a lie, and thus became the victim of a contract killing in her home.

The horrific death of Mel ignited much fear in the community. In the wake of this shocking murder, many senior parishioners living alone approached me with a proposition. They suggested constructing a senior living center on parish grounds, where they would feel safe and secure. Drawing upon my successful experience in building senior housing in Ireland, I met with the finance council. Together, we crafted a detailed plan, mirroring the one I had implemented in Ireland. As per custom, I submitted this proposal to the diocese for approval, eagerly awaiting their response to this much-needed initiative.

I received no response concerning our proposal.

To my surprise, the diocese came up with an alternative project that would not benefit the parish. The project proposed by the diocese would involve donating part of the parish property to the government, the department of Health and Urban Development (HUD), to build housing for seniors in Okeechobee according to their rules and regulations. After discussing this government project proposed by the diocese with the parish finance council, it was rejected because it didn't meet the crucial and pressing needs of our parishioners. I relayed this decision of the parish council to the monsignor in charge of Catholic Charities at the diocese.

But there was another equally disturbing incident. I had long been bothered by the cruel tactics used by the diocese to remove priests. Father Tom was a beloved priest, and good friend of mine who was removed as pastor of his parish.

One fateful day during my time as secretary of the Priest Personnel Board, he reached out to me, revealing that he was asked to step down as pastor because a woman in Canada would bring a charge of alienation of affection against him. Despite the absurdity of the claim, which I knew to be false, I found myself appalled that such an allegation could be weaponized against a man of Father Tom's character. The diocese's motivation to remove him stemmed from a desire to replace him with his associate, a priest who actually held nothing but respect and admiration for Father Tom.

"This charge is fake and total nonsense," I assured Father Tom, adding: "Stepping down could not solve the problem even if one existed."

But it was all too heavy a burden for Tom to bear.

He called me back again: "Hugh," the word catching in his throat, "emotionally I cannot handle this."

Father Tom's voice on the phone was barely audible, a shadow of his usually robust tone. In that moment, I could almost see him, a man once standing tall in his vocation, now bent and broken by the weight of a false accusation.

Thus, a good man was shamed into submission, forced to step down as pastor on a trumped-up sexual peccadillo to make way for another priest.

When the transfer of authority process was completed, he called me once more.

"I asked the diocesan official about the woman in Canada," he said. "I was told not to worry because there never was any such woman!"

The entire ordeal had been nothing more than a scam, a deplorable tactic to remove Father Tom as pastor.

As I pondered Annabelle's odd behavior, memories of the past two incidents began to unravel, connecting what I had once considered isolated. The rejection of the senior housing project following Mel Gentry's murder, and Father Tom's cruel dismissal—these weren't random incidents. Slowly, like pieces of a puzzle falling into place, they formed a picture: a web of manipulation spun by forces within the diocese. It felt like each event was part of a game I was unwittingly playing.

As I pieced together these incidents, I was overcome by an uneasy feeling. Was I witnessing a pattern of systematic manipulation? The thought that the institution could be capable of such deceit shook me to my core. Yet, even as doubt crept in, I felt a steely resolve forming within me. If this was indeed a battle for the soul of our parish, I knew I couldn't back down.

I tried to remain calm. I had prepared myself, mentally and spiritually, for the worst, but the events of the past, Annabelle especially, kept gnawing at my innards.

Later that evening, I was thrust out of my seat again to answer the doorbell. This time it was the police.

Chapter 25

THE SPECTACLE OF TWO men in blue at my doorstep, so soon after my encounter with Annabelle, made my blood curl.

"Here are your keys, Father Duffy," said Officer Conlon (not his real name), dangling them in my face. "Annabelle asked me to return them to you."

Shocked but not surprised at this sudden turn of events, I said: "I asked Annabelle for those keys earlier today. Why did she get you to return them?"

With the coolness of an iceberg, he replied: "Annabelle has filed a battery charge against you. Since she didn't want to deal with you in person, she asked me to return the keys."

These words were like a knife to the heart. But everything about Conlon's demeanor had the air of pretense. His voice sounded cold and dull and his speech rehearsed. This made it all the more difficult to bear.

A rush of thoughts flooded my mind. I had heard rumors in the community about Annabelle and Conlon's romantic relationship, but I dismissed them as scandal mongering. Now, however, these rumors seemed plausible. I felt that Officer Conlon was Annabelle's man, and he would go to any lengths to please her. This included taking a sidekick with him, Officer Sweitzer (not his real name), as a backup or witness. The presence of Sweitzer, however, might prove to my advantage, I felt, if he was an innocent bystander, unwittingly roped into a sinister plot.

Anxious to get to the bottom of this scam, I invited both officers into the rectory. I'm told it is unwise to say anything to the police if an accusation is made against you, but I had absolutely no fear of the truth, since my conscience was clear. I felt I could only benefit from hearing what they had to say about this accusation.

Both men took their places in the living room, standing to attention. I plonked into my old easy chair, its familiar embrace offering me little comfort in this charged atmosphere. I invited the officers to take their seats on the sofa to my right so they could be more comfortable. Conlon declined and Sweitzer followed suit. The air felt threatening, thick with unspoken intent. This meeting was not going to be that comfortable, I figured.

"What's this about a battery charge?" I inquired of the two men facing me.

"The State's Attorney has the report," replied Conlon.

"The State's Attorney," I exclaimed. "It's actually gone that far."

Sweitzer said nothing. He stood there motionless, both hands clutching the belt around his rotund frame. My interest now was in getting as much information from Conlon as I could. The truth would emerge, I felt, in its own good time, but I needed to help it along.

"Who wrote the report?" I asked.

Without hesitation Conlon replied: "I did."

So, Conlon wrote the report. That made sense. But where did he write it? I had a sneaking suspicion that this phony report might have been written at the house that belonged to the parish, now at the center of a canonical dispute between the diocese and the parish. The diocese, as mentioned earlier, had taken possession of this house as an office for Catholic Charities.

The bishop and Catholic Charities, who were operating under the concept of corporation sole, were not giving up the parish property that easily, I realized. Thus, they occupied it. If this report was indeed written up in the parish house, I believed it would link the whole nasty affair to the diocese's attempt to seize the house from the parish.

"Where did you write the report?" I asked Conlon.

He was totally shaken, as if he had been hit by a freight train. Normally such a report, if genuine, would be written at police headquarters, but I strongly suspected this was not the case. Conlon lost his rehearsed composure and looked at Sweitzer, whose eyes flickered about uneasily. This was Sweitzer's first sign of life or emotion. I don't know if he was taken aback by Conlon's sudden loss of control, or if it was my question that threw him off. At any rate, my question struck a nerve and Conlon's obvious unease was a dead giveaway. He was unwilling to answer this simple question, so I prodded him further: "Was the report written at the property that the diocese and Catholic Charities are trying to take from the parish?"

"It's in the report," he replied, after regaining his composure.

He was not giving anything away that might have implicated him in a bigger plot, but he did not refute or rebut what I was asking. An uneasy silence followed. I thought best not to press this aspect of the matter further and I did not want to provoke him.

I had other questions.

"Where did the alleged battery take place? I asked.

Quick came the reply: "At the parish office."

I could not have been more relieved when I heard this response. Thank God, the office had been closed all afternoon. Annabelle had left the premises around noon when she learned the office was closed.

But I had another question for Conlon: "What time does the report say the alleged incident occurred at the parish office?"

"Around 1:30 p.m.," he answered.

My sense of relief was complete.

"So, you say this alleged battery took place around 1:30 p.m. or thereabouts in the church's office. Is that right?" I continued.

Conlon glanced nervously at Sweitzer and replied: "That's right. That's what's in the report."

These people appeared to be a bunch of bunglers, thinking they could make a preposterous charge like this stick. I wanted to confirm with Sweitzer what his colleague had just admitted, that the alleged battery took place around 1:30 p.m. in the church's office.

"Is it true that the alleged battery, according to the report, took place a 1:30 p.m.?" I asked Sweitzer.

"Yes," he muttered.

"Well, that does it," I said. "My secretary, Faye, had closed the office at noon for the New Year, and Annabelle was told this when she stopped by the rectory."

How anyone could fabricate such a ridiculous story amazed me.

Conlon and Sweitzer cast glances at each other without uttering a word. Finally, Conlon's attitude went through a sea change.

"You could meet," he said, "with Tony Young, the State's Attorney, after the New Year to see about dropping these charges."

I don't know if I felt assuaged or disgusted by this remark. But I did know that the plot to frame me on a false battery charge was disintegrating before my eyes.

What ultimately protected me from a terrible fate were two women, Faye and Fran, my ministering angels, who came to my rescue when I needed them most and when I least expected it. It was Faye's idea to close the office at noon, on the vigil of the New Year, that removed any shred of credibility to the allegation of battery there at 1:30 p.m. And it was Fran's appearance at the door of the rectory that sent Annabelle hunkering away in confusion, thus foiling any other plans she or her collaborators might have been hatching to entrap me.

Annabelle's poor mastery of English worked in my favor also, because it made it difficult for the plotters to formulate and implement their scheme.

I learned later that this scam originated in the parish house that was taken over by Catholic Charities. The false report, it turned out, was written by Officer Conlon, in conjunction with and at the instigation of a Catholic Charities employee residing in the parish house.

There was no official report from the police department, and there were no charges made against me. This was a scam, pure and simple.

After the two policemen left, Fran returned to the rectory with Rocky, our little Shi-tzu, whom she took care of like her own child.

"What were those two policemen doing here?" she asked, having seen them leaving the rectory.

"Oh, they were returning the keys Annabelle had to the office," I replied nonchalantly.

Fran shrugged her shoulders, puckered her lips, and moved on about her business. Her earlier remark about Annabelle: "What's she up to?" was wringing in my ears.

I picked up pen and paper and committed myself to writing down everything that had transpired that day. Although I've always kept a journal, I decided to keep another detailed record on this plot to frame me on a false battery charge. I wrote down everything in detail pertaining to this outrageous scam, and I continued to keep accurate notes on everything else that transpired after that.

As I laid down my pen, the suffocating weight of the day pressed in on me. The false battery charge was no isolated incident, but the opening salvo in a much larger battle, one I hadn't even known I was fighting. The church, the institution I had devoted my life to, now appeared riddled with unseen forces, hidden in the shadows and pulling strings I had barely begun to comprehend. Annabelle, Conlon, even Sweitzer—they were just pawns in a game played by far more powerful and devious hands that remained unseen.

As the last light disappeared from the window, I felt a cold determination settle in. I would need every ounce of faith and strength for what lay ahead, for this fight was not merely for my reputation but for my very soul.

Chapter 26

THE NEW YEARS' CELEBRATION on the eve of 1995 at the pavilion was a moving event for the parish. We felt we had come a long way to arrive at this point and had surmounted many obstacles through the grace of God.

Our social ministry was ecumenical in its embrace, partnering with other agencies to extend a broader outreach into the community. Thus, we worked hand in hand with the Quaker's American Friends Service Committee (AFSC) to provide free legal assistance to immigrants; with Martha's House to help victims of domestic violence, with the Federal Emergency Management Agency (FEMA) to help family households with rental assistance, with the Children's Service Council (CSC) to offer essential services to youth, with Women, Infants and Children (WIC) to provide prenatal and nutrition care to the children of migrants, and with Job Referral Services to provide employment.

There had always been a strong women's club and men's club in the parish. But over the past ten years these were augmented by an equally strong outreach to the needy. Our youth groups—the Martial Arts Club, the Soccer Club, and the Drama Club that produced our *Christmas Around the World* celebration every year—were all part of the Family Outreach Center. In addition to these groups, we offered a food pantry, which served not only the children and families of the parish, but the children and families of the town and county.

As the clock struck midnight, a shower of brightly colored balloons rained down from the ceiling of the parish pavilion. The pop of champagne corks mingled with the joyful laughter of parishioners. We hugged tightly as tears of joy dampened cheeks. The room buzzed with warmth and gratitude, the joy of the moment a brief reprieve from the trials we were facing.

Even amid the laughter and the joy, a dark undercurrent ran just below the surface. While most of us celebrated the accomplishments of our parish, unseen forces were already working against us, hidden in the shadows. As I looked around at the smiling faces, so full of hope, I couldn't shake a growing unease. How could these good people know what was unfolding beyond their view, plotting to tear down what we had built?

Jesus's parable of the wheat among the weeds was not just a biblical message to be contemplated, but a dismal reality that we were experiencing in the parish. We had to tread lightly and wisely to protect the flock (the good wheat) from the bad weeds within the church itself.

Thus, as I was quietly making notes a few days into the new year about my meeting with the two officers of the law, a welcome visitor was ushered into the living room by Faye. It was Detective Alan "Bingo" Le Vin, and he was a ray of sunshine. He was all smiles and took a seat beside me.

Bingo had been around for a long time, and knew almost everybody in town. An old hand with his ear to the ground, Bingo appreciated the delicate balance between the different components in the community: the city mayor and the city councilmen, the Fire Chief and the county commissioners, the State Attorney and the police.

He knew who belonged to what church, who gave the most lavish parties in town and who was likely to be there. When a petty crime took place in the community, you could depend on Bingo to know who did *not* do it before finding out who actually did.

When our church's office had been broken into and the collection of offertories stolen, Bingo solved the crime. Jimmie Winnie, another guardian angel, had called me beforehand about this theft and told me about an earlier one at the First Baptist Church before we were burglarized. Jimmie always had a knack for helping, like Faye and Fran, whenever he was needed.

I shared Jimmy's information with Bingo.

"It's the same guy," Bingo said. "I was on the case at the Baptist church, and this guy has learned from the previous one because both safes are the same, except he has gotten better at breaking into them."

When I asked Bingo who it might be, he replied: "A stranger who moved into town."

"That's odd," I said. "A total stranger came to our Monday night bingo, Jimmy told me, asking to join the church, not knowing anything about the process of becoming a member."

Jimmy was the secretary of the Bingo Committee. He and a few other bingo workers observed this newcomer casing the property.

Based on this information, and a good description of the newcomer, Bingo easily tracked down the robber, and the crime at both churches was solved in a matter of days.

I was very heartened this time to see my old friend, Bingo, so soon after my ordeal with Annabelle and the police officers.

Part 2—Chapter 26

"So, you heard the news about the false battery charge levelled against me," I said, sadly.

Bingo smiled and shook his head.

"Yes, I know about that," he said. "The report about the alleged battery is not a valid police report. It was written up at the parish house, which the diocese and others are trying to steal from the parish."

Bingo had been advised about the problems with the parish house a few weeks earlier at the police station by Roger Azcona. In his capacity as leader of our Family Outreach Center, Roger had come into contact with the plotters, who tried to involve him in their ugly intrigue. Roger would have nothing to do with them, and told me about the plot.

After Roger had told me everything, I drove him to the police station to report the plot to Detective Bingo Le Vin. That's how Bingo knew about the plotters' attempt to frame me. Thus, he had written up a full account of the plot, and how it related to a wider scheme by Catholic Charities to wrest control of the guest house from the parish. When he came to see me now, at the rectory at the turn of another new year, he was able to connect the dots.

It was fortunate that Bingo was in possession of this information beforehand so we could evade the subtle snares set to entrap us. To my amazement, Bingo shared some very disturbing new developments coming out of the diocese. He had received an upsetting call from the chancellor, who told him that I was "being investigated by the diocese." This was obviously a deliberate attempt to discredit me, but Bingo was not having any of it.

If Bingo had not been told in advance about the machinations of the diocese to wrest the guest house from the parish, he could easily have been prejudiced by the chancellor's call. The plot had now worked its devious way, through false innuendo, into the inner workings of the police department itself. Fortunately for me, the police department was not deceived by such chicanery.

I knew I had to tread carefully now. One little slip here, another one there, and I could come a cropper without any means of defending myself.

But Bingo knew the truth, and was not taken in by diocesan intrigue. And, thank God, Roger had shared vital information about the plot to the police department before it was set in motion. In times like this, you see the importance of solid friends like Roger and Bingo and others to steer you safely through the storm.

Bingo, however, found it hard to get his mind around the diocese's attempt to interfere in the proper conduct of the law. He asked me if I would accompany him to meet with Tony Young, the state attorney in Okeechobee. I told him I would be more than happy to do so.

When we arrived at the Okeechobee County State Attorney's office, I volunteered to take a lie detector test, and asked that my accuser do the same.

"That won't be necessary," replied Tony Young. "I took a photo of the accuser's arm where she claimed she had suffered bruises and told her to come back again to see if they were still there. She did not come back."

I recounted what had actually taken place to the state attorney. He didn't need any convincing. The fact that the parish office was closed at noon on New Year's Eve, 1994, made the claim of battery totally preposterous.

The trumped-up allegation was preposterous for another reason as well. It could not have taken place in the office as alleged because Faye and Jack, who worked there, would have been witnesses to it. Obviously, they had witnessed nothing of the sort at the office before they left on New Year's Eve.

Relieved that the police detective and the state attorney had seen through this scam, I returned to the parish in a good mood. It was there, when I got back, I decided to call the monsignor in charge of Catholic Charities to let him know what was going on.

Faye bustled efficiently around the office, her steady presence as comforting as a well-worn prayer book. She put in the call to the monsignor at the diocese for me. When he called back, I was mid-conversation with Al Roussel, our volunteer, parish manager. Al, a retired shop owner, had been an indispensable help, looking out for the material needs of the parish.

"Do you want me to step outside?" Al graciously suggested.

"Not at all," I replied. "This is a matter of parish administration, and you need to be in on it since you're the parish manager."

I was glad to talk to the head of Catholic Charities, a colleague and fellow priest. I told him how I was being framed on a false battery charge and that it was fabricated at the parish property, which Catholic Charities was occupying.

His response was totally unexpected and very upsetting.

"Now the matter is in the hands of the police," he replied, coldly.

"Is that all you have to say about this outrageous skullduggery? Now the matter is in the hands of the police?" I retorted.

The abrupt click of the phone, ending the conversation, left me stunned. I sat there, the receiver still clutched in my hand, my mouth hanging open in disbelief after hearing these words, so cold and dismissive. How could a fellow priest brush off something so serious with such callous indifference? I hung up the phone, shaken, wondering if loyalty and support within the church was nothing more than a fragile illusion.

Al was beside himself. He was never prepared for anything like this.

Part 2 — Chapter 26

"I only heard one part of the conversation," Al said, "but it's enough to tell me this man is part of the plot to destroy you."

Shaking his head in frustration, he added, emphatically: "I wouldn't have your job for all the tea in China!"

"I was never prepared for this kind of job either, Al," I replied. "I feel like Jeremiah, who cried out in the midst of persecution: 'You duped me, O Lord.'"

I realize that doing God's will is never easy. It means carrying your cross and following Christ. Trying to live by this teaching, in spite of human weakness, in a world of sin, is no joke. The eighth beatitude of Jesus makes it clear that persecution for the sake of his kingdom is a cross we must all be prepared to bear. The bishop I met down in Mexico also warned me that I'd face persecution. But what disappointed me most was that the persecution was perpetrated by the church itself. This was the worst form of corruption, for it was corruption of the highest.

Corruption by those highly placed is the gravest of scandals and is not new in the church's history. It was an alarming wake-up call to discover that the institution I thought would support me in doing the Lord's work was actually my biggest obstacle. Prepared for it or not, I realized I was dealing with something far worse than I ever expected: the dark underbelly of church politics. I had no choice but to oppose this ungodly behavior with every fiber of my being.

Chapter 27

Bad news travels fast.

As word of the false battery charge spread outward from the diocesan pastoral center to the rest of the diocese, the seeds of rumor were sown, giving rise to a twisted tangle of gossip and conspiracy. The tongues of diocesan talking heads were cocked and loaded, ready to spit out outrageous gossip, the last resort of weak minds. These rumors, nourished by whispers and lies, wound their way from the diocesan headquarters, threatening to choke the truth beneath their relentless growth.

Officials spread rumors that I was hospitalized, or that I was arrested, or that I was taken to prison in an unmarked police car. These were just some of the wild stories I heard from a few trusted friends working in the Diocesan Pastoral Center. The *Palm Beach Post* was fed these outrageous rumors, and a reporter contacted the Okeechobee Police Department, only to learn that these offensive claims were entirely false. To its credit, the *Post* would not pursue any story out of the diocese based on lies and false allegations.

Things were heating up, and I needed to talk to Faye privately about what was going on. She was on the front line in the front office and would need to be extra careful amid the pernicious intrigue welling up around us. I walked to the office from my study in the rectory, where I do most of my daily work of preparing sermons and attending to parish administration. I noticed that the door to the inner office where the parish files were kept, normally left open, was closed.

"Why is this door closed?" I asked Faye, taken aback. "It's always left open."

"Oh, a few nice people wanted to make copies of some paperwork and asked me if they could use the copying machine," she replied graciously, as usual.

Before I could utter another word or check out what was going on in the inner office, the door flung open and two people rushed out, heading

Part 2—Chapter 27

for the street. Clutching bundles of material in their arms, they left without saying a word, making a quick getaway. The ugly intrigue had stolen its way, not only into the Okeechobee Police Department, but into the parish office, unbeknownst to me and the parish secretary.

Faye and I looked at each other, dumbfounded. Her usual warmth drained from her face as the weight of what had happened dawned on us both. Her eyes were wide with disbelief.

"I'm so sorry," she murmured, her voice breaking with guilt.

Her trusting nature had been manipulated in ways neither of us could have anticipated, and my heart ached for her, knowing how she had been exploited and used in a web of deceit.

"You acted in good faith, Faye, so don't accuse yourself," I said. "I'll have to tell Al Roussel to replace this door with a half-door, so this doesn't happen again. No one must be allowed to enter this inner office without permission."

The plot thickened further after this break-in. The two collaborators had stolen the files of George McKay's estate. But they didn't stop there. They got together with the representative of Catholic Charities in Okeechobee and went with the information they had stolen to the chairman of the parish finance council, Vincent La Mariana.

They claimed that the attorney for the estate, Tom Conley, and the personal representative of the estate—myself—had embezzled approximately $157,000. They had in their possession a copy of a check they stole from the office.

It was made out to "Sacred Heart." The plotters, in their eagerness to accuse me and the estate attorney of embezzlement, jumped to the false conclusion that the check was made out to the parish of Sacred Heart in Okeechobee without checking the facts. In reality, the check was made out to Sacred Heart, a *seminary* in Hales Corners, a village in Milwaukee County, Wisconsin!

The plotters were confident that they had developed a convincing case of embezzlement, but Vinny was buying none of it. Tom Conley was his personal attorney, and Vinney knew that Tom, a devout Baptist, and I myself would never be involved in something like that.

So, Vinney raised himself up to his full height and told the plotters: "You are involved in a fishing expedition and have only caught yourselves. I'm going right now to see Tom Conley to tell him about this and to get the facts."

The plotters left, disappointed that Vinney would not back them and had refused to accompany them to Diocesan Headquarters. As they made their way to the Diocesan Pastoral Center, Vinney made his way to meet with attorney Tom Conley.

Upon hearing what happened, Conley was infuriated at the accusations.

"Who's that bishop's boss?" he asked Vinney.

"Someone in Washington D.C.," said Vinney, hesitating. "He's called the Papal Nuncio."

"Can you get me his address?" asked Tom.

"Father Duffy should have it," Vinney replied.

"Leave Father Duffy out of this," said Tom, decisively. "We know what he's going through, and we don't want to create more anxiety for him."

Vinney called Faye at the parish office. Faye perused the *Catholic Directory* and found the address of the Papal Nuncio in Washington.

A few days later, I received in the mail a blind copy of the letter that attorney Conley sent to the Papal Nuncio. I was flabbergasted when I read it, because I had no idea of this development at that time. Not only had I been falsely accused of battery, the plotters were doubling down by adding another false allegation of embezzlement of parish funds.

Attorney Conley addressed this allegation in his letter to the Nuncio and included a letter from the Provincial of Sacred Heart Seminary in Hales Corners, Wisconsin, thanking me and the attorney for the professional way in which we handled the entire McKay Estate. The attorney also included a letter from the state attorney in Okeechobee, exonerating me from the battery charge.

After reading the blind copy of the letter, I rushed out of the rectory and drove directly to Tom Conley's office. When he saw me, he crossed both arms over his chest, and asked, pleadingly: "Did I do something wrong?"

"No, you did everything just right, and thanks for keeping me out of this," I replied, gratefully.

I sat down with Tom at his office. He went over everything that had transpired regarding this latest plot to accuse both of us of embezzlement from the McKay estate. Tom was now personally involved, and his reputation as an attorney was at stake.

We had a long conversation. I understood clearly now that the robbers had stolen the files of the Mc Kay estate from the inner office in order to frame me and my attorney on a false charge of embezzlement. I also understood clearly that this plot to frame me involved the diocese.

I had to tread cautiously, because the diocese possessed nearly unlimited resources to get its way.

Sometimes we mistakenly think only the right things, the benevolent things, are part of God's will for us. Then when bad things happen, we wonder what went wrong, and question God's will. Maybe nothing went wrong here, and maybe it was all part of God's plan to bring the truth to light. The conspirators who stole the files from the parish office were responsible for bringing to light what was happening in secret. This was a blessing in disguise, an example of how out of evil can come good. My attorney, who was personally, falsely accused, was left no option but to write to the Papal Nuncio in Washington, outlining the real facts of the case. The robbery backfired, leading, eventually, to a good outcome for the parish.

I had been waiting and hoping for God's timing to run its course, realizing that He only permits as much trouble to befall us as we can handle. This latest allegation of embezzlement was actually an answer to my prayer, because it blew the whole plot wide open.

In the meantime, I shuddered to contemplate what might come next. I expected I would be hearing from the diocese, at some stage, about these trumped-up allegations. So far, the diocesan leadership was holding its cards close to its chest while others did its bidding.

I kept wondering when the call would come, but I was not going to contact the diocesan offices in Palm Beach Gardens, simply because I hadn't done anything wrong. It would do me no good anyway, as I discovered when I talked to the monsignor in charge of Catholic Charities. Bingo's revelation about the chancellor's interference in the process of law also made me wary about turning to him for support.

Thus, I went about my business confidently.

Chapter 28

ON JANUARY 4, 1995, my foreboding was realized.

"You've got a visitor," said Fran, as she ushered the second bishop of the Diocese of Palm Beach, into my study. A small, rotund figure of a man, he entered the study full of his wee self. A rim of dyed, dark hair encircled his shiny bald head from ear to ear, giving the impression he was wearing a golden helmet.

I stood up and we shook hands. Taken aback but not surprised by this unexpected visit, I adjusted to the shock as best I could. The bishop took a seat facing me, across the desk where I was working.

Wasting no time, he got to the point: "I'm here because I got a report from the Okeechobee Police Department of a battery charge against you."

"You got a report from the Okeechobee Police Department of a battery charge against me?" I repeated, my tone casting doubt on the veracity of what he had just said.

"Yes," he insisted. "It's the custom of the police department to let the bishop know when one of his priests is in trouble."

The bishop's remarks were delivered in such a condemnatory tone that I was ready to explode. But that would have served no purpose and would have made things worse, so I forced myself to stay calm. I knew well that somebody was in trouble, but it wasn't me.

I responded calmly: "The report you got was not from the police department. It was from a police officer acting at the behest of Catholic Charities to get me arrested. In fact, this phony report was written up at the parish property that you have taken from Sacred Heart."

Just then, Roger walked into my study and handed me a typewritten report from Detective Le Vin at the police department. This was the genuine police report: the one that implicated diocesan personnel in wrongdoing. I looked it over and it clearly outlined the malfeasance of my detractors, working with the diocese, to frame me. The timing of this report could not have been better.

Part 2—Chapter 28

The bishop wanted to see it.

"You can look at it," I said, forcefully, "but I want it back."

The bishop flipped through the report and handed it back to me without discussing it. It was as if the very act of holding it was beneath him, an inconvenience he wished to forget as quickly as possible.

While not expecting much sympathy from the bishop for all the abuse I had been subjected to by him, I was dismayed when he got irate with me because I dared to defend my rights and the rights of the parish. He doubled down on the lies about battery in the phony police report he received even after I showed him the real one. He accused me of battery, saying I dragged the accuser out of the parish office on New Year's Day, causing bruises to her arm. Then he continued.

"These are very serious charges. As your bishop, I am asking for your resignation as pastor of the parish."

I responded: "I cannot resign over something I did not do. That would be spiritual suicide. The allegations you're making are scurrilous and have been proven to be false. The fact that the office was closed at the time of the alleged battery incident certainly demonstrates that it was totally fabricated."

I kept watching his reaction and waited for his answer, but there was none. He knew he was in trouble and shifted uneasily in his seat. Dropping the subject of the false battery charge, he took another track.

He decided to pull rank: "What about your oath to the bishop?" he asked. "You're not going to disobey your bishop, are you?"

I was ready for this classic Catch-22. Even though the allegations he brought up were proven false, he still felt I had no option but to go along with them, simply because of my oath to him as bishop.

"Name one example," I challenged, "when I did not support your office as bishop to promote the ministry of Christ which we both share?"

He was unable to come up with a single example of my refusal to support his office as bishop. His own actions were so clearly opposed to that shared ministry that he didn't want to go there.

He turned his gaze away in embarrassment. Obviously, he didn't want to expose his own wrongdoing; his own corruption of that office, a very serious matter, and the unlawful pressure put on me to go along with diocesan corruption.

The next question was surprising: "What did you do with the $157,000 that should have gone to the Sacred Heart Seminary in Hales Corners, Wisconsin?"

The bishop knew about this donation to the Sacred Heart Seminary in Wisconsin because my attorney had sent him a copy of the will, as was proper. But why would he assume the money was not sent to the seminary?

I suspected that those who stole a copy of the check from the parish office for the same amount managed to convince him of this nonsense. Even though he possessed a copy of George McKay's will, he still pushed the false charge of embezzlement.

"What do you think I did with it?" I asked, stunned by the tone and audacity of the question.

"That's what I'm asking you", he replied.

"That's where it went," I emphasized emphatically. "It went to the Sacred Heart Seminary in Wisconsin. Where else do you think it went? You have a copy of the will."

The bishop shifted in his seat again and seemed to lose his cool. I could see that he was flummoxed by my responses, especially to this latest try. Both he and his collaborators had blundered into this one, and botched it the same way they botched the earlier, false battery accusation.

He had nothing more to say, and he rose to leave.

I accompanied him outside as a gesture of respect for his office. I saw him to his car, parked in the little driveway in front of the rectory. As he drove off, my little dog, Rocky, ran after his car. I watched as both of them took off. I feared for my little dog, but the bishop did a U-turn and drove back by the entrance with the dog behind. He ended up where he began, in front of the rectory where I was standing. He stepped out of the car as I bent down to pick up Rocky.

"At least there's one creature," he said, "that's willing to follow me."

We both laughed for a change. I was glad he hadn't taken himself too seriously, at least for now. The allegations he leveled at me so intently during our meeting had vanished like dust in the wind, and I could see he was embarrassed. He would have a lot to ponder on his way back to Palm Beach Gardens.

"We can learn a lot from these harmless creatures," I said, petting Rocky. "They are very loving and not at all judgmental."

With that, he drove off.

The sun slid slowly behind the field of trees in the distance, and the magic light of the setting sun laced the leaves with a sparkle of diamonds. The birds were chirping, and I felt a surge of inner joy in the midst of all this beauty. This was the timeless pulse of nature itself, indifferent to the reckless whims of man. These natural sights and sounds raised my spirits after the strange, off-the-wall encounter with the bishop. Our little lives are but a drop in the ocean of God's mysterious plan, achieving its purpose in his good time, not ours.

I closed the door behind me as Fran, lovingly, set the dinner table for Father Finn and myself.

Chapter 29

THE PAPAL NUNCIO IN Washington responded affirmatively to attorney Tom Conley's letter of January 9, 1995. Soon after, the bishop called me, summoning me to a meeting at the Diocesan Pastoral Center.

"This whole Okeechobee situation is festering," he began, angrily.

"Who's making it fester, Bishop?" I replied, frankly. "It's not me. All I want is to do my work as pastor of the parish. I can only do this if you put a stop to these false allegations, circulating in the community and in the diocese."

Ignoring this remark, he continued: "I want you to be here on January twenty-fifth for a meeting about this."

He gave me the time of the meeting.

"That's when we're having our general meeting for the parish festival," I replied. "Could you not make it some other time, bishop?"

"The meeting is on January twenty-fifth, and if you aren't here, I'll hold the meeting without you," he declared officiously.

There was no getting out of this January 25th meeting.

"How many people will you be bringing with you?" continued the bishop, apprehensively. "Around twenty?"

I didn't expect to bring anyone with me, but twenty sounded too many.

"Not that many, Bishop," I replied. "Just the attorney for the estate, the chairman of the Parish Finance Council, and myself."

At dinner the night before this meeting, Father Jim Finn opened up about what was going on.

"I've been giving a lot of thought to this persecution by the bishop and Catholic Charities," he said. "It's obvious that Sacred Heart is doing more to help people in need than Catholic Charities, and that's why the diocese is trying to steal the parish property and social programs."

"I'm actually aware of that, Jim," I replied. "I found the executive director of Catholic Charities in the parish hall one afternoon with one of his assistants taking materials from our files without permission. Later, we received, in the mail, copies of our own social programs, which were sent out to all parishes as if they were being conducted by Catholic Charities."

"You'll have to be very firm at tomorrow's meeting," Jim persisted. "You're dealing with a secret society, and these people have shown you no mercy. They have tried everything to destroy you."

A secret society—I was surprised to hear Jim characterize the diocesan operation, a church institution, in this way. But I couldn't disagree with him. Jim was a man of vast experience, and he painted a stark but true picture of what I was dealing with. I was up against an aberrant church institution that conducted its dealings in secrecy and threatened to engulf the parish in its own corruption.

"My sole purpose at tomorrow's meeting," I replied, "will be to clear the air and put this whole affair behind us. I pray for this outcome. We cannot adopt the same tactics as our accusers, Jim. Lord knows, it's time for this to end."

On January 25, Tom Conley drove Vinney and myself to the Diocesan Pastoral Center. We drove along Highway 701 to Indiantown Road, where we took a sharp left to Palm Beach Gardens. The afternoon sun cast a mercurial sheen across the asphalt, while lances of light skewered through the trees lining our route.

A chill was in the air. Flocks of wild geese were aiming their huge, feathery arrow formation to the south. As we entered the Palm Beach Gardens area, the landscape changed from the raw and natural countryside we knew in Okeechobee County to carefully manicured hedges and flowing expanses of lawns. It was a glorious winter's afternoon. A pity our minds were heavy with the pressing anxieties of the meeting we were summoned to.

When we arrived at the Pastoral Center, we were escorted into the upstairs conference room where I often attended the Presbyteral Council meetings as representative of the Northern Deanery, and again as secretary of the Diocesan Personnel Board. This was familiar territory for me.

The bishop and his retinue entered the conference room after we got there. We shook hands and I introduced the bishop to my attorney for the estate, Tom Conley, and to the chairman of the Parish Finance Council, Vincent La Mariana.

The bishop's aides consisted of lay members of the board of Catholic Charities, the executive director of Catholic Charities, the monsignor who presided over this organization, and the diocesan chancellor. The meeting was chaired by the bishop himself.

Part 2—Chapter 29

The bishop wasted no time, and turning to me asked: "How did your attorney get the Papal Nuncio's address? You must have been the one to give it to him."

His tone dripped with suspicion, leaving no doubt that he expected my admission. Obviously, the bishop thought I was responsible for the attorney writing to the Nuncio. Nothing could have been further from the truth since I had only learned about the attorney's letter when I received a blind copy of it in the mail. He wasn't bothered, it seemed, that his collaborators had stolen the files of the McKay Estate from the parish office and brought them to him at the Pastoral Center.

"You'd better ask the attorney," I replied, pointing to Tom sitting beside him.

Turning to Tom, he asked: "Where did you get the address of the Papal Nuncio?"

Tom seemed to be enjoying the charade. With a broad smile, and without uttering a word, he pointed his index finger towards Vinney, his good friend, sitting next to him.

"So, where did *you* get the address of the Nuncio?" the bishop asked Vinney.

"I called the secretary at the parish, and she gave it to me," Vinny replied, succinctly.

The bishop was embarrassed, and grudgingly admitted: "This kind of information is readily available to anyone nowadays, I suppose."

He next began by distancing himself from Catholic Charities, which came under his jurisdiction. He said it was a separate entity from the diocese, in an effort to absolve himself of any wrongdoing. He then asked me what I had to say.

I addressed the abuses of both the diocese and Catholic Charities in taking over parish property, in trying to take over parish programs, and falsely accusing me of battery and embezzlement. I mentioned how the monsignor, who was present at this meeting, refused to support me when I was falsely accused of battery, saying the matter was now in the hands of the police.

The monsignor, twirling a toothpick in his mouth, offered no reply.

Then I asked the chancellor if he had met with my accusers at the Diocesan Pastoral Center, as I had been told.

In an effort to distance himself from the conspirators, he replied: "I only saw them in the corridor."

I continued: "The local director of Catholic Charities in Okeechobee, together with other collaborators, told Vinney they were bringing a copy of a check for over $157,000 stolen from the parish office to the bishop at the Pastoral Center."

Vinny confirmed what I reported.

"Did the robbers give you the copy of the check for $157,000 which they stole from the parish office?" I asked of the bishop.

No response.

"On January fourth when you visited the parish," I continued, "you asked me what I did with the check for $157,000 that should have gone to the Sacred Heart Seminary in Wisconsin. I told you it went to the seminary."

No response.

I continued: "When you visited me at the parish, Bishop, you made a false allegation of battery against me."

No response.

No explanation was offered regarding the serious, false allegations of battery and embezzlement.

At the end of this perplexing meeting, the bishop announced he was returning the property occupied by Catholic Charities to the parish.

I could hardly believe my ears. This was a very welcome surprise. It made a mockery of the bishop's earlier assertion that Catholic Charities was a separate entity from the diocese. But I didn't go there. I was happy with the outcome. I could see the hand of the Nuncio in this decision to return to the parish what belonged to the parish.

"The transfer will not happen right away," the bishop continued. "The present occupants need some time to get it ready to hand over to the parish."

It took a month to get the property back, and when we did, it had been swept clean of anything that could be traced to the previous occupants who worked for the diocese.

After the meeting adjourned, a lay member on the Catholic Charities board approached me. Publicly, he made clear that not all backed the unethical behavior of diocesan administrators. Speaking from the heart and with moral conviction, he voiced strong objections to such unchristian behavior. I was heartened to know that voices of conscience still spoke within the ranks, though tragically silenced until now. This lone layman gave me hope that truth and justice might yet prevail.

Eavesdropping on our conversation, the bishop, perhaps nudged by his conscience, casually mentioned that Okeechobee parish was to receive a multimillion-dollar donation. But his words, though surprising, stirred no hope within me.

From my experience in dealing with the property donated by George McKay, and how the diocese, as corporation sole, tried to take if from the

Part 2—Chapter 29

parish, I was not optimistic that the parish would receive this new donation, either.

A short time before this meeting, my old friends Tom and Barbara Garrity visited me in Okeechobee. Tom was very impressed by the parish and particularly inspired by the video, *A Parish for All Seasons*. He wanted to donate his shares in the Kimberly-Clark Corporation to our church. It was a rather substantial donation but, in conscience, I could not accept it, since I was engaged in the dispute with the diocese over a much smaller donation of property by George McKay.

"I don't want to put you through what I'm being subjected to over another property that's been donated to us," I told Tom.

Tom, a Glasgow man, was awfully surprised, but thankful that I had spared him a bad experience with the diocese.

"I didne ken that sorta thing went on in the Kirk, Faither," he said, with a heavy heart in his lilting Scottish brogue.

"I didn't know until recently that this type of thing went on in the church either, Tom," I replied.

It obviously shocked Tom to hear about this, but I had to tell the truth to spare him the anguish caused by the institutional church. A parish, I believed, was about more important matters than money.

We departed the Pastoral Center after that January 25 meeting in a better mood than when we entered it. Getting into the car for the home journey, Vinney, seated in the passenger seat, turned around to me and exclaimed: "What a crock of bull!"

He was, of course, talking about the meeting we had just attended.

Tom Conley sat there in the driver's seat, tapping his fingers on the wheel. He was in a pensive mood.

"I'm looking for another way to describe that meeting," he said.

I leaned over and suggested: "Inquisition!"

Tom reacted strongly: "That's it! That's exactly the word I've been looking for, Inquisition."

Vinney was very disappointed at the blatant disregard for truth and the slick way facts were covered up, even though the cover-up didn't work.

"Do they go to school to study this?" Vinney asked, puzzled.

"I don't know about going to school for this, but they're obviously well-schooled in these practices," I responded.

We drove back to Okeechobee.

The sun was setting over the big lake. The anxiety we experienced on the way to the Pastoral Center was now lifted. I was able to absorb, unperturbed, nature's bounty. When you are beaten down with cares and worries, you see little of nature's loveliness. But once these worries are dispelled, the beauty of nature comes rushing back again.

An orange glow settled on the wide water of the placid lake as the sun slid beneath the horizon. What a blessed ending to an otherwise excruciating day.

By the time we returned to Okeechobee, the parish festival was in full swing. Volunteers hurried about, preparing meals for the weekend's crowds. From the succulent Polynesian feast on Friday and the French-Canadian Cajun delicacies on Saturday to the traditional American barbecue on Sunday, the festival brought the community together in joyous celebration. The warmth of the festival lifted our spirits, reminding us that in the end, service to the people was our true calling. In all, over a thousand meals were served during the three-day festival at the pavilion.

On Saturday evening, the chairman of the festival tracked me down on the grounds and said: "The bishop is here and is looking for you."

Surprises never cease, I thought.

We located the bishop, who was accompanied by a seminarian at the big Ferris wheel. I welcomed him to the festival. All's well that ends well, I felt. He wanted me, surprisingly, to join him for a ride on the Ferris wheel, where everybody could behold us, seated together in harmony. I had to decline the invitation because I had a problem with vertigo.

We had dinner instead in the pavilion. At the dinner, the bishop was telling me about meeting a group of Jews recently, and that he had apologized to them for the Holocaust.

"They had tears in their eyes as I apologized to them," said the bishop.

The seminarian, accompanying him, swooned in admiration.

As much as I found the Holocaust abhorrent, I would have been grateful if the bishop showed some compunction for what he and his collaborators had put myself and the parish through. But remorse seemed to be a rare attribute among those who abuse power in the church. Thus, he continued to talk about the Holocaust rather than what was really on our minds.

The unfortunate events of the past were over, and now we could set our sights on doing what we enjoyed: taking care of the real needs of the people of God.

I usually visited the hospital on Mondays. During my routine visit, one of the pink-clad ladies at the front desk handed me a list of the sick who needed to see a priest. On the list, to my surprise, was the name of the police officer involved in trying to frame me on a false battery charge. I didn't know he was Catholic, since he never attended church. But he was on my list and he wanted to see a priest.

Part 2—Chapter 29

Standing at the doorway to his room, I felt a storm of emotions rising inside me—anger, betrayal, confusion. This moment, more than most, tested my ability to set aside personal grievances. I knew that ministry demanded more than just service—it called for humility and compassion, even toward those who had wronged me. Compassion, I realized, is often the heaviest burden to carry, but also the most necessary.

I have found it helpful not to take the human weaknesses of others too seriously, for you don't know what they're going through or what terrible trauma brought them to this point in their lives. Only God knows, and everyone is in need of his mercy.

My former enemy was glad to see me, and happier still to receive the anointing of the sick. I was pleased to give him the sacrament, because the act lifted a heavy burden from both of us. I was elated to let bygones be bygones, and he was overjoyed to be back in the fold. I did not feel bitter over what he had tried to do to me. He was a pawn in a terrible game, and had succumbed to the weakness of the flesh for the woman he craved. He was being used, regrettably, by diocesan officials who should have known better and thus carried the greater guilt.

I left the hospital that day feeling like I was walking on air.

Chapter 30

Reconciliation surged through me like a gentle breeze, cleansing the lingering bitterness and filling me with a renewed sense of my vocation. It was more than mere relief—it was a spiritual rebirth, one that freed me from the chains of resentment, allowing peace to settle in its place.

Knowing we had been vindicated and that the property had been returned to its rightful owner, the parish, was an enormous relief.

Yet, this euphoria proved as ephemeral as morning mist. The tranquility I had briefly savored vanished as the familiar shadows of old conflicts creeping back, threatened once again to darken the peace.

Those who had fought to seize the property and programs from the parish did not go meekly into the night. Their intrigues ran deep, and turning back was not an option, it seemed. So immersed were they in their own machinations, like Macbeth stealing Duncan's crown, that it was easier for them to persist in perfidy than to relent.

Rather than abandoning their false claims, they doubled down, sowing alarm and dismay among the good people in the parish.

In the midst of this confusion, Goldie Gibbons, a friend and Purple Heart recipient for his heroism during the Korean War, came to talk to me. A straight-talker, Goldie was a man of respect in the community, and was genuinely upset by what he was hearing.

"I want to talk to you man-to-man," he said, entering the rectory unannounced.

"Sure, Goldie," I replied brightly, getting up from my seat and shaking his hand before we sat down together.

"Ask me whatever you want," I said.

"Well," said Goldie, his voice gravelly with the weight of years, "I'm not one to beat around the bush. What I've been hearing out there—it isn't purty, and I'm here to lay it all out, straight as it comes."

He recounted the rumors to me in detail. I was glad to have this opportunity to clear the air with somebody as decent and open-minded as

Goldie. I answered every one of the allegations he recounted, and I provided documentation, especially the detailed letter of attorney Conley to the Nuncio, proving the rumored accusations totally false.

Goldie was appalled that people could spread lies like these, especially after they were debunked, and he thanked me for being so frank and truthful. He told me he knew nothing about the parish property being confiscated by Catholic Charities or the involvement of my detractors in this chicanery, but he was glad the property had been returned to the parish. He was flabbergasted at how people, caught telling lies and robbery of files from the parish office, could continue to spread slander.

"It doesn't make sense to me," he said.

"Nor does it make any sense to me," I added.

"I'm going to give these people a good piece of my mind when I see them," said Goldie, with gusto, as he got up to leave. Knowing Goldie's character, I knew he would tell these people where to go with their lies.

"You were in the heat of a fierce battle in Korea," I said, "and you've been decorated with a Golden Heart for saving a thousand lives in the battle for the Eastern Corridor. You carry the scars of battle. How is this any different?"

"A big difference," insisted Goldie, as he strode to the door.

Turning back, he said: "In war, it was kill-or-be-killed. What these people are doing is knifing you in the back. That's what low-down cowards get up to."

Parishioners like Goldie, armed with the facts, soon turned the tables around among those inclined to believe or spread malicious gossip.

Most people, fortunately, saw through these unfounded rumors, and never gave them the slightest credence. I kept my counsel, and never dropped a hint of what was going on from the pulpit. There was no need. The facts sufficed to disprove the lies. Life went on as usual and the parish weathered the storm, calmly.

Goldie was not the only one who came to see me for a man-to-man talk. An old friend, a member of the Okeechobee Council of City Commissioners and vice-mayor of the town, Andy Rubin, stopped by. Andy was a Jew, and we became friends on account of his adopted son, Richard, whom he raised Catholic. Richard's mother, who was married to Andy, was Catholic and had passed away. After his high school graduation, Richard suffered a terrible car accident that left him crippled for life. That did not deter Andy from adopting him and raising him Catholic. I frequently visited Andy at his home, bringing the Sacrament of the Sick and communion to Richard.

"Father Duffy, we've been friends for many years, and I don't want to see you get hurt," he said. "I worked with Father Baker in Buffalo, and I've seen up close how Catholic Charities and these bishops act. They're worse than the Mafia."

The Mafia. I had heard this term used by priests before to describe the behavior of certain bishops. I did not tell Andy about the meeting we had with the bishop and Catholic Charities at the Diocesan Pastoral Center.

"Andy, if I were to roll over and let this injustice succeed, I couldn't live with myself."

Andy did not dispute what I said. He was my friend, and he was only looking out for me.

We talked about the capricious nature of life, and the trying circumstances we're often thrust into through no fault of our own. Andy, like Goldie, bore the scars of war, having fought in the blood-drenched killing fields of Okinawa. A man of deep compassion, he wept when recounting tales of cruelty towards the vulnerable and disabled. He was the first to suggest having a free day for the handicapped at our festival, and he generously covered the cost of all meals himself.

Yet Andy was also a seasoned politician, and viewed my situation politically. But I was different, and couldn't allow myself to be entangled in the complexities of church politics. My role was pastoral, answering to the gospel and meeting the needs of the parishioners in a mixed-up world and, if that meant persecution, so be it. I was not promised a rose garden. I held fast to the belief that God's will was stronger than political machinations. We conversed amiably with the fervent hope that more reasonable and charitable minds might prevail.

There was a most disheartening turn of events, however, after this meeting with Andy, as if to confirm his political savvy. The bishop suddenly reignited the dying embers, deciding to meet with the same people who were spreading the same allegations against me that had been proven false and, as I thought, were now ended for good.

He arranged a meeting with my accusers for 3:00 p.m. on March 26, 1995 in the parish hall. Accompanied by a young man, who stayed in the rectory while the meeting was taking place, the bishop asked me to open the door to the parish building. The meeting consisted of four or five people, including the two who stole the files of the McKay estate from the parish office. I was forbidden to attend.

This secretive meeting concluded, and the bishop met with me in the corridor between the rectory and the church. He asked if I had in my possession a copy of the false battery report drawn up at the parish guest house which the diocese had tried to wrest from the parish. I told him I did. Irate, he then repeated what my accusers told him.

Part 2—Chapter 30

I answered everything with facts, but his response floored me: "I don't care if you can answer these accusations. The fact that they are being made is good enough for me."

What a turnaround! My response was simple: "In that case, I have nothing more to say."

He repeated his old demand that I offer my resignation as the pastor of the parish. I did not answer him.

On April 11, 1995, attorney Conley wrote to the Nuncio again about these regrettable developments, stating that I welcomed full disclosure and the opportunity to clear my name.

Miraculously, things died down again as they always did, and everything continued as usual. People, I've found, have a knack for ignoring the ridiculous and getting on with what is right. There's something about the Christian sense of the faithful that easily deciphers truth from falsehood. It's called *Sensus Fidelium* or Sense of the Faithful. Faith is a gift, and those who are led by it are not going to be led astray by mischief and wrongdoing, no matter where it comes from. Deep down, I trusted the community's sense to know right from wrong and to do the right thing.

I also knew where the loyalty of the parishioners lay. What had transpired had nothing to do with the real business of the gospel to uplift and help one another. The good parishioners knew that, too. This was about institutional abuse. The best way to deal with it, I realized, was to ignore the craziness and concentrate on the real needs of the people of God.

This approach paid off, thank God, for people came up to me, uninvited, and told me what they thought about the false allegations swirling around. I did not have to volunteer any information to them. They saw what was happening as a nasty business and ignored it. It was alien, they knew, to the true mission of the church, which was to spread the good news of the gospel, not bad news.

Sensing that the conflict was far from over, I meticulously documented every incident, compiling a detailed dossier. The Papal Nuncio's support had reached its limit—our only hope now was Rome. With approval from my trusted canonist, Father James A. Coriden, I sent a full report to the Congregation for Bishops (now called the Dicastery for Bishops) in the Vatican on September 15, 1995. I hoped the Vatican would finally put an end to the abuse.

The bishop, it appeared, had got himself mixed up with the wrong crowd, and he couldn't control them. God knows I had no control over them and that's why I decided to bring the matter to Rome. Everybody is answerable to a higher power, and even a bishop must answer to his superiors, and to God. My sole purpose in bringing this matter to Rome was to stop these abuses.

I continued to do my work quietly, ignoring the false allegations of my accusers.

I didn't hear back from the Congregation for Bishops, but I knew my correspondence got there, since I received the green, return receipt from the post office by mail.

During my vacation in July of 1996, at my canonist's strong recommendation, I flew to Rome concerning this matter.

Chapter 31

I HAD LONG AVOIDED Rome, the Eternal City. Tales of corruption within the Vatican's ancient walls kept me at a distance. But now, driven by duty and necessity, I had no other choice but to go there if I wanted to put a stop to abuses that threatened to overwhelm the parish. My canonist emphasized the importance of a personal meeting with Vatican authorities, and I appreciated the wisdom of his advice.

My relationship with the Congregation for Bishops, up to this point, had been conducted on paper, including the dossier I sent that was not acknowledged. Paper correspondence has a logic all its own, as Saint John Henry Newman pointed out in the *Grammar of Assent*.[1] It fails to capture the complexity of concrete life, and is no substitute for personal, face-to-face encounter. What I needed was a personal meeting with the head or heads of the Congregation for Bishops in the Vatican.

On July of 1996, the sun scorched the runway as I stumbled out of Fiumicino International Airport, exhausted from my red-eye flight from Miami. I flagged down a battered Fiat taxi, its driver gesticulating wildly as he whisked me through narrow streets to Casa Romana del Clero, near the ancient center of Rome. This is where I would be staying during my stopover in Vatican City on the way to Ireland for my annual vacation. I was hoping it would be a brief interlude.

A small, oriental man met me at the door of Casa Romana. Casually dressed and barefoot, he helped carry my bags to my room. Once inside the room, he sat on the bed, and asked: "What brings you to Rome?"

"I am here on business," I replied, but didn't elaborate. He told me he was part of a delegation of Asian bishops making their *ad limina* visit to the Pope.[2]

---

1. *An Essay in Aid of a Grammar of Assent* (commonly abbreviated to the last three words) is John Henry Newman's 1870 book on the assent of faith.

2. An *ad limina*—from the Latin *ad limina apostolorum* ("to the threshold of the apostles") is an obligatory visit that all bishops make to Rome to pray at the tombs of

"So, you're a bishop," I declared, somewhat startled but not really surprised. It looked from what he told me that he was head of the delegation.

I could then share with him the nature of my visit, which intrigued him. He was not bewildered in the least. On the contrary, he was fascinated and wanted to know more.

When I finished my story, he leaned back on the bedrest and asked: "Is there any hope of redemption in the American Church?"

Surprised at his question, I probed: "Why do you ask that?"

"When the American bishops," he said, "come here on their *ad limina* visits, they stay in the best five-star hotels and are chauffeured around in expensive limousines. We all notice how money seems to be their great love," he rejoined, matter-of-factly.

I understood what he was saying, because where money was concerned the Christian code of conduct tended to take a holiday in the corporate American Church.

"I know what you're getting at," I concurred. "It's the basic reason why I'm here."

"I wish you the best," he returned. "You're a brave man to take on that Goliath."

"I did not want to confront this Goliath," I replied. "But I was left no other choice."

I tried to imagine some of the American bishops I knew staying in these simple quarters. It would not have been a good match for their expensive tastes.

This self-effacing prelate then invited me to offer Mass with the rest of the delegation at 8 a.m. every morning while in Rome. I accepted the invitation gladly.

"I cannot wait to get away from this city," he remarked.

"That bad," I remarked, as I wondered what kind of reception awaited me at the Vatican.

First impressions are always important. My encounter with this sympathetic prelate in Casa Romana was a propitious start to my Vatican visit. It was still early in the day and, even with the window open in my room, I felt like I was being roasted in a hot oven. There was no air-conditioning in the room. Moreover, I was hungry, and I needed to eat. I hailed a taxi outside Casa Romana and told the driver to bring me to the center of Rome.

Maria Maggiore, he cried, enthusiastically.

St. Peter and St. Paul, and then to meet the Pope and Vatican officials and present a quinquennial (five-year) report of their dioceses.

Part 2—Chapter 31

The Basilica di Santa Maria Maggiore, or Basilica of St. Mary Major, is one of four major basilicas in Rome. The other three are Saint Peter's, Saint John Lateran and Saint Paul Outside the Walls.

Santa Maria Maggiore is a remarkable edifice in that it combines various stages of Christian art and architecture. The fifth century mosaics and Ionic columns, taken from ancient Roman buildings, are from the early Christian period. The exquisitely designed marble floors and mosaics are from the Medieval period. The lattice interior design of the ceiling is from the Renaissance. The renovations undertaken during the eighteenth-century account for the Baroque features, the high domes and side-chapels.

What first struck me about this great structure was its massiveness. The steps leading to the huge front doors were wide and long and reminded me of the steps to the pyramid of Chichén-Itzá in Yucatan, Mexico.

Entering the vestibule, or foyer, where worshippers gather before and after Mass, I got lost in the enormous space. It was as big, if not bigger, than any church I had encountered in my travels. And that was just the vestibule.

I slipped into the interior of the basilica as Mass commenced—a stroke of luck. Yet, as I scanned the sparse congregation, my heart sank. Back home in Florida, even our smallest services drew more worshippers than this, here at the very heart of Catholicism.

The people in the basilica were tourists walking around, albeit respectfully, admiring its many attractions. This basilica is home to the relics of St. Jerome, the renowned Scripture scholar, who translated the entire Bible into the Latin vernacular, called the Vulgate (ordinary). Too bad, I thought, that the church dropped the ball, and didn't follow the spirit of St. Jerome by having the Bible translated into the new modern vernacular languages, when they were widely used, as Martin Luther did when he translated the Bible into modern German.

Ironically, I discovered that Mass attendance in Rome, the center of Catholicism, was among the lowest in the world.

After visiting the great Basilica, I decided to have lunch. It was the centenary of the invention of radio by Italy's inventor-hero, Marconi, and many buntings, banners and signs were on display throughout Rome honoring the occasion.

As a child is drawn to a candy shop, I was drawn to a restaurant, called The Old Marconi, just a short walk away. The waitress who served me spoke good English, with a touch of an Irish accent.

I asked her: "Where are you from?"

"I'm from here, but my mother is from Galway," she replied with an easy smile.

"I have some friends from Letterkenny, my hometown in Ireland, whose name is Bianconi," I said.

As soon as I uttered the name Bianconi and my town in Ireland, a man seated at the end of the restaurant cried out, excitedly: "Did you say Letterkenny? And Bianconi?"

"Yes. That's what I said," I returned.

"Well," he replied, "I'm married to Donna."

He was the owner of the restaurant, and he got up from his seat and hurried to where I was sitting. I couldn't stop laughing at the coincidence as he approached me excitedly. Taking his wallet out of his pocket, he showed me photos of his wife, Donna, and all his relatives in Letterkenny, my hometown. We then had a great time and laughed at this providential encounter in the heart of Rome.

My new friend in Rome invited me to join his family at the enchanting Parco di Colle Oppio, on one of the seven storied hills gracing the Eternal City. This twenty-seven-acre oasis of landscaped gardens and splashing fountains offered a spectacular vista of the Colosseum.

At this magical locale, ordinary Romans gathered to pass the time in congenial company. Overlooking the magnificent Colosseum, the park provided a rich variety of food and drinks, served at different cafes. My friend owned one such cafe, where I whiled away the hours making new acquaintances and meeting some new friends from Ireland. The lively sounds of games like table tennis, volleyball, and badminton mingled with the sound of music wafting through the sylvan setting. Like the Irish, Italians know how to celebrate. Among the merry crowd, I met Donna from Letterkenny and a lovely lady from Galway, mother of the waitress from The Old Marconi. This fair lady was married to Donna's Italian brother-in-law, whom I also met.

The Colle Oppio had become my sanctuary, a place I could find solace and peace amidst the chaos of Rome. I felt a comfortable sense of belonging among these ordinary folk with spontaneous emotions and genuine warmth. It reminded me of our parish festivals, full of community and camaraderie. I became immersed in the mood, and for a few blissful hours forgot my troubles. As I sat there, I knew that no matter what lay ahead, I would always have this special place to return to in Rome. It offered the perfect respite before meeting with officials of the Vatican.

As night settled over the city, I braced myself for the meetings that awaited me in the Vatican. Tomorrow, I would enter the Holy See's domain, armed with nothing but my conscience and the hope that truth would stand firm against the politics and bureaucracy of the institutional church.

Chapter 32

I GOT OUT OF bed to prepare for my big meeting at the Vatican as the first light of dawn crept over Rome's skyline. Today, I would face the formidable heart of the church's power structure. With eager anticipation threading through me, I dialed the Office of the Congregation for Bishops, seeking to secure a meeting with Prefect Cardinal Gantin—the man who had ignored my correspondence for ten long months.

The prefect was away on vacation, but the general secretary of the congregation, Archbishop Jorge María Mejía, took my call.

"How can I be of help to you?" he asked, amiably. His voice, polite but edged with an undertone of formality, intoned through the receiver.

"I'd like to discuss important matters detailed in correspondence I sent to the Congregation for Bishops," I said.

He asked for more details. I filled him in.

He listened carefully and hastened to reply: "I'll be glad to meet with you, but can you give me about twenty minutes or so to retrieve the information."

I was heartened by this prompt response.

"That would be fine," I said, adding: "I appreciate your generosity in arranging a meeting so soon."

I had expected it would take days, at least, to get an appointment with someone at the Congregation for Bishops, and I was prepared to wait in Rome if that was necessary. So, I was very surprised the meeting would take place so quickly. I knew, when it came to the Vatican, you needed to talk to the top person if you wanted anything done. The institution employs over five thousand functionaries. The general secretary was an important figure, so I was glad I could talk with him.

Half an hour later, I was on my way to the meeting. I entered a large, spacious office, where several lay secretaries, seated behind desks, were working the phones. I introduced myself to one of them and told him I had an appointment with Archbishop Jorge María Mejía. He asked for identification and told me to be seated until someone would come for me.

I sat there for perhaps ten minutes until a cleric finally emerged through a door, behind where the secretaries were seated. He motioned for me to follow him and directed me, in silence, along a corridor to another room where I was left alone to wait again.

The room was bathed in a quiet austerity—a simple coffee table and four cardinal-red chairs. Through the window, St. Peter's Square unfolded like a vast chessboard, with pilgrims and tourists walking amidst the grandeur of Bernini's impressive colonnade, four columns deep. The neighboring Vatican offices looked out onto the movements of people below.

On the mantlepiece above an unused fireplace, a thick volume of the *Acts of the Holy See* lay patiently, waiting to be perused. I thumbed through its pages, my mind pondering the significance of the appointments detailed within, while awaiting my own.

Silence persisted as another wordless cleric opened the door and ushered me along a corridor to a third chamber. Our silent, three-chamber procession felt like a symbolic journey, intended or not, through the cycle of the Trinity.

In the final room, time stretched until the archbishop arrived, flanked by a boyish-looking priest.

"I retrieved this dossier from the archives, Your Eminence, after much effort," said the young priest, congratulating himself.

The archbishop attempted to hand me the dossier, thinking I should have it, but I told him I already had a copy and knew what was in it. This prelate wore a simple clerical suit with no pectoral cross or any insignia indicating rank. A modest man by all accounts, he was from Argentina and happened to be friends, I discovered, with a boyhood friend of mine who had worked at the Vatican and was now bishop in my home diocese in Ireland. Moreover, I learned that his housekeeper in Argentina was also from County Donegal, and it was from her that he learned to speak English.

To make conversation with the assistant, I asked him where he was from.

"The Archdiocese of Philadelphia," he replied with a broad grin.

"Oh, then you must have known Father John Morley from your diocese," I offered. He was pastor of St. Richard's Parish and helped me out in Florida after he retired.

"Never heard of him," was his reply.

As soon as the assistant left, the archbishop's demeanor changed. He raised his right arm, dramatically, and asked: "Why is that bishop persecuting you?"

This question was a clear give-away. He was well acquainted with the information in the dossier. I was hesitant to respond to his loaded question, since the answer surely could be deduced from a reading of the dossier in his possession. But I was glad he expressed indignation that I was being persecuted.

"I'll know better what is behind this persecution," I replied, "if and when I can see my personnel files at our diocesan pastoral center."

The diocesan personnel files, containing lies and misinformation, would reveal the truth of what was going on. What they would clearly show would be a compromised institution that had lost touch with its true purpose. In the dossier I sent to the Vatican, I emphasized the need to review these personnel files, and to be allowed to set the record straight.

The archbishop then invited me to take a seat on one of the red-colored chairs in the room. After we were seated, I showed him the green return receipt slip I received from the post office as proof of my dossier's delivery to the Congregation for Bishops back in September 1995. I emphasized that I received no acknowledgement of any kind from the Congregation that it had received my correspondence.

The archbishop examined the green receipt with the Vatican stamp and accompanying signature.

Once he understood this, he apologized for the failure to acknowledge the correspondence.

He picked up a church directory from the table and began thumbing through it.

"How old is this bishop?" he asked.

"I don't know," I replied. "Perhaps he's in his sixties, but I'm only guessing."

He closed the directory he was perusing in frustration and inquired: "Are there any other disturbing instances you are aware of?"

"I haven't talked to anyone about this, except my canonist and spiritual director," I said.

Then, on second thought, I did recall a disturbing article in the *Palm Beach Post*, a paper which covers the five-county diocese, about the bishop giving his approval to some way-out homosexual ministry.

As soon as I dropped this tidbit of information, the archbishop grasped his head with both hands, as if he was trying to keep it from flying off. I could see that I had touched a nerve, and I wondered what he knew that I didn't.

Focusing on the matter at hand, I continued.

"My reason for coming here is to put a stop to these abuses by the diocese, detailed in the dossier," I said. "God knows I cannot stop them and I've tried, but I trust you can."

At the mention of the abuses detailed in the dossier, he remarked: "That diocese is run by a bunch of incompetents."

This unexpected remark got my attention, and I hastened to ask: "Will you stop these abuses?"

He recoiled at my question, so I probed: "Isn't that your job?"

"I'm just the general secretary of the Congregation for Bishops," he replied. "That's my job."

I now felt I was in a difficult situation and wondered what to do. I did not come all this way to Rome to be sifted through the intricacies of Vatican diplomacy. I needed real, concrete help, and I wanted it now. I wondered if I could count on the Vatican.

"What do you expect me to do then in this situation?" I retorted. "Or what would *you* do in my situation?"

His reply was encouraging, if evasive: "Continue doing what you're doing. Be a good priest and defend your rights."

"I appreciate this personal endorsement," I replied, "but it doesn't stop the abuses I'm talking about. These abuses have been going on for a long time and the Congregation for Bishops has known about them for over ten months, yet they continue unabated."

I paused and asked again: "Will you stop these abuses?"

No answer.

I was used to this kind of non-response back in my own diocese, so I persisted: "Will you stop these abuses?"

Again, he did not want to commit himself. This conversation appeared to be going nowhere, but I didn't come all this way for nothing. I needed a concrete answer, some assurance of real help.

"If these abuses are not stopped, I will stop them," I said, "but it is not going to look good. You'll leave me no option but to litigate the facts against my diocese and the Holy See."

When I mentioned litigation, he rose up from his seat like a shot from a sling.

"Don't do that," he said firmly. "We'll stop them."

A feeling of relief wafted over me, momentarily lifting the heavy weight of uncertainty. For the first time, I felt as though my journey to the Vatican might not have been in vain.

Before the meeting ended, the archbishop, shrugging his shoulders and with a wry smile, remarked: "Not to pass the buck, but you need to discuss this with the Congregation for Clergy. This congregation has competence in this matter, and it has your material."

It was news to me that the Congregation for Clergy also had my dossier. The archbishop directed me to meet with the general secretary of that congregation, whose offices were close by.

I was intrigued by the archbishop's good command of English, even colloquialisms like "pass the buck." His Donegal housekeeper had taught him well.

The archbishop's hand fell lightly on my shoulder as I turned to leave.

"Father," he said softly, "remember, not all bishops are the same. So don't judge us all the same way."

His words were uplifting. "I'm heartened to hear that," I replied, nodding my head. "But I'm not judging anybody; I just want to stop abuses."

With a touch of dark clerical humor, he added: "The only thing you are guaranteed in the church is a Christian burial."

"Even that is not guaranteed," I assured him. "I've known priests, sorry to say, who passed away without the benefit of a Christian burial."

We parted in a jovial mood.

My subsequent meeting with Archbishop Crescenzio Sepe at the Congregation for Clergy happened almost instantly and did not involve the protracted procession through multiple rooms.

Archbishop Sepe received me graciously and, after a brief discussion about the case, he handed me over to his English-speaking secretary, a priest from Colorado, I think.

As we discussed the matter briefly, I asked him, earnestly: "Is there any need for you and me to discuss this matter further since you have all the information you need in the dossier?"

"I'm just a mere functionary, a nobody, a cog in the machine," he replied. "You've talked to the main people in charge: Archbishop Mejía at the Congregation for Bishops and Archbishop Sepe at this congregation."

Glad to hear this, I simply asked him: "What's going to happen now, and going forward?"

He was helpful: "Now we'll be working on a letter to the bishop."

I was glad to hear this. Hoping to depart soon on my vacation to Ireland, I was anxious to get confirmation that this matter would be attended to before I left.

"Can I call you tomorrow?" I asked.

"That would be fine," he responded.

The following day, I spoke to this priest at the Congregation for Clergy on the phone, inquiring about the status of my case.

"As we are speaking, the letter to your bishop is being written," he affirmed.

Thanking him for his attention to the matter, I immediately set about making preparations to continue on to Ireland. But first, I wanted to see as much of Rome during the next few days as possible, since I'd never before visited the city.

Rome is called the Eternal City for a reason. Unique among cities of the world, it has a living history going back to its legendary founding by Romulus and Remus on April 21, 753 BC. It blends the old and the new: The Roman Forum where the Senate and emperors met standing beside modern skyscrapers housing some of the world's biggest hi-tech companies. Wherever you walk in modern-day Rome, you encounter monuments of antiquity, such as the Colosseum, the Pantheon and the beautiful eighteenth century Trevi Fountain.

As I walked along a street the day following my meetings at the Vatican, I saw some Asian tourists sitting on the steps of a church. I went over to them and asked, politely: "What are you waiting for?"

One of them pointed to a brochure, containing a photo of a sculpture by Bernini. Just then, an old monk or friar opened the doors, and moved off to the side. We proceeded as a group down the center aisle.

The sculpture was of the Ecstasy of St. Teresa of Avila, a magnificent, detailed depiction of the ecstasy, carved in white marble by Bernini, the same artist who designed the famous colonnade and columns in St. Peter's Square. Strange, I thought, how I could have discovered this priceless treasure while sauntering through the streets of Rome. The Eternal City was full of surprises.

One of my favorite experiences in Rome was a visit to the Vatican Museum. It should be called the Vatican Museums, in the plural, for they consist of several chapels constructed by different Popes, all now converted into museums. Each of these chapel/museums display magnificent tapestries and works of art produced through the centuries. Passing from one to the other revealed one marvel after another. Nothing was played down or disguised in these museums. They depicted the history of the church and western civilization in works of art, warts and all. Just when I thought my experience couldn't get any better or more enlightening, I suddenly found myself borne along with the crowd into the Sistine Chapel.

Suddenly, the usual tourist chatter subsided. Complete silence and awe took over. Michelangelo's incredible ceiling frescoes hung over our heads like a vision from heaven. What surprised me most was the Sistine Chapel's smallness. The ceiling could be taken in at one glance while standing or sitting at one end of the chapel, without the illusion of grand size you

Part 2—Chapter 32

see created by the wide-angle camera lenses used in documentaries. The Sistine Chapel's ceiling, painted by a sculptor-turned-painter, is perhaps the greatest monument to Renaissance creativity.

Moreover, the Pietà, sculpted by the 21-year-old Michelangelo, sits in St. Peter's Basilica, not too far from the Vatican Museums, and is free to be enjoyed by all who visit Rome. There is an entrance fee to visit the museums, but none to enter St. Peter's Basilica, because it is a church.

The catacombs of Rome were my next discovery. They were not what they are popularly known as: obscure areas where the early Christians celebrated Masses away from the prying eyes of hostile Roman authorities. On the contrary, they were public burial grounds, dug deep into the earth, consisting of descending tunnels, tombs atop tombs, and some ornate alcoves with altars, where the wealthy could have Masses celebrated for themselves.

The Roman catacombs were well worth seeing, if only to dispel the myth that these were solely the gathering spaces where early Christians congregated to celebrate their Masses in secret.

During these last few days in Rome, I managed to visit the Pantheon, the Trevi Fountain, the Colosseum, St. Peter's, where I saw the reverential Pieta and, of course, the Roman Forum, which is impossible to miss, right in the center of the city.

On the eve of my departure to Ireland, I was invited to dinner by an acquaintance at a private club near the Spanish steps, the Circulo de La Cacce. This was another slice of Roman life I never expected. My host was the Marquis Cosimo. His wife had passed away sometime earlier and he was eager to meet me because I had offered Mass for her. Also invited to the dinner was the grandson of the inventor Marconi, who was being celebrated all over Rome.

To my surprise, Marconi's grandson told me he had Irish roots. His grandmother was a Jameson from Ireland, the brewers of the famous Irish whiskey. I was very surprised to learn that he knew so much about the history of my homeland. We got along well together, and he was genuinely excited when I told him about my good fortune to come across another Italian-Irish family at the Colle Oppio overlooking the Colosseum, where I spent a few pleasant evenings.

What were the odds, I thought to myself, as I was flying over the English Channel the following day, that I would be able to meet up with people in Rome with Irish roots at both the popular Colle Oppio and the exclusive Circulo de La Cacce?

It was, indeed, a small world after all.

Chapter 33

RETURNING TO MY FLORIDA rectory, the weight of my visit to Rome still pressed upon me. There, on my desk, lay an envelope stamped with the unmistakable Vatican seal, dated July 10, 1996. The Congregation for Clergy had been in possession of my material since the previous April, I learned. But now, after my visit, it was prepared to act. It needed more time, the letter stated, to review both sides of the case.

I was quick to acknowledge this correspondence from the Holy See.

On October 4, nearly three months later, the next letter from the Congregation arrived. It was no surprise to me that the Congregation interpreted the issues of abuse as resulting from miscommunication and misunderstanding. Nevertheless, it set up a meeting between the bishop and me so that we could have a frank discussion over the issues, and that the matter be brought to a speedy resolution.

This was good news since all I ever wanted was to bring this matter of abuse to a speedy resolution. The letter also mentioned that my bishop, our second diocesan bishop, would be getting in touch with me to set up the meeting.

The bishop wasted no time, for he soon called me for a meeting at the pastoral center on October 23, 1996.

This was going to be, perhaps, the most important meeting of my life. The other meetings with the bishop were significant, too, but not like this one. The Holy See had come through. Although it asked for a frank discussion of the matters I raised, I knew I could not do this alone. I put the matter in God's hands.

It is my custom to spend quiet time in meditation on Scripture every morning after breakfast. My secretary, Faye, respected this, and she would hold all calls for me, excluding emergencies, during this time. There is nothing better for the mind than to start the day with good news, and where better to ponder this good news than in Scripture.

Part 2—Chapter 33

The meditation I chose was from Matthew 18:15–17, where Jesus addresses differences among members of the community, and how to resolve them. I drew comfort from this beautiful Scripture, and also courage to approach my bishop with the facts in a Christian manner. I have preached on this passage often, but now I was challenged, not to talk about it, but to put it into practice. I prayed to the Holy Spirit to help me swallow hard and apply this teaching at my meeting with the bishop. It had always worked like a charm in settling disputes among members of the parish. Now I prayed it would be just as effective in settling those thorny abuse issues relating to the bishop and the diocese.

The meeting on October 23, was unlike any I ever had. It was frank, but cordial. I was able to present the list of abuses that needed to be stopped. This was essentially the same list of abuses I detailed in my correspondence with the Vatican:

1. False allegations, proven to be false, of embezzlement, and criminal battery.
2. Misappropriation of parish funds, property, and the Family Outreach Center by the diocese.
3. The bishop's meeting with my accusers on March 26, 1995 while excluding me from the meeting.
4. Failure by the bishop to make the proper parish visitation which he is obliged to do, and which would have demonstrated my effectiveness as a pastor with reference to church law: canons 384, 396.
5. Finally, the most important request: to be given access to all data and information in my personnel files, with permission to remove from my files any false and defamatory information and to provide clarification for anything that was false or harmful to my good name (canon 220).

I was heartened to hear the bishop agree to take responsibility to end these abuses. He said, however, he didn't meet with my accusers as mentioned in the above number three, even though he did. I even opened the door of the hall for that meeting. When I presented him with the evidence, he let it drop, embarrassingly.

After a very frank though cordial discussion of the items presented, the bishop noted: "I've been ten years a bishop, and twenty years a priest, and this is the first time I've been reported to Rome."

I replied as honestly as I could: "You left me no choice. I made every effort through many letters and several meetings to have these abuses stopped, but it was to no avail. What other recourse was left to me?"

He made no attempt to offer an answer.

Changing the subject, he continued: "What's going to happen after this meeting?"

I said I was just happy that things could now return to normal, and that I would do everything in my power to ensure that this would happen.

"What are you going to write to the Holy See?" he asked.

That's what was bothering him.

"I'll write to the Congregation for Clergy," I replied, "and let it know I met with you and that the meeting went well."

I didn't know what else to say. The meeting, in my view, went well. As well as it could, I thought. It now depended on good will (on both sides) to put the past behind and move forward, and I was fully committed to do that.

He seemed happy with my response, and the meeting ended cordially. As I was leaving, he asked me to exit by the fire escape.

"The fire escape—I might break a leg going down there," I said, jokingly. "I'd feel safer leaving on a sure footing by the way I came in—through the front door."

The soft carpet swallowed my footsteps as I moved down the corridor, passing a gauntlet of closed doors. Ahead, I could see the chancellor fidgeting nervously with his watch, his movements jittery, betraying his discomfort. When our eyes met, he turned abruptly, disappearing into the sanctuary of his office with the swiftness of a man fleeing judgment.

I approached his office, opened the door and, putting as much cheeriness as I could into my greeting, cried out: "Good-day, Barnie!" (not his real name).

He didn't respond.

I continued the way I came in, down the elevator and out the front door to my car in the parking lot. Relieved, after having had such a cordial and successful meeting with the bishop that put an end to the abuses of the past, I drove home with a good feeling that a new day had dawned.

Peace and laughter reigned again as things got back to normal in the parish. Even the bishop, it seemed, was enjoying the new dawn. He called me at the rectory a few days after the meeting. His voice dripped with enthusiasm.

"Wasn't that a good meeting we had, Hugh?" he exclaimed.

"It sure was, Bishop. I am so relieved this whole saga is over."

"Did you write the letter to the Holy See?" he asked, inquisitively.

"Yes, I did. I mailed it off the day after our meeting."

The bishop was delighted to hear this and asked if I had mentioned that the meeting went well.

"Absolutely," I told him.

I even read to him what I wrote to the Pro Prefect of the Congregation: "I am happy to let you know that I met with the bishop on Wednesday, October 23, 1996. The meeting went well."

The bishop was pleased, and the mood was very upbeat. I couldn't have felt happier.

About a week later the bishop called me again.

That letter you wrote to the Holy See? he inquired. "I'd like to have a copy of it."

I was shocked that my word was not good enough. People, I've come to realize, tend to judge others in terms of themselves and their own conduct. I did not pry into what he would do, following our meeting, nor did I think it would be appropriate to ask. Thus, I was disappointed he didn't trust me.

"I don't think it would be appropriate to do that, bishop," I replied. "I told you what I wrote, and I have absolutely no objection if you ask the Holy See for a copy of my correspondence. It will confirm what I told you".

Immediately the conversation ended abruptly and the phone went dead.

As the dial tone echoed in my ear, an old, familiar dread stirred in the silence. I could sense the bishop's simmering resentments rising, like old grievances waking from a troubled nightmare, threatening to unleash the storm all over again.

Just as the darkness seemed to close in, a single light broke through. It came on February 23rd—an unexpected letter, one that bore the seal of Archbishop Re, the Pope's substitute. As I read it, expressing the Holy Father's deep appreciation for my gesture of congratulations on his fiftieth ordination anniversary, I realized we were not alone.

The letter also conveyed the assurance of the Pope's prayers for the parish. I published the letter in the parish bulletin, to the great delight of the parishioners.

On May 12, 1997, a different kind of letter arrived from the bishop. He stated that I told him I had no record of my correspondence with the Holy See. I wrote back on May 30, stating: "I do have copies of my correspondence with the Holy See." For good measure, I included a reference to canon 220 regarding protection of the clergy's right to privacy.

The whole saga went through another disturbing sea change. The old allegations, proven to be false, were now replaced by a new set of equally false allegations, this time pertaining to matters canonical.

I got my first clue to this development when my secretary, Faye, told me that a diocesan canonist, working at the Tribunal and later to become the first lady chancellor, had been trying to obtain a copy of the marriage documents of a couple from Sacred Heart. Faye would not send her the paperwork without my permission, so it remained where it belonged, in the parish archives.

There was a strange, double irony to this little scam. Firstly, the marriage paperwork was strictly in accord with diocesan policy. Secondly, the husband in the marriage had already passed away, making any attempt to create a canonical case ridiculous.

The diocesan canonist didn't know what she was doing and was evidently barking up the wrong tree.

Then, we were dealt another disturbing blow. The icons for the stations of the cross were abducted from our warehouse and transported to the diocesan warehouse. This was done to sabotage our parish project to build outdoor stations of the cross on the grounds of the church. It was a particularly disturbing development, for it was a direct attack on the church's pastoral ministry. In the past, apart from false allegations, the failed attacks had been over parish property and our social ministries.

On June 5, 1997, the bishop paid another unexpected visit to the parish. We met in the living room of the rectory. By this time, I was so exhausted dealing with false allegations and attempts to undermine both our social and pastoral ministry that I decided to say as little as possible. Instead, I listened carefully to what was being alleged and wrote it all down in his presence.

No doubt, the matters raised by the bishop about marriage preparation for a certain couple made no sense, since the husband was already dead.

At this meeting, the bishop informed me he had revoked the faculties of my two assistants: Father James Finn, and Deacon Roman Harwas.[1]

Father Finn was a retired priest from Ireland, and would be returning there for the summer. When I told him the bishop had revoked his faculties, he waved the matter away with a flick of his hand. His infectious smile said everything.

As for the deacon, whose wife, son, and grandchild lived in the parish, it was a different matter entirely. They would be mortified by such a cruel blow.

---

1. Diocesan faculties refer to the official permission from the bishop for the exercise of clerical ministry.

Part 2—Chapter 33

My heart skipped a beat when the bishop handed me a letter from the previous year, removing the deacon's faculties without my knowledge. I hadn't seen a copy of that letter until now.

"Why did you not inform me of this decision back then?" I asked. "If the deacon could exercise the faculties of the diocese all that time in spite of the previous year's letter, why not now?"

I pointed out that this action was contrary to the church's agreement with the Congregation for Oriental Rites.

He got nervous and immediately revoked his decision there and then.

It was clear to me that these abuses of authority were a normal *modus operandi* by some bishops to force clerics into line with their agendas.

The bishop's actions in removing the faculties of two good men, Father Finn and Deacon Harwas, was deeply disturbing. I feared I might be next.

Faced with this behavior, I asked to be given the opportunity to go through my personnel files, a request that had been agreed to at our October 23 meeting. The personnel files were the key to everything and would reveal the truth about abuse and cover-up. He now refused, point blank, to honor the request he had agreed to.

As of this June 5 meeting, everything had reverted to the way they were before I reported the abuses to the Holy See. What was I to do? If ever I felt trapped, it was right now. I needed some kind of breakthrough, and I prayed for a miracle, a sign. I had written positively to the Holy See about my October 23 meeting with the bishop, and I was not going to take it back.

As I stood at this crossroad, weighing the cost of continuing this struggle against the price of surrender, divine providence intervened. It came not in a burning bush or a heavenly choir, but in the form of a dear friend: Archbishop Flavio Calle Zapata. His arrival reminded me that even in the convoluted politics of the church, God's hand could still be discerned—if one had the faith to see it.

He came by the church to celebrate Mass with me. Our acquaintance traced back to his days as a seminary rector in Columbia. He loved our parish and our ministries, meeting the community's spiritual and practical needs, and he deemed Sacred Heart a *perfect* parish. I knew there was no such thing as a perfect parish, but it was good to know he held the parish in high esteem. His brother owned a ranch in Okeechobee and his family were active parishioners, always willing to help. Archbishop Flavio's technologically adept nephew helped to print our bulletins in-house, allowing us to create our own publishing system for English and Spanish parishioners.

When I shared my predicament with my friend after Mass, he listened intently, offering a sympathetic ear. If he possessed more information about the matter, he did not divulge any.

Before leaving, he kindly penned a letter of introduction to his fellow Columbian, Cardinal Darío Castrillón Hoyos, the new Prefect of the Congregation for Clergy at the Vatican. Archbishop Flavio's support came at the right time. It was the sign I needed as I knew I had to pay yet another visit to the Vatican.

Thus, during my summer vacation of 1997, I set off once more for Rome, enroute to Ireland.

Chapter 34

THE OPPRESSIVE HEAT OF a Roman summer greeted me as I stepped out of Fiumicino Airport in 1997. Burdened with both exhaustion and anticipation, I flagged down a taxi to Casa Romana del Clero.[1]

When I got settled in, I called Archbishop Mejia at the Congregation for Bishops. We met the following day in his office in Vatican City. Gone was the previous protocol, passing through different rooms before a meeting was granted. This time was different.

"This is my secretary, Mr. Ganancias," said the archbishop, gesturing toward his aide. "He's at your service should you require anything or wish to phone Ireland or Florida."

Mr. Ganancias approached me with a broad, warm smile, like an old friend reunited after years apart. The father of seven children, if memory serves me correctly, he was from Argentina also.

"What can I do for you, Father?" he inquired politely. I assured him I was quite comfortable. We had a pleasant conversation, and he informed me that his surname, Ganancias, translated to "prophet," a fitting name for a secretary to the archbishop, I thought.

After Mr. Ganancias left, the archbishop said to me, excitedly: "You and your bishop are getting on well."

Obviously, he was familiar with the contents of my letter to the Congregation for Clergy. The Vatican is a close-knit community, and news within those walls travels fast.

The archbishop's face lit up with joy when I told him about the positive outcome of my meeting with my bishop. But then I could see his spirit dim as I related the unfortunate turn of events since then. Though I hesitated to be the bearer of bad news, I had to apprise him of the troubling new developments.

---

1. Also known as *Domus Romana Sacerdotalis* ("Roman House of Clergy").

I took a deep breath and described how the outdoor icons of the stations of the cross were abducted from the parish. Then I presented the fabricated canonical allegations contained in a file I had brought with me. At this, his face fell and a cloud of sadness seemed to envelop him. He didn't bother to look at the file I had with me, but asked, distressingly: "When did you leave the parish?"

"A few days ago," I replied.

"What day and what time?"

His insistence on knowing the exact day and time hinted at an unspoken urgency.

I told him the exact day and time I left the parish.

I sensed his concern that, with me absent, the bishop of my diocese might seize the chance to force my removal before anyone could intervene. But with only two days having passed, it seemed there was still time.

Not wasting a moment, he pointed to the file in my hand and directed: "Take that information to the Congregation for Clergy. Most are away on vacation, but you'll find someone."

The archbishop quickly left. The time for pleasantries was over. There was critical work to be done.

I made my way after this brief meeting to the office of the Congregation for Clergy, where I met with an English-speaking monsignor. To my surprise, he was someone I knew. I had no idea he was working in the Vatican.

"I've been dealing with your case, Hugh," he said, walking towards me.

"Fancy that," I replied, and we both laughed.

I showed him the file with the trumped-up canonical allegations. A canon lawyer himself, he found it amusing that a case could possibly be made about a dead person.

The diocesan canonist for my bishop was not aware of that vital piece of information, I explained.

It was a comedy of errors. Changing the subject, he asked, curiously: "How do you and the bishop get along on the personnel board? You are the secretary of the board, are you not?"

"Yes, I'm the secretary and we get along," I replied. "I always show him the minutes of the previous meetings before we meet in session, and he has nothing but praise for them. He even proposed to the board that I be re-elected to the post again by acclamation."

The monsignor shook his head.

"It's very hard to get rid of a bishop," he said.

Part 2—Chapter 34

His remark pierced me like a winter chill. Unseat the bishop? The very notion of removing the bishop left me reeling. Why did he think that was necessary? I had to remind him that was not my intent at all.

"I've no wish to unseat the bishop," I replied. "My sole aim is to end these abuses."

My words seemed to stir something in him, prompting another startling comment: "Consider Al Capone! He could only be caught on tax evasion, not his notorious crimes."

"Al Capone," I gasped. "What's he got to do with this?"

I was struck by the allusion to the Mafia, as if he were trying to make a point about the untouchability of church corruption.

"This is not about winning; it's about integrity," I emphasized. "I only want to see these abuses stopped. Nothing more."

Apparently moved, he agreed.

"Yes, yes," he conceded haltingly. "It's about integrity."

Concerned that I should be prepared if the bishop attempted to force me out of the parish, he proceeded to dictate a letter for that eventuality. I chose not to reveal Archbishop Flavio's letter to the Prefect of the Congregation for Clergy, since the Prefect was away on vacation.

"The perceptions of bishops vary so drastically," I said. "I know an archbishop from Colombia who has a high regard for our parish. No parish is perfect, obviously, but he seemed to give it high praise. Ironically, my own bishop seemed intent on its destruction."

After this meeting at the Congregation for Clergy, my business at the Vatican was concluded. I made arrangements the following day to fly to Ireland for my annual vacation.

When I stepped through the doors of the rectory after my return from Ireland, a profound stillness greeted me. It felt as if the chaos of recent months had evaporated, leaving behind a quiet peace that lingered like the final note of a distant hymn. It was like waking up from a bad dream where all the ugliness that had transpired had never happened. Happy days, it seemed, were back again.

The bishop decided to return the icons of the stations of the cross to the parish. He called me and told me he had found them at his door, not knowing where they came from. I went along with this doubtful scenario, simply glad to have them returned. The ever-faithful Al Roussell drove to the pastoral center in Palm Beach Gardens to retrieve them.

I endeavored to reach out to the bishop when he called me about the stations of the cross, and asked him if he would be kind enough to bless them when they would be installed at Sacred Heart.

He declined to do so.

When the icons arrived back at the parish, Tom Blair, who had designed the outdoor area expressly for the stations of the cross, took one look at them and burst out laughing.

"So, these little bronze icons were the cause of all this commotion," he said, between laughs.

The theft of the icons was only a small part of the commotion, but it was the straw that broke the camel's back. The attempt by the diocese to undermine the pastoral ministry of the parish by stealing the icons was a bridge too far for the Vatican.

The dust settled slowly, almost imperceptibly. Days turned into weeks, and the storm over Father Finn's faculties withered to a faint murmur, then faded into the background. Life at the parish resumed its steady rhythm, a quiet restoration after the chaos.

Father Finn continued to serve alongside myself and Deacon Harwas.

Another positive development: The deacon was ordained a priest by his bishop of the Ukrainian Catholic Rite, and he gave his first blessing to the parishioners at Sacred Heart. We now had a married priest of the Ukrainian Catholic (Byzantine) Rite serving at Sacred Heart.

Father Harwas was well-established at the church, visiting hospitals and prisons, and officiating at marriages when he was a deacon. His transition to the priesthood was smooth and well-received by the parishioners. But his ministry at the parish was short-lived. He was not allowed to minister as a married priest, due to the celibacy requirement in the Latin Rite. He was offered a position as pastor in Pittsburgh by the Ukrainian-Rite Bishop. We lost a good and faithful man.

Many people think that there are no married priests in the Catholic Church, but this is not true. Unlike the Latin Church, the Eastern or Oriental Catholic Churches, have an unbroken tradition of a married priesthood from the earliest times of the church's history.

Father Harwas served out his ministry in Pittsburg. When he passed away, I was privileged to celebrate his Funeral Mass alongside the priests and bishop of the Eastern Catholic rite.

It was a relief to have things back to normal, and to experience the freedom of the children of God once again.

One day, Archbishop Flavio's nephew phoned to convey his uncle's wish to join me for Mass the next morning at the usual time, an invitation I accepted eagerly.

In the sacristy before Mass, I welcomed the archbishop warmly. As we proceeded toward the altar, I saw his brother and his sister-in-law in the front pew. I smiled at them and Mr. Calle offered a discrete bow. I sensed that something was afoot.

Part 2—Chapter 34

The archbishop gave an effusive homily praising the parish very highly. It was only later, in the rectory, that I learned the purpose of his visit.

"Has the bishop left yet?" the archbishop asked, his question cloaked in subtle ecclesiastical-speak.

He was talking about my bishop, the second Ordinary of my diocese. I did not know what to say because I was not privy to any developments. Ever wary of the intricate web of church politics, I kept my distance from it, engaged only when forced to defend the gospel, the parish and my ministry.

"I've just returned from Washington where I met with the bishops," the archbishop continued. "The decision has been made."

The revelation struck me with the force of a thunderbolt, leaving me reeling in its wake. The bishop was stepping down. A maelstrom of emotions swept through me: shock, disbelief, and an unexpected pang of sorrow. This was never my goal, never my desire. In that moment, I realized the true weight of my struggles—not a personal vendetta, but a crucible in which the very essence of my calling was tested.

When Archbishop Flavio left, I went to Father Finn's room. In stunned silence, I told him the bishop was stepping down. Imperturbable as always, Jim took it all in stride, not saying a word, but listening carefully to the monumental news.

"The bishop is coming here for Confirmation soon," I said, "and we'll have to be extra careful to treat him with respect. I doubt if this news has reached the priests of the diocese yet."

The Confirmations were conducted reverentially, as usual. The bishop spoke to the congregation at the end of the Mass, saying he had been to Rome, met with the Pope, and was wearing a cross the Holy Father had given him.

Holding up the cross, he said, for the edification of everyone: "From the Pope, through me, I bless you with this cross."

Before he left for Palm Beach Gardens, he had a telling encounter with me outside the rectory. Gone was the antagonism I had become used to. It was as if his humanity had flicked back on and he treated me with unusual kindness. Shaking my hand over and over again, like he was pumping a well, he kept repeating: "Thank you, Hugh! Thank you, Hugh! Thank you, Hugh!"

Father Finn had a clear, one-way view of this scene through the picture window in the rectory.

"What was that all about?" asked Jim, smiling, after I went inside. "I could see the two of you through the window."

"I don't really know," I replied. "Perhaps it was a form of reconciliation. I never harbored any bad feelings towards the man, as you know, and maybe he's acknowledging this in some strange way before he steps down. He was being very gracious and, impelled by the better angels of his nature, he needed to express his thanks to me."

That was the last time I spoke to the second Ordinary of the Diocese of Palm Beach.

Chapter 35

I WAS SEATED IN the living room of the rectory, preparing a young couple for marriage on the day the news broke. The living room, usually a sanctuary of peace and quiet, buzzed with the nervous energy of a young couple on the cusp of matrimony. As we discussed the sacred commitments they were about to undertake, I received an urgent call to turn on the television.

When we watched the announcement on June 2, 1998, about the resignation of the Bishop of the Diocese of Palm Beach on TV, and the reasons given for it, the three of us needed a break to absorb the news and its implications. The news was framed in cold, bureaucratic terms—*inappropriate sexual conduct with minors*. This announcement ushered in a seismic shift in the diocese, leaving priests and parishioners alike shaken and searching for solid ground in a suddenly uncertain landscape.

The bishop had grown up in Florida and was ordained a priest for the Diocese of Saint Augustine, which covered the entire state back then. He became chancellor of the Diocese of Saint Petersburg and was ordained bishop of the Diocese of Pensacola-Tallahassee before becoming the second Ordinary of the Diocese of Palm Beach in 1990.

I was surprised at the way the bishop's departure from the diocese occurred. My discussion with Archbishop Flavio the past year came rushing back—I understood it was to be a discreet exit, a quiet retreat like retirement.

But nothing about this scandal was quiet. It roared through the global, Catholic community, uprooting trust.

The Vatican appointed an apostolic administrator to administer the diocese until a new bishop could be appointed. This new appointee, a bishop from elsewhere in Florida, startled everyone by opening up about the outgoing bishop's "dirty little secrets." This was very surprising, given the fact that, as it turned out, he had to face accusations by his own diocesan spokesperson for inappropriate touching. This led to a severance payment of slightly more than $100,000 to the spokesperson, as reported in the *Tampa Bay Times* of March 23, 2002.

People wondered at the time, why the apostolic administrator was so eager to air the dirty laundry of the outgoing bishop in public.

What apparently brought about the resignation of the former Bishop of Palm Beach were abuses of authority. But so many cracks had developed within the institution itself, it seemed, that it could no longer hold out against the warped ambitions and machinations of its own leadership.

The Sunday before the announcement of the bishop's resignation was a normal Sunday, like any other. We had no idea what tomorrow would bring.

After the last Mass, Roy and Bianca Padgett came up to me in church. They looked worried and frightened. Roy, in charge of parish maintenance, had endured a lot of pressure from the plotters to join them in their schemes to remove me as pastor. He had told me earlier that he got a call at his home from a diocesan official, telling him to remain neutral when charges (trumped-up as usual) would be brought against me. He was a loyal staff member and did not take part in wrongdoing. This time, he and his wife shared something that disturbed them deeply.

Bianca said nervously: "Roy woke up in a sweat last night and he woke me up too. He had a bad nightmare and it frightened me."

I then asked Roy to tell me what happened. He looked like someone who had just seen a ghost.

"You're in church now, Roy," I said, laying my hand gently on his shoulder. "Don't be afraid."

Roy explained what he'd dreamt: "I saw a big snake crawling out of the roof of the church. It went into the woods behind the stations of the cross."

Roy's dream had come on the eve of the announcement of the bishop's resignation, before the public knew anything about it. I didn't know what to say, but I could see that it troubled Roy deeply. For Roy it was very real, and had something to do with what was going on in the diocese and in the parish.

I put him at ease.

"Roy, don't be afraid," I said. "The snake of your nightmare has left our church. We've been set free, thank God."

Roy and his wife were much relieved after that.

Subsequently, on the following day, the big announcement of the bishop's demise became international news.

We had a Mexican celebration for a young girl's fifteenth birthday, during the Spanish Mass. The youngsters invited to the event were in the throes of excitement preparing for this big occasion. They were carrying flowers to the altar, seating the girl's family, and posing for photographs by Björn, a Swedish photographer. While this ecstatic commotion was taking place, Björn sidled up to me, his camera hanging around his neck. His eyes glittered with the hunger of a journalist scenting a story.

"So, Father," he said, voice low and conspiratorial, "what do you think of your boss now?"

The question hung between us, loaded with unspoken implications.

Pointing to the glowing youngsters preparing for the celebration, I inquired: "What do *they* think about it?"

Björn laughed. "They couldn't be bothered," he answered.

But the Catholics in Florida and throughout America *were* bothered by the fallout from this scandal. The media never let up. The apostolic administrator summoned all the priests to a meeting at the Passionist Florida Center in North Palm Beach to be briefed on what took place and on how to respond to the crisis from the pulpit. I attended this meeting and listened, in dismay, to the narrative he presented to the priests. His account of the events was later contradicted by the *St. Petersburg Times*, a newspaper that covered his own diocese.

Accompanied by the vicar general, the apostolic administrator then came to the parish to meet with me. To my surprise, this administrator continued the old harassment by trying to remove me from the parish. I had thought the days of persecution were over, but apparently not. It was business as usual.

The apostolic administrator asked me to take another parish.

I replied: "I'm happy where I am."

"If you were in my diocese," he said, "I'd be after you."

How lucky, I mused, *I wasn't part of his diocese.*

He left without achieving his objective. Later, he met with the college of consultors, communicating to the priests that he failed to remove me from the parish.

At a meeting of the parish men's club, I asked what they thought I should say about this scandal from the altar.

"Don't say anything," was the response. "There's more than enough being said in the media, and you don't know how far back it goes or what is still to come."

These were my sentiments exactly. I knew too much anyway, and I couldn't tell the truth from the altar. It wouldn't serve any purpose. So, I said nothing, except to pray for our former bishop at Mass.

Nobody in the parish came up to me with any questions about the scandal.

In rare moments of stillness, amid the chaos, something stirred within me—pity. Despite everything, despite the battles fought and wounds inflicted, I couldn't shake the sadness of seeing a man fall so far from grace. I penned a letter, expressing the sorrow I felt, but as fate would have it, that letter would never be sent.

Just as the letter was being typed by Faye, a realtor and a parish member, came by to show me a contract by the diocese regarding property in Okeechobee. The contract contained a handwritten note reading: "Don't tell Father Duffy about this."

"I'm not *telling* you this," said the realtor. "I am *showing* you."

The second bishop of our diocese had told me after our meeting on January 25, 1995 at the Pastoral Center about a donation to Okeechobee, but I never held out any expectations of receiving it. Sure enough, I now discovered from the realtor that the diocese had purchased property in Okeechobee, presumably from that donation.

As a result, the letter I drafted was never sent, since the same old abuses didn't stop.

Ironically, a group of evangelists from Hobe Sound in Martin County, Florida, had stopped by the rectory to discuss a mission they were asked to conduct on this property. The diocese, it seemed, was attempting to undermine the ministry of Sacred Heart by supporting this evangelical group on property it had purchased in Okeechobee. The evangelicals didn't realize how they had been providentially directed to me, unwittingly ending up at the rectory where they broke the news in my presence.

Nothing came of this sinister scheme. The property that was bought in Okeechobee was later sold by the diocese during another administration.

So much for a donation that was meant to benefit Okeechobee. It had been quietly redirected to suit other agendas.

* * *

We had a deanery meeting in Fort Pierce, and I had arrived early. The dean, who was about to retire, called to me from the door of the rectory: "Come on inside, Hugh. Let's have a drink."

I went inside, and the dean poured a small whiskey for both of us.

"Didn't the bishop get caught with his pants down, Hugh?" he commented.

"Thanks to people like you," I told him. "You aided and abetted those abuses as a member of the bishop's college of consultors."

The dean didn't try to defend himself. We knew one another well, and I always spoke frankly to him.

"Why did you back the abuses of the bishop against me?" I prodded.

"Ah, but Hugh, you were a marked man," he exclaimed. "But that's over now."

"A marked man," I repeated. "Why?"

"You threatened the system, Hugh."

"I threatened an abusive system. Is that it?"

"Yes, that's it."

"I drink to your health," I said, "and wish you a decent normal life in your coming retirement."

"Thank you, Hugh."

It struck me as disappointing that a fellow priest would go along with such abuses simply out of loyalty to a flawed system.

This was a good time, I felt, to correct the defamatory information in my personnel files. I asked the apostolic administrator for permission to go through them and correct them along with a canonist, Father William Martin.

"Why don't you let me and the vicar general go through the files for you and remove whatever needs to be removed?" he urged.

He wanted to cover up the wrongs of the institution, it appeared to me. But I couldn't trust him after he had tried, like the others, to remove me from the parish without cause.

"That wouldn't be a good idea," I answered.

The vicar general then called me. He was responsible for much of the false information in my files, especially the parts involving him. He described the information as rubbish and wanted, as he put it, to close the file.

"So, now it's *rubbish*," I replied, "and you want to close the file. When you were using this rubbish against me, you didn't call it that. My request is simply to review these personnel files with my canonist, and ask that they be corrected. It's my right," I insisted.

After these difficult episodes with the apostolic administrator and the vicar general, Father Martin and I were finally given permission to review my personnel files.

Chapter 36

THEY SAY THE TRUTH will set you free. As Father Martin and I stood on the brink of viewing the contents of my personnel files, I pondered: *How would we go about the task of uncovering the contents of my files?*

Thankfully, my trusted friend, Father William Martin, pastor of St. John Fisher Parish in West Palm Beach, would be by my side to help me through this process. His integrity was matched only by his legal acumen—a rare combination of civil and canon lawyer. I was confident that, with him at my side, we would be up to the task. He was honored that I would ask him to help me.

Father Martin would often get me to celebrate a Spanish Mass on Sunday evenings at his parish. This arrangement suited me since I was free then, and I always enjoyed getting together with my friend over in the rectory after Mass. We had built up a relationship of friendship and trust over the years.

On September 22 and 23, 1998, we reviewed my files in the formal confines of the Pastoral Center.

As we approached the room housing my personnel files, I couldn't shake the feeling that we were about to open Pandora's box. Little did I know how prophetic that sentiment would prove to be.

The first thing we noticed about my personnel files was that they were in no way real or authentic documents. They were essentially character assassination documents, the kind you would associate with shady organizations, such as the KGB in the old Soviet Union. No wonder I was prevented from seeing them. These so-called personnel files did not offer an objective record of my ministry, but instead offered a caricature of my record, containing throughout false and derogatory information.

As we pored over these files, Father Martin's face grew increasingly ashen.

"I've never seen anything as bad as this," he remarked. Chills ran up and down my spine. If a seasoned canon lawyer was this disturbed, what horrors still lay buried in these pages? I steeled myself, knowing that each revelation would test not just my resolve, but my trust in the very institution I had devoted my life to serving.

"The reason you've never seen anything as bad as this," I said to Father Martin, "is probably because you were never allowed to see anything like this."

There was abundant evidence of tampering and the files contained many redactions. My academic background, which I hadn't shared with the diocese, was falsified. Why?

"What is this strange interest in my academic background?" I asked Father Martin. "And why did they falsify it, rather than contact me for the proper documentation?"

Father Martin just shook his head.

"You were never asked by the diocese for this information because they didn't want it," he remarked, sadly.

"According to these files," I said, "they were making all kinds of inquiries, both at the University of Hull, where I got my PhD, and at Harvard University, where I did research."

When I checked later with my doctoral advisor, Professor McClelland, at the University of Hull, and with Mr. Montelbano in charge of students doing PhD research at Harvard University, they had no knowledge whatsoever of any inquiries from the Diocese of Palm Beach concerning my academic records or research. So, what were they trying to do, and who did they supposedly talk to?

Another interesting note in these files, going back many years, was written by the chancellor of the Diocese of Orlando, with reference to myself: "He's intelligent, so don't give him a wide berth."

There was still another baffling note, from the first bishop of the diocese of Palm Beach, asking how it might be possible to remove a pastor who didn't do anything wrong.

"Why did the diocese adopt these positions?" I asked my friend.

"Well, it is obvious from a study of these pathetic files they're opposed to right reason," he replied, laughing.

As we I sifted through the files with a mixture of shock and righteous anger, we unearthed a document that would forever change my understanding of the internal workings of the church bureaucracy. Dated May 30, 1994, this memo wasn't just a piece of paper—it was the smoking gun, the genesis of a meticulously crafted conspiracy to remove me from my position as pastor. The words on the page, clinical and devoid of Christian charity, laid bare the true motives behind the diocese's machinations: a desire to seize control of our parish's thriving social programs. In that moment, within the walls of the Pastoral Center, I felt the full weight of institutional betrayal.

This memo was written by the executive director of Catholic Charities and addressed to the chancellor and the vicar general.

Before reading through these files, I had sent a dossier to the Vatican, outlining the abuses of the diocese as I had experienced them. Now, reading the files in person, especially this memo, I was alarmed to realize that they were even worse than I could ever have imagined. No wonder every effort was made to prevent me from seeing them.

The memo began by taking exception to the parish housing project for the elderly that I had proposed together with the parish council. This housing project was similar to one we successfully concluded in Ireland, when I was director of Christian Community Action (CCA). In its place, the executive director proposed a Catholic Charities housing project to be initiated in conjunction with the U.S. Department of Housing and Urban Development (HUD). The conspiracy memo continued by proposing that the chancellor act as an arbiter to deal with allegations against the pastor "that would be forthcoming."

Horror of horrors! The allegations against the pastor, according to the memo, *would be forthcoming*. Thus, the diocesan officials had formulated, in writing, a scheme to fraudulently discredit me before setting in motion their awful plan of action.

The executive director further wrote that future actions should be based upon forthcoming documentation by one of their allies in the parish. He also requested that his own name, as executive director, not be used in any discussion regarding these allegations, but that the accuser be requested to put his concerns in letter form and forward them to the bishop for his attention.

The executive director's memo went on to say that he would offer to assist the pastor with the development of a housing project proposed by Catholic Charities in conjunction with HUD. This was obviously a smokescreen to deflect my attention away from what was really going on. He concluded that he did not want to get into the middle of any "pastoral issues."

We were appalled to learn that this whole charade to remove me as pastor had been put into action way back in May of 1994, and was laid out clearly in the memo in my personnel files. I had heard from my contacts at the Pastoral Center that before he left the diocese, the executive director had been busy shredding documents and letters linking him to his history of wrongdoing. What he didn't seem to realize was that my files at the diocese contained his conspiracy memo, which revealed the plot in detail. Nor

Part 2—Chapter 36

did he seem to realize I was in possession of copies of his letters to me and others in the parish.

The Machiavellian behavior of diocesan officials first came to my knowledge on the last day of 1994, when two policemen showed up at my door. But the genesis of this plot to undermine me and my ministry was set in motion seven months earlier in May of 1994. It had all the appearance of an acquired *modus operandi*, a process and procedure that the perpetrators were schooled in, and knew all too well. Vinny had said it first: "Do they go to school for this?" The proposed actions detailed in this memo were confined to social matters, but once carried out, they crossed the line into pastoral matters when the icons of the stations of the cross were abducted from the parish. This was something the executive director, in his memo, had wished to avoid.

As a result of this outrageous conspiracy, abuses began to pile on without let-up. The files contained a copy of the check for $157,455.25, which was stolen from the parish office and used as the basis for the accusation of embezzlement. But it was not the only false embezzlement charge revealed in these files. They contained pages of hand-written notes by the chancellor, falsely alleging, on the word of Annabelle, that she saw $10,000 of offertory money on the office table, which was stolen, plus $4,000 more still uncounted.

How Annabelle could, allegedly, arrive at these calculations without actually counting the money herself or being present when it was counted boggles the imagination. The chancellor accepted this nonsense without checking the facts. It didn't bother him that Annabelle was never present during the counting of the offertory or that it always took place on Monday mornings by two reliable and trusted parishioners, not in the parish office, but in the archival office. The weekly offertory (published every week in the parish bulletin), never amounted to $14,000 at any time of the parish's history.

Of course, I was never contacted about any of these allegations. They were part of a hidden conspiracy to discredit me by the diocese itself.

"How would you like a weekly collection of $14,000?" I asked my friend. He shook his head, eyes wide in disbelief.

"We don't see anything close to that, not even during Christmas," he uttered, "his voice laced with incredulity."

Still, the nonsense continued, unabated.

"Can you imagine they never even took the time to find out where the check for $157,455.25 went?" I remarked to Father Martin.

"Where did it go?" He asked, since he had no knowledge of this.

"It went to the Sacred Heart Seminary in Hales Corners, Wisconsin, according to the terms of the McKay estate," I said.

"It's obvious they weren't interested in the facts," he replied. "They were only interested in building up a case, any kind of case, against you. The memo has made that abundantly clear."

And there was yet more: slanderous letters, written in block letters to avoid any identifiable handwriting, each signed by a *different* person. I showed them to Father Martin.

"These are fictitious letters by non-existing parishioners," I explained, "and they go back to the time of the first Ordinary of the diocese."

Father Martin looked at the letters and shook his head.

The parish video that was produced in response to the Year of Evangelization in 1992 was viewed, in the copious notes of the chancellor, with suspicion.

"I saw that video on television and it was very good," commented Father Martin.

I wasn't surprised he had seen the video, since it was widely aired on different television channels.

"The bishop actually called me about the video," I explained further, "asking if I was making money from it. I told him I wasn't."

Hoisting his full frame back in his chair, Father Martin soberly commented: "These file comments display a high level of sour grapes and jealousy."

The files contained tapes of my sermons and copies of my bulletin messages. We listened to the taped sermons and read the bulletin messages, but could find nothing that warranted any criticism. There were no criticisms of them in the files either. We wondered: Why were these tapes of my sermons and parish bulletins being collected and stored in my files? My mind flashed back to the two monsignors Roy had caught collecting bulletins and other materials in our church on the day of the second bishop's installation.

It made no sense.

The big lie about the phony battery charge, in the files, got even crazier after it was proven it couldn't have taken place in the office, which had been closed. A new lie was concocted, claiming that the battery happened in the rectory. This was inserted into the files to replace the old lie contained in the phony police report. No wonder the bishop asked me if I had a copy of the police report after he met with a few conspirators in the parish hall. The new lie was an implicit admission that they'd lied in the phony police report. But it was equally preposterous, since Annabelle never set foot inside the rectory.

Part 2—Chapter 36

The problem with lying, is that it creates a domino effect that eventually runs out of control. That's what happened. As the poet Walter Scott wrote: *Oh, what a tangled web we weave, when first we practice to deceive.*

The many letters we discovered in the files were a flagrant violation of diocesan policy, which stated that every priest had a right to receive letters written about him, and be given the opportunity to respond. This never took place.

"Here's another bit of blatant nonsense," I said. "It states that the parish guest house was in my name when they had to know it was actually in the name of the diocesan bishop."

"The only word I can find to describe these outrageous files," said Father Martin, "is *sacrilegious*."

"Sacrilegious," I repeated the word, pausing to take it in.

"That's a very strong word, Bill," I returned. "But I think it's an appropriate word to describe these files. They have no relationship to the gospel for which we stand."

The church managed to get away with this malfeasance by its code of secrecy. Secrecy and an absence of accountability enabled this to happen, it seemed. No wonder the bishops, the apostolic administrator, the vicar general and chancellors didn't want me to see the personnel files and have them corrected. They were only interested in covering up their own malfeasance, and protecting the institution rather than witness to the gospel.

As we delved deeper into the files, a chilling realization settled over us.

This was not the church we had pledged to serve.

These secret machinations, these lies and calculated deceptions—they were the antithesis of Christ's teachings.

Page after page, we searched for a glimmer of gospel truth.

We found none.

In its place, only the cold, calculating language of institutional self-preservation, and unlawful condemnation.

Another disturbing aspect, apart from false allegations, tampering, and redactions, was that all responses by myself and others to this defamation had been removed, leaving only a one-sided and deliberately erroneous viewpoint.

Thus, the letters from myself and responsible parishioners, such as the chairman of the parish finance council and others, were missing.

Neither did I see the letter from the Congregation for the Clergy, requesting that the matter of abuses be dealt with in an appropriately Christian fashion and brought to speedy resolution.

When Archbishop Mejia had asked me, during my first visit to the Vatican, why this persecution was taking place, I said I'd know when I had an opportunity to see my personnel files. Now I had the answer to his question. From the date of the conspiracy memo onward, good parishioners and myself were constantly put in jeopardy and a relentless campaign of vilification was waged to undermine the ministry of the parish.

The depth of abuse was astounding. It was inconceivable to me and Father Martin that anyone, let alone so many diocesan officials, could go along with this.

"Did they not have a conscience?" I asked my good friend.

"No, it appears they didn't," he said.

As we stared at the mountain of evidence before us, the question continued to burn in my mind: *Do these diocesan officials not have a conscience?* Bill's shoulders rose and fell in a helpless shrug, the gesture speaking volumes. In that moment, we realized we were grappling not just with individual failings, but with systemic corruption that threatened to corrode the foundations of the church.

How does one reconcile the teachings of Christ with this betrayal by his supposed stewards? This question hung between us, unanswered and perhaps unanswerable.

There is a dangerous psychological condition that seems to explain this kind of moral bankruptcy. It is called Loyalty Blindness or Blind Loyalty.[1] It allows immoral and unethical behavior to take place in the name of protecting allegiance to a superior or institution, but it is ultimately a form of collusion. One good example of this would be the defense of Nazi war criminals who pleaded not guilty for the crimes they committed because they were following orders. Hannah Arendt in her book, *Eichman in Jerusalem*, coined the term, the banality of evil, to describe the criminal behavior of nondescript bureaucrats like Eichman.

It is, of course, natural for someone to feel torn between loyalty to a person, cause, institution or group, and risk rejection and punishment by opposing and outing misconduct. But there is no excuse for knowing something to be wrong and acting against that knowledge. Loyalty blindness involves a form of cognitive and moral dissonance, in which a person turns a blind eye to the truth itself in favor of personal allegiance or self-interest.

The analysis of the files by Father Martin and myself on September 22 and 23, 1998 provided a trove of evidence confirming everything—and much more—that I had compiled in my dossier to the Holy See three years

---

1. There are many studies concerning Loyalty Blindness or "blind loyalty." *Obedience and Authority: An Experimental View*, by Dr. Stanley Milgram is an in-depth study of how obedience to authority regardless of morality takes place. *The Lucifer Effect: Understanding How Good People Turn Evil*, by Philip Zimbardo, is another study of this phenomenon.

earlier. Far more damning evidence than I had originally exposed now lay bare in these duplicitous files.

Meeting again with the apostolic administrator after reviewing these files, was very disappointing, but not surprising. I encountered the same urge to conceal. He asked that he and the vicar general address matters privately. This came across to me as more cover-up, a sad response to outrageous malfeasance, when he should have welcomed genuine reform and accountability.

The apostolic administrator would not give permission to Father Martin and I to take the next step to have these files corrected. Prevented from seeking justice, we had to leave the files as is, in their sealed imprimatur under him and his successors.

Father Martin and I now had an important job to do, and plenty of time to do it. We had to compile a full report on my personnel files or as full as was possible, to be presented to the incoming ordinary, the third bishop of the Diocese of Palm Beach.

During the period when the diocese was without a bishop, the *Palm Beach Post*, which covers the five-county diocese of Palm Beach, wanted some good news about the church after all the bad news. The *Post's* religion reporter, Steve Gushee, called me and asked if he could stop by for an interview. As it happened, I was working with the athletic director at the Okeechobee Correctional Facility to bring one of our adult soccer teams to play against the prison team, and I was asked to be the referee. When Steve heard about this he was overjoyed, and wanted to report on the game for his paper. The game took place in the afternoon, to the wild excitement of the prison inmates.

Nobody ever heard of this kind of prison ministry before, but that's what it was, an effective ministry of joy to prison inmates.

The positive article in the *Palm Beach Post* about the parish's outreach to prisoners was very well received in our five-county diocese, after all the bad news.

Chapter 37

With the resignation of the second Ordinary of the Diocese of Palm Beach, the diocese once again found itself without a leader, drifting in a sea of uncertainty. Unlike before, when Mexico offered me a temporary escape, this time I remained grounded, tethered to the very earth where our faith had been shaken by another scandal. Healing could not be sought elsewhere—it had to happen here, amidst the shattered trust of a wounded community.

Parishioners beat a steady path to the rectory to unburden themselves to me and to Father Jim. Deeply distraught over what had happened, they needed answers and, if no answers were available, they needed at least some degree of comfort and understanding. There were lots of conversations, lots of head-shaking, and lots of puzzled expressions and sighs of frustration.

During this grieving period—and it was a time of deep grieving—a group of ladies from the Kampgrounds of America (KOA) in Okeechobee came knocking on my door.

"We're not Catholic," announced the spokesperson of the group, "but we're very concerned over one member of your church."

"What's the matter?" I asked, deeply touched by their concern.

"She can't stop crying," the lady replied.

"Why?" I asked.

"She's torn to pieces by the revelations of sex abuse in her church," she explained.

"She's the nicest person in our park," interjected another lady, "and it pains us to see her suffering like this. We thought you might be able to help her."

I knew the lady they were talking about. She was indeed a beautiful soul, and would be the type to be shocked to the core by what had transpired in the diocese. I drove to her home in my car, following the lead of her good neighbors.

Part 2—Chapter 37

Meeting with this woman, still moaning from the depths of her being over the revelations of sex abuse in the church, was a heart-rending experience. I hardly knew what to do. I'd never witnessed anything like this before. This was a new kind of grief, a grief deeper and more poignant than anything I'd ever seen in my life. When I offered to give her the sacrament of the sick, she nodded her head several times in approval, tears flowing down her cheeks.

After receiving the sacrament, she stood up and embraced me so tightly I could feel the pain draining away from her body. She stopped crying and her good Christian neighbors threw their arms around her and myself, creating a circle of strength and comfort.

Even in the worst of circumstances—and the circumstances we were dealing with in the diocese could hardly have been worse—we managed to slowly come out of our grief. By the time the third bishop was installed we were over the worst of our lamentations.

* * *

The installation of the third bishop of Palm Beach was a low-key affair. Gone was the excessive triumphalism of the previous installation at the West Palm Beach Auditorium. This installation was held in the diocesan cathedral, quietly and without fanfare.

After the installation of the new bishop, the diocese resumed business as usual. The new bishop met with his priests and, at the deanery meeting I attended, he told us he would not attempt to alienate (a church term meaning confiscate) parish property. This was a direct reference to what the previous bishop had done by trying to wrest parish property from Sacred Heart in Okeechobee. Thank God that abuse was behind us.

Things were looking up in the parish. The talented Tom Blair took advantage of the situation to usher in a new day by completing the design of the outdoor stations of the cross with a rock garden, a Japanese bridge, and flowing water, issuing from a centrally-located fountain. As part of this project, he created a repository for a time capsule containing a written history and video about the parish, and a list of all parishioners to date.

A generous couple came forward and donated $125,000, which led to further improvements. With this money, Tom and his volunteer crew were able to work miracles.

"Won't you be needing a new church in the near future?" Tom asked me.

"Yes, we surely will, Tom," I replied. "We've grown beyond the capacity of the present chapel."

"Why not start preparing the site plan now?" he suggested.

"You're right," I said. "I'll meet with the finance council to seek its approval and I'll get back to you."

Once the council approved the project, Tom, our volunteer project manager, set to work preparing the site plan for a new church. He had considerable help. Hurly Electrical in Hobe Sound donated its services free of charge and many parishioners also volunteered to work on this site plan, gratis. The owner of Hurley Electrical had a vacation home in Okeechobee, and attended Sacred Heart when he and his wife were in the vicinity.

This project drew great excitement in the parish; it meant new, angled parking, lighting throughout the parking lot for the first time, and a new paved road leading all the way down to the pavilion, where extra parking would also be created. With this site plan, we laid essential groundwork for a new church of the future.

The new bishop of the diocese (its third) arrived for Confirmations in June.

Confirmations were never as exciting or uplifting as First Communions. The level of enthusiasm and involvement of children and families at First Communions could not be equalled at confirmations. Perhaps this was because First Communions tapped into a rich well of childlike innocence, pulling the parents and families into its warm embrace. Who could not be moved by the innocence of a child?

Confirmations, however, always attracted the bishop, because it was his opportunity to visit the parish, deliver a sermon to the parishioners, meet with them and interact with the youngsters.

The third bishop of the diocese, a stately, rotund man with a florid look, had the common touch, and demonstrated it by connecting with the youngsters when they approached him to be confirmed. He knew how to draw people out of themselves with just the right word, at the right time and in the right tone. He brought something personal and appealing to Confirmations, and the youngsters loved it.

"What Confirmation name have you chosen?" he would ask.

If the name was Peter, he'd say: "You've chosen Peter, my favorite saint. He was not perfect, he had his faults just like me, but he did not give up. Always remember, never give up."

This type of personal connection brought smiles to the faces of the youngsters during an otherwise very solemn ceremony.

Part 2—Chapter 37

There was a reception for the youngsters and their families in the pavilion. The bishop and I made an appearance together to congratulate them all and to spend some time with them.

As we made our way back to the rectory, the bishop lumbered along and I kept pace with him. It was one of those magic Florida sunsets. The sky had exploded into a multicolored quilt of orange, red and amber. These rainbow tones were interspersed with sparks of clear light, accentuating the dazzling array of colors. It was a spectacular June evening, still bright and festive with the sound of birdsong everywhere.

Ahead of us, a group of young Mexican Americans formed an arc in the middle of the road. They looked like figures in a Grecian frieze, plucked from reality by the radiant emanation of the many-colored sky.

"It looks like these lads want to talk about something," the bishop said to me, suddenly quickening his pace.

"Yes. I think they want to talk to you, bishop," I replied. "They've never spoken to a bishop before, more than likely."

"Well, lads," the bishop said, approaching the youngsters.

"What do you do?" asked one of them, unexpectedly.

"I'm Father Duffy's boss," replied the bishop.

The youngsters began to shuffle, shifting their weight from one foot to the other uneasily, as they are inclined to do. They didn't know what to make of the bishop's response but continued in their questioning.

"But, what do you do?" another youngster repeated the question.

"Father Duffy is over the parish," replied the bishop. "I'm over the diocese."

This answer didn't enlighten them either, so again one of them asked for the third time: "What do you do?"

The bishop was tongue-tied and couldn't give an answer. I was just as perplexed as the youngsters at his inability, with all his eloquence, to tell them what he did. But it looked like he wasn't sure what he could say that would make sense to them.

Meandering forward again past the group of curious youngsters, the bishop stopped at the outdoor stations of the cross.

"So, these are the famous stations of the cross," he remarked.

Obviously, he knew something of the history of these items of devotion. I didn't know what he had heard, since he hadn't heard anything from me.

"Yes," I replied. "Our volunteer workers did a great job constructing this beautiful setting."

The bishop could not remove his gaze from the scene before him for the longest time. I was wondering what was going on in his mind. Then, he declared, in a rather reflective mood: "These stations have taken on a significance way beyond their importance."

It was an interesting statement and had nothing to do with the spirit of piety they evoked. But I understood perfectly what he meant. He was referring to the battle that had raged over these stations of the cross. This controversy reached all the way to the Vatican and back again before being returned to the parish where they rightfully belonged.

Before he left Okeechobee, I got the bishop to inspect the church's pastoral records. I've always had to ask every bishop to perform this simple task, which was his pastoral responsibility, so that he might appreciate what was being done, and be given an opportunity to ask any questions. The bishop seemed to lose his verbal eloquence when I showed him the pastoral records of the parish. He silently affixed his signature to the records like every other bishop before him, without saying a word.

I decided then to bring to his attention a matter concerning the diocesan seminary, involving two of our young parishioners.

"Two young men, Jose and Roberto, attended a discernment weekend for vocations at the seminary," I said. "Jose, the son of my housekeeper, and his friend, Roberto, were shocked to be accosted constantly by homosexuals. Naturally, they lost all interest."

The bishop made no response. All I got was a blank stare.

Then I moved to the other serious matter of my personnel files. I gave him a copy of the detailed report that Father Martin and I had prepared during the interregnum. He was surprised to receive the document and he discussed its contents and the grave injustices, as he put it, which were outlined in it. I emphasized the urgency to correct the false information in these files. He agreed, and I was heartened by his interest in pursuing this. I was also touched when he assured me again that he would not attempt to alienate any parish property as the previous bishop had tried to do. After this bishop's visit to the parish, I felt that a new era of collaboration between the diocese and the parish had begun.

It didn't take long, however, for me to be disillusioned with that idea.

In early 2002, the *Boston Globe* published results of an investigation that thrust the sex abuse of minors by Catholic clergy into the national spotlight again. The *Globe's* coverage encouraged other victims to come forward. This resulted in an onslaught of allegations and lawsuits, some without merit, against Catholic clergy. What first appeared to be a few cases of abuse became a nationwide scandal affecting every Catholic diocese throughout the United States.

A major factor in the abuse scandal was the action of Catholic bishops to keep the matter secret, reassigning priests to other parishes where the abuses continued unchecked.

One evening after the Boston scandal broke, I was having dinner in the rectory with Father Finn. The phone rang. The call was from a priest of the diocese. He was not a diocesan official, but he was a priest I happened to know very well.

"Go over to your office," he said, in a conspiratorial tone, "and you'll find a fax about a meeting tomorrow at Our Lady of Florida Passionist Monastery in North Palm Beach."

"What's this about?" I asked, upset at being drawn into another conspiracy.

"The bishop will be addressing the clergy about sex abuse," he replied, adding nothing more.

I went over to the office and found the fax announcing a meeting for the clergy at the monastery at 11 a.m. on Friday, March 8, 2002. Returning to the rectory, I spoke with Father Finn about this unexpected announcement, and what the subsequent meeting in the monastery might be about.

"Could it be that the seminary in Tennessee, where the bishop was in charge, is also in trouble over sex abuse?" I remarked.

"I have no idea," replied Jim, shaking his head.

I went to bed that night wondering what awaited me the following day.

It was a blistering, sunny morning as I drove along Highway 710 to North Palm Beach, where the monastery was located. The sun's rays were bouncing off the highway, suffusing the car with its ubiquitous light.

The phone in my car rang. It was Faye.

"Father, the monastery meeting is canceled," she informed me,

"On whose word?" I asked.

"Sister Consilio, the bishop's secretary, just phoned to tell you not to come."

My suspicion rose at this attempted exclusion. I pulled the car over and called the priest I had talked to the previous night.

"My secretary was told that the meeting was off," I asserted. "Can this be accurate?"

"That cannot be right," he replied. "Let me check it out and I'll get back with you."

Ten uneasy minutes passed until his call back.

"The meeting is still on. See you there," he concluded.

When I arrived at the monastery, I knew at first sight something was amiss. The clergy were solemnly suited in black suits, unlike the casual garb we wore at retreats and other meetings. It was a sure sign that this meeting was portentous. I was the only one in casual attire.

The omnipresent vicar general was running the meeting from the podium up front. He spoke about a prepared letter to the Nuncio and to the *Palm Beach Post* for which he solicited signatures from all the clergy present. Priests took to the floor one after the other, supporting the bishop and condemning the media in any way they could. I didn't know what was going on, but it was obvious that it involved the new bishop.

Was the bishop being accused of sex abuse? Could this actually be happening again? I wondered.

I was sitting in the back of the hall when suddenly the third bishop of the diocese entered and took a seat beside me. He had a woebegone look and sat there silently until the vicar general called him to come up front. His appearance at the podium was greeted with loud applause.

He explained to the assembled clergy the ins and outs of an accusation against himself for inappropriate sexual behavior involving a former priest and seminarian in Tennessee.

It was very difficult to watch.

Each word the bishop spoke seemed to weigh heavier on the room. A gnawing unease settled deep in my gut. This bishop was very well liked by all, but why was he drawing us into his personal turmoil? As the meeting stretched on, I felt more and more uneasy. The bishop had our sympathy, but he was also responsible for his own actions.

When the vicar general announced that the bishop would be facing the media, surrounded by a bunch of supporting priests, clerically clad, well, that's when I decided to leave. I understood all too well why I was not welcome at this meeting.

I drove back to Okeechobee and told Father Jim what had transpired.

"We need to do something, Jim," I said.

"Like what, Hugh?"

"We need to send a fax to the Nuncio in Washington and to the Congregation for Bishops in Rome, stating our position that the bishop should not involve the priests of the diocese in his own personal problem."

Jim pondered this course of action carefully.

"If we don't say something like this," I continued, "it'll look like all the clergy in the diocese are supporting serious wrongdoing. The vicar general has already solicited signatures of support from all the clergy for the bishop in the letter to the Nuncio."

Jim and I signed our names to the fax, under the statement I proposed. As we sent our message to Washington and Rome, I couldn't shake the feeling that we were casting a pebble into an ocean of indifference. But even the smallest ripple, I reminded myself, eventually reaches the shore.

The meeting in the Florida Monastery was followed soon after by the bishop's television interview on Friday, March 8. He was surrounded by a supportive cadre of priests of the diocese in full clerical garb, a sad symbol of misguided loyalty. He took questions from reporters. It was an unmitigated disaster. He admitted that there could be another case of abuse in addition to the one that had just become public. This sent the media scurrying to find more incriminating evidence against him.

After the disastrous television interview, which was viewed widely, many priests called the *Palm Beach Post* and asked that their names be withdrawn from the letter defending the bishop. In the end, the *Palm Beach Post* announced it would not publish the letter.

Only a few years after the first revelations of sex abuse by our second bishop, the diocese was plunged into darkness again by more revelations of sex abuse by our third bishop.

On March 13, 2002, Pope John Paul II accepted the resignation of the third Bishop of Palm Beach.

Chapter 38

As news of the third bishop's resignation rippled through our community, a collective sigh of resignation echoed through the pews. Here we go again, the weary glances of parishioners seemed to say. In the shadow of this latest ecclesiastical earthquake, we clung to our faith like a lifeline.

One day, in a poignant symbol of transition, Fran, our housekeeper, was removing the photograph of the outgoing bishop from its place of honor on the wall in the dining room. This simple act underscored the transient nature of leadership within the diocese and marked the beginning of another chapter in our collective journey of faith.

"What are you trying to do?" I asked her.

"I am removing this photo," she replied. "It has too many hurtful memories."

As she removed the photo of the outgoing bishop, she uncovered another photo behind it of the previous bishop who had also been forced to resign due to sex abuse.

She looked at me askance, and we both laughed.

"Wait a minute," I said to Fran. "I have a non-threatening photo for you that is sure to make you happy."

I retreated to my quarters and reemerged cradling a sizeable photograph of Rocky, our pint-sized Shih-Tzu guardian. Fran's face lit up with delight as she carefully placed Rocky's photo in the frame.

In the absence of a bishop, I found that the parish thrived. Indeed, it was remarkable how smoothly everything functioned.

Fulfilling our financial obligations to the diocesan administration was a breeze during this period. The annual diocesan appeal and assorted special collections were honored quickly and even painlessly, with the efficiency of a Swiss clockmaker. We had the freedom to engage in the work of the gospel, allowing us to focus on the truly important matters, like tending the flock and spreading the good news.

Part 2—Chapter 38

And so, unfettered, we pursued God's work joyfully. The parish's ministries blossomed. With the interregnum came a sense of freedom, of possibility. Unencumbered by bureaucratic red tape, we could get on with the real business of the church, devoting ourselves to meaningful labor and parish ministries.

March 2002 brought our annual St. Patrick's celebration: a three-day festival capped by a parade down Main Street. But this year promised something special. None other than NASCAR legend Bobby Allison would serve as Grand Marshal, thrilling our racing-frenzied town. Everyone was abuzz with anticipation.

The charismatic Billy Dean at WOKC radio was instrumental in fueling the fervor. With Billy at the helm, the station became the epicenter of the growing excitement. As he continually fanned interest, he invited me to the studio for a radio interview.

"Could you get Bobby Allison on the phone?" he asked.

I rang Bobby straightaway.

"I'm at WOKC in Okeechobee, Bobby," I said. "Billy Dean wants a word."

Billy conducted an electrifying interview. Soon the phone jingled with locals keen to meet their hero at the festival.

A native-grown, Florida *cracker*, Billy was Okeechobee's radio celebrity. He was the radio host, the announcer, the interviewer, and the disk-jockey. In the good old days, Billy would have been the town crier, awakening the citizenry to the new morning and heralding the end of another day. Loved by Okeechobee residents for his down-to-earth interviewing style, he discussed with Bobby the upcoming festival, but above all he enjoyed talking about Bobby's extraordinary career as a NASCAR champion driver.

All the major needs for the three-day festival—volunteers, dinners, raffle, gifts for children, food and drinks, vendors, porta-potties, dumpsters, parking, entertainment and parade floats—were organized in advance by Big Tom Peer and his crew. All the food was donated by the Harvest Meat Company in Orlando. The media in Okeechobee and surrounding counties covered the event. They came to our meetings to write about the festival and the stupendous career of Bobby Allison, winner of eighty-six grand national championships.

The town came alive on Saturday, March 16, 2002, with a parade that would be long remembered. More than twenty floats, adorned creatively and with care, proceeded through the streets. Irish bagpipers played their pipes, Mariachis strummed guitars, Irish dancers stepped lively beside martial artists, striking poses. The procession, in its splendid diversity, wove its way back to the church grounds, the festival ongoing.

Bobby Allison ran out of his stock of autographed photos that first day. Not to be deterred, we supplied him with a fresh batch of scenic cards from our gift shop, which he graciously signed for the throngs of enthusiastic well-wishers.

The jubilation could not have been better timed. It shifted our parishioners' gaze away from the troubling headlines plaguing the institutional church, and towards uplifting news and the power of community. As people from all walks of life came together to have fun and celebrate their shared values, the festival served as a testament to the power of unity and the resilience of the human spirit. It was not just a celebration of heritage, but a demonstration of our collective ability to rise up and find joy and solidarity in the face of adversity.

And then there was Holy Week, a time for spiritual renewal and reflection.

Palm Sunday marked the commencement of Holy Week Services. The church was transformed into a community, brimming with life. An extraordinary tide of the faithful flowed through the doors, filling the pews to capacity. Never had our 12:30 p.m. Spanish Mass, the day's last, seen such crowds.

Typically, the parking lot would lie empty until the Latino parishioners' late arrival. But this Sunday at noon, vehicles crammed into every cranny of the new lot. Astonishingly, the overflow spilled all the way to the pavilion, even to the grassy rise behind the soccer pitch.

What provoked this unprecedented turnout amid institutional turmoil? I wondered. Perhaps it was the community's instinct to turn towards prayer and reflection when faced with such alarming uncertainty.

The media storm raged on, the latest blow being a Cardinal's handling of past sex abuse in Connecticut.

Yet personal faith, it seemed, remained firm despite these revelations.

Little children came to church on Palm Sunday decked out in multi-colored costumes, bearing intricately woven palms in the shape of crosses, hearts, and sundials.

We began Mass with a flowery procession that snaked its way outside the church to southwest Sixth Street and back again. This line was so long and large that it was still leaving the church as the first batch of participants were returning. The Mass ended with multiple baptisms of children dressed in luminous white costumes. The families' photo-taking after the baptisms took longer than the baptisms themselves, but this did not bother anyone, for it was a thrilling, uplifting event.

Never did I see anything as moving as the outdoor stations of the cross on Good Friday of 2002. Tom Blair had built an electronic stage that could be moved from place to place. It offered the perfect backdrop for the stations of the cross outdoors, and was equipped with microphones, a portable organ, podium and chairs for the choir, celebrant and readers.

A gentle breeze wafted melodiously through the trees behind the stations of the cross that Good Friday. As if by design, a canopy of clouds hovered over the worshippers during the service, shading them from the scorching sun. As the congregation left the grounds in solemn silence, a flock of geese flew over in orderly fashion in the sun-lit, evening sky.

Nature was going about her business as usual, undisturbed by the wiles and machinations of man, obedient to the mysterious order of creation. A feeling of peace and oneness enveloped us all as we bade farewell to one another and retired to our homes on that Good Friday evening.

* * *

Then, on September 14, 2002, the Vatican announced the appointment of the fourth Bishop of the Diocese of Palm Beach.

The month leading up to the installation on October 19 was a flurry of preparations, each parish, including ours, curating lists of attendees to accompany every pastor.

The morning of the installation was cloaked in a solemn air of anticipation. Our parishioners and I gathered in the church parking lot at 9 a.m. This was a familiar starting point. Father Clem, who had joined me after Father Finn's retirement, accompanied me to the cathedral, followed by others in their own cars.

As we neared the cathedral, an unexpected fortress loomed before us. Stern-faced officers stood guard behind a maze of barricades, their eyes scanning each approaching car with cold suspicion. The air was filled with tension, a far cry from the warm embrace of brotherhood you'd expect. This wasn't like a gathering of the faithful; it was more like a siege, the church seemingly at war with the very flock it was meant to shepherd.

"You'll have to pass through the designated entrance," an officer directed, pointing us further down the barricaded road to an alternate, equally guarded gate.

After navigating the second entrance, we managed to find parking in a large grassy area within the cathedral grounds. We were instructed to vest for Mass in another building, not in the cathedral building itself. This shift from a space of welcome to a guarded fortress resonated with distressing irony. The very institution meant to exude trust now stood ensnared in a web of suspicion and fear.

As we lined up, at a safe distance from the cathedral, a priest announced: "A bomb squad with sniffing dogs was called in forty-five minutes ago to clear the cathedral of danger. We're all clear now."

This was the atmosphere in which we walked to the cathedral for the Mass of installation of the fourth bishop of Palm Beach. We walked in groups of two from the building to the cathedral. To my surprise, I was paired alongside my nemesis, the vicar general. He had overseen the diocese during the Interregnum. He made no bones about wanting to be the next bishop, going so far as to write in *The Florida Catholic* newspaper that he could not refuse this position if offered to him, given the life he led.

As the procession made its way to the cathedral, I remarked: "Well, Jim, your ardent politicking to become bishop didn't work."

"What are you talking about?" he replied, irritated: "'Tis politics that does it."

"I'm aware of that," I answered. "All I'm saying is that your politicking didn't work, and even if it did, would it be worth it?"

"What are you talking about?" He rebutted.

"I'm just saying, Jim, to paraphrase Christ: What does it profit a priest if he rises to the top of the institution at the expense of his vocation?"

He gave no answer as we continued to walk in silence towards the cathedral.

But our relationship changed for the better after that. Every time we got together at clergy gatherings, he'd call me over to sit beside him, his old superior attitude giving way to jollity and camaraderie. It's an extraordinary fact that, when people abandon the poison of careerism, their attitudes change, and they become normal in demeanor and practice. It was a change that I welcomed wholeheartedly, for we could now relate as friends, not opponents.

I could not wait to get back to Okeechobee after the installation ceremony. Clem and I breathed a sigh of relief, driving into the grounds of Sacred Heart without having to worry about bomb scares.

The new bishop did not waste any time in visiting the parish. He came out the following December to attend the Christmas Around the World festival outdoors, and he spoke from the portable stage to the large gathering of parishioners and townspeople who turned out for the occasion. He was happy to be there, and we were happy to welcome him.

Each of the roughly 400 children who attended Christmas Around the World received a personal gift in the spirit of Christmas, as was the custom.

The bishop visited the parish again for Confirmation. We had dinner in the rectory with priests from neighboring parishes. Everything was very cordial. When we were gathered in the hall for a reception after the

Confirmation, a young man, very distressed, came up to me. His mother had just passed away and he wanted me to come to his home. The bishop reacted compassionately and understood that I had to leave him for this grieving young man and his family. He decided then to take his leave and return to North Palm Beach. I was not able to show him the parish records or discuss with him the matter of my personnel files.

* * *

Around this time, a couple came to the office with a picture of their 450-acre farm in Tuscola, Illinois.

"We would like to donate this farm to the church," Harold told Faye, the secretary.

"I think you need to talk to the pastor," replied Faye. "Would you like to meet him? He's over in the rectory."

Faye brought Harold and Betty to the rectory and introduced them to me.

They sat down. Harold, who did the talking, explained why they wanted to donate their farm to the church.

"We've been visiting Okeechobee since the 1950s and this parish is our favorite place. We've seen it grow in the last decade and we like everything about it. We think you need a new church, and we'd like to help by donating our farm."

"That's very generous of you," I said. "But does your family agree with this?"

Harold explained that he and his wife had no children of their own.

I then asked Betty, his wife: "What do you think of this? Does it meet with your approval?"

Betty hesitated for a while but eventually nodded her head.

This was an unusual development. As unusual as it was, it was soon complemented by another fortuitous development, when a husband and wife in the parish made a generous cash donation for the construction of a new church.

I shared with the parishioners these developments, and they were delighted.

A new church was something they had always wanted, it seemed. The old chapel building was too small to accommodate all the parishioners at the various Masses, and we had to continually use the adjoining hall for an overflow crowd.

The fact that Tom Blair and his helpers had already prepared the new church's site plan had a lot to do with the final decision to construct a new church. The cost of the site plan was taken care of by another generous donation from the estate of a deceased parishioner.

On January 13, 2003, I met with the fourth Bishop of the Diocese of Palm Beach to get his approval for the project, a necessary step. It was granted at a 45-minute lunch meeting held at Paddy Mac's Irish Pub in Palm Beach Gardens. Father Richard Murphy, head of the diocesan building department, attended. The bishop and Father Murphy approved of our plans to begin a capital campaign to raise funds to construct a new church.

When the meeting was over, I drove the bishop back to the pastoral center for a follow-up meeting. Every priest of the diocese had been invited by the new bishop to meet with him at a mutually convenient time to discuss common concerns. This was excellent news. No other bishop had ever done this. I saw this meeting as a good chance to talk to him about my personnel files.

As we were seated in his office at the pastoral center, the bishop began this welcome discussion by asking about my age and health. He then inquired if I attended the clergy retreats.

"No, I don't," I replied. "I prefer to make a private retreat."

"Why?"

"The clergy retreats are too gossipy," I explained with a smile.

He smiled back at me. "I've heard that before from others," he conceded.

Turning his attention to another matter, he asked: "How are you handling the crisis in the church?"

I looked at him, waiting for further clarification.

"I mean the sex abuse crisis and how you're handling it," he said.

"Now that you bring the matter up," I replied, "I see this as an institutional problem in the church, straying from its mission to be guided by the gospel."

Wanting me to elaborate, he asked: "What do you mean?"

"I think it is pretty obvious," I continued, "that systemic abuse in the church has nothing to do with the gospel. It has been conducted, regrettably, in terrifying secrecy."

He made no reply and was simply content to nod his head.

"How is the parish reacting to all this?" he asked.

"The crisis of institutional abuse hasn't made much of a dent on the parish it seems," I replied. "People relate to the local church, their priests, and to each other in the parish. After all, we've been dealing with institutional abuse for most of twenty years, the evidence of which is contained in my personnel files in this building."

Part 2—Chapter 38

"You have a clean slate with me," he said.

I went on to outline some of the abuses committed by various diocesan administrations, explaining that evidence of these abuses was contained in the Report that Father Martin and I had drawn up on my personnel files, and given to his predecessor. He did not seem familiar with this report and seemed shocked at what I related. Perhaps the report was removed from my files.

I mentioned also interference in the pastoral ministry of the parish.

"What do you mean?" he inquired.

"The second bishop of the diocese had one of his conspirators take the new stations of the cross from the parish and put them in diocesan storage," I explained.

"And what happened?" he again inquired, becoming very curious.

"The Vatican ordered the bishop to return them to the parish," I said.

He was anxious to know more, and I explained that the second bishop actually called me to say that the items showed up at his door, and that he wanted to return them to the parish.

This struck him as funny.

"I asked the bishop if he would bless the stations when they would be installed."

He roared laughing.

"I thought it would be a good way of letting bygones be bygones," I continued.

More loud laughter.

He seemed to find this whole incident of the stations of the cross very amusing.

"What do you want to do?" he asked, getting serious again.

"I want to have my personnel files corrected and cleansed of all false accusations against me," I firmly replied.

"That could be easily managed," he said.

I was very heartened to hear him say this, feeling I was getting somewhere at last.

But when he added: "Arlene [not her real name], the chancellor, can help you with this, my hopes were dashed again."

Of all people to help me! She was involved in inserting false and defamatory information into my files. Putting the matter of the personal files into the hands of an adversary was like putting a robber in charge of the bank. She had contacted my secretary in the past, attempting to persuade her to send the marriage files of a particular parishioner to her, without my knowledge, so the bishop could build a fake canonical case against me.

But I did not give up hope on this bishop who, for all intents and purposes, meant well and demonstrated his good faith by meeting with me.

Thus, I let the matter drop for the time being, not wishing to throw cold water on an otherwise warm and open conversation.

I next told the bishop that I had related these outrageous goings-on in the diocese to Archbishop Jorge Maria Mejia during my visits to the Vatican.

"I met Archbishop Mejia," he remarked.

"Would you like to know what he said about the Diocese of Palm Beach?" I asked.

"Yes, I would," he replied.

"The diocese," he said, "was run by a bunch of incompetents."

He gave no response.

Regrettably, my hopes of someone dealing professionally and responsibly with my personnel files were squashed once again. It was announced on July 1, 2003, that the fourth Bishop of Palm Beach was appointed to the Archdiocese of Boston.

The only bishop willing to rectify my personnel files was leaving the diocese. He had served as the Bishop of the Diocese of Palm Beach for only nine months.

Chapter 39

WHILE FAITHFUL CATHOLICS BEWAILED the mounting sex-abuse revelations in the church, the Diocese of Palm Beach celebrated the installation of its next bishop, the fifth, with all the pageantry of the church triumphant.

The newly appointed bishop had held the position as auxiliary bishop and chancellor to the Bishop of Brooklyn, who had been the first bishop of the Palm Beach diocese.

When asked about the widely reported sex abuse scandals in the Diocese of Brooklyn, the new bishop told the *Palm Beach Post* he didn't know anything about them.

And thus, another solemn procession entered the Cathedral of St. Ignatius Loyola on August 28, 2003. During the installation Mass, there was just a single mention of the victims of abuse in the Vietnamese reading of the Prayers of the Faithful.

On the drive back to Okeechobee, the sky was overcast. A blanket of gray clouds stretched from horizon to horizon. Even nature was somber and silent. Nobody in the parish said anything to me about the installation of the new bishop, even though it was covered on local television.

I later wrote to the new bishop, the fifth ordinary of the diocese, about the personnel files, and met with him at the pastoral center on Tuesday, September 23, 2003. When I arrived at 11 a.m. for the meeting, the door to the bishop's office was open but inside it was empty. The secretary spotted me looking around and rushed over to tell me the bishop was at an auditor's meeting and would soon be available. He arrived, all smiles, and greeted me cordially.

A bust of President John F. Kennedy loomed large on top of the bishop's desk.

"So, you are fan of President Kennedy," I began.

"Yes," replied the bishop. "He's one of my heroes."

Taking my seat, I thanked him for seeing me.

"Do you have the Report by Father Martin and myself on my personnel files?" I asked him.

He was silent.

I then handed him some letters I received from the Holy See in 1996.

"These letters," I explained, "were not in my files when Father Martin and I reviewed them."

Awkwardly, the bishop made as if to read the letters I gave him, but he looked disinterested and said nothing.

"My main concern," I explained, "was the complete disregard by diocesan administrations for the church's own teaching and policy when it came to false accusations. My personnel files contain ample evidence of malfeasance."

Since I was keenly aware of the reason for the cover up of these abuses by different administrations, I asked the new bishop if this malfeasance would continue.

He assured me it wouldn't.

I told him I had received similar assurances in the past, but was encouraged to hear him say that I would not be exposed to the same kind of persecution in the future.

He gave me his word again that he would not be similarly involved and seemed interested in making amends for past wrongdoings.

He did not give permission, however, to correct the false information in the personnel files.

Before I departed, he had only one question:

"Should I keep the letters from the Holy See that you gave me?"

"Yes, you may," I replied.

That's how the meeting ended at 11:45 a.m.

On Friday, October 10, 2003, I hand-delivered to the fifth bishop of the diocese the report by Father Martin and myself on my personnel files, which I suspected was missing from the diocesan files.

* * *

Meanwhile, in the parish, plans to launch a campaign to raise funds for a new church got underway. Building a new church is a challenging ordeal. You need more than goodwill or good intentions. You need a detailed plan and the overwhelming support of the parishioners, which we fortunately had. We also had access to a company with experience in running such a campaign. So, we hired the company, Guidance and Giving, to walk us through the process.

Part 2—Chapter 39

In the middle of the process, tragedy struck. I received the very sad news that my sister Cathleen was in critical condition in a hospital in Sligo, Ireland.

Cathleen was the inspiration behind the work we undertook in Ireland in the 1970s to help the needy. She motivated me to found Christian Community Action (CCA), an ecumenical organization to build facilities for the handicapped, housing for seniors, and other worthy causes. Our first project had been a facility for handicapped in Sligo.

I told Faye the news of my sister's critical condition. Plans to build the new church had to be put on hold. Faye got on the phone to arrange a transatlantic flight to Dublin while I sought outside help for the New Year's and weekend Masses in the parish.

Faye scheduled the flight to Ireland that same day. I got four priests to cover for me at all the Masses during my absence. My brother, Pat, and my sister, Hannah, my siblings in America, were also flying to Ireland on the same day to be at Cathleen's bedside.

As soon as I arrived in Dublin, I went to a Vodafone shop to purchase a cell phone to use during my time in Ireland. As I was cell phone shopping at the airport, Pat came up from behind and surprised me. He had just arrived an hour before from Chicago and was waiting for Hannah to emerge from Customs.

When Hannah finally appeared, we got a rental car and drove to Sligo General Hospital, situated on top of a hill overlooking the sprawling town below. We found the rest of my family already gathered there, huddled like sheep around my sister's bed. I immediately administered the sacrament of the sick.

The first day was a long and dreary one. The following days converged like dark clouds in a somber sky. Between my visits to the hospital, I had to see a doctor about a bloodshot eye and an irritating head cold, contracted from both my extensive travels and the piercing coldness of the Irish winter.

The doctor who treated my sister informed us that she was being moved to the Beaumont Hospital in Dublin. I checked out of my hotel, got my own rental car and followed the ambulance transporting my sister to Dublin. The rest of my family went to Donegal. It was another miserable day: rain all the way to Dublin, and very poor visibility. It was a relief to finally arrive at the hospital without an accident.

Once my sister was comfortably settled in, I booked a room at the Great Southern Hotel at Dublin Airport. My sister appeared to be on the mend, and I booked my return flight to Florida.

Just as I was driving to the airport for the return flight, Dr. Conlon, a consulting physician at Beaumont Hospital, called me on my cell phone.

"Your sister's condition is very critical," he said. "She will not survive much longer."

"Could you please meet with the family?" I asked. "They all left for Donegal, but I'll get in touch with them to return immediately."

"I'd be glad to meet with your family," he answered, kindly.

My brothers, Michael and Pat, and my sisters Hannah and Marie, drove back from Donegal to Dublin as soon as I alerted them about Cathleen's grave condition.

We all met Dr. Conlon at the hospital waiting room. Listening to his diagnosis of my sister's condition, we reconciled ourselves to the reality that Cathleen was dying, and there was nothing we could do but keep vigil and make her as comfortable as possible.

In the dimly lit hospital room where my sister lay dying, I sat quietly reading a book by her bedside. My sister, Hannah, and the chaplain were seated at the foot of the bed, engaged in rambling philosophical musings about life's journey, with its many twists and turns, ups and downs, pitfalls and surprises. Their words, weaving through my consciousness, resonated with my own experiences.

Suddenly, in a moment where the boundaries between the earthly and the ethereal seemed to blur, an oceanic calm swept the room. It was a serene embrace, transcending the ordinary, halting the passage of time and thought. It was so real, so personal, that I stopped reading and looked up from my book towards Cathleen who lay serenely in bed. Her face beamed with an otherworldly glow, a radiant smile of profound peace gracing her features.

I gently whispered to Hannah and the chaplain: "Do you see what's happening?"

Startled, Hannah leapt up shouting, her voice a mix of awe and revelation: "She's saying goodbye! And she's smiling."

This sacred moment rippled outwards, reaching my anxious, gathered siblings in the hospital waiting room. They rushed in at the cries, just as Cathleen silently and peacefully slipped away, her face still radiant with joy.

And as quick as it came, the moment passed. The extraordinary atmosphere lifted, returning us to an ordinary Irish, winter's day. The chaplain recited psalms while I, with a heart both heavy and uplifted, bestowed the final blessing upon my sister, gone to eternal rest in the Hamilton ward of Beaumont Hospital, Dublin.

We laid Cathleen to rest in our native Donegal. It was not until January 8, 2004 that I found myself on a plane back to Florida, carrying with me the memory of that sacred, fleeting moment.

Part 2—Chapter 39

I resumed the task of building a new church, stalled midstream. Our fundraising regained momentum, reaping over a million dollars pledged initially. We deposited over half a million in cash in the diocesan building fund, accruing interest.

Some parishioners demurred on pledges, preferring to drop affordable contributions monthly into the collection basket. This I understood well from our previous Education Center project, and gladly agreed to their request. We banked these cash contributions locally for now. This auxiliary income would prove vital in time, though we little realized it then.

Following the initial success of the campaign, we met with the diocesan building committee. Our architect presented the design of the church, and I filled the committee in on the financial status of the campaign. The diocesan building committee approved the project.

We did not set a specific timeline to complete the new church, since both the old church and the hall had served the parishioners for forty years and would continue to do so while we were collecting funds for the new one. Our goal was to collect the money first then build the new church, debt-free. This is what we always did during all construction projects. As a result of this policy, the parish never incurred a debt.

In late 2008, four years into our capital campaign, the U.S. was plunged into the Great Recession by the collapse of the American housing market. Money was suddenly scarce and as a consequence, new pledges for the church stopped just as suddenly. Fortunately, time was on our side. The money we had accumulated in the bank was earning good interest and this steadily grew our capital.

Finally, when we decided we had enough funds to build, we experienced another unexpected setback. A donor who had pledged one million dollars to the project from a charitable remainder trust, decided to withhold payment of funds unless he could personally take charge of the church's construction.

"This was not acceptable," I told him on a Sunday morning, as he was walking to his car after Mass.

"The bishop will sign the contract when all the money is deposited in the diocesan building fund," I explained. "Here is his phone number if you care to call him on Monday. He'll be glad to talk to you."

"I'll give the money," he replied.

I told him that lifted a big burden off my shoulders.

But when I spoke with the bishop later, he said the donor had reverted to his old position.

Faced with this dilemma, we agonized over what to do.

The diocese suggested we should solicit more funds from parishioners. But the parishioners were already maxed out, especially now, during the Great Recession.

The parish's building committee and finance council met with me to address this problem. I explained what had happened, but pointed out that all was not lost because we had an ace in the hole: We had collected over half a million from the monthly collections deposited locally. This news brought a smile to the faces of the members. If we could now get a loan for the other half from the diocese, the project would be saved and the new church would be built. Everyone was heartened by this news.

I called the bishop and asked for a loan of $500,000 to complete the project. This was not an extravagant request, I felt, for the parish had an excellent track record of paying its way and had never incurred an expense it couldn't handle.

The bishop replied: "No."

Downhearted, I reported this gloomy news back to our building and finance committees. Naturally, we were disappointed. We now needed a miracle if the new church at Sacred Heart was to be built.

One afternoon, while this crisis was still brewing, a parishioner, Helen Walker, and member of the finance council came to see me.

"I'll give the $500,000 you need to build the new church," she said, emphatically.

"You really mean that, Helen?" I asked, incredulously.

"Yes, I do," she emphasized. "I've been a member of this parish since its inception, and I want to see this church built."

And so, we had our miracle. We got the million dollars we needed: $500,000 from the second collections, and another $500,000 from Helen's matching funds. We did not need the million dollars from the charitable remainder trust, nor did we need a loan from the diocese.

Okeechobee is a small town, and disturbing rumors about money gone missing from the church's building fund were being spread through the local grapevine. It was the month of March, and I was invited by friends to visit Santa Cruz in Bolivia to celebrate St. Patrick's Day. On the morning of the flight, I told my traveling companion, Bill Laier, a snowbird from Michigan, that I had to cancel the trip to Bolivia in order to squelch the false rumors about money gone missing from the church's building fund.

"Can it not wait until we get back?" asked Bill, innocently.

"No, it cannot," I replied. "These rumors take on a life of their own, and I have to be here to answer them. They could derail the building project if they are not checked in time."

The following day, a reporter from the *Okeechobee News* called me.

Part 2—Chapter 39

"There's lots of interest in the community about missing funds for a new church at Sacred Heart," he said. "What do you have to say?"

"No funds are missing at all," I replied. "We have one million dollars in the Bank of America, and over a million and a half dollars more in our building fund at the diocese. That's sufficient to build our new church since the site plan is already completed and paid for."

"How can I verify these figures?" he asked.

"You have my permission to call the Bank of America and the diocese of Palm Beach to verify these figures," I told him.

The reporter thanked me for my candor. We then discussed the origin of these false rumors throughout the community. I explained to the reporter how we had made up for the million dollars that was promised but never given from a charitable remainder trust.

The reporter checked with the Bank of America, confirming what I told him.

"The diocese would not release any information," he declared.

"I can give you my statement from the diocese on these funds," I said, helpfully.

"It won't be necessary," replied the reporter. "I believe you and I trust you."

The upshot of this affair was that the reporter wrote a very positive article about our new church building project, and the false rumors faded away like morning dew on grass.

The parishioners, however, had a right to know, from me, the truth about the status of the new church. I wrote a bulletin article, explaining in detail how we had the required funding. I also spoke about the matter, in place of a homily, at all the weekend Masses, and took questions from parishioners. People I had never seen before turned up at church that weekend. It was the biggest news in town, and the largest attendance we had ever seen in our church.

One man, who I had never seen in church before, seemed very amused by it all, and asked a question: "Was the donor who reneged on his million-dollar donation a local Bernie Madoff character?"

The whole church burst into laughter. Bernie Madoff was national news at the time. He had defrauded wealthy clients in Palm Beach of millions of dollars.

"He is nothing like Bernie Madoff," I replied.

When I finished taking questions at each Mass, the congregation applauded.

You Duped Me, O Lord

The new church at Sacred Heart was built, debt-free. It was erected on the site of the old church, and we were able to use the parish pavilion for daily and weekend Masses during construction.

We launched the campaign to build the new church in 2004, and finally completed its construction and dedicated it in 2012.

* * *

Of all the setbacks, obstacles, and interference I had to deal with, none was as strange and bewildering as an affair involving my little dog, Rocky.

On small things, it is said, great issues hang. A diocesan official working in Hispanic Ministry called me shortly after two violent hurricanes, Frances and Jeanne, rocked the East Coast of Florida in August 2004. These hurricanes had left a trail of devastation. I thought, naturally, that the official was calling me about hurricane damages to parish property.

I was shocked to the bone when he announced: "Some Latino parishioners at Sacred Heart are disturbed by your derogatory comments about them from the altar."

"You have to be kidding," I replied. "I don't know what you're talking about."

I asked him to send me the comments in writing so I could reply to them.

The official grew nervous, humming and hawing, when I made this request. He refused to send me the comments.

I reminded him it was diocesan policy to be given the actual facts in writing, not just hearsay, when a complaint is made against a priest.

He ignored this and continued: "You said from the altar that these people were not as intelligent as your dog, and that, if they were, they'd be better off."

I laughed out loud, wondering in the name of all that was high and holy where this rubbish was coming from, and how a diocesan official could swallow such trifles hook, line, and sinker. But I was no stranger to this nonsense.

"The bishop," he continued, "is shocked that you could put your dog above the parishioners."

The fifth bishop of the diocese, I now learned from the official, was part of this, even after he gave me his word that he would not continue the abuses or witch-hunts of the past.

"I never made such preposterous comments from the altar," was my answer.

Again, I asked him to send me the comments in writing and stop repeating this defamatory hearsay. But it was a losing battle, and I was unable to get anywhere with him. He was covering up, it seemed, for whoever spread these malicious rumors.

I wrote to the fifth bishop asking that I be sent the comments attributed to me from the altar, in writing, so I could reply to them. Surely, he would respect the church's own policy after his earlier assurances to me that he would.

The bishop's surprising response was that I should continue to dialogue with the diocesan official. But how could I dialogue about something when I didn't know the facts and was even prevented from knowing them?

With no evidence or facts to go on, I ransacked my memory to unearth the origin of this allegation. It is extraordinary how memory works, like when you want to wake up at a certain time. The thought worms its way into the subconscious, and *voilà*! You wake up at that exact time. It is the same with memories that seem to lie dormant in the subconscious. At the appropriate time, they can resurface as fresh and clear as the day they were born.

My daily journals were a great help in recalling events connected, in some way, to these strange allegations.

At last, I saw the light. The incident in question occurred during the parish Blessing of Animals. Rocky was loved by everyone, and I spoke about him fondly from the pulpit, to the delight of parishioners. Every year, at the beginning of October, people would bring their pets to church before the actual Blessing at the pavilion. My housekeeper, Fran, always brought Rocky to church before the Blessing, and he always behaved remarkably well.

On this occasion, a parishioner, Marisela Aguilar, commented to her daughter on how good Rocky was in church, and held up my little canine as an inspiration to her little girl. When she told me this innocent story, I shared it with the parishioners from the pulpit. My comments in church were received with good humor by everyone, until now, many years later, when the fifth bishop and his assistant saw fit to interpret them negatively, even though they weren't present at the event.

I spoke to Marisela about this curious development at the diocese, and she was utterly shocked that something so innocent that took place long ago could be so misconstrued by the bishop and his assistant.

The mind of man is a strange thing, I told Marisela, quoting Milton's *Paradise Lost*: "It can make a Hell of Heaven, or a Heaven of Hell."

Marisela wrote to the bishop laying out the facts about her comments on Rocky's exemplary behavior at Mass, and expressed her dismay that such an innocent thing could be perverted by him and his assistant. The bishop did not respond to her letter, so she sent it to him a second time.

Finally, the bishop called me, evading Marisela. In a baffling turn-around, he thanked me for being so "gracious," and he then invited me to have lunch with him. I told him I had to take a rain-check on his gracious offer.

He had no further interest in continuing the outlandish dialogue about my little dog. That's the way the bizarre affair ended.

When it was all over, I wondered to myself, as I had often wondered before, how diocesan bishops could find time to create mischief over such trifling matters. Did they not have more important things to do?

At this time, my good friend, General Vernon Walters, had passed away, and I was asked by his nephew, Peter Adams, to deliver a benediction at a ceremony honoring him at the Defense Intelligence Agency Center (DIAC) in Washington, D.C.

These words, carved in stone, caught my attention on one of the Washington buildings: *The truth will set you free.*

"Are these words to be taken seriously?" I asked another friend, Ambassador Hugh Montgomery.

"Absolutely," he replied. "Democracy can only survive when it respects the truth."

I was impressed by this openness to the truth, and asked him another question: "What do you think is happening to the bishops in the church?"

"They got caught," was his reply.

It struck me as strange that some secular leaders would seem to have a higher regard for truth than prelates in the church.

The peculiar incident about the dog gave me pause. After this petty incident, it was clear to me that nothing had changed, despite promises to the contrary. If such a big deal could be fabricated over such a trifling matter as an innocent dog, what would happen if a more serious allegation could be hatched?

I knew I had to be on guard again from now on.

Chapter 40

ONE DAY, I WAS having dinner in the rectory with O.L. Raulerson, county sheriff. I asked him if he'd heard that we were building a new church.

"That's a big step," he returned. "It can break or make a congregation."

O.L. was a Baptist, one well-acquainted with the ins and outs of Baptist politics.

"Why do you say that?" I inquired.

"I've seen congregations torn apart over building a new church," he noted.

"That's not a problem we have," I told him. "Our congregation is unanimously in favor of the building project."

The church building project did not break the congregation as O.L. had warned, but it nearly broke me. It took its toll on my health. Feeling the strain, I went to a cardiologist for a check-up and was told I needed bypass surgery.

If word about this got out, I guessed, it might jeopardize the entire project, just like the unfounded rumors of missing funds nearly did. Thus, I arranged to undergo the operation—for what turned out to be *quadruple* bypass surgery—during my annual vacation in July.

I came out of the operation feeling good without the parishioners, as far as I could tell, knowing about it and was able to see the happy conclusion of the church's dedication in the following November of 2012. As noted, the new church was completed debt-free.

After the dedication, other health issues surfaced to plague me.

My balance badly faltered, leaving me weaving tipsily even at Mass. My primary doctor, in attendance in church, noticed my unstable gait as I walked down the aisle. I was urgently advised to seek medical help.

The crisis reached its zenith during Sunday Mass. As I raised the chalice, my vision blurred, and a wave of dizziness came over me. I whispered a desperate prayer: "Lord, don't let me fall with Your cup raised."

Somehow, I lowered the chalice and knelt for the Act of Adoration, but my body let me down. The next thing I knew, I was lying down on the floor, surrounded by doctors from the congregation.

Before I'd even become aware of what weas happening, paramedics arrived, strapping me to a gurney as the congregation looked on, stunned but praying. Lying there, vulnerable yet enveloped in the care of my flock, I was starkly reminded that you never know what life will hand you next.

As the dizziness began to fade, I asked the Eucharistic ministers to distribute Communion. When Communion was over, I called for the sacramentary book to be brought to me while prostrate on the floor, so I could read the final prayer and impart the final blessing.

The paramedics hoisted the gurney, bearing me up on its legs and they walked it down the aisle to an ambulance waiting outside. The congregation respectfully applauded.

My primary doctor was already at the hospital before I got there. Dr. Ladia had ordered an MRI as soon as I arrived and before I was assigned to a room. Later, in my hospital room, the results of the MRI were revealed.

"You have a pituitary adenoma, and it is a macro," my doctor declared.

I had no idea what a pituitary adenoma was, but I knew it was serious. Doctor Ladia explained it was a growth on the pituitary gland and needed to be removed.

"This means another big operation, I take it?"

"Yes. We'll make the arrangements right away."

Preparations for the operation were made. The day came and this operation too was successful.

But after this second operation, I knew it was time finally to retire. I had served the parishioners of Okeechobee for thirty years. We had done many wonderful things together, and had just constructed a new church. But given my recent health issues, I knew I would have to retire from parish administration.

In the meantime, the diocese of Palm Beach was having financial problems. At Sacred Heart, we were fortunate to have raised the bulk of the money to build the new church prior to the financial crisis of 2008, when the Great Recession began. Thankfully, we were not affected by the financial crisis. But for the diocese, it was a different story; deficit financing caught up with it. To solve its own problems, the diocese decided to pass its increasing financial burden onto the parishes.

A meeting over diocesan finances was held for all the clergy. The diocesan comptroller asked for more money from the parishes to pay for expenses. The parishes were already contributing more than $6 million.

There was time for questions at this first meeting.

"What is the diocese doing with over six million dollars annually?" I inquired.

The vicar-general sprung to his feet.

"We're helping the poorest of the poor," he said forcefully.

"The poorest of the poor," I repeated. "Where are they? I work in a parish that serves the poorest of the poor, but we don't get a cent from the diocese."

"I don't know where they are," said the vicar-general with a shrug of his shoulders. "Perhaps the comptroller knows."

The assembly burst out laughing at this response.

Another priest spoke up, and asked in a humorous tone: "Is there a stenographer here to keep a record of these proceedings?"

There was no stenographer present.

More laughter.

Still another priest asked: "Why does the diocesan administration not balance its budget the way parishes are expected to balance theirs?"

At this point, the fifth bishop of the diocese sneaked over to the comptroller and whispered something into his ear. The comptroller nodded approvingly.

"We're taking care of the poorest of the poor in Riviera Beach," the comptroller explained, "providing schooling free to poor African Americans."

"Is that school not closed?" I inquired.

There was a long pause while the comptroller gave some thought to the question.

"That school is closed," he admitted, gravely.

The assembly howled with laughter.

As the meeting ended, the bishop took to the podium.

"We need to consider whether we want a poor diocese or a rich diocese," he said in response to the discussion that had taken place.

What he said made sense. Helping the poor defines the church's mission more than anything else. What would be the point in building up earthly treasures in the church when the reason for its very existence was the following of Jesus who became poor himself and the servant of all.

This unsuccessful meeting was not the last word on the fiscal problems of the diocese, however. We were told, at Cathedral meetings in November 2009 that the diocese, as corporation sole presumably, would take control of the finances of every entity under its purview—including parishes. Thus, parish finances were centralized and its payroll transferred to the Diocesan data base.

This decision solved the diocese's problems with deficit spending as it was able to invest these monies and create a multi-million-dollar reserve. But it changed the collegial nature and role of parishes within the diocese.

The pastor and the parishioners were no longer in control of parish finances. I had strong reservations, mainly canonical, and I raised them at one of the meetings. When I was appointed as the proper shepherd of the parish in accord with canon law, the pastor had responsibility (working with the finance council) for the financial needs of the parish as well as its spiritual needs. From now on, however, the finances of the parishes were under the control of diocesan bureaucrats.

I realized, after these developments in the diocese, that it was a good time to retire. On February 13, 2013, after the successful completion of the new church, I wrote to the fifth bishop of the diocese tendering my resignation. A few days later, as I was finishing breakfast, the doorbell rang. I opened the door, and a mail carrier presented herself,

"Are you Father Duffy?" she asked.

"That's me," I replied, wondering what this was about.

"I have a registered letter for you, and I need your signature."

I could see that the large, registered envelope was from the bishop. I signed it in the presence of the mail carrier, who left with a smile and a goodbye.

Inside the large envelope was a smaller one, containing the bishop's acceptance of my resignation, effective immediately.

I reached out to the fifth bishop a few days afterwards, and asked to remain in the parish to conclude the season and leave the following June, when my successor would take over. He graciously agreed to this arrangement.

The additional time allowed me to personally inform the parishioners of my impending retirement, sharing the news through the parish bulletin and from the pulpit at all weekend Masses. While many were disheartened by my departure, I explained the reason behind my decision, citing the serious medical problems I had experienced in 2011 and 2013. My congregation was understanding and supportive.

As I contemplated retirement from the parish I had shepherded for three decades, a kaleidoscope of emotions overpowered me. Sadness, yes—how could there not be? But also, a sense of deep gratitude. Each face in the congregation held a story, each handshake a memory. We had laughed together, mourned together, grown in faith together, and faced dangers together. As I prepared to step away, I realized that these bonds, forged in the crucible of shared experience, would endure long after my formal role had ended. The parish had shaped me as much as I had shaped it, and that mutual transformation was a gift beyond measure.

Part 2—Chapter 40

Before I took leave of the parish, the parishioners, the mayor of Okeechobee and city commissioners all assembled at the pavilion during the last St. Patrick's Day festival.

It was there, to my surprise, that I received two special gifts.

The first was a decorative quilt, embedded with an image of the new church. A mosaic of vibrant colors and warmth, this quilt also carried the heartfelt well-wishes of parishioners.

The second gift came from the mayor of the city, James. E. Kirk, in the presence of parishioners, city commissioners and other citizens of Okeechobee. He presented me with the Key to the City.

It was a good way and a good time to retire.

As I held the Key to the City in my hands and traced the intricate stitches of the quilt, I realized these were more than just gifts. They were symbols of love and trust, woven through three decades of shared service. The key represented not just access to a place, but the love of the community of Okeechobee for our commitment to the welfare of its citizens. The quilt, adorned with the image of our new church, was a testament to what the parishioners and I had built together—not just a building, but a living, breathing community of faith.

As I stepped away from the parish and community of Okeechobee, I knew these connections would remain, their roots deeply intertwined with my own journey.

# Part 3

Chapter 41

MY FIRST PRIORITY UPON retiring was to get my health back.

I had bought a home in Palm Beach County in 2007 and was accustomed to go there to relax on my day off. While I was preparing to retire in 2013, Gloria and José, my housekeeper and her husband, were heart-broken and worried about their future. They had lived in the parish guest house, and had worked effectively in Spanish ministry for seventeen years. I put them at ease when I invited them to come live with me, if they wished. It says in the book of Ecclesiastes, it's not good to be alone: If one person falls, the other can reach out and help.[1]

For decades, the comforting presence of family and fellow priests had been my constant companions. Now, as Gloria, José, and I embarked on this new chapter under one roof, the waters of cohabitation proved choppier than anticipated. Our shared history of seventeen years was put to the test as we navigated the delicate art of household harmony, each day a lesson in compromise and understanding.

Oddly, it was the times of most friction that brought us closer together. These challenging moments gave us chances to prove our worth to each other through acts of kindness, encouragement, and forgiveness. Gradually, we grew into a happy household.

I'll never forget when José lost his hearing. One morning he awoke, deaf in one ear from his jackhammer work on a construction site. Still, he went to work as usual. Returning from an errand that day, I spotted José through the window, clutching his weeping wife. As I stepped inside, I was met with the devastating news: He had now lost hearing in both of his ears. José had gone from hearing to silence in a single day, his world collapsing into quiet oblivion.

It was a mournful moment for us all, for you cannot share a home without sharing each other's pain. Into such agony Our Savior was born,

---

1. Ecclesiastes 4:9–10.

enduring suffering as a means of shepherding us to new life. This was a moment of pure pathos, the kind that makes you want to cry and hug everyone involved. And that's exactly what we did. We commiserated, and resolved to do everything in our power to help Jose. I pursued the best medical help available, finding a good doctor who fitted Jose with quality hearing aids. He could now hear again for he did not lose his hearing entirely. Life went on.

As the sun set on my years of service, I found myself cast adrift, left to chart my own course through the uncharted waters of retirement. The diocese offered no safe harbor. It was at a deanery meeting that I stumbled upon two fellow priests who had fashioned their own lifeboat of mutual support, and had inspired me to do the same.

We couldn't afford to retire on our own, one of them said, so we decided to share and share alike so we could scrape together enough to live on.

One priest had a meagre pension from the Boston Archdiocese, the other an inadequate one since he lacked sufficient service years in my diocese. Having opted out of Social Security, it seemed, both were without that income stream and Medicare eligibility. So, everything was shared: house, mortgage, car, and food until the Boston priest died, leaving the other to live alone. This surviving priest eventually joined a monastery.

Their story offered a sober lesson: When it came to retirement, you were on your own, the future uncertain. For over thirty years I had paid into a diocesan long-term care program (Unum) matched by the diocese: a fine policy on paper. Without any meeting to discuss the matter, a letter announced the discontinuation of diocesan support. I lost the long-term care program as part of my retirement, and the decades of contributions.

Retired nuns faced a similar tale of woe. Collections were taken up in parishes to support them, but the question on everyone's lips was: How could this have gotten so far out of hand?

The nuns, someone said to me, "educated us, preparing us for life, and look at them now."

How could the church, others asked, "not prepare for the retirement of these sisters who had dedicated their lives to serve others?"

These questions lingered, unanswered, in the air of uncertainty that surrounded my twilight years. The plight of my fellow priests and nuns served as a poignant reminder of the importance of personal foresight. While the church had nurtured our spiritual lives, it seemed that in matters of our earthly lives, we were called to take care of that ourselves: "to be as wise as serpents and as innocent as doves." This realization became a guiding principle as I prepared for my own future.

Part 3—Chapter 41

When Gloria and José's children got married, they moved away to create families of their own. To add to their sorrow, our precious little dog, Rocky, also passed away. I gave Gloria a gift of another little female Shih Tzu. She named her Fiona—Gaelic for "fair"—as advised by her little grandchildren. It was a perfect fit for Fiona because of her fair, furry fleece. The grandchildren chose the name not because of its Gaelic origin (they were, after all, Mexican Americans), but after Princess Fiona in their favorite movie, *Shrek*.

And so, Fiona, a spry little dog, brought her vivaciousness and mischief to our retirement household. Her playful nature soon caught the attention of Vega, a roguish Yorkshire Terrier living next door.

I first realized something was amiss when Fiona's ceaseless panting kept me awake one night. I tried every trick in the trade to soothe her discomfort, from draping her in a sweatshirt, to giving her water, to taking her out for a stroll in the wee hours of the morning, all to no avail. Nothing could ease her distress.

In the morning, I shared my concerns with Gloria and José. We decided to take Fiona to the animal clinic for a thorough examination. The doctor's verdict was nothing short of astonishing. Fiona was pregnant and required an immediate caesarian section to deliver the puppy, she said. Gloria was incredulous, her disbelief tinged with a hint of Mexican cynicism.

Como es possible? Siempre ha estado en una correa. ("How is this possible? She's always been on a leash.")

True, except when mischievous Vega had slipped in the door, I reminded her. To Gloria the homely Vega seemed an improbable suitor: *Muy feo* ("very ugly"), she moaned, at the thought.

Despite the initial shock, we decided to embrace the situation and welcome Fiona's impending motherhood with open arms. After all, life is full of surprises, and sometimes the most unexpected ones bring the greatest joys.

We called the newborn puppy Rocky, after our first little Shih Tzu in Okeechobee. Half Shih Tzu and half Yorkie, Rocky soon developed into a highly spirited dog. Fiona showed Rocky nothing but love while he suckled. As he grew older, and whenever Fiona was given an edible bone, she would let Rocky have it. If Rocky needed anything, Fiona was instantly at his side. Whenever they were out for a walk, Rocky insisted on holding Fiona's leash in his mouth. Fiona took all this in her stride and played along with her hyperactive little puppy, who never left her side or ran out of steam. Both of them played constantly around the house and in the back garden. With all this new activity, Fiona got younger and Rocky got livelier by the day.

These adorable canine creatures have given us so much joy over the years. Our furry little bundles of fun jump with excitement whenever we return home after a short or extended absence. They are an integral part of our household: trusting, loyal, and loving all the time. They never disappoint.

You cannot turn the clock back, but you can wind it up again, says an old Irish proverb. My health would never be the same as it was before I had two serious operations, but I could improve on it. I was convinced I could do that if I engaged in regular exercise, was able to relax and enjoy good, wholesome meals every day. My dietary needs left nothing to chance for Gloria saw to that. I pushed myself to walk at least a mile every morning, and it became easier and easier with each passing day. I was able to explore my surroundings and discovered three wooded paths to choose from. One path covered over a mile, another was over a mile and a half, and a third stretched more than two.

I could feel my health improving, eating well and exercising daily in my new environment. When I visited Dr. Miller, my cardiologist, he told me he was amazed at the difference the first month of retirement made to my health.

"I watched you walking here from the window," he said, "and couldn't believe the liveliness of your step."

"That's good to hear," I replied, gratefully.

I told the doctor I'd been eating good meals regularly, taking long nature walks, and doing some swimming.

"Keep it up," he remarked. "It's working."

"I feel much better now, mentally and spiritually," I offered, "because I can go to bed when I want, get up when I want, and do whatever I want in between."

"You're making me envious," he said, with a touch of sadness. "I'd love to be able to do that."

"I know too well what you're getting at," I replied, "because I was in the same boat."

For years, I was absorbed with the responsibilities and challenges of running a parish, and in the later years, especially, with the pressures of building a new church. Parishioners by and large knew little of what was involved. One evening I recall, as I was rushing out the rectory door to drive to the hospital, one of the volunteers was locking the office door. Alaine threw me a curious smile and shook her head. I turned back to ask her what she found so amusing.

"Father," she replied with a laugh, "they'll never know."

She was talking about parishioners in general.

Alaine and her husband Kenny had a car dealership in town, and she volunteered one day a week at the parish office. What she witnessed

Part 3—Chapter 41

throughout the range of our daily duties at the church blew her mind. Alaine was right—They'll never know.

The competent doctors who detected the cause of my illnesses and successfully performed the surgeries I needed, along with the good care I received at my new home in Woodland (not its real name) throughout my recuperation, effectively saved my life.

And what a difference my new life made. When I stepped out the door of my new home at the break of dawn on the first morning of my retirement, it was exciting to observe the rising sun, bright and glorious, trailing wisps of cloud like delicate lace in the sky.

These morning walks were a little bit of paradise. The scenery was Eden-like, with placid lakes mirroring the heavens above, care-free ducks effortlessly gliding on the water, and exuberant hydrangea bushes in full bloom along the pathways, like nature's own welcome committee. All was quiet and peaceful, but for the chirping of birds and the whirring of lawn sprinklers.

This was how I lived my new life from that first day of my retirement. I felt like a new man, imbued with a sense of freedom walking through the grounds first thing every morning, with the sun and gentle breeze on my face and the hum of nature everywhere.

In the back garden of our home, my new friend and neighbor, Francisco, built a pergola for hanging flowers and ferns, bird and animal feeders for our new neighbors in the wild. This was Francisco's gift for celebrating Mass for him and his wife on Sunday mornings. The pergola-garden resonated with all kinds of birds and animals: blue finch, cardinals, doves, blackbirds, stately egrets, squirrels and rabbits. And, there was enough food for all.

This abundant natural life could be viewed through the glass window-doors of our living room every morning; a scene that most people flock to parks to see.

Settled in my new surroundings, I was inspired to start reading *Walden,* by Henry Thoreau, who had famously retired to the woods to live his life as part of nature. His accounts of the differing seasons, especially spring, are vivid and beautiful, with glowing depictions of the sounds and sights of nature.

I could relate. Florida has a vibrant springtime, when nature comes alive with new growth, energy, and hope. You can see it, hear it, and feel it in the soft days of sunshine playing on your face, in the gentle and sometimes gushing rains renewing the earth, and in the harvest of all kinds of fruit and vegetables in the farmers' markets: tomatoes, strawberries, cucumber, broccoli, peas, potatoes, avocado, oranges, and kiwi.

It was not long after we settled into Woodland that we were invited to a block party for everyone in the neighborhood. In a short time, we got to know new friends, reclining in chairs around the long table in the middle of the street, or serving ourselves, buffet-style, during the meal.

It felt good to be living among friends I had never met before. For a full year before retirement, on my day off, I had searched from Sabastian to Delray Beach for a place to settle. I finally chose Woodland for its rich natural environment and ethnic diversity; black, white, and brown. It was a mix of all ages and backgrounds, a place where people were friendly to one another and to animals.

Friends are a great blessing, but to have a friend you have to be a friend. My old friends from different parts of Florida where I served over the years, from Daytona to Lakeland to Okeechobee, were glad to visit and renew old acquaintances in my new surroundings.

After four restorative months of blessing-filled, improved health, I felt called to purposeful work once more. It was then that Cross International (later renamed Cross Catholic), an ecumenical organization dedicated to serving the poor in various parts of the world, reached out to me. I was glad to support Cross International's outreach since years before, as pastor, I had invited representatives to speak at Sacred Heart. Now, in my retirement, I volunteered my services as an Outreach Speaker, traveling to Catholic parishes across the continental United States to raise funds to aid needy people in forty countries around the world.

This work held special allure, as it echoed my 1970s Irish charitable initiatives to help the needy and vulnerable. As I embarked on this new journey of service, I found myself reflecting on the events of my life. The threads of my early charitable work in Ireland now intertwined with this international mission, creating a pattern of continuity I had not anticipated, but welcomed enthusiastically. The challenges of retirement—the health scares, the financial uncertainties, the adjustment to a new way of life—had not dimmed my passion for service but rather fueled it. In the faces of those I now sought to help through Cross International, I saw echoes of the old struggles I had witnessed and experienced. It seemed that my own trials had prepared me for this new chapter, allowing me to approach this work with a deeper empathy and understanding. As I stood at this new crossroads, I felt a sense of gratitude for the journey that had led me here, and a renewed sense of purpose for the path that lay ahead.

Chapter 42

AMERICA POSSESSES A UNIQUE quality that's hard to describe. Were it possible for me to capture its essence in a word, it would be "energy."

This country is constantly in motion, evolving and adapting with an unparalleled vitality. Whether it be the endless technological leaps revolutionizing life, or the cascading societal upheavals transforming it, the American spirit is in a class of its own. This torrent of kinetic activity infuses the works of the nation's literary giants, such as Mark Twain, F. Scott Fitzgerald, John Steinbeck, Ernest Hemingway and William Faulkner, whose vivid voyages of imagination and discovery reveal intriguing facets of the American experience. The country's literature was like a magic carpet, carrying me through a broad and magnificent landscape, opening up new vistas and depths of the human spirit. Through physical and literary travel, I was given a deeper understanding of the ever-changing culture and landscape of America.

My new job with Cross allowed me to physically travel the length and breadth of the United States, being able to experience firsthand America with all its faults, achievements and variety. It also showed me how the church functioned in different parts of this vast continent.

I met and spoke with priests and people in over a hundred different parishes. What struck me most about the parishes I visited, celebrated Masses and preached in, was just how different they were.

Differences were to be expected, since the church has to adapt to different circumstances to be relevant. But the differences I discovered ran much deeper than mere variations of place and time. They had to do with the way the mission of the church was viewed and implemented.

The changes ushered in by the Second Vatican Council (1962–1965) served as the most visible demarcation line between parishes in terms of operation, whether they conducted themselves in accord with the developments introduced by the Council, or modeled themselves on a pre-Council type of church.

You Duped Me, O Lord

The contrast was startling.

I preached at a parish in South Carolina which still adhered to the old model of church before the Second Vatican Council. The priest, Father Don (not his real name), was courteous, and picked me up at the airport to drive me to his church. His mode of dress was the first thing I noticed. He turned up at the airport in a black cassock, buttoned from chin to the toes, and wore it everywhere we went, whether to a restaurant or even to a bar.

Father Don celebrated all the Masses in the pre-Vatican II manner. While I preached at all of them, I was not allowed to be the celebrant at any. The liturgy was a throwback to the rubrics of the 1950s and early 1960s. I was very familiar with them, having celebrated Masses in Latin myself before it was changed into the vernacular in the late 1960s.

Nothing had changed, as far as the liturgy was concerned, in this American parish. The vestments were the old Roman-style vestments, accompanied by a fabric armpiece, or *maniple,* as it was called. The maniple hung from the priest's arm, symbolizing the cloth worn by the disciples in ancient days to wipe sweat from the brow. It didn't have any real function other than a symbolic one, which no one in the congregation, as far as I could tell, understood. The chalice, covered by a cloth canopy and pall (a stiffened square card within a white linen), was carried to the altar by the priest in procession, following ancient custom.

As for the Mass itself, the liturgy adhered to the old Tridentine Rite.[1] The only concession to the signs of the times was that the liturgy was in English, but all the hymns were sung in Latin. This was not the case in some other parishes, where even the language of the Mass was in Latin. Moreover, when I entered the confessional box, I discovered that the words of absolution were typed up in Latin and posted on the wall for the priest to recite. The priest, it seemed, did not even know the words of absolution by heart and had to read them. Additionally, the congregation received Communion on the tongue, kneeling at altar rails that were no longer in use in most churches.

As both of us became more relaxed and acquainted with each other, we were able to engage in informative discussion.

"The church," Father Don insisted after we concluded the Vigil Mass, "is a perfect society that doesn't need to change. I don't agree with you referring to the church in your sermon as the People of God."

I acknowledged his viewpoint because I had also been taught in the seminary to view the church as a perfect society. But that was before the

---

1. The Tridentine Rite also known as the Traditional Latin Mass, is the liturgy in the Roman Missal of the Catholic Church published from 1570 to 1962 until Vatican II introduced the new rite.

Second Vatican Council, which adopted the old biblical description of the church as the People of God.

"The church," I replied, "consists of all the faithful people, not just clerics. That's why it is called the People of God. It is a flawed institution because it is made up of sinners, while entrusted with the mission to preach the gospel in spite of human weakness."

Father Don didn't know how to respond.

"Do you not regard yourself as a sinner?" I asked.

"Oh, yes," he replied. "We're all sinners in need of redemption."

"Good," I replied. "We can agree on that. We're not perfect, nor is the church, which is made up of people like you and me."

"Let's agree to disagree," said Father Don.

"That sounds like a good compromise," I concluded.

We had this discussion about the church in the sacristy after the Saturday Vigil Mass. In the process we arrived at a mild reconciliation that lasted throughout the weekend.

I was not surprised when Father Don told me he was asked to join a breakaway or schismatic group created by Archbishop Lefebvre.[2]

Father Don was only 28 years old, but told me that he had been taught to celebrate Mass according to the old Tridentine Rite in the Seminary. He added that he was part of a new, younger generation of priests in the church today. My other travels bore this out; while pre-Council adherence was a minority trend and did not represent the American Church in general, some of those priests who were drawn to the old liturgy were indeed part of a new and younger generation.

At the end of the weekend, Father Don asked for my blessing. I was glad to oblige and gave him a blessing entirely in Latin. This both surprised and pleased him, and we parted on the friendliest of terms.

* * *

Another Cross mission brought me to remote Mount Angel, Oregon, a secluded settlement founded by Benedictine monks from Austria in the nineteenth century. The monks, hailing from a place called Angel Mount, named their new American settlement Mount Angel, simply reversing the two words for this American namesake. They erected a formidable abbey, which served as a seminary for many West Coast dioceses, as well as a

---

2. Archbishop Lefebvre rejected the theological developments of the Second Vatican Council, demanding among other things, a Traditional Latin Mass.

striking neo-gothic church, hewn from granite, that towered over town and countryside.

As I drove from Portland and approached Mount Angel, the church's neo-gothic spires beckoned to me like the sound of a long Alphorn in the Austrian Alps. The grandeur brought to mind the neo-gothic cathedral in my own hometown of Letterkenny, which similarly dominated the surrounding countryside. Upon entering the church, I was struck by the awe-inspiring vaulted ceiling, stretching towards heaven. People were inside, gazing upwards. I said hello, and one of them turned to me, mouth agape with hands spread out in wonder: "How could something like this be built in such a remote area?"

"I don't know," I replied. "I'm asking myself the same question."

When I met the pastor, I asked him the same question that was on my mind.

"The original Gothic church was destroyed by an earthquake," he explained. "The monks and parishioners rebuilt the present one in its place."

"A Gothic church was built here, not just once but twice," I enthused.

Father Paul, the church's pastor, was a personable and hospitable man.

"Is hospitality a big thing with the Benedictines?" I asked during a delicious Saturday evening dinner.

"Yes, it is," he replied. "It's in our rules that we must treat the guest as though he were Christ."

"That's Christian to the core. It's a pity hospitality has gone out of style in the church of today," I continued. "It used to be a big part of Celtic Christianity in Ireland."

"What happened?" he asked.

"I don't really know," I replied. "Some people say the Roman emphasis on rules and regulations caused its disappearance. A few Irish poets, like Padraic Colum, wrote about the absence of hospitality in the later Irish Church, causing it to become rigid and domineering."

"This kind of deviation from native tradition," said Father Paul, "is most distressing in a country famous for the hospitality of its people."

"That's the sad part," I admitted. "We were trained in the seminary to reject rather than incorporate our natural hospitality into our priestly formation."

Father Paul had been rector of the large seminary that served several dioceses on America's west coast. Our conversation quite naturally turned to seminary training, and I asked him: "Why are some young priests in the U.S. reverting to the way things were done prior to the Second Vatican Council?"

Part 3—Chapter 42

"Broken homes," he replied. "These young men want a safe, unchanging church to protect themselves from the brokenness of the society from which they came."

"Broken homes?" I repeated. "That's not something I would have thought."

But that's how Father Paul described this backward trend by some new priests, based on his experience as a seminary rector.

"It seemed to me," I said, "that it was difficult to have an authentic tradition of formation in the seminary that would prepare young priests to take their place in the world today."

Father Paul agreed.

"I read an interesting article," I continued, "by Bishop Ruiz from the State of Chiapas in Mexico about the problems of a seminary formation. It concerned a young priest who returned from Rome after several years of seminary formation there, and could not relate to his own people back home."

"Why was that?"

"It seemed his seminary training in Rome didn't prepare him to fit in," I replied. "But after a year working with the people in his parish, he adjusted so well to them that they held a celebration for him, welcoming him back as one of their own."

"That makes sense," said Father Paul.

"I heard first-hand accounts about this bishop from Mexicans I knew from Chiapas, who were working in the Florida citrus fields," I continued. "They spoke very highly of this bishop, and his ability to relate personally to them. He was totally one of them, from what I could gather."

"It looks as if that bishop was a people's person, the kind we need today," said Father Paul.

"Yes, he was," I was told. "I've been to Mexico several times and couldn't help but be impressed by the priests in parishes who serve more people than many dioceses in America which are burdened by a large and expensive bureaucracy."

These are the kind of conversations I've had with priests in various parts of the country.

* * *

When I was visiting Utah, I had dinner with three Irish priests who were part of the Salt Lake City Diocese. I was very impressed by what they had achieved, building schools and churches and providing effective social services to the needy.

"Did your seminary training back in Ireland prepare you for the work you did over here?" I asked the three of them over dinner.

The very question was greeted with a collective burst of laughter.

"Of course not," I was told in no uncertain terms.

"How then did you prepare yourselves for this work?" I asked

"We went back to school."

"You re-educated yourselves? Is that it?"

"Yes, that was it," they returned.

My next question was: "How did your seminary formation compare to your formation in the home?"

"There was no comparison," one of the priests assured me. "Our seminary formation brought us backwards, and we've been trying to get over it ever since," he said with a laugh.

I had many a good laugh talking about seminary formation with these priests. Yet they were very dedicated. They had made their own way in a foreign land, carving out for themselves the kind of Christian ministry that met the needs of the people they served in Utah.

* * *

On another occasion, I met with priests who served in a somewhat idyllic parish, deep in the Pocono mountains of Pennsylvania. One of them was a retired pastor, like myself, who was helping out in the parish. We were talking about the challenges presented by the new developments in the church, when the retired priest suddenly introduced a new twist on the topic: "Have you ever heard of a grieving program for priests?" he asked.

"No, I haven't."

"It's a program to help priests deal with grief over loss—the loss of the church we once knew and loved," he said.

"I never knew such a program existed," I said. "But it sounds very interesting."

"Jesus wept," he continued, "and so can we. This program provided healing for me and others like me who were grieving over the death of the church we grew up in."

I listened carefully to him as he described his personal struggles, coming to terms with ecumenism, freedom of conscience, the role of the laity, and other developments of the Second Vatican Council. He spoke especially of how the process of healing changed his life.

"It helped me make the transition psychologically from the way I was trained in the seminary to how I exercise my ministry today," he said.

What this priest shared with me made sense, and I was excited to hear that there was a program to help priests in the way he described. Resistance to change runs deep in the human psyche. What he said reminded me of a close friend in Ireland, Provincial of the Divine Word Society. A model priest, he had shocked everyone who knew him by leaving the priesthood because he couldn't adjust to the changes. Psychologically he was on the brink of a nervous breakdown, he told me, and felt compelled to leave the priesthood for his sanity, since he could no longer take the pressure. I wondered if he might have been able to survive the ordeal, had he had access to a program like this one in Pennsylvania.

The retired priest continued: "You and I are about the same age. We've had the same kind of seminary formation, one that prepared us for a different kind of church and ministry, before Vatican Council II. How did you make the transition in your life?" he inquired.

"I made the change when I was studying English literature as a student priest at University College Dublin," I said. "It helped me transition from a scholastic mindset to a pastoral understanding of the gospel. It was during this time that I felt the intellectual rigidity of scholastic thought begin to melt away, replaced by a more pastoral vision of the church."

"In what way did your literary studies help?" he probed.

"Well, the study of literature—and the Bible—opened my eyes to the real world of emotions and personal experience that was lacking in my rather abstract scholastic formation," I answered.

Asked for an example, I offered George Herbert's poem, "Love," dealing with the Eucharist. "This poem," I explained, "was revelatory. It was as if a veil had been gently lifted from my mind, allowing me to see into the very depths of Christ's love in the Eucharist."

"That's interesting," he remarked.

"In the seminary, we were accustomed to approach the real presence rather abstractly," I explained, "from the perspective of intellectual distinctions and categories. While this knowledge was helpful, it could not fully capture the depths of Christ's love and the living connection with Him."

As our conversation unfolded, it took an unexpected turn, focusing on Pope Francis's remarkable admission of seeking help from a female, Jewish psychiatrist during a challenging period in his life when he was 42 years old. The Pontiff's willingness to pursue counseling brought hope to many because it revealed how human he was.

In an unprecedented admission, Pope Francis revealed to a French interviewer: "My authoritative and quick manner of making decisions led me to have serious problems and to be accused of being ultraconservative."

We discussed Pope Francis's acknowledgement of rigidity, accounting for a closed mindset or need for security. This Pope, just like ourselves, seemingly transitioned from a strict doctrinal rigidity to a pastoral approach grounded on lived experience and the example of Christ in the gospel.

The pastor of the parish was a younger man, ordained several years after the Second Vatican Council. Listening carefully, he said: "Many newly ordained priests are still harking back to the way things were when both of you were ordained. For the life of me, I don't understand any of this."

This trend was indeed puzzling to many, since the younger priests in question didn't know Latin, nor did they have any experience of the church's practice prior to the Second Vatican Council.

I relayed the explanation I'd heard from the former rector of a seminary in Oregon, the one who'd attributed this yearning for the past to broken homes, and the broken state of the society they yearned to escape.

"That makes sense," the pastor replied. "My own young associate [who was not present] comes from a broken home himself, and yearns to return to a pre-Vatican II church."

* * *

During my travels in the Upper Peninsula of Michigan, I came across a young, hardworking priest who was very devoted to his parish.

One of the parishioners called me after I returned from my mission appeal there.

"I stopped by the church and noticed that my pastor was depressed and downcast. I said to him, let's go for a drive."

John, the parishioner, was a good man, and I wouldn't expect any less from him. I got to know John rather well when I was offering Masses and preaching in his parish church. We had met in the rectory for a friendly talk.

"That was real kind of you, John," I now remarked. "I'm glad you reached out to your parish priest."

"I'm glad too," John said. "I had no idea what priests were going through until we started talking."

"The priest," John explained, told him the following: "I'm living on my own without any support from my fellow priests or bishop. If I get close to a woman, I'm afraid of being accused of having an affair, and if I go near

Part 3—Chapter 42

youngsters in the parish, I run the risk of being accused of pedophilia. I'm consigned to live alone and be lonely."

"John didn't know what to say when he heard this from the priest, and that's why he called me."

"Should I talk to the bishop and make him aware of what the priest is going through so he can help him?" he asked me.

"That doesn't strike me as a good idea," I replied.

"Why not?"

"Bishops, on the whole," I replied, "are lonely, isolated men, especially since they don't have a community to relate to, like priests. They are inclined to hear only what they want to hear."

"So, what can I do?" asked John in frustration.

"Do what you're doing," I answered. "Be a trusted friend to the priest, and draw a circle of friends around him who will always be there when he needs them. We cannot live without the support of others," I explained. "Good friendships are as necessary to our spiritual lives as the air we breathe."

"When you visited the parish, you told me that you have people living with you," John said.

"That's correct," I replied. "I wouldn't have it any other way. We're taking care of one another, including our two little dogs. There's nothing like having the support and company of friends."

I knew this was all new to John, who found it difficult to imagine that priests, whose vocation was to help others, needed support and comfort themselves. John had written a book about a dedicated priest he admired and gave me a copy to read. Now, I was asking him to stop putting priests on a pedestal, and to see them as fellow travelers in the flesh who needed support.

"Isn't that what Jesus demanded?" I said to John. "Didn't he call his followers, *friends*? And didn't he say that by our love for one another we will be known as his followers? The Lord put no stock in social positions, John, and he made no distinction when it came to friendship. We're called to be friends with Christ and with one another."

John soon realized he had another purpose besides writing a book about the life of a priest he admired from afar. He could be a true friend to the priest close-by in his parish.

***

You Duped Me, O Lord

When in parishes, I always found it easy to speak on behalf of the needy, the most vulnerable among us, because the message was so thoroughly Christian. And I was gratified by the generous response of parishioners to my appeals. At times, however, the local pastor would not be happy if the contributions of parishioners to the mission of Cross was greater than the regular parish offertory. I never had misgivings about this whenever I invited a Cross speaker to Sacred Heart when I was pastor. I always felt the Lord would repay our generosity to the poor.

On one occasion, I spoke at a parish on Long Island. I was resting in bed on Monday morning after a busy weekend, and I could hear the pastor shouting in the dining room, which was next to my bedroom: "He has taken all our money!"

The other two priests laughed out loud, but I had to face the pastor when I entered the dining room a little while later. The other priests took off when they saw me coming, but the pastor stayed there.

He had an unwelcome scowl on his face, and he stared me down.

"You took all our money," he protested, before I was even seated.

"Don't worry yourself," I replied as graciously as I could while sipping a cup of coffee. "You're doing the Lord's work, and it will come back to you."

"Come back to me? Is that what you think?" barked the pastor, shaking his head in disbelief.

"Yes, I believe that. It always worked for me whenever I invited Cross to the parish."

Suddenly, a bright smile, like a ray of sunshine, dispelled the dark scowl.

"It'll come back to me," he said, relishing the thought, and left the dining room like he was walking on air.

I was pondering the extraordinary, almost miraculous transformation in the pastor's demeanor.

He returned to the dining room in an equally upbeat mood. He was a different man. His new appearance was so unexpected I raised my eyebrows in disbelief.

"I've decided to deposit all the monies collected from your appeal into our bank," he declared shrewdly. "You don't have to worry about taking the envelopes back with you. I'll make it easy for you by depositing the contributions into our parish account and mailing a check from the parish to Cross."

I was caught off guard by this announcement and made no response. He'd figured out a way the money would come back to him, just not in the way I meant. There was nothing I could do but accept the reality of the situation. So, I went to my room, packed my case, and left. I shortened my time on Long Island, missing interesting places I planned to see, and some friends I had planned to visit.

* * *

Whenever and wherever I traveled, I made time to explore the history and culture of the places I visited. The priests in the parishes were very hospitable, allowing me to stay at the parish residences after the weekend Masses so I could check out the sights. But it was the friendly parishioners I enjoyed meeting with most, because they were really glad to show me around.

In Little Rock, Arkansas, I visited the Central High School that was the site of forced desegregation in 1957.[3] As a high school student back in Ireland that year I remember clearly how shocked I was to read about this event in the Irish newspapers, and to see the photos of the angry mob opposed to Blacks entering their school. But now I could visit the actual high school for myself and watch Blacks and Whites going to classes together without the least bother. It was all utterly changed.

My guides from the parish took me to a museum, a little walk from the high school, that told the history of desegregation. I got the surprise of my life when I was led into another museum, within this museum, dedicated to Free Derry and the civil rights movement in Northern Ireland. Here, the struggle of Irish nationalists for equal rights in Northern Ireland was equated with the struggle of Blacks for civil rights in the USA.

I also visited the President Clinton Library in Little Rock. It was very well crafted and laid out. The first to arrive when the doors opened, I was handed a portable audio guide so I could follow the former president's actual commentary. I learned from Clinton's comments that his Inaugural Address was based on the notes of Father Timothy Stafford Healy S.J., president of Georgetown University. Another section in the library was of particular interest to me, dealing with Northern Ireland and the Clinton administration's successful efforts to broker the Good Friday Agreement.[4] This historic agreement did much to develop a political, non-violent solution for the region and bring an end to "the troubles," as they were called.

---

3. The Central High School, Little Rock, Arkansas, was where nine Black students faced an angry mob of over 1,000 Whites protesting integration. This historic event lit the fire that sparked the civil rights movement of the 1960s in America.

4. The Good Friday Agreement in Northern Ireland, was a pivotal democratic breakthrough brokered by the Clinton Administration, envoy George J. Mitchell and leaders of the Irish Republic and Britain, to cease hostilities in favor of a democratically-elected assembly.

Who could have imagined that 26 years later in 2024, an Irish nationalist, Michelle O'Neill, would become the first minister of the Northern Irish Assembly?

To my surprise, Little Rock displayed a strong interest in Irish culture, apart from the Free Derry Museum and the Clinton Library's coverage of the Good Friday Agreement. I had the pleasure of attending a large St. Patrick's Day parade downtown, followed by a traditional Irish dinner in an Irish pub.

* * *

While traveling is undoubtedly one of the best forms of education, it can also be a risky business. I discovered just how risky it could be when I was traveling by car from Seattle to Yakima in the state of Washington. I wanted to climb Mount Rainier or part of it on the way to Yakima. I looked forward to spending the night at the Paradise Inn at the foot of the majestic mountain. The scenery was spectacular; not only the humongous mountain in the distance, but the expanses along the way: natural vistas and gorges everywhere, as far as the eye could see.

I was skirting the rim of another mountain to my right, overlooking an enchanting chasm of natural beauty to my left, when I could hear a great rumbling. An avalanche of stones and debris was coming down the mountains. I kept driving forward, praying for the best. I could hear the barrage of falling stones and pebbles everywhere around me, in front, behind, and even under my car. The damage to the car, however, was the least of my worries; my life was in grave danger.

I managed somehow to round a curve out of harm's way. I stopped the car and got out. I could have danced a jig; I was so happy to be alive. I expected to see a wreck of a car but that didn't bother me, since I was alive. But to my surprise, the car survived unharmed, without a scratch.

"What's this?" I exclaimed to myself out loud. I couldn't believe it.

I drove to the Paradise Inn and had lunch beneath the glorious Mount Rainier. But my near-death experience along the way had dampened my interest in climbing the legendary mountain. I did not spend the night at the Inn.

Glad to be alive, I drove directly to Yakima, arriving a day early. It was dusk. I entered a pub displaying a bright neon sign with a big green shamrock. It looked hospitable. The customers and barman inside were very welcoming.

Part 3—Chapter 42

"What brings you to town?" asked the barman, as I walked up to the bar.

"I'm passing through," I replied.

"Is that an Irish accent I hear?" one of the customers asked.

"It sure is," I returned.

"So, you came all the way from Ireland to visit us?" asked the barman with a jolly grin.

"More or less, by a long, circuitous route," I replied. "When I saw the shamrock outside, like a siren beckoning to me, I couldn't resist."

"We're happy to have you," said the barman, shaking my hand.

We had an enjoyable time. My cell phone had run out of power, but the barman charged it for me. Then I called the parish secretary. She told me the rectory was conveniently just around the corner from the pub with the green shamrock. One of the customers, hearing my conversation with the secretary, showed me the directions on his iPhone.

"Here you are," he whispered, "and there's where you need to go, only a minute away."

"I'll meet you at the rectory in ten minutes to let you in," said the secretary.

I bade farewell to my new-found friends at the Shamrock, and drove to the rectory.

The main industry in Yakima, I was told in the pub, was agriculture: hops, vineyards, vegetables and every kind of fruit. The ground depended on artificial irrigation, without which nothing could grow. It was desert country, not full of sand, but rocky without vegetation.

The parishioners at the various Masses over the weekend were cheerful givers, applauding me after each sermon. This was unusual but heartwarming, considering I had been asking them to part with their money.

On the way back to Seattle to catch my plane home, I left by another route. The countryside was barren, I could see. All I could take in for miles were rocks and dust. As I was told in the Shamrock, desert country.

* * *

A singular experience awaited when I visited St. Christopher parish in Las Vegas. From the airplane's gate all the way through the terminal to baggage claim, lines of slot machines and their spellbound gamblers assaulted my vision. The gambling capital of the world, the Las Vegas Strip, confronts you with glittering and noisy slot machines wherever you go. That's the tourist's Las Vegas, and it starts at the airport.

The community of St. Christopher, however, offered a different view of Las Vegas life. Not the Strip, this Las Vegas had an entirely different feel, with people going about their normal lives: working in factories, offices and malls, looking after children and the elderly, shopping, taking care of each other, and discussing their daily preoccupations. You couldn't even see the Strip from the city of Las Vegas.

I had met a young man, a Las Vegas native, on the plane when flying in. I asked him what growing up in Vegas was like.

"It was very boring," he replied. "It was only for adults and kids had no part of it."

"But you are flying back. It must have some appeal for you."

"The only appeal it has for me is my family," he answered. "I'm going there to spend time with my folks."

This young man's perspective was no different from that of the parishioners I met at St. Christopher. Home is where the heart is, and the Las Vegas Strip was not home. It was for people who craved excitement.

My weekend at St. Christopher in the city was taken up with pastoral activity. The Saturday Vigil Mass was the easiest part, but on Sunday I had four Masses, all in a row, and I was exhausted. A man came up to me after the last Mass on Sunday when I was about ready to collapse.

"I am sixty-seven years old," he said, "and I've been holding the Devil by the tail, but this Mass has changed my life."

He was crying when he told me this. He got my attention. You never know when you are tired and worn out how much your ministry means to someone until you hear words like these.

After the weekend Masses, I finally had time to explore. I signed up for a helicopter tour of the Grand Canyon. I rested on Monday in preparation and on Tuesday morning took a Lyft to the helicopter pad. There were five other people taking the tour with me in addition to the pilot. The pilot gave us a mini seminar before we parted, explaining in detail how to buckle up, what to do inside the helicopter, how to enter and exit, and what to do in case of an emergency. He made sure we would change places during the journey after we landed in the canyon, in order to have the maximum visual experience.

I thought to myself: *We're landing in the Grand Canyon. I can't wait to experience this.*

We all made friends quickly, and this made our flight very enjoyable.

We flew over the mighty Hoover Dam. From our line of vision high up in the helicopter, the bridge over the dam looked like a large, white thread with little hanging chads between two mountains. To the west of the dam was Lake Mead, which provides fresh water to Las Vegas. The pilot told

Part 3—Chapter 42

us that the lake was over five feet too low, causing the city and county to consider desalination as an alternative source of fresh water.

The canyon was a breathtaking marvel. The multi-colored rock formations and the huge gorges, carved out through millions of years of erosion by the great Colorado River, made me feel like an insignificant traveler on a boundless journey. The pilot had a good knowledge of geology, and he was able to offer a fascinating account of how the canyon was formed and reformed over millions of years. When he effortlessly slowed the helicopter to hover inside a many-crayoned canyon, I lost all sense of time and place. I was in a deep, silent trance. When he once more put on speed, I was suddenly startled back to reality, as if I had awoken from a beautiful dream.

The tour took two and a half hours. We flew over the Grand Canyon and into it, landing alongside the Colorado River, which runs through it. Here we had lunch inside one of God's most impressive creations. We took off again, feeling grateful to have seen the canyon from within as well as from above. We flew over flatlands and saw wild horses grazing, as well as solitary cabins where mountain men lived apart from civilization. We landed a second time in the desert, at an appointed spot, to refuel the helicopter.

On the way back to our starting point, the pilot flew us over the Las Vegas Strip. One of the casinos, called Rio, was undergoing a billion-dollar renovation. As a man-made creation it was impressive, but it didn't hold a candle to the natural wonder of the Grand Canyon.

As I prepared to leave Las Vegas, the biggest surprise of all awaited me. In the dead of night, I was roused from my slumber by the movement of the bed beneath me and the rattling of furniture around me. It was no illusion, like the David Copperfield show I saw the night before. This was reality. I recalled a similar experience in Mexico City, and I knew it was an earthquake. As the reverberations faded, I hastily packed and fled my room into the gray dawn, where I hailed a Lyft to the airport.

On the plane, I watched the news of the earthquake in southern California that had sent shock waves as far away as Las Vegas.

* * *

My journeys unveiled many marvels, each outshining the last. The humble home of Abraham Lincoln in Springfield, Illinois, and the modest room where he lay in state in Washington, DC, after his assassination, evoked a sacred reverence. Alaska's dancing Aurora Borealis lit the wee hours of the morning with a majesty exceeding anything in Hollywood or Disney World.

But it was the people I met who left the most enduring impression on me.

Take the interesting case of Billy. I met him in Sparta, Wisconsin. To get there, I took a flight to Atlanta, Georgia, where I got a connecting flight to Rochester, Minnesota. At the Rochester Airport I picked up a rental car, a GMC SUV, for the long, hundred-mile drive to the rural town of Sparta, population 11,000. Sparta is best known as the biking capital of America. Avid bikers, fleeing the smog-filled, concrete canyons of American cities, have the opportunity here not only to enjoy the fresh, clean air of the countryside, but to take in the area's stunning natural beauty.

It was a beautiful, spring day in May when I was driving to Sparta, and nature was alive with a rich renewal. The rolling hills, the rising bluffs, and the winding La Crosse River were not features I typically associated with the flat midwestern region of the U.S. But I was glad of it, and the drive was scenic all the way. At the town of La Crosse I stopped for dinner, a fish medley in a sauce with a nice kick to it. It gave me the burst of energy I needed after the long, arduous and multi-step journey. After dinner, I drove thirty more miles to Sparta and to the rectory of St. Patrick, where I would be spending the weekend. Susan, the kindly parish manager, was waiting for me.

I was the only one staying in this lonely rectory, since the pastor, glad of the weekend coverage, had given himself a mini-vacation. Rather than spend the whole night alone there I drove to a pub, drawn by the sound of music and dancing. The place was packed with jolly people. Squeezing my way past a throng of revelers to the very back of the pub, I found a seat, and that's when I met him.

Billy greeted me kindly and asked if he could buy me a beer. I accepted his kind offer and, after my eyes adjusted to the semi-darkness of the place, I noticed he had no arms and no legs. Despite the absence of arms or legs, Billy filled the room with a quiet magnetism, outshining those around him not by stature, but by the sheer force of his jolly presence.

"Is this the only entertainment place in town?" I asked, paying no attention to his infirmity and trying to engage him in conversation.

"There's another place in town called The Lighthouse," Billy replied. "I could take you there if you wish. It is only a short walk away."

"Thanks," I returned. "I'd like to check it out with you."

We made our way to The Lighthouse for another experience. Billy was driving his electric scooter while I walked beside him. I left my car at the pub, for it was only a short walk. As we entered the establishment, everybody greeted Billy while he introduced me as a new acquaintance to his circle of friends. It was a karaoke place, and one of the performers was giving an impressive imitation of Willie Nelson, singing *You're Always on my*

Part 3 — Chapter 42

Mind. It was a wonderful night of entertainment. When I parted company with Billy, I thanked him profusely.

"I'll never forget you, Billy, or this evening," I said. "And I cannot thank you enough for your kindness to a mere stranger passing through."

Billy returned my thanks with a warm smile. He was a man of few words.

The Sunday morning Mass was at 8:15 a.m. It was Mothers' Day, and the ushers were handing red roses to mothers entering church with their children. As I entered the foyer, I couldn't believe my eyes. The man seated beside the parish bulletins was my new friend, Billy, smiling as usual. If he recognized me from the night before, he didn't let on. Everyone was greeting him with a hearty: Hello Billy.

I walked up to him and did the same.

He smiled and simply nodded his head.

"Tell me something," I asked. "How do you manage to be so jolly all the time?"

"If I knew the answer to that I'd bottle it and make a fortune," he replied.

"You don't know?" I returned, in amazement.

"That's right," said Billy meekly. "I don't know."

"So, it's a gift," I remarked.

"That's it," Billy whispered, wide-eyed. "It's a gift."

This encounter with Billy will be forever etched in my mind. After meeting him, I did not feel tired celebrating two Vigil Masses and four Sunday Masses in two different churches in Sparta, Wisconsin, that weekend.

Billy may have been crippled in body, but not in spirit. He possessed a glow, an infectious joy which everyone who knew him felt in their bones.

Chapter 43

There's a saying that if you love what you're doing, you'll never work a day in your life. In retirement, this adage became my truth. As an Outreach Speaker, I found a delightful irony in being retired yet as active as ever, crisscrossing America, meeting people from all walks of life, sharing their stories and chronicling my adventures in my blogs.

Just when I thought the days of persecution by the institution were behind me, it raised its ugly head again in a way I couldn't possibly have imagined. This chapter chronicles a tumultuous period beginning in 2019, during which I had to fight against institutional machinations and a virulent attempt to besmirch my good name.

The storm began brewing in 2004, though I wouldn't feel its effects until much later. Unbeknownst to me, I was falsely accused of abuse dating back to 1997, but it had been promptly dismissed by the Orange County Police Department for lack of evidence. Normally, that should have been the end of the matter.

The Diocese of Orlando, in a move that would later haunt me, passed this toxic slander to the fifth Bishop of Palm Beach, under the pretext of seeking an interview. That interview never came.

The fifth Bishop of Palm Beach, rather than interview me, attempted to persuade the alleged accuser to support the false accusation, already discredited. To his credit, the accuser resolutely refused, showing contrition for the earlier false claim. But this wasn't enough for the bishop, who conveniently buried the false information in my personnel files, a ticking time bomb waiting for the right moment.

That moment arrived in 2019 when the bishops of Palm Beach and Orlando found themselves under investigation by the State's Attorney. Suddenly, the false allegation from 2004 resurfaced. I found myself blindsided by an accusation I had known nothing about—the very same allegation that had been outrightly dismissed by the police, and which the contrite accuser wanted nothing to do with.

Part 3—Chapter 43

On a bright and sunny Saturday morning in September 2019, I stepped out of my bedroom oblivious to the hidden machinations that threatened to ensnare me. A peculiar sense of peace and contentment enveloped me like a warm blanket on a cold winter's night. Little did I know how quickly this tranquility would be shattered.

My mood buoyant, I set off for a morning of leisurely shopping. My local HomeGoods was a convenient stop. Meandering through the store, a figure in black approached: a picture of melancholy with head downcast. Feeling so upbeat myself, I felt empathy for this man on this glorious morning. My initial instinct was to offer a sympathetic smile, but as he drew closer, I was taken aback. It was the fifth bishop of my diocese who stood before me.

I greeted him kindly. He stretched his face upwards because he was very stooped. Upon recognizing me, his face lit up like a lamp that turns on and off at the clapping of hands. He became so giddy with excitement that his reaction caught me off guard. We were never that close, *so why this unusual display of emotion?* I wondered.

I spoke about hurricane Maria that narrowly bypassed Florida. Surprisingly, he had nothing to say about this perilous storm; instead, he was lost in some lighter, almost whimsical kind of laughter. I left the encounter puzzled. Had I really made so profound an impression on him?

The Monday after my odd encounter, I was having breakfast with my webmaster, Richard Grigonis, at the Country Kitchen Café on Military Trail and PGA Boulevard.

We stopped at my mail box to collect the mail on the way home. Seated in the car, I sifted through fliers and bills. One envelope caught my attention: a personal letter from the bishop himself. My mind flashed back to our chance encounter just days prior at HomeGoods, when his mood pivoted strangely from gloom to giddy elation at the mere sight of me.

Still in the car, I opened the envelope and read the contents. I was dumbfounded as I read the stark words in a letter dated September 9, 2019. I was curtly informed of an allegation of abuse lodged against me during my tenure in the Orlando Diocese.

The news was delivered with a detachment that only added to my incredulity. I was summarily placed on administrative leave, my priestly faculties "to carry out any public ministry" withdrawn, and my name put on the Diocese of Orlando's list of church personnel, credibly accused of abuse.

The bishop's peculiar behavior just days prior took on a new light. Was this bad news the reason for his uncharacteristic glee?

I couldn't help but reflect on my past experiences with abuses in the church. This wasn't the first time I had faced unfounded allegations. There were the recent and absurd accusations regarding my little dog, which this bishop (the fifth) had to abandon to his embarrassment.

Before that, there were the false accusations and innuendos by previous bishops. Each time, I had stood my ground, fought for the truth, and been vindicated. But this . . . this felt different. More sinister. More calculated. It seemed eerily reminiscent of the strange case of Cardinal Pell, a man assigned to clean up abuses in Vatican finances. Sex abuse accusations were suddenly weaponized against him back in his native Australia, forcing him to return there to defend himself. Although he was finally exonerated, he was forced to spend over a year in jail.

In a matter of days, my tranquil life was turned on its head. I was thrust out of the warm womb of retirement back into the cruel and muddy swamp of church politics.

I remembered how Saint Ignatius described the spiritual life as a battle, so I armed myself to fight in what would soon develop into a protracted struggle. I didn't know where the fight would lead, but with a clear conscience I had to commit to it. All I could do was pray for the strength to keep going and the faith to wait for God's timing.

The bishop's letter went on to provide me with the name of a contact, a canonical consultant or "appropriate contact" for both the Orlando and Palm Beach Bishops. I digested the information in stunned silence, opting not to share the contents of the letter with Richard, still in the car with me.

The allegation's sudden announcement after four decades left me with a multitude of questions:

Why had I been told nothing about this accusation? Why was it kept hidden for so long? Why was I denied the fundamental right to a hearing and the opportunity to be interviewed?

The Gospel of Matthew, chapter 18, insists on the need to listen to an accused person's response to any allegation. Moreover, the church's own policy mandated that accused priests be apprised of the details of any allegations, allowing them to offer a defense. As a pastor, I had always adhered, when dealing with staff members, to these principles in faith and practice. But it seemed that these two bishops had chosen to disregard their own guidelines. Why?

Here I was dealing with the frigid language of the institution, not the Gospel of Our Savior. What was so disappointing was that I was already judged guilty without any evidence, and my name put on a public list of credibly accused without a hearing. This amounted to a most serious abuse of authority, it would seem: defamation of character, if not libel.

Part 3—Chapter 43

The two bishops, as mentioned, engaged a canonist or so-called "appropriate contact" outside their dioceses, and it was recommended that I use him.

I couldn't help but think how ridiculous that would be. Using the same canonist who was presumably pursuing an accusation aggressively against me seemed as absurd as expecting Judas to pass the collection plate without skimming off the top.

I researched the background of the "appropriate contact," discovering a list of complaints that made me chuckle in disbelief. These included a parental revolt on the west coast of Florida for prying into the sexual fantasies of their youngsters; information about two DUI incidents issued by the police; and nonpayment of taxes to the IRS.

I knew from experience that bishops used vulnerable members of the clergy to do their bidding. This particular canonist, with a resume as colorful as stained glass, seemed to fit the bill. Rather than contact him, I sought out a canonist to represent me, fairly and justly.

Once I selected a canonist, I asked him to send registered copies of all his correspondence, not only to the so-called "appropriate contact" but to each bishop of the two Dioceses.

My canonist soon got on the case. On September 17, 2019, he wrote to the Bishop of Palm Beach, stating I had the right to know the evidence marshalled, and requested the entire file regarding this investigation to date pertaining to me. He also insisted that my canonical services be reimbursed by the diocese.

Shockingly, my canonist was offered no disclosure whatsoever regarding the information requested. It was as if both bishops had taken a vow of silence on the matter.

Pointing out that this new investigation was illegitimate, my canonist explained that a person was innocent until proven guilty according to the law. Yet I was adjudged guilty by two bishops even after the alleged accuser had recanted and the abuse allegation was demonstrated to be false by the police. My canonist also provided documentation from the Holy See, stating that the name of an accused person must not be placed on a list of abusive personnel without first being granted the right of defense.

In a court of civil or criminal law, lack of disclosure would be unethical. But in the byzantine maze of canon law, this refusal to disclose relevant information seemed to be the norm. Thus, my canonist and I were reduced to operating in the dark when it came to dealing with these two underground prelates, communicating through their intermediaries. In this sad state of affairs, I felt as vulnerable as a turtle without a shell.

We were prevented from knowing the name of the accuser (albeit his change of heart), and the date and time of the alleged allegation. All we knew was what we were being told, but had no way of verifying any of it. We were given no facts, no evidence. I, on the other hand, have kept journals over the years that record where I've been and what I was doing at all times.

What followed was a Kafkaesque nightmare. We were operating in the dark, much like Kafka's protagonist in *The Trial*, forced to defend against unknown charges.[1]

To shed light on the matter, I hired an attorney to investigate the records of the Orange County Police Department for any evidence of any accusation of abuse brought against me in Orlando in 1977, the year the alleged incident was supposed to have occurred. My attorney's diligent investigation revealed there was no evidence whatsoever of any such allegation, nor was there any record that I was ever accused by anyone of abuse.

On October 1, 2019, the Bishop of Palm Beach had his own, separate diocesan canonist craft a reply to my canonist, weaving a narrative that placed the blame squarely on the Diocese of Orlando, seeming to pass the buck in a game of clerical cover-up. This letter clearly distanced the Palm Beach bishop from the affair, stating through his canonist that: "the matter against Father Duffy has been determined by the Diocese of Orlando, where the alleged incident occurred, and with which the Diocese of Palm Beach fully respects and complies."

In other words, on paper, it appeared that the Palm Beach bishop had nothing to do with this allegation and was only accepting the decision of the Orlando Diocese.

But this interpretation of the facts was shown to be false by the "appropriate contact" for both bishops whose letters, unwittingly, provided a trove of valuable information that shed light on what was going on.

In his letter of October 22, 2019, the "appropriate contact" explained that the Diocese of Orlando transferred the false allegation over to the bishop of the Palm Beach Diocese back in 2004, *after* it was promptly dismissed by the police. He then conceded that this new investigation was conducted against the objections of the accuser, stating: "lacking the participation of the accuser," who "was not interested in pursuing the matter further," the Diocese of Palm Beach was "forced to conclude that there was insufficient proof to move forward."

The "appropriate contact" concluded that "the new investigation on behalf of the two Ordinaries [the diocesan bishops] . . . should be brief and

---

1. Franz Kafka's *The Trial*, is a novel where the protagonist is arrested and prosecuted by a remote, unapproachable authority.

conclude within a few weeks." It actually took much longer, dragging on laboriously for over a year.

Why did this silly abuse investigation, dismissed by the police and contrary to the objections of a contrite accuser, drag on for over a year? It dragged on because of the strange actions of the fifth bishop of Palm Beach.

In a twist, bordering on the absurd, the Bishop of Palm Beach widened the investigation to include "historical allegations" in my personnel files. This decision, ostensibly to gather "further proofs" against me, inadvertently opened a Pandora's Box of past injustices and false accusations by the diocese itself.

You couldn't make this stuff up. This strange investigation had now become as complicated as the trial depicted by Charles Dickens in *Bleak House* which, as he wrote, "no man alive could figure out." And like the awful investigation itself by the Chancery Court in Dicken's novel: if you were expecting a resolution, you'd have to wait "On the Day of Judgment."

It was an appalling act of deception but, ironically, it worked to my advantage since Father Martin and I had written a full Report, exposing the falsity of these so-called "historical allegations" in my files.

I had also personally delivered this Report on the files to the same bishop.

To confirm what I've stated above the "appropriate contact" wrote that "the Dioceses reviewed historical allegations and decided that Father Duffy's [case] needed to be reopened with the possibility of gathering further proofs."

So, there it was. The discredited allegation of abuse was replaced by a new investigation into "historical allegations" for the purpose of finding incriminating information (further proofs) against me.

The absurdity of this witch hunt did not escape me. Did these bishops not know they were walking into a trap of their own making? Hadn't I personally delivered to the fifth Bishop of Palm Beach the detailed report by Father Martin and myself exposing these false "historical allegations"? This Report offered a very detailed exposé of Diocesan malfeasance conducted over the years.

It struck me as farcical now that these two bishops could possibly try to weaponize old, discredited, diocesan abuses against me in this new investigation. Were they not aware that similar deviousness in the past had spectacularly backfired? The truth would all be revealed in God's good time.[2]

---

2. See Luke 8:17. "For all that is secret will eventually be brought into the open, and everything that is concealed will be brought to light and made known to all."

You Duped Me, O Lord

The opportunity to set the record straight came on July 16, 2020, when I was interviewed by two officials of the Review Board of the Orlando Diocese in Melbourne, Florida. My canonist had requested this interview many times since the inception of the investigation in September, 2019. The interview, which had been cancelled by the Orlando attorney three times before, focused solely on the discredited 2004 allegation, oddly ignoring the so-called "historical allegations" that had supposedly prompted this new investigation.

The attorney for the Orlando Diocese at the meeting informed me of the source of the trumped-up allegation of abuse. The source was the notes of the former chancellor of the Diocese of Orlando, who had placed the false information in my files in 2004. After this libel was discredited, the notes were sent to the Diocese of Palm Beach, where they were held, it appeared, as ammunition to be used at some future time along with discredited "further proofs" in my personnel files.

The two members of the Review Board who interviewed me were cordial and even apologetic. One of them expressed high praise for my service of over fifty years in the priesthood.

"You are only doing your job," I told them. "I have no problem with you."

My personal lawyer, Roger Ascona, was present at the interview and requested that he be allowed to make a tape recording of the proceedings, in the interest of accuracy. The diocesan attorney would not agree to this. My canonist could not make it, personally, to Melbourne, but he was allowed to listen in electronically to the entire interview.

It was all weirdly similar to the false allegation of battery back in the 1990s that was promoted by the second Bishop of the Diocese of Palm Beach. The basis for that allegation was also the defamatory notes placed in my files in 1994 by the chancellor of the Palm Beach Diocese, without evidence and without my knowledge.

Nothing, I realized, had changed since then.

During this interview, the absurdity of the old accusation became clear. I was accused of abuse that allegedly occurred when I was a coach for a team I had never coached, on a soccer field in plain sight of parents and players, yet without a single witness.

The interview in Melbourne did not take as long as I had expected. It lasted less than an hour, but it struck me as entirely strange because the interviewers only spoke about an already dismissed false allegation and never uttered a word about "historical allegations," the real reason for this new investigation.

The questions I was asked made no sense.

Part 3—Chapter 43

"Could the accuser," the attorney asked, "be retaliating against you for something that upset him?"

"What kind of question is that?" I replied. "I have no idea who the alleged accuser was, if there was one. His identity has been kept secret, and I've been told by the appropriate contact for the two bishops that the alleged accuser wants nothing to do with this investigation. Surely you understand I cannot respond to this question."

The attorney shifted uncomfortably, then tried again. "Let me put it another way. Sometimes, a priest can provoke someone's anger simply by denying them what they want. These things happen, you know."

"Of course, these things happen," I replied. "Everybody in authority is bound to upset somebody."

The irony of the moment struck me like a bolt of lightning. Here I was, being interrogated about upsetting some imaginary figure, when it was the two bishops themselves—embroiled in their own machinations—who seemed most perturbed. The so-called accuser wanted no part of their scheme, yet the bishops continued to weaponize his alleged grievance against me.

"Were there any other allegations made against you?" he asked.

Now we were getting somewhere. I was glad he introduced, even indirectly, the matter of what the Bishop of Palm Beach called "historical allegations" in my files, the real cause of this second investigation, according to the letters we received.

"Yes, there were other allegations," I replied.

"What were they?" he continued.

"Two previous bishops of the Palm Beach Diocese tried to discredit me by making false and defamatory allegations," I said. "There were even attempts to get me arrested."

"Can you explain," asked the attorney.

I described how the first Bishop of the Diocese of Palm Beach had tried to discredit me with a false allegation in the presence of the chairman of the parish finance council because I would not go along with diocesan abuses in the immigration program. The chairman called his bluff by inviting me into the meeting to answer this false allegation. I refuted the allegation and the bishop had nothing to say.

I went on to relate how the second Bishop of the Diocese of Palm Beach, removed from office by the Vatican after I reported him to Rome for grave abuses of authority, tried to have me arrested on a false charge of battery. He also made allegations of embezzlement, without any evidence, which were also disproved.

You Duped Me, O Lord

I wondered how much these diocesan investigators knew about the false "historical allegations" contained in my personnel files, and if they were familiar with the report Father Martin and I submitted to the bishops, exposing them. If they were at all familiar with the truth concerning the files, they kept it to themselves. At any rate, no honest action was ever taken regarding my personnel files, except to subject me to a sham investigation concerning discredited "historical allegations" contained in them.

I was glad for the opportunity to expose the false "historical allegations" by previous bishops. This latest attempt by the fifth Bishop of the Diocese of Palm Beach to incriminate me was merely a continuation of the old trumped-up allegations. It was all, it seemed, part of a dangerous pattern.

A month of heavy silence followed the interview. Finally, on August 20, 2020, we were informed that the allegation of abuse was unsubstantiated. But we already knew that, and so did the two bishops. My name, we were assured, was removed from the list of accused church personnel, and it was the unanimous recommendation of the review board that my priestly faculties be restored.

This was how the pathetic affair ended.

This ordeal, stretching over a long period, tested my faith, my resolve, and also my trust in the institution I had served for decades.

As I ponder this tumultuous chapter of my life, I'm struck by the irony that retirement, far from being a peaceful denouement, became a crucible for my faith and vocation. The golden years I had envisioned transformed into a battlefield where truth clashed with institutional abuse. Yet, in this crucible, I discovered reservoirs of strength I never knew I possessed. The ordeal, painful as it was, honed my spirit and reaffirmed my vocation in ways I couldn't have imagined. It taught me that our calling to serve the Lord doesn't fade with the passing of years. Rather, it evolves, taking on new forms and demanding from us an ever-deeper wellspring of faith, courage and conviction.

In the end, the storm passed, and I emerged not bitter, but more confirmed than ever in my vocation. The adage about loving what you do held true, even in the face of adversity. In fighting the good fight, I found a purpose that transcended the abuses of the institutional church, a purpose that was, in every sense, my life's calling.

Chapter 44

THE GRUELING INQUISITION HAD left me bruised, undoubtedly, but little did I know, it was merely the prelude to another harrowing ordeal. The fallout from having my name placed on a list of abusive priests by two bishops led to aberrant and bizarre repercussions even after the investigation—if one could grace it with such a term—concluded in my favor.

In August 2020, my canonist and I received a letter from the diocesan consultant or "appropriate contact," claiming my name had been removed from the Diocese of Orlando's list of abusive priests. I naively thought that would bring closure to the matter. How wrong I was.

Contrary to what we were led to believe, my name remained like a haunting specter, refusing to be exorcized from the Orlando Diocesan list, and stubbornly resurfaced on various websites that seemed eager to castigate the church. When I brought this unsettling discovery to the attention of the Orlando Diocesan attorney, expecting a swift resolution, I was met with nonchalance.

"That's an old list," he said dismissively.

This, too, was false. My name was still posted on the Diocese of Orlando's list and kept ending up on other sites critical of the church. The whole thing bordered on the absurd. It was clear the diocese had lost its grip on its own narrative, tripping itself up with one false statement after another.

The diocesan attorney seemed to have a ready-made explanation for every error committed in the diocese's name. When he finally acknowledged the lingering presence of my name on that list, his explanation was almost creative in its simplicity. He blamed a computer glitch, an IT hiccup within the diocesan website. I failed to see how the simple act of removing a name from a website could be prevented by a computer glitch.

A peculiar blame game ensued, reminiscent of Adam and Eve pointing fingers at each other over the forbidden fruit. The diocesan investigator, directed the spotlight on the Bishop of Palm Beach, suggesting he had a golden opportunity to put an end to this charade back in 2004 but opted to do nothing.

The diocesan attorney's next suggestion was a study in bureaucratic evasion. He proposed I demand that the attorney for the Diocese of Palm Beach remove my name from sites circulating the libel. I couldn't help but wonder why I should do that when it was the Orlando Diocese that wrongly put my name on their list, and failed to remove it when they were aware of the truth.

So, the buck was passed back and forth, with neither diocese taking responsibility for its actions.

Frustrated by the bureaucratic evasion, I decided to get to the bottom of the mess by calling the Bishop of Orlando himself. On Ash Wednesday, February 17, 2021—ironically, a day when Catholics are reminded of the need for reconciliation and repentance—I put a call through to him. His secretary picked up the phone.

"Could I speak with the bishop?" I asked.

"The bishop is in a meeting," she said, then asked: "Is this urgent?"

"Yes," I replied. "It's very urgent."

"What's your name and phone number?"

I gave her both.

"I'll walk this message over to him at the meeting," she said with real concern in her voice.

I thanked her, ended the call, and waited for the bishop to call me back.

He did, and within minutes.

"How are you doing, Hugh?" he asked.

"Not good at all, bishop," I replied. "You'll know how I'm doing when you hear what I have to say."

Straightaway, the bishop proffered a feeble justification for his actions: "I only wanted you to be interviewed when I read the allegation in your file," he said, making it sound so simple and uncomplicated.

He never mentioned anything about the "historical allegations" in my files to gather further proofs, ostensibly the reason for this second investigation after the failure of the first one in 2004.

"Is that why you put my name on your list of credibly accused priests because I wasn't interviewed?" I asked.

No response.

I continued: "My canonist and I fought very hard to get the interview on July 16, 2020, after it was cancelled three times. We had to wait almost a year, having been put through a tortuous inquisition in the meantime."

Still, no response.

Part 3—Chapter 44

I asked him, "Why did two bishops put me through a trumped-up canonical trial in 2019 against the objections of a contrite accuser, and against the judgment of law enforcement, dismissing the allegation for lack of evidence?"

He offered no explanation for the prolonged inquisition but he did have a question: "Were you interviewed by the police?"

"No," I replied. "Why would the police want to interview me when they knew the truth? The first I heard of this allegation was in September of 2019, when I received an accusing letter from the Bishop of Palm Beach."

I moved on to my next concern.

"This process was illegitimate," I pointed out. "It violated the specific instructions of the Holy See, which say that a person is presumed innocent until proven guilty, and that no name should be published on a public list before completion of an investigation."

The bishop's telling silences were the only responses to my questions about the legitimacy of the process and the damage done to my reputation.

"I'm asking you," I continued, "to take my name off the diocesan list and off those sites that are posting this false information about me."

"We might have to sue the law firm responsible for this," he said. "Some priests are being falsely accused."

"The other web sites," I emphasized, "are getting this false information from *you*. If anyone should be sued, it should be you for posting the libel."

The Bishop of Orlando didn't understand or was unwilling to admit that the Dioceses of Orlando and Palm Beach were responsible for this horrific injustice.

At this point, I got a response.

"You're going in circles," he seethed, his anger palpable even through the phone.

"Maybe I am repeating myself," I replied, "but it's nothing like the web of deceit and double-think I had to endure during this absurd, canonical trial."

This bishop was rather thin-skinned, and did not want to be reminded, it appeared, of his own seeming incompetence. I felt remorseful, sensing he had been drawn into this web of deceit by the bishop of Palm Beach.

In a conciliatory tone, I asked: "Will you get your attorney to remove my name from your list, and ask the law firms in question to take down this false information?"

"Yes," he fumed, rather upset.

That's how the conversation ended, but it was not the end of the story.

Though the Diocese of Orlando eventually removed my name from its list, it offered no help in getting it removed from the other sites. Instead, the buck was passed back to the Diocese of Palm Beach. It struck me as ironical that the attorneys, responsible for the other sites, proved more professional and conscientious than the two diocesan bishops. These attorneys graciously took my name off their sites once my canonist made them aware of the serious abuse, committed by two bishops.

The financial toll of this ordeal was significant. I sent a bill for my expenses—over $10,000 incurred in defending my good name—to the Bishop of Orlando. He forwarded it to the Bishop of Palm Beach, who refused to accept accountability. In the end, I was never reimbursed by either diocese.

The President of Cross Catholic, Jim Cavner, was eager to have me return to work. However, he mentioned something in emails to me that was rather disturbing.

He wrote that the Bishop of Palm Beach had "requested copies of any feedback we had received from parishes where you preached."

Apparently, even after the investigation was over, the fifth Bishop of Palm Beach was still carrying on with his witch hunt, still looking for "historical allegations" against me.

Jim went on to explain: "We sent him all the pastor evaluations, which were uniformly positive. Some parishes requested you by name for additional assignments."

Jim continued: "The bishop talked to me briefly after one of the board meetings, which he usually attends, and told me how pleased he was at the positive responses we had received from your assignments."

Despite the pious pedantry and unctuous tone, the fifth bishop continued to search for more "historical allegations" and made no attempt to correct the false "historical allegations" in my personnel files.

He was obliged, however, to acknowledge in a letter of November 16, 2020 that: "The administrative leave, in accord with Canon 1722, on which you were placed on September 9, 2019, is concluded."

Yet he did *not* follow up on the unanimous recommendation of the Review Board, the body he apparently "fully respects and complies with." After being vindicated both civilly and canonically, the bishop abused his power again by preventing me, for no reason, from working for Cross Catholic. There was never a problem with me working for Cross prior to the mock investigation, so why was there a problem now, after being vindicated? My canonist wrote to the fifth bishop about restoring my priestly faculties, but he would not acknowledge his registered letters.

I called the canonist of the two bishops: "Could you give me the date of the soccer incident that was alleged to have taken place in 1977 in Orlando?" I asked, wishing to check where I had been at that time in my journals.

"I could do that, but I'd have to look up that information in my notes," he responded.

"That's fine," I replied. "There's no hurry."

Thinking this over, he added: "I'd have to send this information to your canonist, who represents you."

"That's no problem," I replied.

Some days later, the "appropriate contact" for the two bishops called me back.

"Father Duffy," he said, "I cannot give you the date of the incident you asked about. The case is over."

What changed his mind? Who did he talk to? And why did he not want me to know the truth?

In a gesture that felt more like mockery than reconciliation, the fifth Bishop of Palm Beach sent me a congratulatory letter for my upcoming 55th Anniversary of Priestly Ordination—nine months in advance—accompanied by a check for $550, representing ten dollars for each year of service. This sum, however, paled in comparison to the financial cost I had incurred during a biased, canonical trial.

As I reflect on this surreal nightmare, I am overcome by the bitter irony of an institution committed to truth and justice becoming so hopelessly ensnared in webs of deceit and bureaucratic evasion. My ordeal has illuminated the stark chasm between the church's sacred ideals and the deeply flawed humanity of those entrusted to uphold them. I bear my accusers no ill will for what they put me through for, in their own strange way, they were following their own lights. God alone will be the final judge.

Yet in the depths of disillusionment, however, I found myself clinging—perhaps more tightly than ever—to my faith that had been so grievously tested. The real scandal in this whole affair was diocesan malfeasance and its egregious deviation from the gospel's teachings. For, in the end, the Kingdom of Christ can only be erected on the foundation of the gospel, not on a foundation of lies.

Chapter 45

THROUGHOUT MY LONG JOURNEY in the priesthood, one question has haunted me: *How does the church reform itself?* As I sit in the quiet of retirement, this enigma still pricks my conscience, like a splinter embedded too deep to be removed.

The strange thing is that the answer has always been there, hiding in plain sight, within the message that has guided my life: the clear and pure teaching of the gospel. It's a truth so simple that even a child can grasp it, yet so profound, that it has the power to transform lives and institutions alike.

It was in the bustling confines of Atlanta's Hartsfield Airport, that this truth crystalized for me once again.

As I watched the chaotic scene unfold before me, the struggles of a rotund gentleman lunging for his belongings at the baggage claim caught my attention. Since he looked like he needed help, I felt compelled to offer it. The whole situation was rather amusing. As I approached, I suddenly recognized the man in trouble: the third bishop of my diocese who had been removed from his former position over a sex abuse scandal, now trying desperately to snatch his luggage from the carousel.

Just as he made another attempt to seize a passing case, I moved quickly and beat him to it.

"You'll be needing this," I said, surprising him.

"Hugh," he exclaimed. "Where did you come from?"

"A better question is, where did you come from?" I replied.

"I'm returning from Ireland," he said, "where I was performing a wedding, incognito of course."

As I stood beside my former bishop in the bustling airport terminal, a burning question resurfaced in my mind: *Would the bishops ever reform?*

Seizing this unexpected opportunity, I put it to him directly: "Now that you're retired and out of the loop and can speak freely," I asked, "do you think the bishops will ever reform?"

His swift response sliced the air with its decisiveness: "No," he answered. "Not for a long, long time."

I pressed further: "And why would you say that?"

"They don't have the will," he replied bluntly.

These words, coming from the third bishop of my diocese, were a stark reminder of the disconnect between the church's mission and its institutional practices. Throughout my life, I witnessed many instances where the church's actions have diverged seriously from the gospel's teachings—a divergence that has allowed abuses to flourish.

The failure to live up to the ideal set forth by the gospel is not a new problem. It is a persistent dissonance that has plagued the church for generations. Real reform requires more than just removing problematic clergy; it means transforming the underlying culture that allows abuses to fester.

The irony is that the solution has always been there, in the very first words spoken by Jesus during his public ministry: "Reform yourselves and believe in the Good News" (Mark 1:15). We are all called, individuals and institutions alike, to deny ourselves, to take up our cross to follow the Lord's example. This is the essence of the Christian adventure.

Yet, as my encounter at the airport revealed, those in positions of power often lack the will to enact this fundamental change. The inclination to elevate personal power above the gospel has eroded trust in the church's institution, leading to the emergence of critical secular platforms like www.bishop-accountability.org.

The root of this problem often lies in the very structure of church governance. The corporation sole model, prevalent in America, grants immense power to individual bishops over assets and decision-making. This concentration of power, coupled with the hierarchical nature of the church, can foster environments where accountability is minimal and transparency lacking.

I've seen and experienced firsthand how this structure can lead to abuses of power:

1. A bishop in Ireland who opposed our efforts to aid the handicapped, insisting on written permission for a simple benefit event.
2. The interference in our parish immigration program in Okeechobee, seemingly viewed as a threat to diocesan income rather than as an opportunity to serve.
3. The misappropriation of parish property under the pretext of Diocesan corporation sole, a battle that lasted four harrowing years.

4. False allegations of battery and embezzlement in an effort to remove me from the parish.

5. The filing of false information in my personnel files, leading to my name being wrongly placed on a list of abusive church personnel—a grave injustice that took too long and too much agony to rectify.

Abuses like these have had devastating effects on the church, undermining the trust between bishops and priests. Recent polls[1] paint a grim picture:

1. Only 24 percent of U.S. Priests express confidence in the decision-making and leadership of U.S. bishops in general.

2. A mere 36 percent of diocesan clergy believe their bishops would provide sufficient resources to defend them in court if needed.

3. Just over half (51 percent) of diocesan clergy think bishops would support them if falsely accused.

These numbers tell the story of a priesthood in crisis, a flock drifting into disillusionment. When barely a quarter of today's priests trust in their bishops' leadership, this is not just a crisis of the institution—it's the undoing of the very fabric that holds our church together.

The path to bridging this gulf between institutional practice and the gospel lies not in concealing abuses to protect the institution, nor in persecuting those who expose malfeasance. Rather, it is to be found in an unwavering commitment to embrace the gospel, to be faithful to its teachings, and to follow in the footsteps of Christ.

The synodal process introduced by Pope Francis offers a glimmer of hope—a renewed effort to engage the faithful and reexamine the workings of the institution. However, caution is essential. If the ideals of synodality are only aspirational, untouched by practical application that reshapes authority and governance, they will fall short. Hope, without action, is as hollow as a promise never intended to be kept. For the synodal process to bear good fruit, it must transcend rhetoric. The church must translate dialogue into concrete steps that transform how power is wielded. Only by genuinely incorporating these ideals into its structure can the church begin to heal the breach between its divine mission and the institution.

The gospel is already in our hands, but without living it, we are merely custodians of a dormant truth. The words of Vatican II, full of promise, are

---

1. Francis X. Rocca, "Most U.S. Catholic Priests Fear False Abuse Allegations, Study Finds," *Wall Street Journal*, October 19, 2022. https://www.wsj.com/articles/most-u-s-catholic-priests-fear-false-abuse-allegations-study-finds-11666198699

rendered impotent if they are confined to documents and not breathed into daily life. Jesus made it clear that it is not enough to hear his teachings or to profess our faith in comfortable settings. The true test lies in putting his teachings into action—in loving one another, in serving the least among us, and in ensuring that no one is left to suffer in silence.

The purpose of this memoir, to lay bare the dissonance between what the church professes and what it practices, is drawn from over fifty years of personal witness. True change will come only when those entrusted with authority choose to embody Christ's message, prioritizing the gospel over the desire to maintain power and control.

As I conclude this memoir, I am struck by a final paradox: The very institution that entrusted me with this sacred duty of proclaiming the gospel also motivated me to pen these pages. If the church had been as steadfast in its adherence to the gospel as it was in the pursuit of its institutional agenda, this book would never have been written.

I am reminded of the stained-glass windows through which I've often gazed. These windows, with their intricate beauty, filter light, as if from above, into the dark corners of our hearts. But over time, grime builds, cracks form, and they become clouded. Like the church itself, they need cleaning and repair to once again let the full radiance of God's light shine through. It is my hope that by telling this story, and shining a light on these problems, we can remove the grime and spark the will to reform that has been so sorely lacking.

For in the end, it is not just the institution that must change, but each one of us. We are all called to reform our lives, to do God's will, and to follow Christ's example. Only then can we hope to build a church that truly embodies the transformative power of the gospel.

www.ingramcontent.com/pod-product-compliance
Lightning Source LLC
Chambersburg PA
CBHW060552230426
43670CB00011B/1789